BENGALI (BANGLA)

PRACTICAL DICTIONARY

BANGLA – ENGLISH
ENGLISH – BANGLA

BENGALI (BANGLA)
PRACTICAL DICTIONARY

BANGLA – ENGLISH
ENGLISH – BANGLA

Hanne-Ruth Thompson

Hippocrene Books, Inc.
New York

For information, address:
HIPPOCRENE BOOKS, INC.
171 Madison Avenue
New York, NY 10016
www.hippocrenebooks.com

Library of Congress Cataloging-in-Publication Data

Thompson, Hanne-Ruth.
   Bangla - English, English - Bangla : Hippocrene
   practical dictionary / Hanne-Ruth Thompson.
      p. cm.
   Bengali and English
   ISBN-13: 978-0-7818-1270-2 (pbk.)
   ISBN-10: 0-7818-1270-4 (pbk.)
 1. Bengali language--Dictionaries--English. 2. English
   language--Dictionaries--Bengali. I. Title.
   PK1687.T56 2011
   491.4'4321--dc22

                                                      2011005793

Printed in the United States of America.

CONTENTS

*In memory of my English father-in-law Ross
Thompson and my Bangladeshi village mother
Estella Rozario, who would both have been
pleased with this work.
And to the early morning birds who kept me
company – in Dankbarkeit für das, was nicht
mit Worten auszumessen.*

—HRT 2011

INTRODUCTION

Bangla (Bengali) is by number of speakers the fifth or sixth most-spoken language in the world. It is the national language of Bangladesh, the state language of West Bengal, and one of the official languages of India. Bangla is a language of great beauty, diversity and color. The main aim of this dictionary is to give speakers of English access to good, usable Bangla words without elaborate explanations or too much high language that is unsuitable for conversation. I hope that for speakers of Bangla the flair and flexibility of the English language has been at least hinted at.

Bangla has absorbed a great number of English words, particularly in the field of technical and computer language. If these words (*voucher, website, dry-cleaner, modem*, etc.) are not given in the English–Bangla word-list, it can be assumed that the English word is in use.

Bangla has a wealth of onomatopoeic words. These are not restricted to sound imitation, as in টাপুর-টুপুর ṭapur-ṭupur for *pitter-patter*, but can also include other sensations such as টকটকে লাল ṭokṭoke lal *bright red* or ঢুলু-ঢুলু ḍhulu-ḍhulu *drowsy*. Rabindranath Tagore called these words very appropriately ধ্বন্যাত্মক শব্দ dhvɔnyat-môk śɔbdô *words whose soul is in their sound*. It is not always easy to determine the part of speech of these words. Many of them can be considered nouns but almost all of them can also be used as adjectives and, with a locative ending, as adverbs. Because of this flexibility in use, I have labeled them as *onom* rather than specifying a part of speech.

There are two systems for transcribing one language into another. We can either represent the sounds of the language in a **phonetic transcript** or we can represent the writing of a language in a **transliteration**. This dictionary uses a carefully balanced mixture in that it gives a one-to-one transliteration of all the Bangla symbols as well as indicating the pronunciation of those words that cannot be accurately predicted from the transliteration. The pronunciation of the inherent vowel is given throughout. This blended transliteration system was first used by William Radice in his *Teach Yourself Bengali* and the credit for it should go to him. A detailed guide to transliteration and pronunciation is given below.

There are some differences in vocabulary, word-formation, and pronunciation between the language spoken in Bangladesh and that spoken in West Bengal. These variations are indicated in the Bangla–English dictionary.

Dictionaries are beginnings. Dictionaries provide us with the raw material: girders for building new bridges, thread for weaving new cloths, stepping-stones for making new connections, and of course, words for learning one another's languages. Learning one another's languages is perhaps the single most important step we can take towards mutual understanding and peace in the world. It is my hope that this dictionary will be a stepping-stone in that direction.

ABBREVIATIONS

adj	adjective	*onom*	onomatopoeia
adv	adverb		(*see note in Introduction*)
Bd	Bangladesh	*ord*	ordinary
c	continuous	*p*	past
conj	conjunction	*pf*	perfect
det	determiner	*pl*	plural
expr	expressing	*pol*	polite
f	female	*pp*	preposition,
fam	familiar		postposition
fig	figuratively	*pr*	pronoun
fut	future	*pref*	prefix
hab	habitual	*pres*	present
hon	honorific	*pron*	pronounced
gram	grammatical	*ps*	person
int	interjection	*rel*	relative
intim	intimate	*s*	simple
m	male	*sg*	singular
math	mathematical	*suff*	suffix
n	noun	*vb*	verb
num	numerical	*WB*	West Bengal

THE BANGLA ALPHABET

The order of the alphabet is set out below. Each vowel in Bangla, except for the inherent vowel অ ɔ/ô (see below) has two symbols, (1) a full vowel that stands on its own at the beginning of words and syllables (eg ঈগল *īgɔl eagle*; উকুন ukun *louse)*, and (2) a vowel sign that is attached to consonants.

Vowel signs are attached to consonants in varying positions: after, before, underneath, or around the consonants. The resulting consonant-vowel combination forms a syllabic unit. This means that even though the combination within a syllable can be vowel sign plus consonant (eg ি- i + ম - m = মি) the consonant is always pronounced first: mi.

ক (k) is the consonant given in this demonstration:

full vowel	vowel sign	position		demonstration
অ	(inherent)	ɔ/ô	no vowel sign is written	ক– kɔ
আ	া	a	**after** the consonant	কা ka
ই	ি	i	**before** the consonant	কি ki
ঈ	ী	ī	**after** the consonant	কী kī
উ	ু	u	**underneath** the consonant	কু ku
ঊ	ূ	ū	**underneath** the consonant	কূ kū
ঋ	ৃ	ṙ	**underneath** the consonant	কৃ kṙ
এ	ে, া	e, æ	**before** the consonant	কে ke
ঐ	ৈ	oi	**before** the consonant	কৈ koi
ও	ে া	o	**around** the consonant	কো ko
ঔ	ে ৗ	ou	**around** the consonant	কৌ kou

Alphabetical order of Bangla letters

অ ɔ/ô   আ a   ই i   ঈ ī
উ u   ঊ ū   ঋ ṙ
এ e/æ ঐ oi   ও o   ঔ ou

ৎ ṁ   ঃ ḥ   ˇ ~

ক k	খ kh	গ g	ঘ gh	ঙ ṅ
চ c	ছ ch	জ j	ঝ jh	এঃ ñ
ট ṭ	ঠ ṭh	ড ḍ	ঢ ḍh	ণ ṇ
ত,ৎ t, ṯ	থ th	দ d	ধ dh	ন n
প p	ফ ph	ব b	ভ bh	ম m
য y	য় ŷ	র r	ল l	
শ ś	ষ ṣ	স s	হ h	

Guide to Transliteration and Pronunciation

Bangla letters and sounds

Bangla is a syllabic language. There are four types of syllables:

(1) a single vowel (v), as in আ-মি a-mi
(2) a vowel and a consonant (vc), as in আম am
(3) a consonant and a vowel (cv), as in মা ma
(4) a consonant-vowel-consonant (cvc), as in নাম nam

Consonants cannot stand on their own. Where no vowel is attached to a consonant, the inherent vowel অ ɔ/ô is usually pronounced, as in খবর = kh+b+r, pronounced khɔbôr. The inherent vowel is not always pronounced after the final consonant of a word, eg নাম is pronounced nam, not namô.

A transliteration, as given in this dictionary, has the aim of representing the Bangla spelling. The spelling of a word, however, does not always give us a sufficient guide to pronunciation. As a help to learners, this dictionary gives:

(1) the presence or absence of the inherent vowel
(2) the pronunciation of the inherent vowel: ɔ = open o as in *hot*
    or ô = closed o as in French *mot*
(3) the distinction between e and æ
(4) the distinction between a and æ (*see below*)
(5) any unpredictable or rarely occurring pronunciations

It is important to read the following guidelines carefully in order to be able to work out the pronunciation of words. Explanations and descriptions in books are only ever approximations. The best way to learn the pronunciation of a language is to listen to native speakers and imitate what they say. Some dictionaries, for instance my *Bengali Dictionary and Phrasebook* (Hippocrene, 2010), use a phonetic transcript instead of a transliteration.

Quick Pronunciation Guide

The rules and conventions for the transliteration and Bangla pronunciation are set out in detail below, but here is an overview of the symbols whose pronunciation cannot be guessed from the transliteration:

transliteration		pronunciation
c	→	tch, as in <u>ch</u>air
ch	→	tchh, as in <u>ch</u>air but with more breath
ṅ	→	ng, as in si<u>ng</u>er, or ngg, as in fi<u>ng</u>er
ṁ	→	ng, as in si<u>ng</u>er, or ngg, as in fi<u>ng</u>er
ṅg	→	ngg, as in fi<u>ng</u>er
ṙ	→	ri, as in <u>ree</u>l
ṣ, ś and s	→	sh, s (in conjuncts)
y (at the beginning of words and syllables)	→	ɉ, as in <u>j</u>ab
ŷ	→	y, as in law<u>y</u>er, or w as in a<u>w</u>ay

The following chart shows in columns:

    (1) the Bangla letter
    (2) the transliteration symbol
    (3) a note on pronunciation
    (4) an example word in Bangla
    (5) its transliteration

Vowels

Note on pronunciation: Unlike English vowels, Bangla vowels are pure single sounds that can be open (or short) as in *pat, pet, pit, pot, put*, or closed (long). For the closed sounds it is difficult to find English equivalents as English sounds tend to shift from one vowel to the other. For instance, the vowel sound in *go* shifts from e to o to u. Bangla sounds stay in one place. Examples are given below.

1	2	3	4	5
অ, –	ɔ	open as in *hot*	বলা	bɔla
	or			
	ô	closed ô as in *Roma* (Italian pronunciation)	প্রমাণ	prômaṇ
আ, া	a	open a as in *samba*	রান্না	ranna
		closed a as in *llama*	আম	am
ই, ি	i	open i as in *hit* or	জিনিস	jinis
		closed i as in *bee*	ইদ	id
ঈ, ী	ī	open i as in *hit* or	দীর্ঘ	dīrghô
		closed i as in *bee*	নীল	nīl
উ, ু	u	open u as in *put* or	মুক্তি	mukti
		closed u as in *rude*	দুধ	dudh
ঊ, ূ	ū	open u as in *put* or	মূল্য	mūllô
		closed u as in *rude*	দূর	dūr

The distinction in writing between 'short' and 'long' i and 'short' and 'long' u respectively is no longer mirrored in the pronunciation of these vowels. Pronunciation and spelling have to be learned.

| ঋ, ৃ | ṙ | ri | পৃথিবী | pṙthibī |
| | | | | (*pron* prithibi) |

Note that the pronunciation of this letter, in spite of its consonantal appearance, is always ri.

এ, ে	e	open e as in *met*	কেনা	kena
		closed e as in French *née*	সে	se
	æ	open æ as in *cat*	দেখা	dækha

The pronunciation of এ as æ is given in the transliteration as distinct from e. Note that the *jophola* ্য or the combination of *jophola* (্য) plus a (া) া can have the same pronunciation as æ (see below).

| ঐ, ৈ | oi | diphthong: closed o followed by i as in Italian *boicotto* | তৈরি | toiri |
| ও, ো া | o | closed o as in Spanish *como* | লোক | lok |

Note that the same pronunciation (closed, long o) can also be produced by the inherent vowel ô. There is a move towards replacing the inherent vowel, eg বার barô, with the long vowel in writing, eg বারো baro, but there is no consensus on this issue as yet and this book follows a conservative approach.

| ঔ, ৌ া | ou | diphthong: closed o followed by u | পৌনে | poune |

Consonants

Bangla distinguishes between aspirated (with extra breath, adding h or a puff of air) and unaspirated (no h sound), as well as voiced (g, d, b) and unvoiced (k, t, p) consonants. It also distinguishes between palatal (related to the palate, roof of the mouth) and dental (behind the teeth) sounds. Not all Bangla sounds have English equivalents. See the examples below.

1	2	3	4	5
ক	k	soft k, no aspiration	কলা	kɔla
খ	kh	aspirated k, k + h	খেলা	khæla
গ	g	soft g, no aspiration	গলা	gɔla
ঘ	gh	aspirated g = g + h	ঘর	ghɔr
ঙ	ṅ	ng as in *singer* or *finger*	ভাঙা	bhaṅa
				(*pron* bhanga)

The pronunciation of this consonant as either ng *singer* or ngg *finger* can vary from speaker to speaker and is not given in the dictionary. There is also, however, a conjunct ঙ্গ ṅg whose pronunciation is always ngg.

চ	c	ch as in *chip*	চাবি	cabi
ছ	ch	ch + h	ছবি	chôbi
জ	j	j as in *jam*	জল	jɔl
ঝ	jh	aspirated j, j + h	ঝাল	jhal

ঞ	ñ	nasal n, only used in conjunction with other letters, eg. ঞ (ñ) + চ (c) = ঞ্চ (ñc)	চঞ্চল	cɔñcôl
ট	ṭ	palatal t, similar to English t as in *top*, but with the tongue slightly further back in the mouth	টাকা	ṭaka
ঠ	ṭh	aspirated palatal t	ঠেলা	ṭhæla
ড	ḍ	palatal d, similar to English d as in *day,* but with the tongue slightly further back in the mouth	ডাল	ḍal
ড়	ṛ	a flapped r (needs practice)	আড়াই	aṛai
ঢ	ḍh	aspirated palatal d	ঢালা	ḍhala
ঢ়	ṛh	aspirated flapped r	গাঢ়	garhô
ণ	ṇ	pronounced as n	কারণ	karôṇ
ত	t	dental t (as in Italian *tanto,* the tongue is at the back of the teeth)	তুমি	tumi
ৎ	t̲	pronounced as dental t, occurs at the end of syllables where no inherent vowel is pronounced	সৎ	sɔt̲
থ	th	aspirated dental t + h	থামা	thama
দ	d	soft dental d as in Italian *dio*	দল	dɔl
ধ	dh	aspirated dental d + h	ধান	dhan
ন	n	n as in *not*	না	na
প	p	as English p, but without aspiration	পান	pan
ফ	ph	pronounced as pf or f	ফল	phɔl

These are regional variants between West Bengal (pf) and Bangladesh (f).

ব	b	as English b in *bit*	বাবা	baba
ভ	bh	aspirated b, b + h	ভুল	bhul
ম	m	as English m in *man*	মামা	mama
য	y	(1) pronounced as j in *jam*	যদি	yôdi

য	y	(2) the shortened form of this letter is called *jophola* and written ্য. It appears after consonants and has a doubling effect except when it (rarely) follows the initial consonant of a word, eg. জন্য jonyo is pronounced *jonno*, but জ্যোৎস্না jyôt̪sna is pronounced jôtsna	জন্য	jônyô
য	y	(3) As a vowel ্য is pornounced æ or, rarely, e. Its pronunciation is given in each case.	ব্যথা	bytha
				(*pron* bætha)
			ব্যক্তি	bykti
				(*pron* bekti)
্যা	ya, yæ	(4) Followed by া a: pronunciation varies between a and æ – this difference is incorporated into the transliteration, ie the symbols ya and yæ both stand for ্যা.	বিদ্যা	bidya
				(*pron* bidda)
			ব্যাপার	byæpar

The symbol y essentially represents three different uses of the same Bangla letter. The important thing to remember is that the full consonant য is always pronounced as j.

য়	ŷ	a semivowel (glide) used between vowels, pronounced y as in *mayor* or w as in *away,* also appears at the end of words following a vowel and is pronounced as e after o, a or æ, eg. হয় hɔy, যায় yay, and দেয় dæy are pronounced hɔe, jae, and dæe respectively.	মেয়ে	meŷe
			হাওয়া	haoŷa
			হয়	hɔŷ
			যায়	yaŷ
			দেয়	dæŷ
র	r	rolled r, similar to Italian r	রাগ	rag
ল	l	as English initial l *line,* formed at the front of the mouth	লাল	lal
শ	ś	pronounced as sh in *shine,* in some conjuncts as s in *sun*	শাক	śak

ষ	ṣ	pronounced as sh in *shine*	ষোল	ṣolô
স	s	pronounced as sh in *shine*, in some conjuncts as s in *sun*	সাপ	sap
হ	h	h as in *hot*	হাত	hat

Extra Symbols

ং	ṁ	ng as in *sing*, used instead of ঙ ṅ when no vowel follows	অংশ	ɔṁsô (*pron* ɔngsô)
ঃ	ḥ	a spelling convention with little effect on pronunciation: sometimes the preceding vowel is shortened, sometimes the subsequent consonant is doubled	বাঃ দুঃখ	baḥ duḥkhô (*pron* dukkho)
ঁ	~	nasal: indicates nasalisation of the vowel as in French *pain*, *bon*	চাঁদ	cãd
ব	v	*bophola*, underneath a consonant, doubles the sound of this consonant	বিশ্ব	bisvô (*pron* bisshô)
		When used with the initial consonant of a word or with a conjunct, it has no effect on pronunciation.	জ্বর সান্ত্বনা	jvɔr (*pron* jɔr) santvôna (*pron* shantôna)
ম	m	*mophola*, underneath a consonant, doubles the sound of this consonant	আত্মা	atma (*pron* atta)
		When used with the initial consonant of a word, it has no effect on the pronunciation.	স্মরণ	smɔrôṇ (*pron* shɔrôn)
্র	r	*rophola*, underneath a consonant, is pronounced after the consonant	প্র	prô
র্	r	*reph*, above a consonant, is pronounced before the consonant	কর্ম	kɔrmô

| ` | – | *hasanta*, underneath a consonant: sign to indicate that the inherent vowel is not pronounced | ননস্টপ | nɔnstɔp |

Conjuncts

Bangla has a great number of conjuncts that combine two or more consonants into one symbol. Some common ones are given below but there are many more – see the list of further readings below.

ক্ত	ক + ত	k + t		ক্র	ক + র	k + r
ক্ষ	ক + ষ	k + ṣ *		ঙ্ক	ঙ + ক	ṅ + k
ঙ্গ	ঙ + গ	ṅ + g		চ্ছ	চ + ছ	c + ch
জ্জ	জ + জ	j + j		জ্ঞ	জ + ঞ	j + ñ *
ঞ্চ	ঞ + চ	ñ + c		ঞ্জ	ঞ + জ	ñ +j
ট্ট	ট + ট	ṭ + ṭ		ণ্ট	ণ + ট	ṇ + ṭ
ণ্ঠ	ণ + ঠ	ṇ + ṭh		ণ্ড	ণ + ড	ṇ + ḍ
ত্ত	ত + ত	t + t		ত্র	ত + র	t + r
দ্ধ	দ + ধ	d + dh		ন্ত	ন + ত	n + t
ন্থ	ন+ থ	n + th		ন্ধ	ন + ধ	n + dh
প্ত	প + ত	p + t		ব্দ	ব + দ	bd
ম্ম	ম + ম	m + m		ম্ভ	ম + ভ	m + bh
র্ক	র + ক	r + k		ল্প	ল + প	l + p
ষ্ট	ষ + ট	ṣ + ṭ		ষ্ণ	ষ + ণ	ṣ + ṇ
স্ত	স + ত	s + t		স্থ	স + থ	s + th
হ্ন	হ + ন	h + n *		হ্য	হ + য	h + y *

* Of the above conjuncts, the following are pronounced differently from what might be expected:

transliteration   **pronunciation**

| ক্ষ | ক + ষ | k + ṣ | kh initially: ক্ষমা kṣɔma *pron* khɔma; kkh between vowels: অক্ষর ôkṣôr *pron* okkhor |

ঞ	জ + ঞ	j + ñ	gg between vowels: কৃতজ্ঞ kṙtɔjñô *pron* kritɔggo; g initially: জ্ঞান jñan *pron* gæn. When ঞ jñ is followed by the vowel ৗ a, the pronunciation of the sequence varies between g(g)a, eg জিজ্ঞাসা jijñasa *pron* jiggasha and g(g)æ, eg জ্ঞান jñan *pron* gæn, and is given in each case.
হ্ন	হ + ন	h + n	nh, as in চিহ্ন cihnô *pron* cinho
হ্য	হ + য	h + y	jjh, as in সহ্য sôhyô *pron* sojjho

The following books are useful for learning more Bangla:

Dakshi, Alibha, *Learning Bengali*. Shri K.C. Datta, Kolkata 1995

Nasrin, Mithun and van der Wurff, Wim *Colloquial Bengali*. Routledge 2008

Radice, William, *Teach Yourself Bengali*. Hodder Headline, London 2007 (3nd ed)

Seely, Clinton, *Intermediate Bangla*. Lincom Language Coursebooks, Munich 2002

Smith, W.L., *Bengali Reference Grammar*. Stockholm Oriental Textbook Series, 1997

Thompson, Hanne-Ruth, *Essential Everyday Bengali,* Bangla Academy, Dhaka 2006 (2nd ed)

Thompson, Hanne-Ruth, *Bengali: A Comprehensive Grammar*. Routledge, 2010

BANGLA-ENGLISH
DICTIONARY

Order of letters *(read in columns top to bottom)*:

অ ɔ/ô	ঘ gh	দ d
আ a	ঙ ṅ	ধ dh
ই i	চ c	ন n
ঈ ī	ছ ch	প p
উ u	জ j	ফ ph
ঊ ū	ঝ jh	ব b
ঋ ṙ	ঞ ñ,	ভ bh
এ e/æ	ট ṭ	ম m
ঐ oi	ঠ ṭh	য y
ও o	ড ḍ	য় ŷ
ঔ ou	ড় ṛ	র r
২ ṁ	ঢ ḍh	ল l
ঃ ḥ	ঢ় ṛh	শ ś
ঁ ~	ণ ṇ	ষ ṣ
ক k	ত t	স s
খ kh	ৎ ṯ	হ h
গ g	থ th	

Alternative forms of verbs are given in the Bangla–English dictionary. Distinctions in vocabulary, forms, or pronunciation between Bangladesh and West Bengal are indicated in this part of the book as *(Bd)* = Bangladesh, *(WB)* = West Bengal. As the borders between language variations are fluent, these indications can only be approximate.

Only basic numbers and the nominative forms of pronouns are given in the dictionary. The full sets are given at the end of the book.

অ১/ô

অংশ ɔṁśô (*pron* ɔngsho) *n* part,
share

অংশগ্রহণ ɔṁśôgrôhôṇ *n*
participation

অংশ নেওয়া ɔṁśô neôŷa *vb* take
part

অংশগ্রাহী ɔṁśôgrahī *n* shareholder

অংশত ɔṁśôtô *adv* partly, partially

অংশীদার ôṁśīdar *n* partner

অংশীদারি ôṁśīdari *n* partnership

অংশু ôṁśu *n* beam, ray, glow

অংশুমান ôṁśuman *adj* luminous,
bright, radiant

অংস ɔṁśô *n* shoulder

অকথা ɔkɔtha *n* abuse; abusive
language

অকথ্য ɔkɔthyô *adj* unspeakable,
unutterable

অকপট ɔkɔpôṭ *adj* frank, sincere,
candid

অকম্প ɔkɔmpô *adj* unperturbed,
steady, unmoved

অকাট্য ɔkaṭyô *adj* irrefutable

অকাতর ɔkatôr *adj* ungrudging,
untiring

অকাতরে ɔkatôre *adv* patiently,
unflinchingly

অকারণে ɔkarôṇe *adv* unnecessarily

অকাল ɔkal *adj* premature, untimely

অকু ôku *n* incident, accident

অকূল ɔkūl *adj* shoreless, limitless

অকৃত ɔkṙtô *adj* undone, outstanding

অকৃত্রিম ɔkṙtrim *adj* unadulterated,
pure, natural

অকেজো ɔkejo *adj* unserviceable,
disabled

অক্রম ɔkrôm *n* disorder

অক্রিয় ɔkriŷô *adj* inert, lethargic

অক্লান্ত ɔklantô *adj* untiring,
ceaseless

অক্লিষ্ট ɔkliṣṭô *adj* undefeated,
indomitable

অক্ষ ɔkṣô *n* die, dice

অক্ষক্রীড়া ɔkṣôkrīṙa *n* game of dice

অক্ষত ɔkṣɔtô *adj* unhurt, unwounded

অক্ষম ɔkṣɔm *adj* incapable

অক্ষয় ɔkṣɔŷ *adj* imperishable,
unfailing, inexhaustable

অক্ষর ôkṣôr *n* letter of the alphabet

অক্ষি ôkṣi *n* eye

অক্ষুন্ন ɔkṣunnô *adj* unimpaired,
unaffected

অক্ষুব্ধ ɔkṣubdhô *adj* unperturbed,
unruffled

অখণ্ড ɔkhɔṇḍô *adj* whole, entire,
integral

অখাদ্য ɔkhadyô *adj* inedible

অখুশি ɔkhuśi *n* dissatisfaction,
displeasure

অগণন ɔgɔṇôn *adj* uncountable,
countless

অগণনীয় ɔgɔṇôniŷô, অগণ্য ɔgôṇyô
adj uncountable, countless

অগতি ɔgôti *adj* motionless,
immobile, helpless

অগত্যা ɔgôtya *adv* perforce, by
necessity

অগভীর ɔgôbhīr *adj* shallow,
superficial

অগম ɔgɔm *adj* motionless, static

অগম্য ɔgɔmyô *adj* impassable,
inaccessible

অগা ɔga *adj* stupid, ignorant

অগাধ ɔgadh *adj* bottomless, deep,
profound

অগোচর ɔgocɔr *adj* invisible,
imperceptible

অগ্নি ôgni *n* fire

অগ্র ɔgrô *n* top, summit

অগ্রগতি ɔgrôgôti *n* progress, advance

অগ্রগামী ɔgrôgamī *adj* progressive

অগ্রসর ɔgrôsɔr *adj* moving, leading

অগ্রসর হওয়া ɔgrôsɔr hɔoŷa *vb* advance, progress

অগ্রাধিকার ɔgradhikar *n* priority

অগ্রাহ্য ɔgrahyô (*pron* ɔgrajjho) *adj* unacceptable, rejected

অগ্রাহ্য করা ɔgrahyô kɔra (*pron* ɔgrajjho kɔra) *vb* reject, slight, ignore

অগ্রিম ôgrim *adj* first, elder, chief

অগ্রিম ôgrim *n* advance

অঙ্ক ɔṅkô *n* sum, digit, number

অঙ্কুর ôṅkur *n* sprout, shoot, sapling

অঙ্গ ɔṅgô *n* limb, body, appearance, shape, form

অঙ্গার ɔṅgar *n* coal, carbon, cinder

অঙ্গুলি ôṅguli *n* finger, toe, digit

অঙ্গুষ্ঠ ôṅguṣṭhô *n* thumb

অচঞ্চল ɔcɔñcôl *adj* unwavering, steady

অচল ɔcɔl *adj* out of use

অচলিত ɔcôlitô *adj* obsolete, out of date

অচিরে ɔcire *adv* immediately, without delay

অচেতন ɔcetôn *adj* inanimate

অচেনা ɔcena *adj* unknown, strange

অচেষ্টা ɔceṣṭa *adj* inactive, not trying

অচ্ছ ɔcchô *adj* transparent, pure

অছি ôchi *n* guardian, custodian

অজ ɔjɔ *adj* downright, thorough

অজয় ɔjɔŷ *adj* invincible

অজর ɔjɔr *adj* ageless, unchanging

অজস্র ɔjôsrô *adj* innumerable, plenty, abundant

অজানা ɔjana *adj* unknown, strange

অজিত ɔjit *adj* unconquered, undefeated

অজু ôju *n* ablutions, ritual cleansing

অজুহাত ôjuhat *n* excuse, pretext

অজ্ঞ ɔjñɔ *adj* ignorant, uninformed

অজ্ঞাত ɔjñatô (*pron* ɔggæto) *adj* secret, hidden

অজ্ঞান ɔjñan (*pron* ɔggæn) *adj* unconscious, fainted

অজ্ঞানতা ɔjñanôta (*pron* ɔggænota) *n* ignorance

অঞ্চল ɔñcôl *n* region

অটল ɔṭɔl *adj* unwavering, firm, steady

অটুট ɔṭuṭ *adj* unbroken, intact, firm

অণু ɔṇu *n, adj* atom, minute, small

অত ɔtɔ *adv* so, so much

অতএব ɔtɔeb *adv* therefore, hence, so

অতঃপর ɔtôḥpɔr *adv* hence, so, therefore

অতন্দ্র ɔtɔndrô *adj* vigilant, untiring, alert

অতর্কিত ɔtôrkitô *adj* unexpected

অতল ɔtɔl *adj* fathomless, deep

অতশত ɔtôśɔtô *n* all that, all these things

অতি ôti *pref* over-

অতিক্রম ôtikrôm *n* transgression, violation

অতিক্রান্ত ôtikrantô *adj* passed, elapsed

অতিথি ôtithi *n* guest

অতিমানবিক ôtimanôbik *adj* superhuman

অতিরঞ্জন ôtirɔñjôn *n* exaggeration

অতিরিক্ত ôtiriktô *adj* surplus, extra, too much

অতিশয় ôtiśɔŷ *adj* excessive, too much

অতিষ্ঠ ɔtiṣṭhô *adj* restless, uneasy, irritated

অতীত ɔtīt *n* the past, times gone by

অতীত ôtīt *pp* past, beyond

অতুল ɔtul *adj* incomparable, matchless

অতৃপ্ত ɔtṛptô *adj* unsatisfied

অত্যধিক ôtyôdhik *adv* too much, extremely

অত্যন্ত ôtyôntô *adv* extremely

অত্যাচার ôtyacar *n* oppression, tyranny

অত্র ɔtrô *adv* in this place, here

অথচ ɔthôcô *conj* yet, still

অথবা ɔthôba *conj* or

অদক্ষ ɔdɔkṣô *adj* unskilled, inexpert

অদম্য ɔdɔmyô *adj* indomitable, wild

অদলবদল ɔdɔlbɔdôl *n* interchange, alternation

অদূর ɔdūr *adj* near, close

অদৃশ্য ɔdṛśyô *adj* invisible, imperceptible

অদৃষ্ট ɔdṛṣṭô *n* the unseen, fate, destiny

অদ্ভুত ôdbhūt *adj* strange

অদ্য ɔdyô *n, adv* today

অধঃপতন ɔdhḥpɔtôn *n* downfall, degradation

অধঃপাত ɔdhḥpat *n* downfall

অধম ɔdhôm *adj* lowest, inferior

অধর ɔdhôr *n* lower lip

অধর্ম ɔdhɔrmô *n* sinfulness, wickedness

অধস্তন ɔdhôstɔn *adj* subordinate, inferior

অধস্তন পুরুষ ɔdhôstɔn puruṣ *n* later generation, posterity

অধিক ôdhik *adj* many, much, more

অধিকাংশ ôdhikaṁśô *adj* most

অধিকার ôdhikar *n* right, claim

অধিকারী ôdhikarī *n* proprietor, owner

অধিগত ôdhigɔtô *adj* attained, obtained, acquired

অধিজন ôdhijɔn *n* majority

অধিনায়ক ôdhinaŷôk *n* chief, leader

অধিনিয়ম ôdhiniŷôm *n* legislation

অধিবর্ষ ôdhibɔrṣô *n* leap year

অধিবাসী ôdhibasī *n* resident, inhabitant

অধিবিদ্যা ôdhibidya *n* metaphysics

অধিবেশন ôdhibeśôn *n* meeting, session

অধিরাজ ôdhiraj *n* emperor, ruler

অধিষ্ঠান ôdhiṣṭhan *n* place of residence; presence, appearance

অধীত ôdhītô *adj* read, studied, perused

অধীন ôdhīn *adj* subjugated, subordinate, dependent

অধৈর্য ôdhoiryô *n* impatience, unease

অধ্যবসায় ôdhyôbɔsaŷ *n* perseverance

অধ্যাপক ôdhyapôk *n* professor

অধ্যাপনা ôdhyapɔna *n* teaching, instruction

অধ্যায় ôdhyaŷ *n* chapter, paragraph

অনটন ɔnôṭɔn *n* want, shortage, deficiency

অনধিকার ɔnôdhikar *n* absence of right or claim

অনধিকারচর্চা ɔnôdhikarcɔrca *n* interference, meddling

অনধিকারপ্রবেশ ɔnôdhikarprôbeś *n* trespassing

অনন্ত ɔnôntô *adj* endless, everlasting

অনন্য ɔnônyô *adj* singular, unique

অনবকাশ ɔnɔbôkaś *n* lack of time, want of leisure or respite

অনবরত ɔnɔbɔrôtô *adj* ceaseless, continuous

অনভিজ্ঞ ɔnôbhijñô *adj* inexpert, inexperienced

অনভ্যস্ত ɔnɔbhyôstô *adj* unused to, unaccustomed

অনর্গল ɔnɔrgɔl *adj* unrestrained, profuse

অনর্থক ɔnɔrthôk *adj* futile, useless

অনশন ɔnɔśôn *n* starving, fasting

অনশন–ধর্মঘট ɔnɔśôn-dhɔrmôghɔṭ *n* hunger-strike

অনাচার ɔnacar *n* malpractice, immoral practice

অনাথ ɔnath *(WB) n* orphan

অনাথাশ্রম ɔnathaśrôm *n* orphanage

অনাদর ɔnadôr *n* neglect, disrespect

অনাদিকাল ɔnadikal *n* time immemorial, ancient times

অনাবৃষ্টি ɔnabr̥ṣṭi *n* drought

অনায়াস ɔnaẏas *adj* effortless, easy

অনাশ্রয় ɔnaśrɔẏ *adj* unprotected, helpless

অনাসক্তি ɔnasôkti *n* indifference

অনাস্থা ɔnastha *n* mistrust, lack of confidence

অনাহার ɔnahar *n* starving, fasting

অনিচ্ছা ɔniccha *n* reluctance

অনিচ্ছুক ɔnicchuk *adj* unwilling, reluctant

অনিদ্রা ɔnidra *n* sleeplessness, insomnia

অনিবার ɔnibar *adj* incessant, nonstop

অনিবার্য ɔnibaryô *adj* irresistible, unpreventable

অনিয়ত ɔniẏ̐ɔtô *adj* unregulated, uncontrolled

অনিয়ম ɔniẏôm *n* violation of rules

অনিয়মিত ɔniẏômitô *adj* irregular

অনিদিষ্ট ɔnirdiṣṭô *adj* not fixed, not settled

অনিল ɔnil *n* wind, air, breeze

অনিশ্চিত ɔniścitô *adj* uncertain, indefinite

অনিষ্ঠা ɔniṣṭha *n* non-observance

অনীহা ɔnīha *n* inertia, apathy

অনুকম্প ônukɔmpô *n* compassion, kindness

অনুকরণ ônukɔrôṇ *n* imitation, copying

অনুকল্প ônukɔlpô *n* alternative, substitute

অনুকূল ônukūl *adj* helpful, favorable

অনুক্ত ɔnuktô *adj* unspoken, unuttered

অনুক্রম ônukrôm *n* serial, order, sequence

অনুক্রমণিকা ônukrômôṇika *n* preface, list of contents, index

অনুক্ষণ ônukṣɔṇ *adv* continually, always

অনুগত ônugɔtô *adj* obedient, devoted

অনুগমন ônugɔmôn *n* act of following, obedience

অনুগামী ônugamī *adj* obedient, adherent, conforming

অনুগ্রহ ônugrôhô *n* favor, kindness

অনুচর ônucɔr *adj* accompanying, attendant

অনুচিত ɔnucit *adj* improper, inappropriate, unjustified

অনুচ্ছেদ ônucched *n* paragraph, section

অনুতপ্ত ônutɔptô *adj* repentant, contrite

অনুতাপ ônutap *n* repentance, penitence

অনুদান ônudan *n* grant, scholarship

অনুদার ɔnudar *adj* narrow-minded, niggardly

অনুধাবন ônudhabôn *n* reflection, deliberation

অনুনয় ônunɔẏ̐ *n* entreaty, request, solicitation

অনুনাদ ônunad *n* echo, resonance

অনুন্নত ɔnunnɔtô *adj* backward, underdeveloped

অনুপকারী ɔnupôkarī *adj* harmful, injurious

অনুপম ônupɔm *adj* incomparable, unequaled

অনুপযুক্ত ɔnupôyuktô *adj* unfit, unsuitable

অনুপস্থিত ɔnupôsthit *adj* absent

অনুপাত ônupat *n* ratio, proportion

অনুপায় ɔnupaŷ *n* lack of resources, helplessness

অনুপুঙ্খভাবে ônupuṅkhôbhabe *adv* minutely, thoroughly

অনুপ্রবেশ ônuprôbeś *n* penetration, infiltration

অনুপ্রভ ônuprôbhô *adj* phosphorescent

অনুপ্রস্থ ônuprôsthô *adj* crosswise, transverse

অনুপ্রাণনা ônupraṇôna *n* stimulus, fillip, incentive, inspiration

অনুপ্রাণিত ônupraṇitô *adj* inspired, stimulated

অনুপ্রাস ônupras *n* alliteration

অনুপ্রেরণা ônuprerôṇa *n* stimulus, inspiration

অনুবন্ধ ônubɔndhô *n* start, introduction; context

অনুবর্তী ônubôrtī *adj* subservient, obedient

অনুবাদ ônubad *n* translation

অনুবাদ করা ônubad kɔra *vb* translate

অনুভব ônubhɔb *n* perception, feeling, realization

অনুভব করা ônubhɔb kɔra *vb* perceive, feel, realize

অনুভাব ônubhab *n* influence, power

অনুভূতি ônubhūti *n* feeling, intuition

অনুমতি ônumôti *n* permission, leave

অনুমান ônuman *n* supposition, conjecture

অনুমান করা ônuman kɔra *vb* guess, suppose

অনুমোদন ônumodôn *n* consent, approval

অনুযায়ী ônuyaŷī *adj* according to, following

অনুযোগ ônuyog *n* censure, reproof, reproach

অনুরক্ত ônurɔktô *adj* inclined towards, attracted to, devoted to

অনুরণন ônurɔṇôn *n* resonance, echo

অনুরাগ ônurag *n* love, affection, attraction

অনুরূপ ônurūp *adv*, *pp* similar, like

অনুরোধ ônurodh *n* request, entreaty

অনুলিপি ônulipi *n* copy, duplicate

অনুশাসন ônuśasôn *n* order, command, injunction

অনুশীলন ônuśīlôn *n* exercise, practice

অনুশোচনা ônuśocôna *n* regret, contrition, remorse

অনুষদ ônuṣɔd *n* university faculty

অনুষ্ঠান ônuṣṭhan *n* ceremony, celebration

অনুসন্ধান ônusɔndhan *n* search, research

অনুসরণ ônusɔrôṇ *n* pursuit, imitation

অনুসারে ônusare *adv* according to, following

অনুসূচি ônusūci *n* schedule, timetable

অনেক ɔnek *adj* much, many

অনেকত্ব ɔnekɔtvô *n* plural, plurality

অনেকক্ষণ ɔnekkṣôṇ *adv* a long time

অন্ত ɔntô *n* end, termination, death

অন্তঃকরণ ɔntôĥkɔrôṇ *n* heart, mind

অন্তঃশীল ɔntôĥśīl *adj* unrevealed, hidden

অন্তঃসার ɔntôĥsar *n* core, essence

অন্তত ɔntôtô *adv* at least

অন্তর ɔntôr *n* heart, depth, interior

অন্তরঙ্গতা ɔntôrɔṅgôta *n* intimacy

অন্তরা ɔntôra *n* middle part of a song

অন্তরীপ ɔntôrīp *n* cape, promontory

অন্তরে ɔntôre *adv* within, in the depth of

অন্তর্গত ɔntôrgɔtô *adj* included, inward, enclosed in

অন্তর্ঘাত ɔntôrghat *n* sabotage

অন্তর্ধান ɔntôrdhan *n* disappearance

অন্তর্হিত ɔntôrhitô *adj* departed, vanished

অন্তিম ôntim *adj* final, last, ultimate

অন্ত্র ɔntrô *n* bowels, intestines; *adj* internal

অন্ধ ɔndhô *adj* blind

অন্ধকার ɔndhôkar *n* darkness

অন্ন ɔnnô *n* rice, food

অন্বেষণ ɔnveṣɔṇ *n* search

অন্য ônyô *adj* other, different

অন্যমনস্ক ônyômônôskô *adj* absentminded, preoccupied

অন্যান্য ônyanyô *n, adj* various others, several others

অন্যায় ɔnyaŷ (*pron* ɔnnay) *n* impropriety, wrong-doing, injustice

অন্যায় করা ɔnyaŷ kɔra *vb* do wrong, act improperly

অপকার ɔpôkar *n* harm, injury, disservice

অপক্ক ɔpɔkkô *adj* unripe, immature

অপক্ষপাত ɔpôkṣôpat *n* impartiality, neutrality

অপঘাত ɔpôghat *n* death or injury by accident

অপচয় ɔpôcɔŷ *n* waste, loss, misuse

অপচেষ্টা ɔpôceṣṭa *n* evil-doing, vicious intention

অপছন্দ ɔpɔchôndô *n* dislike, aversion

অপটু ɔpôṭu *adj* unskilled

অপদার্থ ɔpôdarthô *adj* worthless, useless

অপপ্রয়োগ ɔpôprôŷog *n* misapplication

অপবাদ ɔpôbad *n* defamation, slander, ill repute

অপব্যয়ী ɔpôbyæŷī *adj* wasteful, extravagant

অপভাষা ɔpôbhaṣa *n* obscene language, slang

অপভ্রংশ ɔpôbhrôṁśô *adj* corrupted, distorted (*especially of language*)

অপমান ɔpôman *n* insult, disgrace

অপমান করা ɔpôman kɔra *n* insult

অপর ɔpɔr *adj* other, another, later

অপরাজিত ɔpôrajitô *adj* victorious

অপরাধ ɔpôradh *n* fault, crime

অপরাধী ɔpôradhī *adj* criminal, guilty

অপরিচিত ɔpôricitô *adj* unknown

অপরিণত ɔpôriṇôtô *adj* immature, young, green

অপরিমাণ ɔpôrimaṇ *adj* excessive, immeasurable

অপরিমিত ɔpôrimitô *adj* immeasurable, countless

অপরিষ্কার ɔpôriṣkar *adj* unclean

অপরিহার্য ɔpôriharyô *adj* indispensable, inevitable

অপরূপ ɔpôrūp *adj* wonderful

অপর্যাপ্ত ɔpôryaptô *adj* abundant, plentiful

অপলক ɔpôlôk *adj* unblinking, steadfast

অপসরণ ɔpôsɔrɔṇ *n* withdrawal, retreat

অপহরণ ɔpôhɔrôṇ *n* theft, plunder

অপাক ɔpak *n* indigestion

অপাত্র ɔpatrô *n* unsuitable partner, unfit person or thing

অপার ɔpar *n* endless, vast

অপারক ɔparôk *adj* incapable, unable

অপার্থিব ɔparthibô *adj* supernatural

অপুষ্ট ɔpuṣṭô *adj* undeveloped, unripe, undernourished

অপূর্ণ ɔpūrṇô *adj* incomplete

অপূর্ব ɔpūrbô *adj* unprecedented, unusual

অপেক্ষা ɔpekṣa *n* wait, delay

অপেক্ষা করা ɔpekṣa kɔra *vb* wait

অপোগণ্ড ɔpogɔṇḍô *adj* minor, infant

অপ্রকট ɔprɔkɔṭ *adj* hidden

অপ্রকাশিত ɔprôkaśitô *adj* unrevealed, unpublished

অপ্রকৃত ɔprôkṛtô *adj* untrue, false

অপ্রচলিত ɔprôcôlitô *adj* obsolete, out of date, unfashionable

অপ্রচুর ɔprôcur *adj* scanty, scarce, insufficient

অপ্রতিদ্বন্দ্বী ɔprôtidvôndvī *adj* unrivaled, peerless, unparalleled

অপ্রতিহত ɔprôtihɔtô *adj* unopposed, unobstructed

অপ্রতুল ɔprôtul *n* shortage, dearth, insufficiency

অপ্রত্যাশিত ɔprôtyaśitô *adj* unexpected, sudden, accidental

অপ্রয়োজন ɔprôŷojôn *n* needlessness

অপ্রয়োজনীয় ɔprôŷojônīŷô *adj* unnecessary

অপ্রশস্ত ɔprôśôstô *adj* narrow; unsuitable, improper

অপ্রস্তুত ɔprôstut *adj* unprepared

অপ্রাপ্ত বয়স্ক ɔpraptô bɔŷôskô *adj* minor, underage

অপ্রিয় ɔpriŷô *adj* disagreeable, unpleasant

অফুরন্ত ɔphurɔntô *adj* unending, endless

অবকাশ ɔbôkaś *n* leisure, respite

অবগত ɔbôgɔtô *adj* informed, aware, acquainted

অপচয় ɔpcɔŷ *n* waste, decay

অবতরণ ɔbôtɔrôṇ *n* descent, disembarkment

অবতরণ করা ɔbôtɔrôṇ kɔra *vb* descend, climb down

অবতল ɔbôtɔl *adj* concave

অবতার ɔbôtar *n* avatar, incarnation, personification

অবদান ɔbôdan *n* contribution, offering

অবদ্য ɔbɔdyô *adj* vulgar

অবধান ɔbôdhan *n* attention, deliberation

অবধারিত ɔbôdharitô *adj* sure, certain

অবধি ɔbôdhi *pp* since, until

অবনত ɔbônɔtô *adj* stooping, low, depressed

অবনতি ɔbônôti *n* deterioration, baseness, depravity

অবনী ɔbônī *n* the earth, the world

অববুদ্ধ ɔbôbuddhô *adj* enlightened, awakened

অবমাননা ɔbômanôna *n* insult, dishonor, irreverence

অবয়ব ɔbɔŷôb *n* body, limb, organ

অবর ɔbôr *adj* inferior, subordinate, junior

অবরোধ ɔbôrodh *n* blockade, siege

অবরোধ করা ɔbôrodh kɔra *vb* besiege, obstruct, hinder

অবরোহ ɔbôrohô *n* descent; deduction

অবর্ণনীয় ɔbɔrṇônīŷô *adj* indescribable

অবর্তমান ɔbɔrtôman *adj* absent, dead, departed

অবলম্বন ɔbôlɔmbôn *n* support, prop

অবলিপ্ত ɔbôliptô *adj* arrogant, proud

অবলুপ্ত ɔbôluptô *adj* extinct; screened from view, concealed

অবশ ɔbɔś *adj* unmanageable

অবশ করা ɔbɔś kɔra *vb* anesthetize

অবশিষ্ট ɔbôśiṣṭô *n* remainder, surplus

অবশেষ ɔbôśeṣ *n* end, termination

অবশেষে ɔbôśeṣe *adv* finally, at last

অবশ্য ɔbôśyô *adv* of course

অবসন্ন ɔbôsɔnnô *adj* exhausted, tired

অবসর ɔbôsɔr *n* leisure, retirement

অবসাদ ɔbôsad *n* tiredness, fatigue, exhaustion

অবসান ɔbôsan *n* termination, end, death

অবস্থা ɔbôstha *n* situation

অবস্থিত ɔbôsthitô *adj* situated, located, placed

অবহিত ɔbôhitô *adj* attentive, absorbed

অবহেলা ɔbôhela *n* neglect

অবহেলা করা ɔbôhela kɔra *vb* neglect, disregard

অবাক ɔbak *adj* amazed, stunned, speechless

অবাধ ɔbadh *adj* unobstructed

অবাধ্য ɔbadhyô *adj* disobedient, unruly, uncontrollable

অবান্তর ɔbantôr *adj* irrelevant, extraneous

অবাস্তব ɔbastôb *adj* unreal

অবিকল ɔbikɔl *adj* perfect, whole, complete

অবিকৃত ɔbikṛtô *adj* undistorted, uncorrupted

অবিচল ɔbicɔl *adj* unmoved, unshaken

অবিচার ɔbicar *n* injustice

অবিচ্ছিন্ন ɔbichinnô *adj* whole, entire

অবিধেয় ɔbidheyô *adj* improper, unjust

অবিনয় ɔbinɔy *n* impertinence, incivility, discourteousness

অবিনাশী ɔbinaśī *adj* indestructible, imperishable

অবিবাহিত ɔbibahitô *adj* unmarried

অবিবেক ɔbibek *n* unscrupulousness

অবিবেচক ɔbibecɔk *adj* imprudent, inconsiderate

অবিভাজ্য ɔbibhajyô *adj* indivisible

অবিরত ɔbirɔtô *adj* continuous

অবিরাম ɔbiram *adj* ceaseless, non-stop, untiring, unremitting

অবিলম্বে ɔbilɔmbe *adv* promptly, quickly

অবিশ্বস্ত ɔbiśvɔstô *adj* unreliable, unfaithful

অবিশ্বাস ɔbiśvas *n* mistrust

অবিশ্বাসী ɔbiśvasī *adj* untrustworthy, unfaithful, perfidious

অবিশ্বাস্য ɔbiśvasyô *adj* incredible, unbelievable

অবিহিত ɔbihitô *adj* improper, illegal, unadvisable

অবুঝ ɔbujh *adj* obstinate, stupid, foolish

অবেক্ষণ ɔbekṣɔṇ *n* observation, review, supervision

অবেলা ɔbela *n* inauspicious time; *adv* untimely

অবৈধ ɔboidhô *adj* unlawful, illegal, unauthorized

অবোধ ɔbodh *adj* stupid, foolish, ignorant

অবোলা ɔbola *adj* dumb, mute

অব্যক্ত ɔbyktô (*pron* ɔbækto) *adj* indistinct, unspoken

অব্যবস্থা ɔbybôstha *n* mismanagement

অব্যবহার্য ɔbybôharyô *adj* useless, out of order

অব্যয় ɔbyɔŷ *adj* indeclineable

অব্যর্থ ɔbyrthô *adj* certain, infallible

অব্যাকুল ɔbyækul *adj* composed, calm

অব্যাহত ɔbyæhɔtô *adj* unimpeded, unhindered

অব্যাহতি ɔbyæhôti *n* aquittal, release, exemption

অভক্ত ɔbhɔktô *adj* irreverent, apathic, faithless

অভদ্র ɔbhɔdrô *adj* impolite, rude, discourteous

অভয় ɔbhɔŷ *n* fearlessness, courage, confidence

অভয় দেওয়া ɔbhɔŷ deoŷa *vb* reassure

অভাগ্য ɔbhagyô *adj* unfortunate, unlucky

অভাব ɔbhab *n* lack, want

অভাবনীয় ɔbhabôniŷô *adj* unthinkable

অভাবী ɔbhabī *adj* needy, poor

অভিকর্ষ ôbhikɔrʂô *n* gravitation

অভিঘাত ôbhighat *n* stroke, blow, hit

অভিজাত ôbhijatô *adj* aristocratic

অভিজ্ঞ ôbhijñô *adj* experienced, specialized, expert

অভিজ্ঞতা ôbhijñôta *n* experience

অভিধান ôbhidhan *n* dictionary

অভিনন্দন ôbhinɔndôn *n* congratulations

অভিনব ôbhinɔbô *adj* new, strange, novel

অভিনয় ôbhinɔŷ *n* simulation, acting, performance

অভিনেতা ôbhineta *n* actor, player

অভিনেত্রী ôbhinetrī *n* actress

অভিন্ন ɔbhinnô *adj* similar, same, undivided

অভিপ্রায় ôbhipraŷ *n* desire, intention, purpose

অভিপ্রেত ôbhipretô *adj* deliberate, designed, intended

অভিবাদন ôbhibadôn *n* salute, greeting

অভিবাসী ôbhibasī *n* immigrant

অভিভাবক ôbhibhabôk *n* guardian, custodian, caretaker

অভিভূত ôbhibhūtô *adj* stricken, overcome, bewildered

অভিমান ôbhiman *n* hurt pride

অভিমানী ôbhimanī *adj* piqued, hurt

অভিমুখে ôbhimukhe *adv* in the direction of

অভিযান ôbhiyan *n* expedition, exploration

অভিযোগ ôbhiyog *n* complaint, accusation

অভিরুচি ôbhiruci *n* desire, wish, liking

অভিলাষ ôbhilaʂ *n* desire, wish, pleasure

অভিশাপ ôbhiśap *n* curse

অভিষিক্ত ôbhiʂiktô *adj* anointed, initiated, installed

অভিষেক ôbhiʂek *n* inauguration

অভিসন্ধি ôbhisôndhi *n* (evil) intention, scheme

অভিসম্পাত করা ôbhisɔmpat kɔra *vb* curse

অভিসার ôbhisar *n* tryst, love tryst

অভিহিত ôbhihitô *adj* named, entitled

অভুক্ত ɔbhuktô *adj* untasted, untouched (food)

অভেদ ɔbhed *n* similarity, unity, oneness

অভ্যর্থনা ôbhyôrthôna *n* greeting, welcome, reception

অভ্যস্ত ôbhystô (*pron* obhosto) *adj* practiced, used to, accustomed to

অভ্যাস ôbhyas *n* habit, custom

অভ্রান্ত ɔbhrantô *adj* unerring, unfailing

অমঙ্গল ɔmôṅgôl *n* evil, harm, danger

অমত ɔmɔt *n* disapproval

অমন ɔmôn *adj* such

অমনি ômni *adv* at once, instantly

অমর ɔmɔr *adj* immortal

অমরত্ব ɔmɔrɔtvô *n* immortality

অমর্যাদা ɔmɔryada *n* neglect, disrespect, slight

অমলিন ɔmôlin *adj* bright, clean, untarnished

অমানুষিক ɔmanuṣik *adj* inhuman, superhuman

অমান্য করা ɔmanyô kɔra *vb* disrespect, neglect, disobey

অমায়িক ɔmaẏik *adj* candid, frank, guileless

অমার্জিত ɔmarjitô *adj* rough, un-polished, crude

অমিত ɔmitô *adj* boundless, excessive, immense

অমিতব্যয় ɔmitôbyæŷ *n* extravagance

অমিল ɔmil *n* discord, dissension

অমিশ্র ɔmiśrô *adj* unadulterated, pure, genuine

অমুক ômuk *n* someone, unnamed person

অমূল্য ɔmūlyô *adj* priceless, invaluable

অমেয় ɔmeŷô *adj* immeasurable, immense

অমোঘ ɔmogh *adj* infallible, unfailing

অম্ল ɔmlô *adj* sour

অম্লজান ɔmlôjan *n* oxygen

অযত্ন ɔyɔtnô *n* disregard, neglect

অযথা ɔyôtha *adj* baseless, groundless, false

অয়ন ɔŷôn *n* route, path, course (of the sun)

অযোগ্য ɔyogyô *adj* unfit, unsuitable

অযৌক্তিক ɔyouktik *adj* illogical, unreasonable

অরক্ষিত ɔrôkṣitô *adj* unprotected, defenseless

অরণ্য ɔrônyô *n* wood, forest

অরাজক ɔrajôk *adj* anarchical, lawless

অরুচি ɔruci *n* loss of appetite, distaste

অরুণ ôruṇ *n* the morning sun

অর্চনা ɔrcôna *n* worship, homage

অর্জন ɔrjôn *n* gain, profit, earnings

অর্জন করা ɔrjôn kɔra *vb* reap, earn, acquire

অর্জুন ôrjun *n* fox-glove

অর্থ ɔrthô *n* meaning, significance, money, wealth, purpose

অর্থনীতি ɔrthônīti *n* economics

অর্থনৈতিক ɔrthônoitik *adj* economic

অর্থশূন্য ɔrthôśūnyô *adj* meaning-less, nonsensical, vacant

অর্থহীন ɔrthôhīn *adj* meaningless

অর্থাৎ ɔrthaṯ *conj* that is, namely

অর্ধেক ɔrdhek *adj* half

অর্পণ ɔrpôṇ *n* investment, award

অলংকার ɔlôṁkar, অলঙ্কার ɔlôṅkar *n* decoration, ornament

অলক ɔlôk *n* curl, ringlet (of hair)

অলক্ষিত ɔlôkṣitô *adj* unnoticed, unobserved

অলক্ষ্য ɔlôkṣyô *adj* invisible, unseen

অলস ɔlôs *adj* lazy, idle, indolent

অলিগলি ôligôli *n* narrow path

অলৌকিক ɔloukik *adj* superhuman, supernatural

অল্প ɔlpô *adj* a little

অল্প-কিছু ɔlpô kichu *n* a small amount

অল্প বয়সী ɔlpô bɔŷôsī *n* young

অল্পে অল্পে ɔlpe ɔlpe *adv* little by little

অশক্ত ɔʃɔktô *adj* incapable, powerless

অশন ɔʃôn *n* eating, food, repast

অশান্ত ɔʃantô *adj* agitated, restless, worried

অশান্তি ɔʃanti *n* lack of peace

অশিক্ষিত ɔʃikṣitô *adj* illiterate, uneducated

অশিষ্ট ɔʃiṣṭô *adj* uncivil, impolite, rude

অশুদ্ধ ɔʃuddhô *adj* impure, unclean

অশেষ ɔʃeṣ *adj* endless, unending

অশোধিত ɔʃodhitô *adj* unrefined, crude

অশোভন ɔʃobhôn *adj* unbecoming, improper

অশ্রদ্ধা ɔʃrôddha *n* irreverence, apathy

অশ্রু ôʃru *n* tear(s)

অশ্লীল ɔʃlīl *adj* indecent, obscene

অষ্ট ɔṣṭô *num* eight

অষ্টম ɔṣṭôm *num* eighth

অসংখ্য ɔsôṁkhyô *adj* countless

অসংযত ɔsɔṁyôtô *adj* uncontrolled, unrestrained

অসৎ ɔsɔt *adj* dishonest

অসতর্ক ɔsɔtɔrkô *adj* inadvertent, careless

অসত্য ɔsôtyô *adj* untrue, false

অসদ্ভাব ɔsɔdbhab *n* unfriendliness, enmity

অসন্তুষ্ট ɔsôntuṣṭô *adj* displeased, dissatisfied

অসভ্য ɔsôbhyô *adj* rude, uncivil, discourteous

অসমকক্ষ ɔsɔmôkôkṣô *adj* unequal

অসমতা ɔsɔmôta *n* inequality

অসময় ɔsômôŷ *adj* inauspicious, untimely

অসমর্থ ɔsɔmɔrthô *adj* unable, incompetent

অসমান ɔsɔman *adj* uneven

অসমাপিত ɔsɔmapitô *adj* incomplet

অসম্পূর্ণ ɔsɔmpūrṇô *adj* incomplete, unfinished

অসম্ভব ɔsɔmbhɔb *adj* impossible

অসম্ভাবনা ɔsɔmbhabôna *n* improbability, unlikelihood

অসম্মান ɔsɔmman *n* disrespect, indignity

অসরল ɔsɔrôl *adj* crooked, deceptive

অসহায় ɔsɔhaŷ *adj* defenseless, weak, helpless

অসহ্য ɔsôhyô (*pron* ɔshojjho) *adj* unbearable

অসাড় ɔsar *adj* numb, paralysed

অসাধারণ ɔsadharôn *adj* unusual

অসাধু ɔsadhu *adj* corrupt, evil

অসাধ্য ɔsadhyô *adj* unattainable

অসাবধান ɔsabdhan *n* carelessness

অসাময়িক ɔsamôŷik *adj* untimely, unseasonal

অসামান্য ɔsamanyô *adj* uncommon, unusual

অসাম্প্রদায়িক ɔsamprôdaŷik *adj* universal, cosmopolitan

অসীম ɔsīm *adj* endless, vast

অসুখ ɔsukh *n* illness

অসুবিধা ɔsubidha, অসুবিধে ɔsubidhe *n* inconvenience

অসুস্থ ɔsusthô *adj* ill, unwell

অসুস্থতা ɔsusthôta *n* sickness, illness

অস্তিত্ব ôstitvô *n* existence

অস্ত্র ɔstrô *n* instrument, tool

অস্ত্রোপচার ɔstropôcar *n* operation

অস্থায়ী ɔsthaŷī *adj* temporary, transient, unstable

অস্থি ôsthi *n* bone, skeleton

অস্থির ɔsthir *adj* restless, uneasy, perturbed

অস্থিরতা ɔsthirɔta *n* restlessness

অস্পষ্ট ɔspɔʂʈô *adj* indistinct, unclear, hazy, vague, obscure

অস্বস্তি ɔsvôsti *n* discomfort, uneasiness

অস্বাভাবিক ɔsvabhabik *adj* rare, unusual

অস্বাস্থ্য ɔsvasthô *n* ill health, illness; *adj* malnourished

অস্বীকার ɔsvīkar *n* denial

অস্বীকৃত ɔsvīkr̥tô *adj* denied, disavowed

অহঙ্কার ɔhôṅkar *n* pride, vanity, arrogance

অহঙ্কারী ɔhôṅkarī *adj* arrogant, proud

অহরহ ɔhôrɔhô *adv* incessantly, always

অহেতুক ɔhetuk *adj* irrelevant, unreasonable

আ a

আইন ain *n* law, rule

আওতা aota *n* care, guardianship, custody

আওয়াজ aoŷaj *n* sound, voice

আংটি aṁṭi *n* ring

আংরাখা aṁrakha *n* cloak, coat

আঁকা āka *vb* draw

আঁকাবাঁকা ākabāka *n* zigzag

আঁচ āc *n* guess, conjecture

আঁচ করা āc kɔra *vb* guess, surmise, sense

আঁচ লাগা āc laga *vb* feel stressed

আঁচড়ানো ācrano *vb* comb, scratch

আঁচল ācôl *n* loose end of a sari that is pulled up to cover the head

আঁচিল ācil *n* wart, mole, blotch

আঁট āṭ *n* tightness, tension

আঁটা āṭa *vb* tighten

আঁটি āṭi *n* stone (of fruit); bundle

আঁধার ādhar *n* dark

আঁশ āṡ *n* fiber

আঁস্তাকুড় āstakuṛ *n* dump, tip

আকর্ষণ akɔrṡôn *n* attraction, pull

আকাঙ্ক্ষা akaṅkṣa *n* ambition, wish

আকার akar *n* shape, form

আকাশ akaṡ *n* sky

আকস্মিক akôsmik *adj* sudden, unexpected

আকুতি akuti *n* ardor, eagerness

আকুল akul *n* distressed, anxious

আকৃষ্ট akṛṡṭô *adj* attracted, charmed

আক্রমণ akrômôn *n* attack

আক্রোশ akroṡ *n* wrath, grudge, anger

আক্ষরিক akṡôrik *adj* literal

আক্ষেপ akṡep *n* regret, repentance

আখ akh *n* sugarcane

আখ্যা akhya *n* name, title

আখ্যায়িত akhyaŷitô *adj* named, called

আগমন agômôn *n* arrival

আগা aga *n* top, summit

আগাছা agacha *n* weed

আগামী agamī *adj* next, coming

আগুন agun *n* fire

আগে age *adv, pp* before, earlier, in front of

আগ্রহ agrôhô *n* interest

আঘাত aghat *n* blow, stroke, hit

আঙুর aṅgur *n* grape

আঙুল aṅgul *n* finger

আচরণ acɔrɔn *n* behavior

আচার acar *n* pickle

আচার acar *n* rite, ritual

আচ্ছন্ন acchɔnnô *adj* overcast, cloudy

আচ্ছা accha *int* fine, well, OK

আছ– ach- *vb* be, be present, exist

আজ aj, আজকে ajke *n, adv* today, this day

আজকাল ajkal *adv* nowadays

আজগুবি ajgubi *adj* fantastic, absurd

আজব ajôb *adj* strange, queer

আজান ajan *n* Muslim call to prayer

আজেবাজে ajebaje *adj* nonsense, worthless

আজ্ঞা ajña *n* order, request

আঞ্চলিক añcôlik *adj* local, regional

আট aṭ *num* eight

আটকা aṭka *n* obstruction

আটকানো aṭkano *vb* confine, block, obstruct

আটকে পড়া aṭke pɔra *vb* be confined, be blocked

আটা aṭa *n* coarse flour

আঠা aṭha *n* glue

আঠার aṭharô *num* eighteen

আড়ঙ্গ arɔṅgô *n* marketplace

আড়ত arôt *n* warehouse, depot

আড়ম্বর arômbɔr *n* pomp, grandeur

আড়াই aṛai *num* two and a half

আড়াআড়ি aṛa–aṛi *adv* crosswise, diagonally

আড়াল aṛal *n* screen

আড্ডা aḍḍa *n* meeting place, social gathering

আতঙ্ক atôṅkô *n* terror, dread, fright

আতঙ্কিত atôṅkitô *adj* frightened, alarmed

আতপ্ত atɔptô *adj* warm, tepid

আতশবাজি atôśbaji *n* fireworks

আতা ata *n* custard apple

আতিথেয় atitheŷô *adj* hospitable

আতিথ্য atithyô *n* hospitality

আতিশয় atiśɔyyô *n* intensity, excess

আত্ম atmô *adj* own, self

আত্মগৌরব atmôgourɔb *n* conceit, vanity

আত্মবিশ্বাস atmôbiśvas *n* self-confidence

আত্মরক্ষা atmôrôkṣa *n* self-protection

আত্মশাসন atmôśason *n* self-control, self-discipline

আত্মসম্মান atmôsɔmman *n* self-respect

আত্মহত্যা atmôhɔtya *n* suicide

আত্মা atma *n* soul

আত্মীয় –স্বজন atmīŷô–svɔjôn *n* relatives, kin

আত্মীয়তা atmīŷôta *n* relationship

আদত adôt *n* practice, conduct, custom

আদত adôtô *adj* genuine, real

আদব adôb *n* good manners, courtesy

আদবে adôbe *adv* in reality, really

আদর adôr *n* love, affection, caress

আদর্শ adôrśô *n* ideal

আদল adôl *n* similarity

আদা ada *n* ginger

আদালত adalɔt *n* court of law

আদি adi *n* origin, source

আদিম adim *adj* aboriginal, primitive

আদুরে adure *adj* beloved, spoiled

আদেশ adeś *n* order, command

আদেশ দেওয়া adeś deoŷa *vb* order, command

আধবুড়ো adhburo *n, adj* middle-aged

আধা adha *n, adj* half

আধার adhar *n* receptacle, container

আধুনিক adhunik *adj* modern, current

আধুলি adhuli *n* coin; half-rupee

আধ্যাত্মিক adhyatmik *adj* spiritual

আনন্দ anôndô *n* joy

আনন্দিত anônditô *adj* delighted, pleased

আনমনে anmône *adv* listlessly, absentmindedly

আনা ana *n* anna (currency); *vb* bring

আনাজ anaj *(WB) n* vegetable

আনাড়ি anaṛi *adj* inexpert, unskilled, inefficient

আনারস anarɔs *n* pineapple

আন্তরিক antôrik *adj* heartfelt, sincere

আন্দোলন andolɔn *n* agitation, movement

আন্দোলিত andolitô *adj* stirred, agitated

আপত্তি apôtti *n* objection

আপন apôn *adj* one's own

আপনারা apnara *pr* you *(pl, pol)*

আপনি apni *pr* you *(sg, pol)*

আপশোষ apśoṣ *n* regret, chagrin

আপস apôs *n* compromise, reconciliation

আপাতত apatɔtô *adv* at present, for now

আপিস apis *n* office

আপ্যায়ন apyaŷôn *n* entertainment, reception, welcome

আফসানো aphsano *vb* brag, fret, bluster

আফিম aphim *n* opium

আবদার abdar *n* childish insistence, unreasonable demand

আবর্ত abɔrtô *n* rotation, whirling motion

আবহাওয়া abhaoŷa *n* weather

আবাদ abad *n* cultivation

আবার abar *adv* again

আবিষ্কার abiṣkar *n* invention, discovery

আবিষ্কার করা abiṣkar kɔra *vb* invent, discover

আবৃত্তি abṙtti *n* recital, reading

আবেগ abeg *n* passion, force, emotion

আবেদন abedɔn *n* prayer, solicitation, petition

আবোলতাবোল aboltabol *n* nonsense, delirium

আব্বা abba *n* father

আভা abha *n* shine, glow

আভাস abhas *n* trace, shadow

অভিধানিক abhidhanik *adj* lexicographical

আভ্যন্তরীণ abhyôntɔrīṇ *adj* internal

আম am *n* mango

আমড়া amṙa *n* hog plum *(fruit)*

আমতা–আমতা amta–amta *n* stutter

আমদানি amdani *n* import

আমরা amra *pr* we

আমল amôl *n* reign, rule

আমল না দেওয়া amôl na deoŷa *vb* overlook, pay no attention to

আমসত্ত্ব amsɔtvô *n* mango preserve

আমাশা amaśa *n* dysentery

আমি ami *pr* I

আমূল amūl *adj* radical

আমোদ amod *n* delight, pleasure

আমোদ প্রমোদ amodprômod *n* recreation, entertainment

আম্মা amma *n* mother

আয় aŷ *n* earnings, income

আয়তক্ষেত্র aŷôtôkṣetrô *n* rectangle

আয়তন aŷôtɔn *n* breadth, volume; format

আয়ত্ত aŷôttô *n* controlled, subjugated

আয়না aŷna *n* mirror

আয়া aŷa *n* nurse-maid

আয়ু aŷu *n* lifespan

আয়োজন করা aŷojɔn kɔra *vb* prepare

আর ar *conj* and, also, else, more

আরও aro *conj* more

আরক arôk *n* essence

আরক্ষী arôkṣī *n* guardsman

আরজি, আর্জি arji *n* prayer, request

আরব arôb *n* Arab

আরম্ভ করা arômbhô kɔra *vb* begin

আরসোলা arsola *n* cockroach, blackbeetle

আরাম aram *n* comfort, ease

আরে are *int expr* surprise, disapproval

আর্ত artô *adj* distressed, aggrieved; sick

আর্তনাদ artônad *n* groaning

আলকাতরা alkatra *n* tar

আলগা alga *adj* loose, untied, relaxed

আলঙ্কারিক alôṅkarik *adj* rhetorical, figurative

আলতো alto *adj* light (of touch)

আলনা alna *n* rack

আলমারি almari *n* cupboard

আলয় alɔŷ *n* abode, home

আলাদা alada *adj* separate

আলাপ alap *n* introduction *(WB)*, conversation *(Bd)*

আলাপ করা alap kɔra *vb* introduce oneself *(WB)*, talk *(Bd)*

আলিঙ্গন aliṅgɔn *n* embrace, hug

আলু alu *n* potato

আলেয়া aleŷa *n* illusion, false hope

আলো alo *n* light, beam, ray

আলোচনা alocɔna *n* discussion, deliberation

অলোড়ন alorɔn *n* agitation, excitation

আল্লাহ allah *n* God, Allah *(Muslim)*

আশকারা aśɔkara *n* indulgence, lenience

আশঙ্কা aśɔṅka *n* fear, dread

আশপাশ aśpaś *n* surroundings, environment

আশা aśa *n* hope, expectation

আশা করা aśa kɔra *vb* hope, expect

আশাতিরিক্ত aśatiriktô *adv* beyond expectation

আশি aśi *num* eighty

আশীর্বাদ aśīrbad *n* benediction, blessing

আশ্চর্য aścôryô *n* wonder, surprise, marvel; *adj* astonishing, amazing

আশ্বস্ত aśvôstô *adj* assured, heartened

আশ্বাস aśvas *n* hope, promise, assurance

আশ্রয় aśrɔŷ *n* shelter, refuge

আষাঢ় aṣarh *n* third Bengali month

আসক্ত asɔktô *adj* devoted, addicted

আসক্তি asôkti *n* devotion, attachment, addiction

আসন asôn *n* seat; Hindu prayer mat

আসবাব asbab *n* furniture

আসমান asman *n* sky, heavens

আসর asôr *n* meeting, gathering

আসল asôl *adj* real, genuine, true

আসলে asôle *adv* actually, in fact

আসা asa *vb* come, arrive, reach

আসামী asamī *n* defendant, accused

আস্ত astô *adj* whole, entire; real

আস্তানা astana *n* abode

আস্তে aste *adv* slowly, softly, carefully

আস্থা astha *n* trust, faith, reliance

আস্পর্ধা aspɔrdha *n* impudence, effrontery

আহত ahɔtô *adj* hurt, injured

আহা aha *int expr* sorrow, sympathy, alas, woe

আহার ahar *n* food, meal

ই

ইউরোপ iurop *n* Europe

ইংরেজ iṁrej *n* English

ইংরেজি iṁreji *adj* English (language)

ইঁদুর ĩdur *n* mouse, rat

ইঙ্গিত iṅgit *n* sign, hint

ইচ্ছা iccha *(Bd)*, ইচ্ছে icche *(WB) n* wish

ইচ্ছা করা iccha kɔra *vb* want, desire

ইচ্ছুক icchuk *adj* willing, eager

ইট iṭ *n* brick

ইতর itɔr *adj* other; base, mean

ইতরামি itrami *n* mischief, naughtiness

ইতস্তত itɔstɔtô *adv* here and there

ইতস্তত করা itɔstɔtô kɔra *vb* hesitate, procrastinate

ইতি iti *n* end, termination

ইতিমধ্য itimôdhyô *n* interval

ইতিমধ্যে itimôdhye *adv* in the meantime

ইতিহাস itihas *n* history

ইত্যাদি ityadi *adv* and so on

ইদানীং idanĩṁ *adv* at present, nowadays

ইনসাফ insaph *n* justice, equity

ইনি ini *pr* he, she *(hon)*

ইনিয়ে বিনিয়ে iniŷe biniŷe *adv* elaborately, in a roundabout way

ইমাম imam *n* Muslim priest

ইয়ার্কি iŷarki *n* joke, joking

ইলিশ iliś *n* hilsa fish

ইশকাপন iśkapôn *n* spade (in cards)

ইশারা iśara *n* gesture, beckoning

ইস is *int expr* pain, sympathy, regret

ইস্কুল iskul *n* school

ইস্ত্রি istri *n* iron (for clothes)

ইস্পাত ispat *n* steel

ইহুদি ihudi *adj* Jewish; *n* Jew

ঈ।

ঈগল īgɔl *n* eagle
ঈদ īd *n* Eid
ঈর্ষা īrṣa *n* envy; malice
ঈশ্বর īśvôr (*pron* isshor) *n* God

উ u

উঁকি ūki *n* prying

উঁকি মারা ūki mara *vb* peep, pry

উঁচু ūcu *adj* high, elevated

উকিল ukil *n* lawyer

উকুন ukun *n* headlouse

উগ্র ugrô *adj* cruel, rough

উগ্রতা ugrôta *n* violence, harshness

উচিত ucit *adj* proper, right

উচ্চ uccô *adj* high, tall

উচ্চতা uccôta *n* height

উচ্চবিত্ত uccôbittô *n* upper class

উচ্চারণ uccarôn *n* pronunciation

উচ্চাশা uccaśa *n* ambition

উচ্ছৃঙ্খল ucchr̊nkhɔl *adj* wayward, uncontrolled

উজানো ujano *vb* climb, rise

উজ্জ্বল ujjvɔl *adj* bright, radiant

উট uṭ *n* camel

উঠা uṭha *see* ওঠা oṭha

উঠান uṭhan *n* courtyard

উঠে যাওয়া uṭhe yaôŷa *vb* come off, be dissolved; rise

উড়া uṛe *see* ওড়া oṛa

উড়ে যাওয়া uṛe yaôŷa *vb* fly away

উড়ো কথা uṛo kɔtha *n* rumor

উতলা utɔla *adj* worried, anxious

উৎকট uṯkɔṯ *adj* severe, serious

উৎকণ্ঠ uṯkɔṇṭhô *adj* anxious, worried

উৎকণ্ঠা uṯkɔṇṭha *n* suspense, anxiety, worry

উৎকর্ণ uṯkɔrnô *adj* eager, curious

উত্তর uttôr *n* answer, reply; north

উত্তরাধিকার uttôradhikar *n* inheritance

উত্তেজনা uttejɔna *n* adventure, excitement

উত্তেজিত uttejitô *adj* excited

উত্ত্যক্ত করা uttyɔktô kɔra *vb* vex, tantalize

উৎপত্তি uṯpôtti *n* origin, birth

উৎপন্ন uṯpɔnnô *adj* produced, created

উৎপাত uṯpat *n* disturbance, nuisance

উৎপাদন uṯpadôn *n* manufacture, cultivation

উৎসব uṯsɔb *n* ceremony

উৎসাহ uṯsahô *n* encouragement; zeal

উথাল-পাথাল uthal-pathal *adv* topsy-turvy

উদয় udɔŷ *n* sunrise, dawn

উদার udar *adj* generous, liberal

উদারতা udarôta *n* generosity, kindness

উদারনীতি udarnīti *n* liberalism

উদাসীন udasīn *adj* detached, stoical, indifferent

উদাহরণ udahɔrôn *n* example

উদ্দাম uddam *adj* violent, wild

উদ্দীপনা uddīpôna *n* incitement, incentive

উদ্দীপিত uddīpitô *adj* excited, animated

উদ্দেশ uddeś *n* aim, direction

উদ্দেশ্য uddeśyô *n* purpose, aim

উদ্ধত uddhɔtô *adj* arrogant, insolent

উদ্ধার uddhar *n* rescue, deliverance

উদ্বিগ্ন udbignô *adj* worried, concerned, anxious

উদ্বৃত্ত udbr̊ttô (*pron* udbritto) *adj* surplus, extra

উদ্বেগ udbeg *n* worry, concern, anxiety

উদ্বেল udbel *adj* inundated, overflowing

উদ্ভব udbhɔb *n* origin, birth

উদ্ভাবক udbhabôk *n* inventor

উদ্ভাবন udbhabôn *n* invention, creation

উদ্ভাস udbhas *n* manifestation, appearance

উদ্ভিদ-বিদ্যা udbhid-bidya *n* botany

উদ্ভ্রান্ত udbhrantô *adj* confused, agitated

উদ্যত udyɔtô *adj* ready, prepared

উদ্যম udyɔm *n* enthusiasm, endeavor, enterprise

উদ্যোগ udyog *n* preparation, effort, endeavor

উদ্রেক udrek *n* excitement, rousing

উধাও udhao *adj* vanished, missing

উনি uni *pr* he, she *(hon)*

উনুন unun *n* stove, oven

উন্নত unnɔtô *adj* prospering, improved

উন্নতি unnôti *n* improvement

উন্নয়ন unnɔŷôn *n* prosperity, development

উপকরণ upôkɔrôṇ *n* ingredient, equipment

উপকার upôkar *n* favor, benefit

উপকূল upôkūl *n* shore, coast, beach

উপগ্রহ upôgrôhô *n* satellite, planet

উপজাতি upôjati *n* tribe; sub-group

উপজেলা upôjela *n* subdistrict

উপত্যকা upôtyɔka *n* valley

উপদল upôdɔl *n* faction, subgroup

উপদেশ upôdeś *n* advice, counsel

উপনিবেশ upônibeś *n* colony

উপনেতা upôneta *n* assistant leader, deputy

উপন্যাস upônyas *n* novel

উপপদ upôpɔd *n* compound word

উপপত্তি upôpôtti *n* argument, reasoning, proof

উপবন upôbôn *n* garden, grove

উপবাস upôbas *n* fast, starvation

উপবৃত্ত upôbr̥ttô *n* ellipse

উপভাষা upôbhaṣa *n* dialect

উপমা upôma *n* likeness, similarity

উপযুক্ত upôyuktô *adj* suitable

উপযোগ upôyog *n* benefit

উপর upôr *n* top, on top of, on

উপরতলা upôrtɔla *n* upstairs

উপরন্তু upôrôntu *n* in addition, besides

উপরে upôre *pp* on, above

উপলক্ষণ upôlôkṣôṇ *n* omen, foreboding

উপশম upôśɔm *n* relief, alleviation

উপস্থ upôsthô *n* genitalia

উপস্থিত upôsthit *adj* present, arrived

উপহার upôhar *n* present, gift

উপাত্ত upattô *n* data, proven facts

উপাদান upadan *n* ingredient, part, constituent

উপাধি upadhi *n* title, designation

উপায় upaŷ *n* way, method

উপার্জন uparjôn *n* earnings, income

উপোস upos *n* starvation, fasting

উভচর ubhôcɔr *adj* amphibious

উভলিঙ্গ ubhôliṅgô *adj* bisexual, androgynous

উভয় ubhɔŷ *adj* both

উমেদার umedar *n* candidate

উর্বর urbɔr *adj* fertile

উলঙ্গ ulôṅgô *adj* naked

উলটা ulṭa *(Bd)*, উলটো ulṭo *(WB)* *adj* upside down

উলটানো ulṭano *(Bd)*, উলটানো ulṭono *(WB)* *vb* turn upside down

উলটাপালটা ulṭapalṭa *adj* upside down, reversed

উল্লাস ullas *n* delight

উষ্ণ uṣṇô *n* heat, warmth, passion

উসুল usul *n* avengement

ঊ ū

উহ্য ūhyô (*pron* ujjho) *adj* implied

ঋ ṛ

ঋণ ṛṇ (*pron* rin) *n* loan, debt
ঋণী ṛṇī (*pron* rini) *n* debtor
ঋতু ṛtu (*pron* ritu) *n* season
ঋষি ṛṣi (*pron* rishi) *n* sage; saint

এ e/æ

এই ei *pr* this

এইতো eito *int expr* here it is

এইমাত্র eimatrô *adv* just now

এক æk *n* one

একঘেয়ে ækgheŷe *adj* monotonous

একটু ækṭu *adj* a little

একদম ækdɔm *adv* altogether

একনায়ক æknaŷôk *n* autocrat, dictator

একনায়কতন্ত্র æknaŷôktɔntrô *n* dictatorship

একবার ækbar *adv* once

একমাত্র ekmatrô *adj* only

একমেটে ekmeṭe *adj* unfinished, rough

একসঙ্গে eksɔṅge *adv* together

একরকম ækrɔkôm *adj* similar, same

একতা ækôta *n* unity

একলা ækla *adv* alone

একা æka *adj* alone, unaccompanied

একার্থ ækarthô *adj* synonymous

একই eki *adj* same

একেবারে ækebare *adv* completely

এক্ষণি ekṣôṇi (*pron* ekkhôni) *adv* right now

এখন ækhôn *adv* now

এখানে ekhane *adv* here

এখুনি ekhuni *adv* immediately, right now

এড়ানো æṛano *vb* avoid

এত ætô *adj* so, so much

এতক্ষণ ætôkṣɔṇ (*pron* ætôkkhɔn) *adv* for so long (within a day)

এতক্ষণে ætôkṣɔṇe *adv* by now

এতদিন ætôdin *adv* for so long

এতদূর ætôdūr *adv* so far

এতিম etim (*Bd*) *n* orphan

এতিমখানা etimkhana (*Bd*) *n* orphanage

এদিক edik *adv* this way

এপার epar *adv* on this side

এবং ebɔṅ *conj* and

এবার ebar *adv* this time

এমন æmôn *adj* such, so, like this

এমনি emni *adv* just like that, spontaneously

এরূপ erūp *adj* like this

এলাকা elaka *n* area

এলানো elano *vb* relax, recline, slacken

এলো elo *adj* ruffled, dishevelled

এলোমেলো elomelo *n* disorderly

ঐ oi

ঐক্য oikyô *n* unity

ঐচ্ছিক oicchik *adj* optional

ঐতিহাসিক oitihasik *adj* historical

ঐতিহ্য oitihyô (*pron* oitijjho) *n*
tradition, heritage

ও o

ও o *pr* he, she *(ord)*

ওই oi *pr* that over there

ওখানকার okhankar *adv* of that place, that region

ওখানে okhane *adv* there

ওগো ogo *int expr* sympathy, swooning

ওজন ojôn *n* weight

ওঠা oṭha, উঠা uṭha *vb* rise, get up

ওড়া oṛa, উড়া uṛa *vb* fly

ওড়না oṛna *n* scarf

ওত পেতে থাকা ot pete thaka *vb* ambush, lie in wait

ওদিকে odike *adv* in that direction

ওমা oma *int expr* surprise

ওয়ালা oŷala *suff* owner, wallah

ওরা ora *pr* they *(ord)*

ওলকপি olkôpi *n* kohlrabi

ওলাওঠা olaoṭha *n* cholera

ওষুধ oṣudh *n* medicine

ঔ ou

ঔচিত্য oucityô *n* decorum, appropriateness

ঔদার্য oudaryô *n* generosity

ঔপনিবেশিক oupônibeśik *adj* colonial

ঔপন্যাসিক oupônyasik *n* novelist

ঔপম্য oupômyô *n* similarity

ক k

কই kôi *adv* where; *n* type of fish

কওয়া kɔoŷa *vb* speak

ককপিট kɔkpiṭ *n* cockpit

ককানো kɔkano *vb* sob, groan, moan

কক্ষ kôkṣô *n* chamber

কখন kɔkhôn *conj* when

কখনও kɔkhôno *adv* ever

কঙ্কাল kɔṅkal *n* skeleton

কচলানো kɔclano *vb* rub, squeeze

কচি kôci *adj* soft, tender *(of plants)*

কচু kôcu *n* trifle; kind of vegetable

কচুরি kôcuri *n* kind of pancake

কচ্ছপ kɔcchôp *n* turtle

কঞ্জুস kôñjus *adj* miserly

কটমট kɔṭmɔṭ *adj* harsh, angry

কঠিন kôṭhin *adj* difficult, hard, firm

কঠোর kɔṭhor *adj* hard, stern, harsh

কড়া kɔṛa *n* cowrie; *adj* harsh, severe

কড়াই kɔṛai *n* pan, cauldron

কড়াকড়ি kɔṛakôṛi *n* strictness, stringency

কড়িকাঠ kôṛikhaṭh *n* joist

কড়কড়ে kɔrkɔre *onom* sound of munching, crackling noise

কণা kɔṇa, কণিকা kôṇika *n* particle

কন্টক kɔṇṭôk *n* thorn, thistle

কণ্ঠ kɔṇṭhô *n* throat

কত kɔtô *adj* how much, how many

কতক্ষণ kɔtôkṣôṇ *adv* for how long

কতদিন kɔtôdin *adv* for how long

কথা kɔtha *n* word, fact, statement, utterance, voice

কথা কওয়া kɔtha kɔoŷa *vb* speak

কথা দেওয়া kɔtha deoŷa *vb* promise

কথা বলা kɔtha bɔla *vb* speak

কথা বাড়ানো kɔtha baṛano *vb* elaborate

কথা রাখা kɔtha rakha *vb* keep a promise

কথাবার্তা kɔthabarta *n* conversation

কথামত kɔthamɔtô *adj* as promised

কথামাত্র kɔthamatrô *n* mere words, empty talk

কনিষ্ঠ kôniṣṭhô *adj* youngest

কন্যা kônya *n* girl; daughter

কপট kɔpôṭ *adj* crafty, deceitful

কপাট kɔpaṭ *n* lid, cover

কপাল kɔpal *n* luck; forehead

কপি kôpi *n* cabbage

কপি kɔpi *n* copy

কফি kôphi *n* coffee

কবজি kôbji *n* wrist

কবর kɔbôr *n* grave, graveyard

কবল kɔbôl *n* grip, seizure

কবি kôbi *n* poet

কবিতা kôbita *n* poetry

কবুতর kôbutɔr *n* pigeon

কবে kɔbe *conj* when

কম kɔm *adj* deficient, short

কমতি kômti *n* deficiency, shortfall, discount

কম পড়া kɔm pɔṛa *vb* fall short

কমপক্ষে kɔmpôkṣe *adv* at least

কমবেশি kɔmbeśi *adv* more or less

কমনীয় kɔmônīŷô *n* lovely, graceful, pleasant

কমলা kômla *n* orange

কমা kɔma *vb* decrease

কমানো kɔmano *vb* reduce

কম্প kɔmpô *n* tremor, quake

কম্বল kɔmbôl *n* blanket

কয় kɔŷ *adj* how many

কয়েক kɔŷek *adj* a few

কয়েদ kɔŷed *n* prison, jail; *adj* imprisoned, confined

কয়েদ করে রাখা kɔŷed kore rakha *vb* imprison, confine

কয়েদী kɔŷedī *n* prisoner

কর kɔr *n* tax, custom

করা kɔra *vb* do, make

করাত kɔrat *n* saw

করানো kɔrano *vb* cause to do

করুণ kôruṇ *adj* sad, pathetic

করুণা kôruṇa *n* compassion

করে kôre *conj* due to

কর্তব্য kɔrtôbyô *n* duty, obligation

কর্তা kɔrta *n* master, nominative

কর্তিকা kôrtika *n* cutting

কর্ম kɔrmô *n* work, activity

কর্মচারী kɔrmôcarī *n* employee; officer

কর্মফল kɔrmôphɔl *n* consequence, result

কর্মভার kɔrmôbhar *n* commission, assignment

কল kɔl *n* machine, engine

কল-কারখানা kɔl-karkhana *n* mill, workshop

কলম kɔlôm *n* pen

কলস kɔlôs, কলসি kôlsi *n* pitcher of water

কলহ kɔlôhô *n* quarrel, brawl

কলা kɔla *n* banana

কলাবিদ্যা kɔlabidya *n* arts, fine arts

কলিজা kôlija *n* liver

কলেজ kɔlej *n* college

কলেরা kɔlera *n* cholera

কল্পনা kɔlpôna *n* imagination

কল্পনা করা kɔlpôna kɔra *n* fancy, imagine

কল্যাণ kôlyaṇ *n* welfare, good

কশেরুকা kɔśeruka *n* vertebra

কষা kɔṣa *adj* tight, strict; *vb* calculate

কষ্ট kɔṣṭô *n* trouble; grief, sorrow

কষ্ট করা kɔṣṭô kɔra *vb* toil, labor

কষ্টকর kɔṣṭôkɔr *adj* difficult, hard

কসরত kɔsrɔt *n* feat, achievement, effort

কসাই kɔsai *n* butcher

কসুর kôsur *n* fault, offense

কস্তুরী kôsturī *n* musk; musk deer

কাঁকড়া kākṛa *n* crab

কাঁকলাস kāklas *n* chameleon

কাঁচা kāca *adj* unripe, green, immature, raw

কাঁচি kāci *(WB)* *n* scissors

কাঁটা kāṭa *n* thorn

কাঁঠাল kāṭhal *n* jackfruit

কাঁদা kāda *vb* weep, cry

কাঁধ kādh *n* shoulder

কাঁপা kāpa *vb* tremble, shiver

কাক kak *n* crow

কাকতালীয় kaktalīŷô *adj* coincidental

কাকা kaka *n* uncle (*father's younger brother*)

কাকি kaki, কাকিমা kakima *n* aunt (*father's younger brother's wife*)

কাগজ kagôj *n* paper

কাঙ্গাল kaṅgal *adj* wistful, hankering after; miserable

কাচ kac *n* glass

কাছ kach *n* proximity

কাছাকাছি kachakachi *adv* next to, close to

কাছিম kachim *n* tortoise, turtle

কাছে kache *adv, pp* next to, close to

কাজ kaj *n* work

কাজের লোক kajer lok *n* servant, employee

কাজে লাগা kaje laga *vb* be useful, come in handy

কাজেই kajei *conj* so, therefore

কাটা kaṭa *vb* cut, disperse, be sold, pass (*with time*)

কাটানো kaṭano *vb* cause to be cut; spend (*time*); overcome

কাটিম kaṭim *n* spool

কাঠ kaṭh *n* wood, timber

কাঠগড়া kaṭhgɔra *n* witness stand

কাঠবাদাম kaṭhbadam *n* walnut

কাঠবিড়ালি kaṭhbirali *(Bd)*,
কাঠবেড়ালি kaṭhberali *(WB) n*
squirrel

কাঠামো kaṭhamo *n* framework,
structure

কাঠি kaṭhi *n* chip of wood

কাড়া kara *vb* snatch, seize, grab

কাণ্ড kaṇḍô *n* incident, event,
chapter

কাত kat *n* side; *adj* slanted

কাতর katôr *adj* distressed

কাতলা katla *n* freshwater fish

কাতুকুতু katukutu *n* tickling

কাদা kada *n* mud

কান kan *n* ear

কানা kana *adj* blind

কানা kana *n* rim, border

কানাকানি kanakani *n* whispering

কান্না kanna *n* weeping

কান্নাকাটি kannakati *n* continuous
weeping

কাপ kap *n* cup

কাপড় kapôr *n* cloth

কাপড়-চোপড় kapôrcopôr *n* clothes

কাপুরুষ kapurus *n* coward

কাবাব kabab *n* kebab

কাবার kabar *n* end, termination

কাবু kabu *adj* weak, feeble

কাব্য kabyô *n* poetry, poetics

কাম kam *n* desire, passion

কামড় kamôr *n* bite

কামড়ানো kamrano, কামড় দেওয়া
kamôr deoŷa *vb* bite

কামনা kamôna *n* wish, desire,
prayer

কামরাঙা kamraṅga *n* five corner
fruit

কামাই kamai *n* earnings, income

কামাই করা kamai kɔra *vb* play
truant

কামানো kamano *vb* earn (money);
shave

কামিজ kamij *n* loose-fitting shirt,
Kamiz

কায়দা kaŷda *n* system, method

কারখানা karkhana *n* workshop

কারচুপি karcupi *n* trick, device

কারণ karôn *n* reason, cause

কারবার karbar *n* business, trade

কারা kara *pr* who *(pl)*

কারাগার karagar *n* prison cell

কার্ড karḍ *n* card

কার্তিক kartik *n* Bengali month
(mid October to mid November)

কার্য karyô *n* task, job, occupation

কার্যকর karyôkɔr *adj* effective,
feasible

কার্যত karyôtô *adv* actually, indeed

কাল kal *n* time, period; *adv*
tomorrow

কাল, কালো kalo *adj* black, dark-
skinned

কালকে kalke *adv* tomorrow;
yesterday

কালজাম kalôjam *n* dark cherry

কালবৈশাখী kalboiśakhī *n* strong
wind *(in April and May)*

কালা kala *adj* deaf

কালি kali *n* ink

কালিক kalik *adj* seasonal

কালিমা kalima *n* darkness, gloom;
disrepute

কাহিনী kahinī *n* story, anecdote

কাহিল kahil *adj* exhausted, tired

কি ki *pr* what

কিংবদন্তি kiṁbɔdônti *n* rumor,
hearsay

কিংবা kiṁba *conj* or, alternatively

কিছু kichu *n, adj* something, some

কিঞ্চিৎ kiñcit *adj* a little, somewhat

কিনা kina *adv* whether or not

কিনারা kinara *n* border, shore

কিন্তু kintu *conj* but

কিপটা kipṭa, কিপটে kipṭe *adj* stingy

কিমা kima *n* ground meat, mince

কিরণ kirɔn *n* ray, beam

কিল kil *n* fist

কিশমিশ kiśmiś *n* raisin

কিশলয় kiśôlɔy *n* young tender leaf

কিশোর kiśôr *adj* adolescent, teenage

কীট kīṭ *n* worm, insect

কীটপতঙ্গ kīṭpɔtôn̊gô *n* worms and insects

কীর্তন kīrtɔn *n* narration; celebration

কীর্তি kīrti *n* fame, renown

কুঁচকানো kũckano *vb* shrink, contract

কুঁচকি kũcki *n* groin

কুঁজ kũj *n* hump

কুঁড়ি kũṛi *n* bud

কুঁড়ে kũṛe *adj* idle, lazy

কুকুর kukur *n* dog

কুখ্যাত kukhyatô *adj* notorious

কুচকুচে কালো kuckuce kalo *adj* brilliantly black

কুচানো kucano *vb* chop finely

কুটা kuṭa *see* কোটা koṭa

কুটি kuṭi *n* straw (fine)

কুটির kuṭir *n* hut, cottage

কুটিল kuṭil *adj* zigzag, crooked

কুড়ানো kuṛano *vb* gather, collect

কুড়াল kuṛal *n* axe

কুণ্ঠ kuṇṭho *adj* reluctant, unwilling

কুণ্ঠা kuṇṭha *n* diffidence, hesitation

কুণ্ঠিত kuṇṭhitô *adj* shy, reluctant

কুত্তা kutta *n* dog

কুদিন kudin *n* hard times

কুদৃষ্টি kudṛṣṭi *n* evil eye

কুপরামর্শ kupɔramɔrśô *n* bad counsel

কুপানো kupano, কোপানো kopano *vb* strike; dig

কুমড়া kumra *(Bd)*, কুমড়ো kumro *(WB)* *n* pumpkin

কুমার kumar *(Bd)*, কুমোর kumor *(WB)* *n* potter

কুমির kumir *n* crocodile

কুয়াশা kuŷaśa *n* fog, mist

কুল kul *n* family, clan

কুল kul *n* jujube

কুলা kula *(Bd)*, কুলো kulo *(WB)* *n* winnowing platter

কুলানো kulano *(Bd)*, কুলোনো kulono *(WB)* *vb* be sufficient, be adequate

কুলি kuli *n* porter

কুলুপ kulup *n* lock, padlock

কুশল kuśôl *adj* expert, skilled, proficient

কুশ্রী kuśrī *adj* ugly, deformed

কুষ্ঠরোগ kusṭhôrog *n* leprosy

কুসংস্কার kusɔmskar *n* superstition

কুসুম kusum *n* egg yolk

কূট kūṭ *adj* shrewd, subtle

কূটকর্ম kūṭkɔrmô *n* forgery, sabotage

কূল kūl *n* shore, bank, border

কৃত kṛtô *adj* done, made

কৃতজ্ঞ kṛtɔjñô *(pron* kritɔggo*) adj* grateful

কৃতজ্ঞতা kṛtɔjñôta *(pron* kritɔggota*) n* gratitude

কৃতি kṛti *n* performance, achievement

কৃত্রিম kṛtrim *adj* artificial

কৃপণ kṛpɔn *n* miserly

কৃপা kṛpa *n* kindness, mercy

কৃমি kṛmi *n* worms *(in the body)*

কৃষক kṛṣɔk *n* farmer

কৃষি kṛṣi *(pron* krishi*) n* agriculture

কে ke *pr* who

কেউ keu *pr* someone

কেঁচো kēco *n* earthworm

কেক kek *n* cake

কেচি keci *n* scissors

কেন kænô *adv* why

কেনা kena *vb* buy

কেন্দ্র kendrô *n* center

কেবল kebôl *adv* only

কেমন kæmôn *adv* how

কেয়ার keȳar *n* care

কেয়ার করা keȳar kɔra *vb* care

কেরানি kerani *n* clerk

কেরাসিন kerasin, কেরোসিন kerosin *n* kerosene

কেলি keli *n* dalliance

কেশ keś *n* hair

কেস kes *n* lawsuit

কৈফিয়ত koiphiȳɔt *n* explanation

কোঁকড়া kõkṛa *adj* curly

কোকিল kokil *n* cuckoo

কোটর koṭôr *n* crevice, socket

কোটা koṭa *vb* cut into pieces, chop

কোটি koṭi *n* crore, ten million

কোণ koṇ *n* angle, corner

কোথা kotha *adv* where, which place

কোদাল kodal, কোদালি kodali *n* hoe, spade

কোন kon *adv* which

কোনও kono *adj* any

কোমর komôr *n* waist

কোমল komôl *adj* soft, gentle

কোমলতা komôlɔta *n* mildness, gentleness

কোম্পানি kompani *n* firm, company

কোল kol *n* lap

কোলে নেওয়া kole neoȳa *vb* take in one's lap, lift up

কোলাকুলি kolakuli *n* mutual embrace

কোষ্ঠবদ্ধতা koṣṭhôbɔddhôta *n* constipation

কৌতুক koutuk *n* joke, jest, comedy

কৌতূহল koutūhɔl *n* curiosity

কৌতূহলী koutūhɔlī *adj* curious, eager

কৌশল kouśɔl *n* dexterity, skill

ক্যামেরা kyamera *n* camera

ক্রম krôm *n* grade, order, sequence

ক্রমশ krômôśɔ *adv* gradually

ক্রমাগত krômagɔtô *adj* successively

ক্রিয়া kriȳa *n* action, work

ক্রিয়াপদ kriȳapɔd *n* verb

ক্রীড়া krīṛa *n* play, game, sport

ক্রীড়াচ্ছলে krīṛacchɔle *adv* for fun, as a sport

ক্রুশ kruś *n* cross

ক্রোড় kror *n* ten million

ক্রোড় kror *n* lap

ক্রোধ krodh *n* anger, fury

ক্লান্ত klantô *adj* tired

ক্লান্তি klanti *n* tiredness

ক্লাস klas *n* class

ক্লিষ্ট kliṣṭô *adj* troubled, stricken

ক্ষণ kṣɔṇ *n* moment, instant

ক্ষণজন্মা kṣɔṇôjɔnma *adj* fortunate, born at an auspicious time

ক্ষত kṣɔtô *n* wound, sore; *adj* wounded

ক্ষতি kṣôti *n* harm, damage

ক্ষতিকর kṣôtikɔr *adj* harmful

ক্ষমতা kṣɔmôta *n* power, strength

ক্ষমা kṣɔma *n* forgiveness

ক্ষমা করা kṣɔma kɔra *vb* forgive

ক্ষয় kṣɔȳ *n* destruction, defeat

ক্ষান্ত kṣantô *adj* desisted, stopped

ক্ষার kṣar *n* alkali

ক্ষিপ্ত kṣiptô *adj* frenzied, mad, frantic

ক্ষিপ্ততা kṣiptôta *n* frenzy, madness; rabies

ক্ষীণ kṣīṇ *adj* meager, weak, feeble

ক্ষীর kṣīr *n* condensed milk; sweet-meat

ক্ষুদ্র kṣudrô *adj* small, trivial

ক্ষুদ্রতা kṣudrôta *n* insignificance

ক্ষুধা kṣudha *n* hunger, greed

ক্ষুব্ধ kṣubdhô *adj* distressed, offended, mortified

ক্ষুর kṣur *n* razor

ক্ষেত kṣet *n* piece of land

ক্ষেত্র kṣetrô *n* field, area

ক্ষেপ kṣep, ক্ষেপণ kṣepôṇ *n* act of throwing

খ kh

খই khôi *n* puffed rice

খচমচ khɔcmɔc *n, onom* rustling sound

খচিত khôcitô *adj* studded, inset

খচ্চর khɔccôr *n* mule

খঞ্জ khɔñjô *adj* crippled

খঞ্জনি khɔñjôni *n* tambourine

খটকা khɔṭka *n* suspicion, doubt

খটখট khɔṭkhɔṭ *onom* knocking sound

খটমট khɔṭômɔṭô *adj* complicated, difficult

খড় khɔṛ *n* hay, straw

খড়খড়ি khɔṛkhôṛi *n* Venetian blind

খড়ি khôṛi *n* chalk

খণ্ড khɔṇḍô *n* part, fragment, slice

খতম khɔtôm *n* end, termination

খদ্দর khɔddôr *n* coarse cotton, khadi

খন্দ khɔndô *n* ditch, trench

খপ্পর khɔppôr *n* clutch, grip

খবর khɔbôr *n* news

খবরদার khɔbôrdar *int expr* beware!

খবরের কাগজ khɔbôrer kagôj *n* newspaper

খয়রাত khɔŷrat *n* donation, alms-giving

খয়েরি khɔŷeri *adj* dark brown

খরগোশ khɔrgoś *n* rabbit

খরচ khɔrôc *n* expense, spending

খরা khɔra *n* drought

খরিদ্দার khôriddar *n* customer, client

খসখস khɔskhɔs *n* couscous

খসা khɔsa, খসে যাওয়া khôse yaoŷa *vb* come off, become detached

খাওয়া khaoŷa *vb* eat

খাওয়ানো khaoŷano *vb* feed

খাঁচা khāca *n* cage

খাঁজ khāj *n* notch, dent

খাঁটি khāṭi *adj* pure, unadulterated

খাকী khakī *adj* light-brown, khaki

খাগড়া khagra *n* reed

খাজনা khajna *n* rent, revenue

খাট khaṭ *n* bedstead

খাট khaṭô, খাটো khaṭo *adj* short

খাটনি khaṭni *n* hard work, labor

খাটা khaṭa *vb* work, toil

খাটানো khaṭano *vb* cause to work, set up, hoist

খাড়া khaṛa *adj* erect, upright

খাড়াই khaṛai *n* steep rise, cliff, height

খাত khat *n* pit, ditch

খাতা khata *n* notebook

খাতির khatir *n* respect, honor

খাতির করা khatir kɔra *vb* respect, care for

খাদ্য khadyô *n* food

খানা khana *suff det* the

খানা khana *n* place, house, abode

খানা khana *n* food

খানিক khanik *adv* for a moment

খানেক khanek *adj* one, about one

খাপ khap *n* case, container; agreement, congruity

খাপ–ছাড়া khap–chaṛa *adj* inconsistent, irrelevant

খাপ্পা khappa *adj* furious, enraged

খাবার khabar *n* food

খাম kham *n* envelope

খামখেয়ালী khamkheŷali *adj* eccentric, whimsical

খামাকা khamaka *(Bd)*, খামোকা khamoka *(WB) adv* unnecessarily

খামার khamar *n* farm, granary

খামি khami *n* yeast

খারাপ kharap *adj* bad, evil

খাল khal *n* canal

খালা khala, খালী khalī *n Muslim aunt (mother's sister)*

খালাস khalas *n* acquittal, release

খালি khali *adj* empty; *adv* only

খালু khalu *n Muslim uncle (mother's sister's husband)*

খাসা khasa *adj* excellent, fine, superior

খাসি khasi *n* goat's meat

খিঁচানো khīcano *vb* grimace, make faces

খিঁচুনি khīcuni *n* fit, spasm

খিচুড়ি khicuri *n* kedgeree

খিদা khida, খিদে khide *n* hunger

খিমচি khimci *n* tweak, pinch

খিল khil *n* cramp

খিলখিল করা khilkhil kɔra *vb* giggle

খুঁচা khūca, খোঁচা khõca *n* prick, thorn

খুঁটি khūṭi *n* wooden post, pillar

খুঁটিয়ে khūṭiɣe *adv* minutely, meticulously

খুঁড়া khūṛa *see* খোঁড়া khõṛa

খুঁত khūt *n* scar, mark

খুঁত ধরা kūt dhɔra *vb* nag, carp, find fault

খুঁতখুঁতানি khūtkhūtani *n* pevishness, peculiarity

খুচরা khucra *(Bd)*, খুচরো khucro *(WB) n* small change *(money)*

খুন khun *n* murder

খুন করা khun kɔra *vb* murder

খুব khub *adv* very

খুলি khuli *n* skull, cranium

খুশি khuśi *adj* happy

খেই khei *n* clue

খেঁচা khẽca *vb* pull tight

খেঁচাখেঁচি khẽcakhẽci *n* bickering

খেঁচুনি khẽcuni *n* spasm, convulsion

খেজুর khejur *n* date, datepalm

খেত khet *n* piece of land

খেদ khed *n* lamentation, grief

খেদানো khædano *vb* drive away, scare off

খেপা khæpa *vb* go mad, rave, throw a tantrum

খেপানো khæpano *vb* incite, drive mad

খেয়া kheɣa *n* ferryboat

খেয়াল kheɣal *n* attention, thought, fancy

খেয়াল করা kheɣal kɔra *vb* be attentive to

খেয়ালি kheɣali *adj* whimsical, capricious, erratic, wayward

খেয়াল থাকা kheɣal thaka *vb* have in mind

খেলনা khæIna *n* toy

খেলা khæla *vb* play; *n* game, sport

খেলাপ khelap *n* infringement, breach

খেলো khelo *adj* inferior, trivial

খেলোয়াড় khæloɣaṛ *n* player, sportsman

খেসারত khesarôt *n* compensation

খোঁজ khõj *n* search, inquiry

খোঁজা khõja *vb* search, investigate

খোঁটা khõṭa *n* caustic comment; *vb* pick, pinch

খোঁড়া khõṛa, খুঁড়া khũṛa *vb* dig, excavate

খোঁড়া khõṛa *adj* lame, crippled

খোঁড়ানো khõṛano *vb* limp, hobble

খোঁপা khõpa *n* hairbun

খোকা khoka *n* boy; son

খোজা khoja *n* eunuch

খোদা khoda *n* God

খোদাই khodai *n* carving

খোয়াব khoɣab *n* dream, illusion

খোয়ার khoŷar *n* misery, distress,
  harm
খোরাক khorak *n* food, provision
খোল khol *n* cover, case; drum
খোলসা kholôsa, kholsa *adj* plain,
  frank
খোলা khola *vb, adj* open; *n* skin
  (of fruit), shell
খোশ khoś *adj* delightful, pleasant
খোশখেয়াল khośkheŷal *n* delight,
  fancy
খোশামোদ khośamod *n* flattery,
  adulation
খ্যাত khyatô *adj* famous
খ্রিস্টান khrisṭan *n, adj* Christian

গ g

গগন gɔgôn *n* sky, heavens

গঙ্গা gɔṅga *n* Ganges

গচ্ছা gɔccha *n* compensation

গচ্ছা দেওয়া gɔccha deoẏa *vb* compensate

গছানো gɔchano *vb* persuade to accept

গজ gɔj *n* yard (measure of length); elephant

গজ গজ gɔj gɔj *adj* reluctant, grudging, discontent

গজ গজ করা gɔj gɔj kɔra *vb* grumble; push through a crowd

গজব gɔjôb *n* oppression, tyranny

গজরানো gɔjrano *vb* rumble, growl, grumble

গজানো gɔjano *vb* sprout, originate, evolve

গজাল gɔjal *n* peg, large nail

গঞ্জ gɔñjô *n* granary, store, market

গটগট gɔṭgɔṭ *onom* marching firmly

গঠন gɔṭhôn *n* construction, formation

গড় gɔṛ *n* average; fort

গড়ন gɔṛôn *n* shape, act of building/ making/shaping

গড়া gɔṛa *vb* make, shape, mold, model

গড়ানো gɔṛano *vb* roll around, laze around; pour

গড়িমসি gôṛimôsi *n* procrastination

গড়গড় gɔṛgɔṛ *onom* rumbling thunder

গণ gɔṇ *suff* a number more than one *plural suffix*

গণ gɔṇô *n* common people, population

গণতন্ত্র gɔṇôtɔntrô *n* democracy

গণতান্ত্রিক gɔṇôtantrik *adj* democratic

গণ আদালত gɔṇô adalôt *n* people's court

গণ আন্দোলন gɔṇô andolôn *n* mass-movement

গণন gɔṇôn *n* act of reckoning, counting

গণিত gôṇit *adj* reckoned, counted; *n* mathematics

গণ্ডগোল gɔṇḍôgol *n* uproar, riot, tumult, disorder

গণ্ডি gôṇḍi *n* boundary, encircling line, limit

গণ্য gɔṇyô *adj* countable, estimable

গত gɔtô *adj* last, departed, dead, finished

গতকাল gɔtôkal *n* yesterday

গতপরশু gɔtôpôrśu *n* day before yesterday

গতানুগতিক gɔtanugôtik *adj* routine, customary, usual

গতি gôti *n* passage, motion, move-ment; speed

গতিহীন gôtihīn *adj* motionless, still

গদা gɔda *n* club, stick

গদি gôdi *n* mattress, cushion

গদ্য gôdyô *n* prose

গন্ধ gɔndhô *n* smell, scent, odor

গন্ধক gɔndhôk *n* sulphur, brimstone

গপগপ gɔpgɔp *onom* gulping, eating fast

গবাদি gɔbadi *n* cattle

গভীর gôbhīr *adj* deep

গম gɔm *n* wheat

গমগম gɔmgɔm *onom* echoing

গমন gɔmôn *n* departure

গম্ভীর gômbhīr *adj* serious, grave, solemn

গয়না gɔŷna *n* jewelry

গরগর gɔrgɔr *onom* overwhelmed, delighted

গরগরে gɔrgɔre *onom expr* intense

গরজ gɔrôj *n* interest, necessity, attention

গরম gɔrôm *n* heat; *adj* hot

গরমি gɔrômi *(Bd)*, gôrmi *(WB) n* heat; summer; anger; prickly heat; syphilis

গরীব gôrīb *adj* poor

গরিমা gôrima *n* glory; pride, vanity

গরু gôru *n* cow

গর্জন gɔrjôn *n* roar, rumble, howl

গর্জানো gɔrjano *vb* roar, howl, thunder

গর্ত gɔrtô *n* hole, cavity, ditch

গর্ব gɔrbô *n* pride, conceit, vanity

গর্বিত gôrbitô *adj* proud, conceited, vain

গর্ভ gɔrbhô *n* inner part, interior

গর্ভনাশ gɔrbhônaś *n* abortion

গর্ভবতী gɔrbhôbôtī *adj* pregnant

গর্ভাশয় gɔrbhaśɔ̂ŷ *n* uterus

গল gɔl *n* throat, neck

গলতি gôlti *adj* melting, dripping; *n* mistake, shortcoming

গলদ gɔlôd *n* error, mistake

গলা gɔla *vb* melt, soften, rot; *n* throat, neck; voice

গলায়গলায় gɔlaŷgɔlaŷ *adj* close, intimate

গলি gôli *n* lane, alley

গল্প gɔlpô *n* story, tale, fable

গল্পগুজব gɔlpôgujɔb *n* gossip, chit-chat

গহনা gɔhôna *n* jewelry, ornament

গা ga *int filler word*; *n* body

গায়ে দেওয়া gaŷe deoŷa *vb* wear, put on

গাওয়া gaoŷa *vb* sing

গাঁ gã *n* village, hamlet

গাঁজলা gãjla *n* froth, scum; yeast

গাঁজা gãja *n* ganja, cannabis

গাঁজানো gãjano *vb* ferment

গাঁট gãt *n* joint, link, knuckle

গাঁটকাটা gãṭkaṭa *n* pickpocket

গাঁতি gãti *n* pickaxe

গাঁথা gãtha *vb* lay (bricks), build, construct

গাছ gach *n* tree, plant

গাজর gajôr *n* carrot

গাড়া gaṛa *vb* drive in, plant, set up

গাড়ি gaṛi *n* car, vehicle

গাঢ় gaṛhô *adj* solidified, thickened

গাথা gatha *n* poem, couplet, ditty, verse

গাদা gada *vb* cram, stuff, load

গাদা gada *n* heap, pile, stack

গাধা gadha *n* donkey, ass

গান gan *n* song

গাপ gap *adj* concealed, hidden

গাপ করা gap kɔra *vb* conceal, _misappropriate

গাব gab *n* mangosteen

গামছা gamcha *n* thin towel, napkin

গামলা gamla *n* water-container, basin

গায়ক gaŷôk *n* singer

গায়েব gaŷeb *adj* hidden, concealed

গারদ garôd *n* confinement, jail, prison

গাল gal *n* abuse, rebuke, reproach; *n* cheek

গালাগালি galagali *n* abuse, revilings, bickering

গালানো galano *vb* melt, cause to melt

গালি gali *n* rude language

গালিচা galica *n* carpet

গিঁট gĩt *n* joint, knuckle; knot

গিজগিজ gijgij *onom* crowding together

গিন্নি ginni *n* housewife

গিরগিটি girgiṭi *n* chameleon

গিরা gira *n* knot

গিরি giri *n* mountain, hill

গিরিখাত girikhat *n* ravine, gorge

গির্জা girja *n* church

গিলটি gilṭi *adj* gilded

গিলা gila *see* গেলা gela

গিলে ফেলা gile phæla *vb* swallow

গীত gītô *adj* sung, chanted

গীতি gīti *n* song, hymn

গু gu *n* feces, stool, dung

গূজা gūja *see* গোঁজা gōja

গুজি gūji *n* stake, wedge, stick

গুঁড়া gūṛa *(Bd)*, গুঁড়ো gūṛo *(WB) n* powder

গুচ্ছ gucchô *n* cluster, bundle

গুছানো guchano *(Bd)*, গুছোনো guchono *(WB) vb* tidy up, arrange

গুজব gujɔb *n* rumor, hearsay

গুজরানো gujrano *vb* spend (time), pass

গুজগুজ gujguj *onom* whispering

গুঞ্জন guñjɔn *n* buzzing, humming

গুটানো guṭano *(Bd)*, গুটোনো guṭono *(WB) vb* roll up, wind up

গুটি guṭi *n* pill; blister; pawn (*in chess*); fruit (*in early stage*)

গুটিসুটি guṭisuṭi *adv* coweringly, crouchingly

গুড় guṛ *n* juice of sugarcane, molasses

গুণ guṇ *n* quality, virtue

গুণাগুণ guṇaguṇ *n* merits and demerits

গুণী guṇī *adj* virtuous

গুণ্ডা guṇḍa *n* hooligan, gangster

গুনগুন করা gungun kɔra *vb* whisper, lilt, hum

গুনতি gunti *n* computation, count

গুনা guna *see* গোনা gona

গুপ্ত guptô *adj* secret, hidden, unrevealed

গুপ্তচর guptôcɔr *n* spy, detective

গুম gum *adj* secret, hidden; speechless; motionless

গুমট gumɔṭ *n* sultriness, humidity

গুমর gumôr *n* self-esteem, pride

গুমরানো gumrano *vb* suffer from suppressed grief

গুরু guru *n* teacher, guide, mentor

গুরুত্ব gurutvô *n* importance, seriousness

গুরুত্বপূর্ণ gurutvôpūrṇô *adj* important, serious, weighty

গুলি guli, গুলো gulo *suff det: plural (inanimates)*

গুলি guli *n* marble; bullet

গুহা guha *n* cave

গৃহ gṛhô *n* room, chamber; house

গৃহধর্ম gṛhôdhɔrmô *n* family life

গৃহিনী gṛhinī *n* housewife, wife

গেঁজানো gæjano *vb* chatter, gossip

গেঁড়া gēṛa *n* misappropriation, swindling

গেঞ্জাম gæ̃njam *n* trouble, upset

গেঞ্জি geñji *n* vest, T-Shirt

গেট geṭ *n* gate

গেরুয়া geruŷa *adj* ochre-colored

গেরো gero *n* scrape, difficulty

গেল gælô *adj* preceding; last

গেলা gela, গিলা gila *vb* swallow

গেলাস gelas *n* glass, tumbler

গৈরিক goirik *n* red ochre

গো go *n* cow

গোঁ gõ *n* obstinacy, stubbornness

গোঁজ gõj *n* peg, stake, wedge

গোঁজা gōja *vb* drive into, insert, thrust into

গোঁজামিল gōjamil *n* fraud

গোঁড়া gōṛa *adj* fanatic, bigoted, orthodox

গোঁড়ামি gōṛami *n* fanaticism, bigotry

গোঁফ gõph *n* moustache

গোঁয়ার gõŷar *adj* obstinate, stubborn

গোঙানো goṅano *vb* whimper, whine

গোচর gocôr *n* perception, sense

গোছ goch *n* bundle, bunch, sheaf

গোটা goṭa *adj* entire, whole, undivided

গোড় gor, গোড়া gora *n* base, root, foundation

গোড়ালি gorali *n* ankle, heel

গোত্র gotrô *n* clan, tribe

গোনা gona, গুনা guna *vb* count, reckon, calculate

গোপন gopôn *n* act of concealing; secret; *adj* secret, hidden, private

গোপাল gopal *n* cowboy, cowherd

গোবর gobôr *n* cow dung

গোমড়া gomra *adj* sullen, silent, glum

গোমাছি gomachi *n* gadfly

গোয়াল goŷal *n* cowshed

গোয়েন্দা goŷenda *n* spy, detective

গোর gor *n* grave, tomb

গোর দেওয়া gor deoŷa *vb* bury

গোরস্থান gorôsthan *n* graveyard, burial ground

গোল gol *adj* round, circular, spherical; *n* disturbance, clamor, uproar

গোলমরিচ golmôric *n* pepper, black pepper

গোলমাল golmal *n* riot, tumult, uproar, disturbance

গোলমেলে golmele *adj* noisy, disorderly; confusing, intricate, complicated

গোলাপ golap *n* rose

গোলাপি golapi *adj* pink

গোলাম golam *n* slave

গোষ্ঠী gosṭhī *n* family, clan

গোসল gosôl *n* bath, bathing

গোস্ত gostô *n* meat

গ্রাম gram *n* village

গ্রাস gras *n* mouthful, morsel; grip

গ্রাস করা gras kɔra *vb* snatch, devour, seize

গ্রাহ্য grahyô *adj* acceptable, gratifying

গ্রীষ্ম grīṣmô *n* summer, hot season

গ্লানি glani *n* weariness, tiredness

ঘ gh

ঘটনা ghɔṭona *n* event, occurrence

ঘটমান ghɔṭoman *adj* progressive, continuous

ঘটা ghɔṭa *vb* occur, happen

ঘটিত ghôṭitô *adj* due to, involving, concerning, containing

ঘড়াঞ্চি ghɔṛañci *n* step-ladder

ঘড়ঘড় ghɔrghɔr *onom* rattling

ঘড়ি ghôṛi *n* clock, watch, wrist-watch

ঘণ্টা ghɔṇṭa *n* hour

ঘন ghɔnô *adj* dense, thick

ঘনত্ব ghɔnôtvô *n* density, thickness

ঘনানো ghɔnano *vb* thicken; draw near

ঘনিষ্ঠ ghôniṣṭhô *adj* intimate, close

ঘনিষ্ঠতা ghôniṣṭhôta *n* intimacy, closeness

ঘর ghɔr *n* house, building; room

ঘরবাড়ি ghɔrbaṛi *n* buildings, houses, settlement

ঘরোয়া ghɔroŷa *adj* domestic, internal

ঘষা ghɔṣa *vb* rub, scrub, scour

ঘা gha *n* wound, stroke, blow

ঘাঁটানো ghãṭano *vb* vex, irritate

ঘাট ghaṭ *n* landing stage, quay, wharf, ghat

ঘাড় ghaṛ *n* neck, nape of the neck

ঘাত ghat *n* shock, stroke, blow, push

ঘানি ghani *n* oil-mill, handmill for expressing oil

ঘাপটি ghapṭi *n* ambush

ঘাবড়ানো ghabṛano *vb* be taken aback, lose one's balance

ঘাম gham *n* sweat

ঘামা ghama *vb* sweat, perspire

ঘামাচি ghamaci *n* prickly heat

ঘাস ghas *n* grass

ঘি ghi *n* ghee, clarified butter

ঘিঞ্জি ghiñji *adj* stuffy, over-crowded

ঘিরা ghira *see* ঘেরা ghera

ঘুঘু ghughu *n* dove, turtledove

ঘুটঘুট ghuṭghuṭ *adj* black, dark

ঘুড়ি ghuṛi *n* paper-kite

ঘুণ ghuṇ *n* woodworm

ঘুম ghum *n* sleep

ঘুমানো ghumano *(Bd)*, ঘুমোনো ghumono *(WB)* *vb* sleep

ঘুর ghur *n* turn, spin

ঘুরা ghura *see* ঘোরা ghora

ঘুষ ghuṣ *n* bribe

ঘুষঘুষে ghuṣghuṣe *adj* secret, subdued, furtive

ঘুষি ghūṣi *n* punch, blow

ঘূর্ণ ghūrṇô *n* rotation, whirling, revolution

ঘূর্ণাবর্ত ghūrṇabɔrtô *n* whirlpool

ঘূর্ণি ghūrṇi *n* circular current of water (or air)

ঘূর্ণিঝড় ghūrṇijhɔr *n* cyclone, tornado

ঘৃণা ghṛna *n* hate, aversion, disgust, revulsion

ঘৃণা করা ghṛna kɔra *vb* hate, detest, despise

ঘেষা ghæ̃ṣa *vb* touch, come close

ঘেষাঘেষি ghæ̃ṣaghēṣi *adv* closely, crowdingly

ঘেনঘেন করা ghænghæn kɔra *vb* whine, wimper

ঘেরা ghera, ঘিরা ghira *vb* encircle, surround

ঘেরাও gherao *n* enclosure, besiegement

ঘোট ghôṭ *n* conspiracy; rumor; faction

ঘোচা ghoca, ঘুচা ghuca *vb* vanish, cease to exist, pass

ঘোটা ghoṭa, ঘুটা ghuṭa *vb* agitate, stir

ঘোড়া ghoṛa *n* horse

ঘোড়ার গাড়ি ghoṛar gaṛi *n* tomtom, horse-drawn carriage

ঘোমটা ghomṭa *n* veil

ঘোর ghor *adj* dreadful, frightful, awful; *n* obsession, illusion

ঘোরা ghora, ঘুরা ghura *vb* turn, revolve; move, wander, travel, journey

ঘোল ghol *n* whey, buttermilk

ঘোলা ghola *adj* turbid, muddy, dull

ঘোষক ghoṣôk *n* announcer

ঘোষণা ghoṣôṇa *n* announcement, proclamation

ঘোষপত্র ghoṣpɔtrô *n* bulletin, notice

ঘোষা ghoṣa *vb* announce, proclaim, declare

ঘ্রাণ ghraṇ *n* scent, smell

চ c

চওড়া cɔora *adj* broad, wide

চক cɔk *n* square, place

চক cɔk *n* chalk

চকমকি cɔkmôki *n* flint

চকমিলানো cɔkmilanô *adj* built around a square courtyard,

চক্কর cɔkkôr *n* wheel, circle

চক্কর মারা cɔkkôr mara *vb* roam around

চক্র cɔkrô *n* cycle, circle, wheel, orbit

চক্রনাভি cɔkrônabhi *n* axle

চক্ষু côkṣu *n* eye

চঞ্চল cɔncôl *adj* moving, mobile, restless

চটক cɔṭôk *n* sparrow; splendor, glamor

চটকানো cɔṭkano *vb* knead, press, handle

চটচটে cɔṭcôṭe *onom* sticky, cloying

চটপটে cɔṭpôṭe *adv* quickly, promptly

চটা cɔṭa *vb* get angry, be offended

চটি côṭi *n* sandal

চটুল côṭul *adj* quick, swift, nimble

চড় cɔr *n* slap, blow, cuff

চড়া cɔra *vb* climb, mount, ascend; *n* sandbank, island in a river

চড়াই cɔrai *(Bd)*, চড়ুই cɔrui *(WB) n* sparrow

চড়াইভাতি cɔraibhati *(Bd)*, চড়ুইভাতি cɔruibhati *(WB) n* picnic

চড়ানো cɔrano *vb* ride, board; cause to rise

চতুর côtur *adj* cunning, clever, quick-witted, crafty

চতুরালি côturali *n* trick, joke

চতুর্থ côturthô *num* fourth

চন্দন cɔndôn *n* sandalwood

চন্দ্র cɔndrô *n* moon

চপল cɔpôl *adj* restless, swift, fickle

চমক cɔmôk *n* flash; fright

চমক লাগা cɔmôk laga *vb* be dazed, be alarmed

চমৎকার cɔmôtkar *adj* excellent, good

চম্পক cɔmpɔk *n* magnolia

চর cɔr *n* spy, agent; sandbank

চরম cɔrôm *adj* highest, ultimate

চরা cɔra *vb* move about, graze, wander

চরাচর cɔracɔr *n* creation, world

চরিত côrit, côritô *n* conduct, behavior, manners

চরিতার্থ করা côritarthô kɔra *vb* satisfy, gratify

চরিত্র côritrô *n* character

চর্চা cɔrca *n* practice, application, study

চর্বি côrbi *n* fat

চর্ম cɔrmô *n* skin; leather

চল cɔl *adj* restless, moving

চলকানো cɔlkano *vb* spill, overflow

চলতি côlti *adj* current, present; going; colloquial

চলন côlôn *n* motion; currency; vogue

চলমান côlôman *adj* moving, mobile; current

চলা côla *vb* go, move, run

চলাচল côlacɔl *n* movement, traffic

চলিত côlit *adj* colloquial, current

চল্লিশ côlliś *num* forty

চলে যাওয়া côle yaoẏa *vb* go away

চশমা côsma *n* glasses, spectacles

চষা cɔṣa *vb* plow, cultivate, till

চা ca *n* tea

চাই cai *n* need

চাইতে caite *pp* than

চাউল caul, চাল cal *n* uncooked rice

চাওয়া caoŷa *vb* want, desire, look at

চাঁদ cãd *n* moon

চাঁদনি cãdni *n* canopy, awning; moonlight

চাঁদা cãda *n* subscription; contribution

চাঁদাবাজি cãdabaji *(Bd)*, চাঁদোবাজি cãdobaji *(WB) n* extortion

চাঁদনি cãdni *adj* moonlit

চাঁপা cãpa *n* champak flower

চাকর cakôr *n* servant

চাকরি cakri *n* job, employment

চাকলা cakla *n* slice

চাকা caka *n* wheel, tire

চাকি caki *n* grinding stone

চাখা cakha *vb* taste, enjoy

চাগা caga *vb* become stronger; arise

চাচা caca *n* uncle *(father's brother, Muslim)*

চাচি caci *n* aunt *(father's brother's wife, Muslim)*

চাটনি caṭni *n* chutney

চাটা caṭa *vb* lick

চাটাই caṭai *n* coarse mat

চাটি caṭi *n* slap

চাটু caṭu *n* frying pan

চাড় caṛ *n* shove, push; enthusiasm

চাড়া caṛa *vb* raise, lift up

চাতক catôk *n* swallow

চাতাল catal *n* terrace, platform

চাতুরী caturī *n* craftiness, cunning

চাদর cadôr *n* bedsheet; wrap

চান can *n* bath

চানা cana *n* pulse; chickpea

চাপ cap *n* pressure, weight, burden

চাপড় capôṛ *n* slap, blow

চাপা capa *vb* weigh on, press on; suppress, conceal

চাপাটি capaṭi *n* flat bread

চাপানো capano *vb* lay on, place onto, pile on

চাবি cabi *n* key

চাবুক cabuk *n* whip, lash

চামচ camôc *n* spoon

চামড়া camṛa *n* skin; leather

চামেলি cameli *n* white jasmine

চার car *n* four

চার car *n* bait for fishing

চারা cara *n* seedling

চারিত্রিক caritrik *adj* characteristic

চারু caru *adj* pleasant, charming

চাল cal *n* thatched roof

চাল cal *n* manners, behavior

চালনি calni *n* sieve

চালবাজ calbaj *n* snob; *adj* snobbish

চালবাজি calbaji *n* snobbery

চালা cala *n* thatched roof

চালাক calak *adj* clever, cunning

চালানি calani *adj* for export, exportable

চালানো calano *vb* drive, conduct, lead

চালু calu *adj* current, in vogue

চাষ caṣ *n* agriculture, cultivation

চাষী caṣī *n* farmer, plowman

চাহনি cahôni *n* look, glance

চাহিদা cahida *n* need, necessity

চিংড়ি cimṛi *n* shrimp, prawn

চিঁচি cĩcĩ *int expr* distress, anguish

চিকচিক cikcik *onom* sparkling(ly), glittering(ly)

চিকন cikɔn *adj* fine, thin, delicate

চিকিৎসা cikiṭsa *n* treatment

চিচিঙ্গা cicinga *n* snake-gourd

চিটা ciṭa *adj* sticky, viscous

চিটে যাওয়া ciṭe yaoŷa *vb* get stuck, stick

চিঠি ciṭhi *n* letter

চিড় ciṛ *n* crack, fissure

চিড়িক cirik *n* pain, twinge; flicker

চিড়িয়াখানা ciriẏakhana *n* zoo

চিৎকার ciṭkar *n* scream

চিৎকার করা ciṭkar kɔra *vb* shout, scream, yell

চিতা cita *n* funeral pyre; cheetah, leopard

চিত্ত cittô *n* mind, imagination, intellect

চিত্তবিনোদন cittôbinodôn *n* amusement, entertainment

চিত্র citrô *n* picture, sketch, portrait

চিনা cina *see* চেনা cena

চিনি cini *n* sugar

চিন্তা cinta *n* thought, consideration, reflection, worry

চিন্তা করা cinta kɔra *vb* think, consider, worry

চিন্তিত cintitô *adj* anxious, worried

চিবানো cibano *(Bd)*, চিবোনো cibono *(WB) vb* chew

চিবুক cibuk *n* chin

চিমটি cimṭi *n* pinch, squeeze

চির cirô *adj* perpetual; entire, whole

চিরকাল cirôkal *n, adv* forever, eternity

চিরনি ciruni *n* comb

চিল cil *n* hawk; kite

চিহ্ন cihnô *(pron* cinho) *n* sign, mark, trace

চীন cīn *n* China

চীনা cīna *adj* Chinese

চুকচুক cukcuk *onom* sound of sipping, slurping

চুকা cuka *see* চোকা coka

চুকানো cukano *vb* finish, complete

চুক্তি cukti *n* agreement, contract

চুটানো cuṭano *vb* do one's utmost

চুড়ি curi *n* bangle

চুন cun *n* limestone

চুনকালি cunkali *n* disgrace, infamy

চুনি cuni *n* ruby; emerald

চুপ cup *n* silence

চুপচাপ cupcap *adj* silent, mute

চুপিচুপি cupicupi, চুপিসারে cupisare *adv* silently, quietly, stealthily

চুমকি cumki *n* sequin, sparkle

চুমু cumu *n* kiss

চুমুক cumuk *n* sip, draught

চুম্বক cumbɔk *n* magnet

চুয়ানো cuẏano, চোয়ানো coẏano *vb* ooze, leak, drip

চুয়ে পড়া cuẏe pɔra *vb* drip, leak

চুর cur *adj* stupefied, dazed

চুরি curi *n* theft, stealing

চুরুট curuṭ *n* cigar, cheeroot

চুল cul *n* hair

চুলকানি culkani *n* itching; eczema

চুলকানো culkano *vb* scratch, itch

চুলা cula *(Bd)*, চুলো culo *(WB) n* oven, cooker

চুষা cuṣa *see* চোষা coṣa

চুষি cuṣi *n* dummy; pacifier

চূড়া cūra *n* top, crest, summit

চূড়ান্ত cūrantô *adj* final, ultimate

চূর্ণ cūrnô *n* powder, dust

চেঁচামেচি cæ̃cam-eci *n* outcry, clamor

চেঁচানো cæ̃cano *vb* shout, scream, yell

চেক cek *n* check

চেতনা cetôna *n* consciousness, sensibility

চেন cen *n* chain

চেনা cena *vb* know, recognize

চেপটা cæpṭa *adj* flat

চেপে রাখা cepe rakha *vb* suppress, keep secret

চেয়ার ceẏar *n* chair

চেয়ে ceẏe *pp* than

চেরা cera, চিরা cira *vb* split, sever

চেলা cæla *n* disciple, follower

চেষ্টা ceṣṭa *n* attempt, effort

চেষ্টা করা ceṣṭa kɔra *vb* try

চেহারা cehara *n* complexion, appearance, features

চৈত্র coitro *n* month of Chaitra

চোকা coka (*also* চুকা) *vb* be finished, come to an end

চোখ cokh *n* eye

চোখের জল cokher jɔl *n* teardrop, tears

চোখের পাতা cokher pata *n* eyelid

চোঙা coṅga *n* barrel, tube

চোট cot *n* blow, shock, stroke

চোদ্দ coddô *see* চৌদ্দ couddô

চোয়াল coŷal *n* jaw

চোর cor *n* thief, robber

চোরা cora *adj* stolen

চোলাই colai *n* distillation

চোষা coṣa, চুষা cuṣa *vb* suck

চৌকি couki *n* wooden bedstead

চৌকিদার coukidar *n* guard, watchman

চৌদ্দ couddô *num* fourteen

চৌরাস্তা courasta *n* crossroads

চুতি cyuti *n* loss, destruction, ruin

ছ ch

ছক chɔk *n* square; check pattern; outline

ছকা chɔka *n* draft, sketch; *vb* scheme

ছটফট chɔṭphɔṭ *adj* restless

ছটফটানি chɔṭphɔṭani *n* restlessness, impatience

ছটফটে chɔṭphɔṭe *adv* restlessly, fidgety

ছটা chɔṭa *n* radiance, lustre, glow

ছড়া chɔra *n* verse, rhyme

ছড়াছড়ি chɔrachɔri *n* wastage, excess, abundance

ছড়ানো chɔrano *vb* scatter, spread out

ছড়ি chɔri *n* cane, walking stick

ছত্র chɔtrô *n* line of verse, foot (in poetry)

ছদ্ম chɔdmô (*pron* chɔddo) *adj* pretended, faked

ছদ্মবেশ chɔdmôbeś *n* disguise

ছন্দ chɔndô *n* rhythm; manner; control

ছন্দানুগমন chɔndanugɔmôn *n* willfulness

ছন্দানুগামী chɔndanugamī *adj* willful

ছবি chôbi *n* picture, painting

ছয় chɔŷ *num* six

ছয়লাপ chɔŷlap *adj* flooded with, abundant

ছল chɔl *n* trick, deception, fraud

ছলচাতুরী chɔlôcaturī *n* deception, fraud

ছল-ছুতা chɔl-chuta (*Bd*), ছল-ছুতো chɔl-chuto (*WB*) *n* pretext, pretension

ছাই chai *n* ash

ছাইপাঁশ chaipāś *n* nonsense, triviality

ছাওয়া chaoŷa *vb* cover, spread, pervade

ছাঁকনি chākni *n* sieve, strainer

ছাঁকা chāka *vb* sieve, strain

ছাঁচ chāc *n* mold, cast

ছাঁটা chāṭa *vb* prune, crop

ছাঁটাই chāṭai *n* reduction; exclusion

ছাঁটাই করা chāṭai kɔra *vb* exclude, dismiss; reduce

ছাঁদ chād *n* shape, form, cut

ছাগল chagôl *n* goat

ছাড় char *n* release, permission

ছাড়া chara *vb* leave, depart, let go; *pp* except, without

ছাড়ানো charano *vb* release, set off, disentangle

ছাতা chata, ছাতি chati *n* umbrella; mushroom, fungus

ছাতু chatu *n* barley flour

ছাত্র chatrô *n* student, pupil

ছাদ chad *n* roof, ceiling

ছানা chana *n* young animal (*esp birds*)

ছানি chani *n* cataract

ছাপ chap *n* print, mark

ছাপা chapa *vb* print, publish

ছাপাখানা chapakhana *n* printing press

ছাপানো chapano *vb* print

ছায়া chaŷa *n* shade, shadow

ছায়াপথ chaŷapɔth *n* Milky Way

ছায়ামূর্তি chaŷamūrti *n* apparition

ছার char *n* ashes, rubbish, remains

ছারখার charkhar *adj* laid waste, destroyed

ছাল chal *n* bark, outer skin

ছাল তোলা chal tola *vb* peel, flay

ছি chi, ছিছি chichi *int expr* condemnation, disgust, reproach

ছিঁড়া chĩṛa *see* ছেঁড়া chẽṛa

ছিট chiṭ *n* drop of liquid; blob; piece of cloth

ছিটকানো chiṭkano *(Bd)*, ছিটকোনো chiṭkono *(WB)* *vb* splash, sprinkle (liquids)

ছিটকিনি chiṭkini *n* bolt, lock, bar

ছিটা chiṭa *n* drop; pinch

ছিটানো chiṭano, ছেটানো cheṭano *vb* spray, sprinkle

ছিদ্র chidrô *n* hole, perforation

ছিনানো chinano *vb* snatch, seize

ছিনালি chinali *n* flirtation, coquetry

ছিনিমিনি chinimini *n* waste, squandering (of money)

ছিন্ন chinnô *adj* torn apart, rent, split

ছিপ chip *n* long boat; fishing rod

ছিপি chipi *n* cork (of a bottle)

ছিমছাম chimcham *adj* neat, tidy, trim

ছিরি chiri *n* beauty, grace, elegance

ছিলা chila *n* bow, string

ছিলকা chilka *n* chip, piece of wood

ছুঁচা chūca *(Bd)*, ছুঁচো chūco *(WB)* *n* mole, muskrat

ছুঁচালো chūcalo *(Bd)*, ছুঁচোলো chūcolo *adj* sharp, pointed

ছুঁ, ছুঁত chūt *n* touch, contact; contagion

ছুট chuṭ *n* act of running, run

ছুট মারা chuṭ mara *vb* run off

ছুটি chuṭi *n* holiday, leisure

ছুটা chuṭa *see* ছোটা choṭa

ছুড়া chuṛa *see* ছোড়া choṛa

ছুতা chuta *(Bd)*, ছুতো chuto *(WB)* *n* excuse, pretext

ছুতার chutar *(Bd)* *n* carpenter

ছুরি churi *n* knife

ছুলা chula *see* ছোলা chola

ছুলি chuli *n* skin rash

ছেঁচা chẽca *vb* pound, thresh

ছেঁড়া chẽṛa *vb* tear, pull apart

ছেটানো cheṭano *see* ছিটানো chiṭano

ছেনি cheni *n* chisel

ছেবলা chæbla *adj* childish, puerile

ছেলে chele *n* boy; son

ছেলেবেলা chelebæla *n* childhood

ছেলেমি chelemi *n* immaturity, childishness

ছোঁ মারা chõ mara *vb* swoop, pounce upon

ছোঁয়া chõŷa *vb* touch

ছোকরা chokra *n* boy servant; boy, lad

ছোট choṭô *adj* small, young

ছোটখাটো choṭôkhaṭo *adj* small, trivial, insignificant

ছোটা choṭa, ছুটা chuṭa *vb* run, race

ছোট্ট choṭṭô *adj* tiny, small

ছোড়া choṛa, ছুড়া chuṛa *vb* throw, hurl

ছোপ chop *n* stain, spot

ছোপানো chopano *vb* stain, dye

ছোবড়া chobṛa *n* shell, husk

ছোবলানো choblano *vb* strike, snap

ছোরা chora *n* dagger

ছোলা chola, ছুলা chula *vb* strip, peel

জ j

জং jɔṁ *n* rust

জংলি jôṁli *adj* wild, uncivilized, untamed

জখম jɔkhôm *n* wound, sore, ulcer

জগ jɔg *n* jug

জগৎ jɔgôt, জগতী jɔgôtī *n* world, universe, earth

জগদ্দল jɔgôddɔl *adj* oppressive, heavy

জগাখিচুড়ি jɔgakhicuṛi *n* hodge-podge

জঘন্য jɔghônyô *adj* detestable, disgusting

জঙ্গম jɔṅgôm *adj* mobile, movable, dynamic

জঙ্গল jɔṅgôl *n* forest, jungle

জঞ্জাল jɔñjal *n* refuse, rubbish, debris

জট jɔṭ *n* tangle, knot

জটিল jôṭil *adj* difficult, complex, intricate

জটিলতা jôṭilɔta *n* complexity

জড় jɔṛ *adj* inanimate, inert

জড়তা jɔṛôta *n* inertia, lethargy

জড়বাদ jɔṛôbad *n* materialism

জড়বিজ্ঞান jɔṛôbijñan *n* natural science, physics, chemistry

জড়া jɔṛa *adj* clasped, entwined

জড়াজড়ি jɔṛajôṛi *adj* intertwined

জড়ানো jɔṛano *vb* embrace, hug

জড়িত jôṛitô *adj* concerned; connected, related

জন jɔn *n* person, individual

জনক jɔnôk *n* parent

জনতা jɔnôta *n* crowd, assembly

জননী jɔnônī *n* mother

জনপ্রিয় jɔnôpriyô *adj* favorite, well-liked

জনমজুর jɔnmôjur *n* laborer

জনমত jɔnômɔt *n* public opinion

জনসংখ্যা jɔnôsɔṁkhya *n* population

জনসাধারণ jɔnôsadharôn *n* the people, the public

জনাকীর্ণ jɔnakīrṇô *adj* crowded, overpopulated

জনাব jɔnab *n polite address:* Sir

জনিত jônitô *adj* born, begotten

জন্তু jôntu *n* animal, creature

জন্ম jɔnmô *n* birth, origin

জন্ম গ্রহণ করা jɔnmô grôhôn kɔra *vb* be born

জন্মদিন jɔnmôdin *n* birthday

জন্মানো jɔnmano *vb* produce, grow

জন্য jônyô, জন্যে jônye *pp* for

জবজব jɔbjɔb *onom* drenched, saturated

জবর jɔbôr *adj* pompous, splendid, showy

জবরদস্ত jɔbôrdɔstô *adj* forceful

জবরদস্তি jɔbôrdôsti *n* force, violence; *adv* forcefully

জবান jɔban *n* speech, language

জবানবন্দি jɔbanbôndi *n* testimony

জবাব jɔbab *n* answer, reply

জবুথবু jôbuthôbu *adj* decrepit, old, slovenly

জব্দ jɔbdô *adj* outwitted, defeated

জমক jɔmôk *n* pomp, grandeur

জমজ jɔmôj, যমজ yɔmôj *n* twin

জমজমাট jɔmjɔmaṭ *adj* crowded, overcrowded

জমা jɔma *n* capital, savings

জমা করা jɔma kɔra *vb* save (money), accumulate, collect

জমাট jɔmaṭ *adj* congealed, coagulated, thick; inseparable

জমানো jɔmano *vb* save, collect, accumulate

জমি jômi *n* land, soil, real estate

জমিদার jômidar *n* land-owner, landlord

জমিয়ে রাখা jômiŷe rakha *vb* fascinate, arrest attention

জয় jɔŷ *n* victory, triumph

জয় করা jɔŷ kɔra *vb* win

জরদা jɔrda *n* scented tobacco

জরা jɔra *n* decrepitude

জরানো jɔrano *vb* smear; preserve, pickle

জরায়ু jɔraŷu *n* womb, uterus

জরিপ jôrip *n* land-surveying

জরিমানা jôrimana *n* fine, charge

জরুরি jôruri *adj* urgent, essential

জরুরি অবস্থা jôruri ɔbôstha *n* emergency

জর্জরিত jɔrjôrito *adj* stricken, worn out

জল jɔl *n* water

জলতরঙ্গ jɔltɔrôṅgô *n* wave, ripple; musical instrument

জলদস্যু jɔlôdôsyu *n* pirate

জলবসন্ত jɔlbɔsôntô *n* chicken-pox

জলময় jɔlômɔŷ *adj* water-logged

জলসিক্ত jɔlôsiktô *adj* wet, soaked

জলহস্তী jɔlôhôstī *n* hippopotamus

জলদি jôldi *adv* quickly, hurriedly

জলপাই jɔlpai *n* olive

জলসা jɔlsa *n* concert

জলা jɔla *n* marsh

জলীয় jôlīŷô *adj* watery, aqueous

জলো jôlo *adj* watery, thin

জল্লাদ jɔllad *n* executioner

জহর jɔhôr *n* poison

জা ja *n* sister-in-law *(wife of husband's brother)*

জাঁক jāk *n* splendor, ostentation, pomp

জাঁকজমক jākjɔmôk *n* pomp and grandeur

জাঁকাল jākalô *adj* ostentatious, stylish

জাঁতা jāta *n* grindstone

জাঁতা jāta *vb* compress, massage, squeeze

জাগন্ত jagôntô *adj* awake, wakeful

জাগা jaga *vb* wake up

জাগানো jagano *vb* wake s.o. up

জাত jat *adj* born, produced, originating from

জাতি jati *n* class, species, race; nation

জাতিগত jatigôtô *adj* national; racial; communal

জাতিতত্ত্ব jatitɔttvô *n* ethnology

জাতিভেদ jatibhed *n* caste distinction

জাতীয় jatīŷô *adj* national

জাতীয়তা jatīŷôta *n* nationality

জাতীয়তাবাদ jatīŷôtabad *n* nationalism

জাদু jadu *n* magic, witchcraft, enchantment

জাদুকর jadukɔr *n* magician, sorcerer

জাদুঘর jadughɔr *n* museum

জানা jana *vb* know, be aware of

জানান দেওয়া janan deoŷa *vb* announce, proclaim

জানানো janano *vb* inform, make known

জানালা janala *n* window

জাপটানো japṭano *vb* seize, clasp

জাপানি japani *adj* Japanese

জাফরান japhran *n* saffron

জাফরি japhri *n* lattice, trellis

জাম jam *n* blackberry

জামা jama *n* shirt, blouse, jacket

জামাই jamai *n* son-in-law

জামিন jamin *n* bail

জামিনদার jamindar *n* bailsman, surety

জায়গা jayga *n* place, space, room

জায়ফল jayphɔl *n* nutmeg

জারক jarôk *adj* digestive

জারজ jarôj *adj* illegitimate, bastard

জারণ jarôn *n* dissolution

জারানো jarano *vb* digest, dissolve

জারি jari *n* introduction; enforcement

জারিজুরি jarijuri *n* tactics, skills

জাল jal *n* fishing net; counterfeit

জালি jali *adj* net-like; *n* fraud

জালিয়াতি jaliyati *n* forgery

জাহাজ jahaj *n* ship

জাহাজডুবি jahajdubi *n* shipwreck

জাহান jahan *(Muslim) n* world

জাহান্নাম jahannam *(Muslim) n* hell, perdition

জাহির jahir *adj* manifest, demonstrated

জাহির jahir *n* display, exhibition

জিগর jigôr *n* heart; liver; courage

জিজ্ঞাসা jijñasa *(pron* jiggasha) *n* question, inquiry

জিজ্ঞাসাবাদ jijñasabad *n* interrogation

জিজ্ঞাসা করা jijñasa kɔra *vb* ask, inquire

জিঞ্জির jiñjir *n* shackle, fetter

জিত jit *n* victory

জিতা jita *see* জেতা jeta

জিতেন্দ্রিয় jitendriyô *adj* self-restrained, controlled

জিনিস jinis *n* thing, substance, article

জিনিসপত্র jinispɔtrô *n* things, goods, merchandise

জিন্দা jinda *adj* living, alive

জিব jib, জিভ jibh *n* tongue

জিম্মা jimma *n* custody, guardianship, care

জিয়ানো jiŷano *(Bd)*, জিয়োনো jiŷono *(WB) vb* keep alive, preserve

জিরা jira *n* cumin

জিরানো jirano *(Bd)*, জিরোনো jirono *(WB) vb* relax, take a rest

জিরাফ jiraph *n* giraffe

জীব jīb *n* creature, life, soul, spirit

জীবজন্তু jībjôntu *n* animal, living creature

জীবতত্ত্ব jībtɔttvô *n* biology

জীবন jībɔn *n* life, vitality

জীবন্ত jībɔntô *adj* alive, living, vivid

জীবিত jībitô *adj* existent, alive

জীর্ণ jīrṇô *adj* emaciated, worn-out

জুঁই jũi *n* jasmine

জুজু juju *n* apparition, evil spirit

জুঝা jujha *n* contest

জুড়ানো jurano *vb* cool, soothe, calm

জুড়ি juri *n* match, equal

জুত jut *n* comfort, ease, contentment, suitability

জুতসই jutsôi *adj* advantageous, suitable

জুতা juta *(Bd)*, জুতো juto *(WB) n* shoes, footwear

জুয়া juŷa *n* gambling

জুলফি julphi *n* sideburns, whiskers

জুলুম julum *n* force, oppression

জেঠা jæṭha *n* uncle *(father's older brother)*

জেঠী jeṭhī *n* aunt *(father's older brother's wife)*

জেতা jeta, জিতা jita *vb* win, obtain victory

জেদ jed, জিদ jid *n* insistence, doggedness

জেদি jedi *adj* stubborn, obstinate

জেয়াদা jeŷada *adj* excessive, abundant

জের jer *n* balance (of accounts); *fig* smouldering embers; after-effects

জেরা jera *n* cross-examination

জেল jel *n* jail, prison

জেলা jela, জিলা jila *n* district, division

জেলে jele *n* fisherman

জেহাদ jehad *n* religious war *(Muslim)*

জৈব joibô *adj* organic

জোঁক jŏk *n* leech

জোট joṭ *n* union, confederacy

জোটা joṭa *vb* collect, assemble

জোটানো joṭano *(Bd)*, জোটোনো *(WB) vb* cause to appear; gather, collect

জোড় joṛ *n* joint, joining

জোড়া joṛa *n* pair, couple; *vb* join, add, affix

জোড়াতালি joṛatali *n* patchwork

জোনাকি jonaki *n* firefly, glowworm

জোয়ার joŷar *n* high tide

জোয়াল joŷal *n* yoke

জোর jor *n* strength, force, power

জোর করা jor kɔra *vb* force, coerce

জোরজুলুম jorjulum *n* force, oppression, tyranny

জোরাজুরি jorajuri *n* persistence, insistence

জোরালো joralo *adj* forceful, emphatic

জোরে jore *adv* loudly, forcefully; fast

জ্ঞাত jñætô *(pron* gæto*) adj* known, understood, familiar

জ্ঞান jñæn *n* knowledge, perception, understanding

জ্ঞানবিজ্ঞান jñænbijñan *n* arts and crafts; knowledge and wisdom

জ্ঞানী jñænī *adj* learned, erudite, wise

জ্ঞাপক jñæpôk *adj* indicative, expressing

জ্ঞাপন jñæpôn *n* information, communication

জ্বর jvɔr *n* fever

জ্বলজ্বল jvɔljvɔl *adj* sparkling, glittering

জ্বলা jvɔla *vb* burn

জ্বাল jval *n* heat

জ্বালানি jvalani *n* firewood, fuel

জ্বালানো jvalano *vb* kindle, light, set on fire; irritate, vex, annoy

জ্যামিতি jyæmiti *n* geometry

জ্যেষ্ঠ jyeṣṭhô *adj* elder, eldest

জ্যোতি jyoti *n* light, glow, lustre

জ্যোতিঃশাস্ত্র jyotiḥśastrô *n* astrology

জ্যোতির্বিদ্যা jyotirbidya *n* astronomy

জ্যোতিষী jyotiṣī *n* astrologer

ঝ jh

ঝংকার jhɔṁkar *n* jingling, clattering

ঝকঝক jhɔkjhɔk *adj* glittering, sparkling

ঝকমারি jhɔkômari *n* fault, failing, shortcoming

ঝগড়া jhɔgṛa *n* quarrel, altercation

ঝঙ্কার jhɔṅkar *n* clash, clatter

ঝঞ্ঝা jhɔñjha *n* gale, tempest

ঝটকা jhɔṭka *n* pull, jerk

ঝড় jhɔṛ *n* storm, tempest

ঝনঝন jhɔnjhɔn *onom* clanking, jingling

ঝপ jhɔp *adj* splashing

ঝমঝম jhɔmjhɔm *onom* pattering, sound of heavy rain

ঝরঝরানি jhɔrjhɔrani *n* oozing, incessant flow

ঝরঝর jhɔrjhɔr *onom* rapidly dripping

ঝরনা jhɔrna *n* fountain

ঝরা jhɔra *vb* drip

ঝলক jhɔlôk *n* flash, gush

ঝলঝল jhɔljhɔl *adj* flapping, dangling

ঝলসানো jhɔlsano *vb* dazzle; singe

ঝলসিত jhɔlsitô *adj* dazzled, dazed

ঝা jhā *n* quickness, haste

ঝাঁক jhāk *n* flock, swarm

ঝাঁকা jhāka *n* basket

ঝাঁকানো jhākano *vb* shake

ঝাঁজ jhāj *n* heat; pungent aroma

ঝাঁটা jhāṭa *n* broom

ঝাঁপ jhāp *n* leap, jump

ঝাড়া jhaṛa *vb* dust off, brush off

ঝাড়ু jharu *n* broom, brush

ঝানু jhanu *adj* experienced, veteran; cunning

ঝাপটা jhapṭa *n* gust; trials and tribulations

ঝামা jhama *n* pumice

ঝামেলা jhamela *n* disturbance, trouble

ঝালা jhala *vb* solder, mend

ঝালাপালা jhalapala *adj* deafened, stunned

ঝি jhi *n* daughter; maid-servant

ঝিঁঝিঁ jhĩjhĩ *n* cicada, cricket

ঝিঁঝিঁ jhĩjhĩ *n* pins and needles

ঝিনিঝিনি jhinijhini *onom* jingling (*as of ankle bells*)

ঝিনুক jhinuk *n* oyster

ঝিম jhim *n* languidness, lassitude

ঝিমঝিম jhimjhim *n* dizziness

ঝিলিক jhilik *n* flash, glitter, lustre

ঝুঁকি jhūki *n* risk, peril

ঝুড়ি jhuṛi *n* basket

ঝুনা jhuna *(Bd)*, ঝুনো jhuno *(WB) adj* mature; hardened

ঝুরঝুর jhurjhur *onom* bit by bit; in granules

ঝুল jhul *n* soot

ঝুলা jhula *see* ঝোলা jhola

ঝুলি jhuli *n* clothbag

ঝোঁক jhõk *n* inclination, bend of mind

ঝোঁকা jhõka *vb* bend, stoop

ঝোপ jhop *n* small wood, thicket

ঝোল jhol *n* sauce; soup

ঝোলা jhola, ঝুলা jhula *vb* hang, swing, dangle

ঝোলাঝুলি jholajhuli *n* baggage, belongings

ট ṭ

টং ṭɔṁ *onom* ticking sound; *n* high platform, look-out

টক ṭɔk *adj* sour

টকটকে লাল ṭɔkṭɔke lal *onom* bright red

টকা ṭɔka *vb* turn sour, turn acid

টনক ṭɔnôk *n* recollection

টপকানো ṭɔpkano *vb* leap, take two steps at a time

টপটপ ṭɔpṭɔp *onom* dripping of liquid

টমটম ṭɔmṭɔm *n* horse-drawn carriage

টমেটো ṭɔmeṭo *n* tomato

টর্চলাইট ṭôrclaiṭ *n* torch

টলটলানো ṭɔlṭɔlano *vb* stagger, totter, waver

টলমল ṭɔlmɔl *adj* unsteady

টলা ṭɔla *vb* stagger, totter, waver

টহল ṭɔhôl *n* patrol

টা ṭa *suff* the (det)

টাক ṭak *n* baldness

টাকা ṭaka *n* money, Bangladesh currency

টাকা দেওয়া ṭaka deoŷa *vb* pay

টাঙানো ṭaṅano *vb* suspend, hang up

টাটকা ṭaṭka *adj* fresh, not stale

টাটানো ṭaṭano *vb* smart, feel acute pain

টাটি ṭaṭi *n* mat

টাট্টু ṭaṭṭu *n* pony

টান ṭan *n* pull, tug, attraction

টানা ṭana *vb* pull, draw

টাপুর–টুপুর ṭapur-ṭupur *onom* patter of rain

টাল ṭal *n* slant, slope; danger, crisis

টাল সামলানো ṭal samlano *vb* avert a crisis

টালি ṭali *n* tile

টি ṭi *suff* the (det)

টিকটিকি ṭikṭiki *n* gecko, house-lizard

টিকা ṭika *n* vaccination; *vb see* টেকা ṭeka

টিকিট ṭikiṭ *n* ticket; stamp

টিটকারি ṭiṭkari *n* jeer, snicker, sneer

টিপ ṭip *n* mark on a woman's forehead (Hindu)

টিপয় ṭipɔŷ *n* tripod, small three-legged table

টিপা ṭipa *n* massage; *vb see* টেপা ṭepa

টিফিন ṭiphin *n* snack, tiffin

টিয়া ṭiŷa *n* parrot, parakeet

টিলা ṭila *n* small hill, hillock

টীকা ṭika *n* annotation, note

টুকটাক ṭukṭak *adj* of small quantity, light, paltry; easy

টুকরা ṭukra (Bd), টুকরো ṭukro (WB) *n* piece, bit, fragment

টুকরা–টাকরা ṭukra-ṭakra (Bd), টুকরো–টাকরা ṭukro-ṭakra (WB) *n* odds and ends

টুকরি ṭukri *n* basket

টুকিটাকি ṭukiṭaki *adj* trivial, light, negligible

টুনটুনি ṭunṭuni *n* tailor bird

টুপা ṭupa *n* small container, box

টুপি ṭupi *n* hat, cap

টুল ṭul *n* stool

টেকসই ṭeksôi *adj* durable, lasting

টেকা ṭeka, টিকা ṭika *vb* last, endure

টেকো ṭeko *adj* bald

টেড়া ṭæra *adj* cross-eyed

টেপা ṭepa, টিপা ṭipa *vb* massage; squeeze

টেবিল ṭebil *n* table

টের ṭer *n* feeling, sensation, awareness

টের পাওয়া ṭer paoŷa *vb* feel, be aware of, perceive

টেলিফোন ṭeliphon *n* telephone

টোকা ṭoka *n* tap, flip; *vb* copy

টো-টো ṭo-ṭo *onom* rambling, aimless strolling

টোপ ṭop *n* bait

টোপা ṭopa *adj* round, globular

টোল ṭol *n* dimple

ট্রেন ṭren *n* train

ঠ ṭh

ঠং ṭhɔṁ *onom* metallic striking sound

ঠকা ṭhɔka *vb* be cheated, be deceived

ঠকানো ṭhɔkano *vb* cheat, deceive

ঠন ṭhɔn *onom* ding-dong of a bell

ঠাঁই ṭhãi *n* accommodation, place, space

ঠাকুর ṭhakur *n* deity, idol

ঠাকুরদা ṭhakurda *n* grandfather *(paternal, Hindu)*

ঠাকুরমা ṭhakurma *n* grandmother *(paternal, Hindu)*

ঠাট্টা ṭhaṭṭa *n* teasing, jest, banter

ঠাণ্ডা ṭhanḍa *adj* cold, cool, calm

ঠায় ṭhaŷ *adv* incessantly

ঠারা ṭhara *vb* gesticulate, beckon

ঠাসা ṭhasa *vb* thrust in, cram, load

ঠিক ṭhik *adj* fixed, settled, correct, right, proper

ঠিকঠাক ṭhikṭhak *adv* exactly, correctly

ঠিকরানো ṭhikrano *(Bd)*, ঠিকরোনো ṭhikrono *(WB) vb* scatter, disperse

ঠিকা ṭhika *(Bd)*, ঠিকে ṭhike *(WB) adj* part-time, temporary

ঠিকানা ṭhikana *n* address

ঠুঁটা ṭhũṭa *(Bd)*, ঠুঁটো ṭhũṭo *(WB) adj* maimed, mutilated

ঠুনকো ṭhunko *adj* fragile, brittle, unstable

ঠেকনা ṭhækna *n* prop, lean-to, support

ঠেকা ṭhæka *vb* touch; stop and start; be in difficulties

ঠেকানো ṭhækano *vb* obstruct, impede

ঠেঙা ṭhænga *n* club, stave, pole

ঠেঙানো ṭhængano *vb* beat, beat up

ঠেলা ṭhæla *vb* push, shove, thrust

ঠেলাগাড়ি ṭhælagaṛi *n* pushcart, handwagon

ঠোঁট ṭhõṭ *n* lips

ঠোকরানো ṭhokrano *vb* peck, nibble

ঠোঙা ṭhoṅa *n* carton, box

ড ড়

ডগা ḍɔga *n* tip, top, extreme point

ডঙ্কা ḍɔṅka *n* large kettledrum

ডজন ḍɔjôn *adj* a dozen

ডবল ḍɔbôl *adj* double

ডর ḍɔr *n* fear, fright, dread

ডলা ḍɔla *vb* massage, knead

ডাইন ḍain, ডান ḍan *n* right, the right side

ডাইনী ḍainī *n* witch

ডাঁই ḍāi *n* heap, pile

ডাঁট ḍāṭ *n* handle, shaft; vigor, spiritedness; arrogance

ডাঁটা ḍāṭa *n* stalk, stem

ডাঁটো ḍāṭo *adj* hard, difficult; unripe

ডাক ḍak *n* call, summons; postal system, mail

ডাকঘর ḍakghɔr *n* post office

ডাকা ḍaka *vb* call, summon, invite

ডাকাত ḍakat *n* robber, gangster

ডাক্তার ḍaktar *n* doctor

ডাগর ḍagôr *n* large, big, wide

ডান ḍan *n* right, right side

ডানপিটে ḍanpiṭe *adj* daring, reckless, foolhardy

ডানা ḍana *n* wing

ডাব ḍab *n* green coconut

ডাল ḍal *n* branch, twig; lentils, pulses

ডালপালা ḍalpala *n* bramble, foliage

ডালিম ḍalim *n* pomegranate

ডাহা ḍaha *adj* downright, outright

ডিগবাজি ḍigbaji *n* somersault, tumble

ডিঙা ḍiṅa *n* boat, vessel

ডিঙি ḍiṅi *n* small boat, dinghi

ডিম ḍim *n* egg

ডিমের কুসুম ḍimer kusum *n* egg yolk

ডিম্বকোষ ḍimbôkoṣ *n* ovaries, egg cell

ডুব ḍub *n* dive

ডুবডুব ḍubḍub *onom* almost drowned

ডুবা ḍuba *see* ডোবা ḍoba

ডুবুরি ḍuburi *n* diver

ডুবোজাহাজ ḍubojahaj *n* submarine

ডুমুর ḍumur *n* fig

ডুরে ḍure *adj* striped

ডেকচি ḍekci *n* metallic cooking pot

ডেবরা ḍebra *adj* left-handed

ডেরা ḍera *n* lodgings, temporary abode

ডোঙা ḍoṅa *n* canoe, small boat

ডোবা ḍoba, ডুবা ḍuba *vb* sink, drown

ডোবানো ḍobano *vb* plunge, immerse, soak

ডোরা ḍora *n* stripe, streak

ড্যাংড্যাং ḍyæṁḍyæṁ *onom* sound of drumming

ঢং ḍhɔṅg *n* form, shape; fashion, style

ঢক ḍhɔk *n* shape, form, pattern

ঢকঢক ḍhɔkḍhɔk *onom* gulping, swallowing

ঢল ḍhɔl *n* slope, incline

ঢলঢলে ḍhɔlḍhɔle *adj* loosely fitting

ঢলা ḍhɔla *vb* incline, lean

ঢাউস ḍhaus *adj* huge, enormous

ঢাক ḍhak *n* drum

ঢাকনা ḍhakna *n* lid, cover

ঢাকা ḍhaka *vb* cover, screen, envelop, conceal

ঢাল ḍhal *n* shield

ঢালা ḍhala *vb* pour, cast, mold; spend; confer

ঢালু ḍhalu *adj* sloping, inclined downward

ঢিঢি ḍhiḍhi *n* loud noise; reproach; public discussion

ঢিপি ḍhipi *n* hillock, mound

ঢিমা ḍhima *(Bd)*, ঢিমে ḍhime *(WB) adj* mild, slow, low

ঢিলা ḍhila *(Bd)*, ঢিলে ḍhile *(WB) adj* loose, slack, lax

ঢুকা ḍhuka *see* ঢোকা ḍhoka

ঢুল ḍhul, ঢুলুনি ḍhuluni *n* drowsiness, sleepiness

ঢেউ ḍheu *n* wave, billow, surge

ঢেঁকুর ḍhēkur *n* belch, burp

ঢেঙা ḍhæṅga *adj* lanky

ঢেপসা ḍhæpsa *adj* flaccid, flabby

ঢেলা ḍhæla *n* clump, lump

ঢোক ḍhok *n* gulp, gulping

ঢোকা ḍhoka, ঢুকা ḍhuka *vb* enter, go into, be admitted

ঢোল ḍhol *n* tamtam, drum

ঢোলা ḍhola *adj* loose; *vb* grope, fumble

ত t

ত tô, তো to *int expr* question, doubt; reassurance

তক tɔk *pp* up to, until

তকতকে tɔktɔke *adv* sparkling clean

তকদির tôkdir *n* fate, luck

তকমা tɔkma *n* badge

তকলিফ tôkliph *n* trouble, hardship, pain

তক্তা tɔkta *n* plank, board

তক্ষনি tɔkṣôni, তক্ষুনি tôkṣuni *adv* immediately, instantly

তখন tɔkhôn *adv, conj* then, at that time

তছনছ tɔchnɔch *adj* upset, spoiled, messed up

তট tɔṭ *n* beach, shore

তটস্থ tɔṭôsthô *adj* perturbed, busy, worried

তটিনী tôṭinī *n* river, stream

তড়কা tɔṛka *n* spasmodic fit

তড়পানো tɔṛpano *vb* fuss, fret

তড়বড় tɔṛbɔr *adv* hurriedly

তড়িঘড়ি tôṛighôṛi *adv* hurriedly, promptly

তড়িৎ tôṛit *n* lightning; electricity

তণ্ডুল tôṇḍul *n* husked rice

তত tɔtô *adv, conj* so much, to that extent

তৎক্ষণাৎ tɔtkṣɔṇat *adv* immediately, presently

তত্ত্ব tɔttvô *n* truth, essence, theory

তত্ত্বানুসন্ধান tɔttvanusɔndhan *n* investigation, research

তত্ত্বাবধান tɔttvabɔdhan *n* guidance, custody, supervision

তত্র tɔtrô *adv* there, in that place

তথা tɔtha *adv* there, in that place; like, for example

তথ্য tôthyô *n* information, truth, fact

তদন্ত tɔdôntô *n* investigation

তদর্থ tɔdɔrthô *adv* for that purpose

তদুপরি tɔdupôri *conj* furthermore

তনয় tɔnɔŷ *n* son

তনয়া tɔnɔŷa *n* daughter

তনু tônu *n* body, shape

তন্তু tôntu *n* thread, fiber

তন্ত্র tɔntrô *n* cult; system

তন্দ্রা tɔndra *n* sleep

তন্দ্রালু tɔndralu *adj* drowsy, sleepy

তন্নতন্ন tɔnnôtɔnnô *adj* thorough; minute

তন্নতন্ন করা tɔnnôtɔnnô kɔra *vb* search, ransack, rummage

তপ tɔp *n* devotion, meditation

তপন tɔpôn *n* sun, source of heat

তপস্বী tɔpôsvī *n* hermit, ascetic

তপোবন tɔpobôn *n* hermitage

তপ্ত tɔptô *adj* hot, warm; agitated

তফাত tɔphat *n* difference, distinction; distance

তবক tɔbôk *n* stratum, layer

তবলা tɔbla *n* small drum

তবু tôbu, তবুও tôbuo *conj* in spite of, yet, still

তবে tɔbe *conj* then, thereafter, but

তম tɔmô *n* darkness

তমসা tɔmôsa *n* darkness, ignorance

তমসাচ্ছন্ন tɔmôsachɔnnô *adj* covered in darkness; steeped in ignorance

তরকারি tɔrkari *n* curry; vegetables

তরঙ্গ tɔrôṅgô *n* wave, surge of water

তরঙ্গায়িত tɔrôṅgaŷitô *n* undulating, wavy

তরজমা tɔrjôma *n* translation, rendering

তরণী tɔrôṇī *n* ferry

তরতর tɔrtɔr *onom* swiftly flowing (water)

তরতাজা tɔrtaja *adj* fresh, alive

তরফ tɔrôph *n* side; direction

তরমুজ tôrmuj *n* watermelon

তরল tɔrôl *adj* liquid, fluid, watery

তরী tôrī *n* boat

তরু tôru *n* tree, plant

তরুণ tôruṇ *adj* young, fresh, adolescent, immature

তর্ক tɔrkô *n* altercation, argument

তর্ক করা tɔrkô kɔra *vb* argue, debate, discuss

তর্কবিদ্যা tɔrkôbidya *n* science of reason, logic

তর্জন tɔrjôn *n* angry roar, outburst

তর্জনী tɔrjônī *n* forefinger, index finger

তল tɔl *n* base, bottom, foot

তলতল tɔltɔl *adj* oversoft, flabby

তলা tɔla *n* floor, storey, foot, base

তলানি tɔlani *n* dregs, sediment

তলানো tɔlano *vb* be drowned, sink; probe

তলিয়ে দেখা tôliŷe dækha *vb* scrutinize

তল্পিতল্পা tôlpitɔlpa *n* luggage

তল্লাট tɔllaṭ *n* region, locality

তল্লাশ tɔllaś *n* search, trace

তল্লাশ করা tɔllaś kɔra *vb* scout, search

তল্লাশি পরোয়ানা tɔllaśi pɔroŷana *n* search warrant

তসবি tôsbi *n* rosary, string of beads

তহবিল tɔhôbil *n* treasury, cash, fund

তহসিল tɔhôsil *n* revenue

তা ta *pr* that, it

তাই tai *conj* therefore, for that reason; *n* clapping, applause

তাওয়া taoŷa *n* baking pan

তাওয়ানো taoŷano *vb* heat up, provoke, incite

তাঁত tãt *n* loom

তাঁবু tãbu *n* tent

তাক tak *n* guess, conjecture; shelf

তাক করা tak kɔra *vb* aim

তাকানো takano *vb* look at, see, stare, gaze

তাগাদা tagada, তাগিদ tagid *n* demand for payment, reminder

তাচ্ছিল্য tacchilyô *n* slight, contempt, disregard

তাজ taj *n* cap, crown, headdress

তাজা taja *adj* fresh, living, alive

তাজ্জব tajjôb *adj* strange, amazing

তাড়না tarôna *n* chastisement, rebuke

তাড়না করা tarôna kɔra *vb* urge, drive, chastise

তাড়া tara *n* sheaf, bundle

তাড়া tara *n* hurry, rush, urgency

তাড়া খাওয়া tara khaoŷa *vb* be rebuked, get chased away

তাড়াতাড়ি taratari *adv* quickly, hastily

তাড়ানো tarano, তাড়া করা tara kɔra *vb* chase away, drive out

তাড়াহুড়া tarahura *(Bd)*, তাড়াহুড়ো tarahuro *(WB) n* hurry, haste, bustle

তাত tat *n* heat, warmth

তাতা tata *vb* be heated, warm up

তাতানো tatano *vb* heat, warm up; provoke, excite

তাত্ত্বিক tattvik *adj* theoretical, speculative

তাৎপর্য tatpɔryô *n* significance, meaning

তাথ্যিক tathyik *adj* factual, real

তান tan *n* musical note, tune, melody

তাপ tap *n* heat, temperature, fever, warmth

তাপস tapôs *n* ascetic, hermit; devotee

তাবৎ tabôt *pp* until, till then

তাবিজ tabij *n* amulet, bracelet

তামস tamôs *adj* enveloped by darkness; ignorant

তামা tama *n* copper

তামাক tamak *n* tobacco

তামাশা tamaśa *n* joke, jest, fun

তাম্বুল tambul *n* betel-leaf

তাম্র tamrô *n* copper

তার tar *n* metal string, wire

তারকা tarôka *n* star; pupil of the eye; asterisk

তারপর tarpɔr *conj* after that, then

তারল্য tarôlyô *n* liquid state, fluidity

তারা tara *n* star; *pr* they

তারিখ tarikh *n* date

তারিফ tariph *n* praise, applause

তার্কিক tarkik *adj* logical, versed in logic

তার্কিকতা tarkikɔta *n* sophism

তার্পিন tarpin *n* resin, turpentine

তাল tal *n* palmyra tree; rhythm, beat

তাল দেওয়া tal deoŷa *vb* instigate

তালা tala *n* padlock; floor, storey

তালাক talak *n* divorce, separation

তালাকপ্রাপ্ত talakpraptô *adj* divorced

তালি tali *n* clapping, applause; patch

তালিকা talika *n* list, inventory

তালিম talim *n* instruction, lesson, advice

তালু talu *n* palate, roof of the mouth

তাস tas *n* playing cards

তিক্ত tiktô *adj* bitter, distressing, unpleasant

তিক্ততা tiktôta *n* bitterness

তিড়বিড় tirbir *adj* restless, fidgety

তিড়িং বিড়িং tiriṁ biriṁ *onom* gamboling, frisking about

তিতিক্ষা titikṣa *n* forbearance, patience

তিথি tithi *n* lunar day

তিন tin *num* three

তিনি tini *pr* he, she *(hon)*

তিমি timi *n* whale

তিমির timir *n* darkness; cataract

তিরস্কার tirôskar *n* rebuke, reprimand, reproach

তিরিক্ষি tirikṣi *adj* angry, hot-tempered, irritable

তিরোধান tirôdhan *n* disappearance, exit, death

তির্যক tiryɔk *adj* slanting, oblique

তিল til *n* sesame, minute portion, speck

তিলক tilɔk *n* mark of sandal paste on the forehead

তিলেক tilek *adj* tiny

তীক্ষ্ণ tīkṣṇô *(pron* tikhno*) adj* sharp, keen, penetrating

তীব্র tībrô *adj* severe, intense, unbearable

তীর tīr *n* riverbank

তীর tīr *n* arrow, dart

তীর্থ tīrthô *n* place of pilgrimage, holy place

তুই tui *pr* you *(sg, intim)*

তুঁত tũt *n* mulberry tree

তুকতাক tuktak *n* incantation, spell

তুঙ্গ tuṅgô *adj* high, tall, lofty

তুচ্ছ tucchô *adj* trivial, insignificant, small

তুচ্ছ করা tucchô kɔra *vb* neglect, ignore

তুচ্ছতা tucchôta *n* triviality

তুড়ি turi *n* snapping of fingers; easy defeat

তুফান tuphan *n* storm, tempest

তুমি tumi *pr* you *(sg, fam)*

তুমুল tumul *adj* tumultuous, fierce, terrible

তুরপুন turpun *n* drill, gimlet

তুরীয় turīŷô *n* trance, transcendence

তুর্কী turkī *adj* Turkish

তুলট tulôṭ *adj* cotton

তুলতুল tultul *adj* flabby, oversoft

তুলনা tulôna *n* balance, comparison, resemblance

তুলনা করা tulôna kɔra *vb* compare, liken

তুলসী tulsī *n* basil

তুলা tula *(Bd)*, তুলো tulo *(WB) n* cotton

তুলা tula *n* scales

তুল্য tulyô *adj* comparable, similar, *(math)* equivalent

তুষ tuṣ *n* husk, chaff

তুষার tuṣar *n* snow, frost, ice

তুষ্ট tuṣṭô *adj* satisfied, gratified

তুষ্টি tuṣṭi *n* satisfaction, pleasure, contentment

তৃতীয় tṛtīŷô *adj* third

তৃপ্ত tṛptô *adj* satisfied, pleased, delighted

তৃষা tṛṣa *n* thirst

তেঁতুল tẽtul *n* tamarind

তেজ tej *n* lustre, light, glow; energy, vigor

তেজপাতা tejpata *n* bay leaf

তেজস্ক্রিয় tejôskriŷô *adj* radioactive

তেজী tejī *adj* vigorous, spirited

তেজোময় tejomɔŷ *adj* vigorous, energetic, spirited

তেমন tæmôn *adj, adv* such, like, so

তেল tel *n* oil, fuel, petrol; flattery, adulation

তেল দেওয়া tel deoŷa *vb* flatter, praise

তেল মাখা tel makha *vb* massage with oil

তেলা tela *adj* oily, greasy, glossy

তেলানো tælano *vb* grease

তেলাপোকা tælapoka *n* cockroach

তেলো telo *n* palm (of the hand); sole (of the foot)

তেষ্টা teṣṭa *n* thirst, longing

তেসরা tesôra *num third day of the month*

তৈরি toiri *adj* made, manufactured; ready, prepared

তোড় toṛ *n* impact of strong current; speed, fluency

তোড়া toṛa *n* bunch, bundle

তোতলা totla *n* stammer, stutter

তোতলানো totlano *vb* stammer, stutter

তোপ top *n* gun, cannon

তোফা topha *adj* excellent, wonderful, unusual, outstanding

তোবড়ানো tobṛano, তুবড়ানো tubṛano *vb* shrivel, shrink

তোমরা tomra *pr* you *(pl, fam)*

তোয়াজ toŷaj *n* adulation, flattery

তোয়ালে toŷale *n* towel

তোরা tora *pr* you *(pl, int)*

তোলপাড় tolpaṛ *n* agitation, disturbance

তোলা tola *vb* raise, lift, pluck

তোশক tośôk *n* mattress

তোষণ toṣôṇ *n* appeasement

তোষামোদ toṣamod *n* flattery, adulation, sycophancy

তৌল toulô *n* weight, balance

ত্বক tvɔk *n* skin; complexion; texture

ত্যক্ত tyktô *(pron* tækto*) adj* abandoned, given up, relinquished

ত্যাগ করা tyæg kɔra *vb* give up, abandon, relinquish

ত্যাগী tyægī *adj* selfless, self-effacing

ত্বক tvɔk *n* skin, hide; bark (of tree)

ত্বরণ tvɔrôṇ *n* acceleration

ত্বরা tvɔra *n* haste, hurry, quickness

ত্বরিত tvôrit *adj* quick, swift, hasty

ত্রস্ত trôstô *adj* frightened, alarmed

ত্রাণ traṇ *n* rescue, delivery, relief

ত্রাণ করা traṇ kɔra *vb* rescue, deliver, relieve

ত্রাস tras *n* terror, panic, fright

ত্রি tri *adj* three

ত্রিকোণ trikoṇ *adj* triangular

ত্রিভুজ tribhuj *n* triangle

ত্রিভুবন tribhubɔn *n* universe (heaven, hell and earth)

ত্রিশ triś, তিরিশ tiriś *num* thirty

ক্রটি truṭi *n* shortcoming, fault, deficiency, flaw

ক্রটি–বিচ্যুতি truṭi–bicyuti *n* faults and failures

থ th

থ thɔ *adj* stupefied, flabbergasted

থই thôi *n* depth, bottom (of a pool)

থই thôi *int ind* vastness, expense

থকথকে thɔkthɔke *onom* sticky, viscous

থতমত thɔtômɔtô *onom* embarrassed, perplexed

থপথপে thɔpthɔpe *onom* heavily, clumsily; making a thudding noise

থমকানো thɔmkano *vb* stop suddenly, halt abruptly

থমথম thɔmthɔm *adj* heavy; dark; silent

থর thɔr *n* layer, stratum

থরথর thɔrthɔr *onom* palpitating, trembling, shivering

থলথল thɔlthɔl *onom* flabby

থলি thôli *n* bag, purse

থাক thak *n* tier, layer, shelf

থাকা thaka *vb* stay, be, live, remain

থান than *n* sheet, piece of cloth; holy place

থানা thana *n* police station

থাপ্পড় thappôr *n* slap, blow

থাবড়ানো thabṛano *vb* strike, slap

থাবা thaba *n* paw; claw

থামা thama *vb* stop, cease

থামানো thamano *vb* stop, arrest, check, cause to stop

থাল thal, থালা thala *n* plate, dish

থিকথিক thikthik *adj* slimy, sticky

থিতানো thitano *(Bd)*, থিতোনো thitono *(WB)* *vb* sink to the bottom, settle

থিতিয়ে যাওয়া thitiye jaoŷa *vb* subside, abate

থুতনি thutni *n* chin

থুতু thutu, থুথু thuthu *n* spittle, saliva

থুতু ফেলা thutu phæla *vb* spit

থুপ thup *n* heap, pile

থুবড়ানো thubṛano *vb* fall flat on one's face

থেঁতলানো thæঁtlano *vb* smash, pound, bruise

থেঁতো thēto *adj* smashed, bruised, pounded

থেকে theke *pp, conj* from, since, than

থেকে যাওয়া theke yaoŷa *vb* remain

থোয়া thoŷa *vb* put, put down, lay down, deposit

থোক thok *n* net amount

থোকা thoka *n* bundle, cluster, bunch

থোড়া thoṛa *adj* little, few

দ d

দই dôi *n* yogurt
দংশ dôṁśô *n* bite, sting
দংশক dôṁśôk *n* gnat, mosquito
দংশানো dôṁśano *vb* bite, sting
দক্ষ dôkṣô *adj* skilled, expert
দক্ষিণ dôkṣiṇ *n* south
দখল dɔkhôl *n* occupation, possession
দগদগ dɔgdɔg *adj* burning, sore, inflamed
দড়ি dôri *n* rope, string
দণ্ড dɔṇḍô *n* rod, pole; punishment
দণ্ডনীতি dɔṇḍôniti *n* penal system
দণ্ডবিধি dɔṇḍôbidhi *n* criminal law
দত্ত dɔttô *adj* given, awarded, bestowed
দধি dôdhi *n* curd, curdled milk
দন্ত dɔntô *n* tooth
দপ dɔp *n* flame, flare, burst
দপদপ করা dɔpdɔp kɔra *vb* throb
দপাদপ dɔpadɔp *n* repeated kicking
দপ্তর dɔptôr *n* office, records, files
দপ্তরী dɔptôrī *n* clerk
দফা dɔpha *n* installment, division, section
দম dɔm *n* breath, aspiration; strength
দমক dɔmôk *n* blast, flash, burst
দমন dɔmôn *n* subdual, quelling, restraint, suppression
দমা dɔma *vb* be subdued, suppressed
দমানো dɔmano *vb* suppress, subdue
দমিত dômitô *adj* tamed, subdued
দয়া dôẏa *n* kindness, mercy
দর dɔr *n* price, rate
দরকার dɔrkar *n* need, necessity

দরকারী dɔrkarī *adj* necessary
দরখাস্ত dɔrkhastô *n* application
দরজা dɔrja *n* door
দরজি dôrji *n* tailor
দরদ dɔrôd *n* sympathy, compassion
দরদর dɔrdɔr *onom* rapidly flowing, oozing
দরদালান dɔrdalan *n* corridor
দরপত্তন dɔrpɔttôn *n* sub-lease
দরবার dɔrbar *n* court-chamber, court
দরাজ dɔraj *adj* open, free, liberal
দরিদ্র dôridrô *adj* poor, lacking, deficient
দর্প dɔrpô *n* vanity, conceit, pride
দর্শন dɔrśôn *n* observation, vision; knowledge; philosophy
দল dɔl *n* group, company
দলন dɔlôn *n* repression, subdual
দলাদলি dɔladôli *n* partiality, partisanship
দলিল dôlil *n* deed, document
দশ dɔś *num* ten
দশা dɔśa *n* phase, stage; disposition; situation
দস্তক dɔstôk *n* summons, warrant
দস্তা dɔsta *n* zinc
দস্তুর dôstur *n* custom, practice
দস্তুরি dôsturi *n* discount
দস্যু dôsyu *n* robber, bandit
দহ dɔhô *n* abyss; danger
দা da *n* dagger, knife
দাই dai, দাইমা daima *n* midwife
দাওয়াত daoẏat *n* invitation
দাঁড় dãr *n* oar, paddle
দাঁড়ানো dãrano *vb* stand, wait
দাঁড়ি dãri *n* punctuation mark at end of sentence

দাঁত dāt *n* tooth

দাখিল dakhil *adj* filed, registered

দাগ dag *n* mark, spot, stain

দাগা daga *n* shock, heartbreak

দাঙ্গা daṅga *n* riot, fracas

দাড়ি dari *n* beard

দাতা data *n* donor, giver

দাদা dada *n* older brother *(Hindu)*; grandfather *(paternal, Muslim)*

দাদী dadī *n* grandmother *(paternal, Muslim)*

দাদু dadu *n* grandfather *(paternal, Muslim)*; grandfather *(maternal, Hindu)*

দান dan *n* act of giving, offering

দানা dana *n* seed, grain

দানী danī *adj* bountiful, generous

দাবড়ানো dabṛano *vb* bully, threaten

দাবা daba *n* chess

দাবানো dabano *vb* suppress, press down

দাবি dabi *n* claim, right, demand

দাম dam *n* price, cost, value

দামাল damal *adj* unmanageable, indomitable

দামী damī *adj* expensive, costly

দাম্পত্য dampɔtyô *adj* conjugal

দায় daŷ *n* danger, difficulty; need necessity

দায়ী daŷī *adj* responsible, liable

দায়িত্ব daŷitvô *n* responsibility, liability

দার dar *suff impl* causing, producing; owning, possessing

দারচিনি darcini *n* cinnamon

দারুণ daruṇ *adj* great, intense, excessive

দারোয়ান daroŷan *n* guard, gatekeeper

দার্শনিক darśônik *n* philosopher

দালান dalan *n* building

দালাল dalal *n* broker, go-between

দালালি dalali *n* brokerage, commission agency

দাস das *n* servant, attendant

দাসী dasī *n* maid, servant girl

দাস্য dasyô *n* slavery, servitude

দিক dik *n* direction; part, side, region

দিগন্ত digôntô *n* horizon

দিঘি dighi *n* tank; pond

দিদি didi *n* sister (elder)

দিদিমা didima *n* grandmother *(maternal, Hindu)*

দিন din *n* day

দিবস dibôs *n* day

দিব্যি dibyi *adj* divine, delightful

দিয়ে diŷe *pp* with *(instr)*, through

দিল dil *n* mind; heart

দিশা diśa *n* orientation

দিশাহারা diśahara, **দিশেহারা** diśehara *adj* disorientated, confused, lost

দীক্ষা dīkṣa *n* instigation, initiative

দীপ dīp *n* light, lamp

দীপিকা dīpika *n* light, lamp

দীপ্ত dīptô *adj* burning, blazing, hot

দীর্ঘ dīrghô *adj* long, lengthy

দীর্ঘশ্বাস dīrghôśvas *n* sigh

দু du *pref* two

দুজন dujɔn *n* two people, both

দুবার dubar *adv* twice

দুয়েক duŷek *adj* one or two, a few

দুই dui *num* two

দুঃখ duḥkhô *n* sorrow, sadness, grief

দুঃখ করা duḥkhô kɔra *vb* regret, rue, grieve

দুঃখজনক duḥkhôjɔnôk *adj* painful, troublesome, sad

দুঃখিত duḥkhito *adj* sorry, woeful, grieved

দুঃশাসন duḥśasôn *adj* unruly, indomitable

দুঃশীল duḥśīl *adj* misbehaved, wicked

দুঃসংবাদ duḥsɔṁbad *n* bad news

দুঃসাধ্য duḥsadhyô *adj* arduous, difficult

দুঃসাহস duḥsahôs *n* daring, recklessness

দুঃস্থ duḥstho *adj* needy, poor, wretched

দুঃস্বপ্ন duḥsvɔpnô *n* nightmare, bad dream

দুগ্ধ dugdhô *n* milk; juice; latex

দুৎ duṭ *int* hang!, blow!, drat!

দুধ dudh *n* milk

দুনিয়া duniŷa *n* world, universe

দুপুর dupur *n* midday, noon

দুপুর রাত dupur rat *n* midnight

দুম dum, দুমাদুম dumadum *onom* banging, booming, thudding sound

দুরন্ত durɔntô *adj* unruly, unmanageable, disobedient

দুরবস্থা durɔbôstha *n* misery, distress, wretchedness

দুর্গ durgô *n* fortress, castle, tower

দুর্গত durgɔtô *adj* afflicted, miserable, wretched

দুর্গাপূজা durgapuja *(Bd)*, দুর্গাপূজো durgapujo *(WB) n* Durga Puja

দুর্ঘটনা durghɔṭôna *n* accident, mishap, calamity

দুর্দশা durdɔśa *n* misery, adversity

দুর্দিন durdin *n* time of danger, hard times

দুর্নাম durnam *n* disrepute, ill fame, discredit

দুর্নীতি durnīti *n* corruption, malpractice, perversion

দুর্বল durbôl *adj* weak, feeble

দুর্ভাগ্য durbhagyô *n* misfortune, ill luck

দুর্যোগ duryog *n* hard times, danger, difficulties

দুর্লভ durlɔbh *adj* scarce, hard to obtain

দুল dul *n* earring

দুলা dula *see* দোলা dola

দুশ্চিন্তা duścinta *n* worries, anxiety, misgivings

দুষ্কর duṣkɔr *adj* arduous, difficult

দুষ্ট duṣtô *adj* faulty, defective, septic

দুষ্টামি duṣtami, দুষ্টুমি duṣtumi *n* naughtiness, wickedness

দুষ্টু duṣtu *adj* naughty, mischievous

দূত dūt *n* messenger, ambassador

দূতাবাস dūtabas *n* embassy

দূর dūr *n* distance; *int expr* disgust, contempt, disagreement

দূর করা dūr kɔra *vb* remove, expel, banish, dispel

দূরত্ব dūrôtvô *n* distance, length, remoteness

দূরবীক্ষণ dūrbīkṣôṇ *n* telescope

দূরের কথা dūrer kɔtha *n* irrelevancy

দূষণ dūṣɔṇ *n* pollution

দূষিত dūṣitô *adj* corrupted, polluted, defiled

দৃঢ় dṛṛhô *(pron* drirhô) *adj* durable, sound, strong, firm

দৃশ্য dṛśyô *(pron* drissho) *n* view, sight, scenery

দৃশ্য dṛśyô *adj* visible, apparent, obvious

দৃষ্টান্ত dṛṣtantô *n* precedent, example, instance

দৃষ্টি dṛṣti *n* view, sight, faculty of seeing

দেওয়া deoŷa *vb* give, confer, bestow

দেওয়ানি deoŷani *n* stewardship, legal protection

দেওয়াল deoŷal, দেয়াল deŷal *n* wall

দেওর dæor, দেবর debor *n* brother-in-law *(husband's younger brother)*

দেখা dækha *vb* see, look, notice

দেখা করা dækha kɔra *vb* meet, visit

দেখা দেওয়া dækha deoŷa *vb* appear

দেখানো dækhano *vb* show

দেড় deṛ *num* one and a half

দেদার dedar *adj* plentiful, abundant

দেনা dena *n* debt, loan

দেব debɔ *n* Hindu deity, god

দেবতা debôta *n* divinity, image of a deity

দেবদারু debdaru *n* cedar, deodar

দেবী debī *n* goddess, female deity

দেরাজ deraj *n* drawer (of a cabinet)

দেরি deri *n* delay

দেশ deś *n* country, state, homeland

দেশী desī *adj* indigenous, local

দেশলাই desôlai *n* match(es)

দেহ dehô *n* body, physique, corpse

দৈনিক doinik *adj* daily

দৈর্ঘ্য doirghô *n* length

দৈহিক doihik *adj* bodily, physical

দো do *pref* two

দোকান dokan *n* shop, store

দোকানদার dokandar *n* shopkeeper

দোটানা dɔṭana, দুটানা duṭana, *n* indecision, dilemma

দোবজা dobja *n* scarf

দোভাষী dobhaṣī, দুভাষী dubhaṣī *adj* bilingual

দোয়া doŷa *n* blessing, grace

দোয়া করা doŷa kɔra *vb* bless, wish well

দোয়েল doŷel *n* magpie

দোল dol *n* oscillation, swinging

দোলনা dolna *n* swing; rocking cradle

দোলা dola, দুলা dula *vb* swing, oscillate, dangle

দোলানো dolano *vb* cause to swing, cause to rock

দোষ doṣ *n* fault, guilt, vice, crime

দোষ দেওয়া doṣ deoŷa *vb* blame, accuse

দোষারোপ doṣarop *n* recrimination, accusation

দোষী doṣī *adj* guilty, at fault,

দোসরা dosôra *adj* second, another; *second day of the month*

দোস্ত dostô *n* friend, comrade

দোহাই dohai *n* plea

দোহারা dohara *n* double, twice; double thread; medium build

দৌড় douṛ *n* act of running

দৌড় দেওয়া douṛ deoŷa *vb* run, take off, rush

দৌড়াদৌড়ি douṛadouṛi *n* running about, rush, hectic

দৌড়ানো douṛano *(Bd)*, দৌড়োনো dourono *vb* run, rush, dash

দৌবারিক doubarik *n* gatekeeper, guard

দৌর্বল্য dourbôlyô *n* weakness, debility

দৌলত doulôt *n* wealth, treasure, fortune

দ্বন্দ্ব dvɔndvô *(pron* dɔndô*)* *n* strife, quarrel, dispute

দ্বন্দ্বযুদ্ধ dvɔndvôyuddhô *n* duel

দ্বার dvar *n* door

দ্বারা dvara *pp* through, by, by means of

দ্বি dvi *pref* two

দ্বিধা dvidha *n, adj* divided into two; wavering, hesitation, indecision

দ্বিতীয় dvitīyô *adj* second

দ্বিভাব dvibhab *adj* hypocritical

দ্বিভাষী dvibhaṣī *adj* bilingual

দ্বিমত dvimɔt *n* divided opinion

দ্বীপ dvīp *n* island

দ্বেষ dveṣ *n* aversion, dislike, antipathy

দ্বৈত doitô *n* duality, dualism

দ্ব্যর্থ dvyærthô *n* ambiguity

দ্যুতি dyuti *n* radiation, glow

দ্যোতক dyotôk *adj* signifying, indicating, expressing

দ্রব drôbô *n* liquid, fluid, solution

দ্রব্য drôbyô *n* matter, substance

দ্রাঘিমা draghima *n* longitude

দ্রাবক drabôk *n* solvent

দ্রুত drutô *adj* quick, swift, speedy

দ্রুততা drutôta *n* speed, swiftness

দ্রুতিমাপক drutimapôk *n* speedometer

দ্রোহ drohô *n* enmity, hostility

ধ dh

ধকল dhɔkôl *n* stress, pressure, strain

ধড় dhɔr *n* torso

ধড়ফড়ানি dhɔrphɔrani *n* trepidation, palpitation

ধড়াস dhɔras *adv* thudding, thumping, banging noise

ধন dhɔn *n* wealth, riches, treasure

ধনিয়া dhôniýa *n* coriander

ধনী dhônī *adj* affluent, wealthy, rich

ধনু dhônu *n* bow, arc, arch

ধনে dhône *n* coriander

ধন্য dhônyô *adj* fortunate, gratified, blessed

ধন্যবাদ dhônyôbad *n* thanksgiving, thanks

ধপাস dhɔpas *n* loud, thudding noise

ধপধপ dhɔpdhɔp *onom* brilliant white, dazzling

ধবল dhɔbôl *adj* white

ধমক dhɔmôk, ধমকানি dhɔmkani *n* rebuff, snub, scolding

ধমকানো dhɔmkano *vb* rebuff, scold, threaten

ধমনি dhɔmôni *n* artery, vein

ধরন dhɔrôn *n* manner, kind, method, way

ধরা dhɔra *vb* hold, catch, seize

ধরে dhôre *pp* during, over a stretch of time

ধর্ম dhɔrmô *n* religion, doctrine, creed

ধর্মগ্রন্থ dhɔrmôgrônthô *n* holy scripture, sacred text

ধর্মতত্ত্ব dhɔrmôtɔtvô *n* theology

ধর্মবিশ্বাস dhɔrmôbiśvas *n* faith, religious devotion

ধর্মশাস্ত্র dhɔrmôśastrô *n* scripture

ধর্মানুষ্ঠান dhɔrmanuṣṭhan *n* religious rituals

ধর্মান্ধ dhɔrmandhô *adj* fanatical, bigoted

ধর্ষণ dhɔrṣôṇ *n* rape, oppression, force

ধর্ষিত dhôrṣito *adj* raped; forced, oppressed

ধস dhɔs *n* landslide

ধসা dhɔsa *vb* come off, fall down, collapse

ধস্তাধস্তি dhɔstadhôsti *n* scuffle, tussle, fray

ধাই dhai, ধাইমা dhaima *n* midwife, wetnurse

ধাঁ dhā *int expr* suddenness, quickness

ধাঁধা dhādha *n* riddle, puzzle

ধাক্কা dhakka *n* collision, impact, push

ধাক্কা দেওয়া dhakka deôýa *vb* push, shove, collide

ধাত dhat *n* temperament, spirit, nature; pulse

ধাতস্থ dhatôsthô *adj* mentally composed, calm

ধাতা dhata *n* God, Brahma

ধাতু dhatu *n* metal, mineral; verbal root

ধাতুগত dhatugɔtô *adj* constitutional; characteristic

ধাত্রীবিদ্যা dhatrībidya *n* midwifery, obstetrics

ধান dhan *n* paddy; rice

ধানাই-পানাই dhanai–panai *n* nonsense

ধাপ dhap *n* step, leap

ধাপ্পা dhappa *n* hoax, bluff

ধাম dham *n* abode, dwelling-place; receptacle, container

ধার dhar *n* edge, border, brink; sharpness

ধার dhar *n* loan, debt

ধার করা dhar kɔra *vb* borrow

ধার দেওয়া dhar deôŷa *vb* lend

ধারণা dharôṇa *n* idea, concept, notion

ধারা dhara *n* flow, stream, current

ধারাল dharalô, ধারালো dharalo *adj* sharp, keen

ধার্মিক dharmik *adj* religious, pious, godly

ধিকিধিকি dhikidhiki *adv* continuously, stealthily, smouldering

ধী dhī *n* intellect, cognition, knowledge

ধীর dhīr *adj* slow, tardy; calm, composed

ধীরে dhīre *adv* slowly, leisurely, gently

ধুকধুক dhukdhuk *onom* palpitating, thudding, throbbing

ধুৎ dhuṯ *int* hang!, dash!, blow!, bother!

ধুতি dhuti *n* loincloth

ধুম dhum *n* abundance, splendor, excess

ধুয়া dhuŷa, ধুয়ো dhuŷo *n* refrain, chorus; platitude

ধুলা dhula *(WB)*, ধুলো dhulo *(WB) n* dust

ধুম dhūm *n* smoke, fume, steam

ধুমপান dhūmpan *n* smoking

ধূলি dhūli *n* dust, pollen

ধূলিষাৎ dhūliṣaṯ *adj* reduced to dust

ধূসর dhūsôr *adj* grey

ধৃত dhṛtô *adj* taken, held, caught, arrested

ধৃষ্টতা dhṛṣṭôta *n* arrogance, impertinence, audacity, insolence

ধৈর্ষ dhoiryô *n* patience, endurance, composure

ধোঁকা dhōka *n* doubt, suspicion

ধোঁকা দেওয়া dhōka deoŷa *vb* hoodwink, deceive, dodge

ধোঁয়া dhôŷa *n* smoke, fume, vapor

ধোপা dhopa *n* washerman

ধোয়া dhoŷa *vb* wash, cleanse, scrub

ধ্বংস dhvɔṁsô *n* destruction, ruin, wreckage

ধ্বংস করা dhvɔṁsô kɔra *n* destroy, ruin, annihilate

ধ্বনি dhvôni *n* sound, tone, voice

ধ্যান dhyæn *n* meditation

ধ্রুব dhrubô *adj* steady, fixed, unwavering

ধ্রুবতা dhrubôta *n* constancy, certainty, surety

ধ্রুবতারা dhrubôtara *n* pole-star, North star

ন n

ন– nɔ- *vb root* be not

নইলে nôile *conj* if not, otherwise

নকল nɔkôl *n* transcript, copy; *adj* artificial, false, forged

নকশা nɔkśa *n* pattern, design, decoration

নখ nôkh *n* fingernail

নগণ্য nɔgôṇyô *adj* worthless, insignificant

নগদ nɔgôd *n* cash; *adj* prompt, immediate, ready

নগর nɔgôr *n* town, city

নজর nɔjôr *n* sight, vision, view

নজর রাখা nɔjôr rakha *vb* watch, look out for

নজির nôjir *n* case; precedent, example

নট nɔṭ *n* dancer, ballet-dancer; actor

নড়চড় nɔṛcɔṛ *n* movement, deviation, alteration

নড়া nɔṛa *vb* move, stir

নড়াচড়া nɔṛacɔṛa *n* movement

নত nɔtô *adj* bent, bowed down, stooping

নতুন nôtun *adj* new

নতুনত্ব nôtunɔtvô *n* newness, novelty

নতুবা nôtuba *conj* else, otherwise

নথি nôthi *n* file, list, document

নদী nôdī *n* river, stream

নধর nɔdhôr *adj* succulent, luscious, juicy

ননদ nɔnôd *n* husband's younger sister

নন্দিত nônditô *adj* delighted, pleased

নপুংসক nɔpuṁsɔk *n* eunuch, hermaphrodite

নব nɔbô *adj, pref* new

নববর্ষ nɔbôbɔrṣô *n* new year

নবাগত nɔbagɔtô *adj* newly arrived

নবাব nɔbab *n* Nawab *(Indian Muslim ruler)*

নবী nôbī *n* prophet

নব্বই nɔbboi *num* ninety

নমস্কার nɔmôskar *n* greeting, salute

নমুনা nômuna *n* sample, pattern

নম্র nɔmrô *adj* gentle, humble, modest

নম্রতা nɔmrôta *n* gentleness, modesty, politeness

নয় nɔŷ *num* nine

নয়তো nɔŷto *conj* or else, otherwise

নয়ন nɔŷôn *n* eye

নয়নগোচর nɔŷôngocôr *adj* visible

নয়নতারা nɔŷôntara *n* pupil of the eye

নর nɔr *n* man, human being

নরক nɔrôk *n* hell, inferno

নরম nɔrôm *adj* soft, gentle, tender

নরম–গরম nɔrôm–gɔrôm *adj* blowing hot and cold

নর্তন nɔrtôn *n* dance, dancing

নর্দমা nɔrdôma *n* drain, gutter

নল nɔl *n* tube, cylinder, pipe

নলকূপ nɔlkūp *n* tubewell

নষ্ট nɔṣṭô *adj* spoiled, destroyed, rotten

নষ্ট করা nɔṣṭô kɔra *vb* waste, spoil, ruin

নষ্টামি nɔṣṭami *n* wickedness, mischief

না na *adv* not, no

নাই nai *adv* is not *denoting absence*

না করা na kɔra *vb* forbid, veto

নাওয়া naoŷa *vb* bathe, have a bath

নাক nak *n* nose; sense of smell

নাকাল nakal *adj* tired, exhausted, harrassed

নাকি naki *adv* or not; *expr* question

নাখুশ nakhuś *adj* displeased, dissatisfied

নাগ nag *n* snake, serpent

নাগরিক nagôrik *adj* urban, civic

নাগরী nagôrī *n* flirt, coquette, tart

নাগাড়ে nagaṛe *adv* incessantly, continuously

নাগাদ nagad *pp* until, till, up to

নাগাল nagal *n* reach, range, touch

নাগাল পাওয়া nagal paôŷa *vb* reach, have access to

নাচ nac *n* dance

নাচা naca *vb* dance

নাচানো nacano *vb* cause to dance, move, excite

নাছোড় nachoṛ *adj* obstinate, dogged

নাজেহাল najehal *adj* fatigued, harrassed, pestered, persecuted

নাজেহাল করা najehal kɔra *vb* pester, harass, irritate

নাটক naṭôk *n* drama, play

নাড়া naṛa *vb* move, set in motion, stir

নাড়ানাড়ি naṛanari *n* shifting, moving, handling

নাড়ি naṛi *n* pulse; vein; uterus *(any tubular organ of the body)*

নাতনি natni *n* granddaughter

নাতি nati *n* grandson

নাতিশীতোষ্ণ natiśītôṣṇô *adj* temperate

নাথ nath *n* guardian, custodian

নানা nana *adj* various, diverse, many; *n* grandfather *(maternal, Muslim)*

নানী nanī *n* grandmother *(maternal, Muslim)*

নাপছন্দ napɔchɔndô *adj* disliked, disagreeable

নাপিত napit *n* barber

নাবিক nabik *n* boatman, sailor

নাভি nabhi *n* navel, center, focus

নাম nam *n* name

নামকরা namkɔra *adj* famous

নামা nama *vb* descend, get down, alight, dismount

নামাজ namaj *n* prayer *(Muslim)*

নামানো namano *vb* set off, drop off, unload

নামী namī *adj* well-known, eminent

নায়ক naŷôk *n* leader, chief, guide, hero

নায়িকা naŷika *n* heroine, leading lady

নারকীয় narôkīŷô *adj* hellish, infernal

নারাজ naraj *adj* displeased, unwilling, reluctant

নারিকেল narikel, নারকেল narkel *n* coconut

নারী narī *n* woman, girl, female

নার্স nars *n* nurse

নাল nal *n* stalk, reed

নালা nala *n* drain, gutter, channel

নালি nali *n* vein, pipe, tube

নালিশ naliś *n* complaint, accusation

নাশ naś *n* destruction, extinction

নাস্তা nasta *n* breakfast

নাস্তিক nastik *adj* atheistic, agnostic

নি ni *adv* not *negative particle*

নিঃ niḥ *pref ind* out, forth

নিঃশর্ত niḥśɔrtô *adj* unconditional

নিঃশ্বাস niḥśvas *n* breath, breathing, exhalation

নিঃশ্বাস নেওয়া niḥśvas neoŷa *vb* breathe, inhale

নিঃসঙ্গ niḥsɔṅgô *adj* solitary, lonely

নিঃসত্ত্ব niḥsɔttvô *adj* unsubstantial; lifeless

নিঃসন্দেহে niḥsɔndehe *adv* surely, undoubtedly

নিঃসহায় niḥsɔhaŷ *adj* unaided, helpless

নিঃসীম niḥsīmô *adj* unbounded, infinite

নিকট nikɔṭ *n* nearness, proximity; *pp* towards, near

নিকাশ nikaś *n* outlet, discharge, drainage

নিকৃষ্ট nikṛṣṭô *adj* bad, vile, debased

নিক্ষেপ nikṣep *n* throwing, hurling, casting away

নিখিল nikhil *adj* complete, all, entire

নিখুঁত nikhũt *adj* perfect, flawless

নিগ্রহ nigrôhô *n* punishment, chastisement

নিচু nicu *adj* low, down

নিচে nice *pp* below, underneath

নিছক nichɔk *adj* mere, sheer; absolute

নিজ nij *pr* own, self

নিজস্ব nijôsvô *adj* own, one's own

নিজে nije *pr* oneself

নিঝুম nijhum *adj* still, calm, motionless

নিটোল niṭol *adj* perfect, flawless

নিড়ানি niṛani *n* hoe

নিতম্ব nitɔmbô *n* buttocks, hips

নিত্য nityô *adv* always, constantly

নিত্যতা nityôta *n* eternity, immortality

নিতান্ত nitantô *adv* very, extremely, downright

নিথর nithɔr *adj* motionless, calm

নিদর্শন nidɔrśôn *n* example, illustration

নিদারুণ nidaruṇ *adj* extreme, severe, terrible

নিদ্রা nidra *n* sleep, slumber

নিদ্রালুতা nidraluta *n* drowsiness

নিদ্রিত nidritô *adj* asleep, sleeping

নিধি nidhi *n* store; fund

নিনাদ ninad *n* sound, noise

নিন্দা ninda *(Bd)*, নিন্দে ninde *(WB)* *n* blame, discredit

নিন্দা করা ninda kɔra *vb* blame, censure, reproach

নিপাত nipat *n* downfall, ruin; death

নিপীড়ন nipīṛɔn *n* oppression, persecution

নিপুণ nipuṇ *adj* adroit, clever, dexterous

নিবদ্ধ nibɔddhô *adj* bound, chained, fettered

নিবদ্ধীকরণ nibôddhīkɔrôṇ *n* registration

নিবন্ত nibɔntô *adj* faint, flickering, weak

নিবন্ধ nibɔndhô *n* dissertation, essay

নিবন্ধন nibɔndhôn *n* registration

নিবা niba *see* নেবা neba

নিবানো nibano *see* নেবানো nebano

নিবারণ nibarôṇ *n* prevention, restraint

নিবাস nibas *n* dwelling, habitation

নিবিড় nibiṛ *adj* close, intimate

নিবিষ্ট nibiṣṭô *adj* absorbed, concentrated

নিবৃত্ত nibṛttô *adj* desisted, stopped, prevented

নিবৃত্তি nibṛtti *n* renunciation, cessation

নিবেদক nibedɔk *n* narrator

নিবেদন nibedɔn *n* narration, declaration, announcement, submission, offering

নিবেদিত nibeditô *adj* told, offered, communicated

নিভৃত nibhṛtô *adj* secret, private

নিম nim *pref* half, middle; indigenous tree

নিমক nimɔk *n* salt

নিমকহারাম nimôkharam *adj* disloyal, ungrateful, treacherous

নিমক হালালি nimôk halali *n* gratitude, fidelity, loyalty

নিমজ্জন nimɔjjôn *n* submersion, immersion

নিমন্ত্রণ nimôntrôn, নেমন্তন্ন nemôntɔnnô *n* invitation, summons

নিমিত্ত nimittô *n* cause, motive, ground, reason

নিমিষ nimiṣ, নিমেষ nimeṣ *n* twinkle, wink

নিম্ন nimnô *adj* low-lying, down, sunk

নিযুক্ত niyuktô *adj* appointed, employed, engaged

নিযুত niyut *num* million

নিয়তি niŷôti *n* order, rule, fate

নিয়ন্ত্রণ niŷɔntrôn *n* control, restraint

নিয়ন্ত্রিত niŷôntritô *adj* controlled, regulated

নিয়ম niŷôm *n* system, rule, custom

নিয়মিত niŷômitô *adj* regular, prescribed

নিয়ামক niŷamɔk *n* regulator, controller

নিয়োগ niŷog *n* employment, appointment

নিরক্ষ nirôkṣô, নিরক্ষ রেখা nirôkṣô rekha *n* equator

নিরক্ষর nirɔkṣôr *adj* illiterate

নিরক্ষীয় nirôkṣīŷô *adj* equatorial

নিরত nirɔtô *adj* attached, devoted to

নিরপরাধ nirɔpôradh *adj* innocent

নিরপেক্ষ nirɔpekṣô *adj* impartial, unprejudiced

নিরবকাশ nirɔbôkaś *adj* incessant, continuous

নিরবধি nirɔbôdhi *adj* endless, infinite, boundless

নিরহঙ্কার nirɔhôṅkar *adj* unassuming, humble, modest

নিরানন্দ niranɔndô *adj* joyless, cheerless

নিরাপত্তা nirapɔtta *n* security, safety

নিরাপদ nirapɔd *adj* safe, secure

নিরামিষ niramiṣ *adj* vegetarian

নিরাশ niraś *adj* disappointed, without hope

নিরাহার nirahar *n* starvation, fasting

নিরিবিলি niribili *adj* forlorn, lonely, secluded, forlorn

নিরীক্ষা nirīkṣa *n* observation, auditing

নিরীহ nirīhô *adj* innocent, gentle, mild

নিরোধ nirodh *n* imprisonment, confinement

নির্গত nirgɔtô *adj* emerged, issued

নির্ঘণ্ট nirghɔṇṭô *n* index, table of contents

নির্ঘাত nirghat *adv* certainly, for sure

নির্জন nirjɔn *adj* lonely, secluded

নির্জনতা nirjɔnôta *n* solitude, loneliness

নিজীব nirjīb *adj* lifeless, dead

নির্ণয় nirṇɔŷ *n* determination

নির্ণায়ক nirṇaŷôk *adj* conclusive, decisive

নিদিষ্ট nirdiṣṭô *adj* determined, appointed, fixed

নির্দেশ nirdeś *n* order, instruction, direction

নির্দোষ nirdoṣ *n* faultless, spotless

নির্ধার nirdhar *n* evaluation, specification

নির্বংশ nirbɔṁśô *n* childlessness

নির্বাক nirbak *adj* speechless, silent

নির্বাচন nirbacôn *n* election, vote, poll, choice

নির্বাচিত nirbacitô *adj* elected, chosen

নির্বাণ nirbaṇ *n* extinction, disappearance

নির্বাসন nirbasôn *n* banishment, exile

নির্বাহ nirbahô *n* execution, completion, accomplishment

নির্বিকার nirbikar *adj* stoical, unmoved, unperturbed

নির্বিচার nirbicar *adj* indiscriminate, thoughtless

নির্বীজ nirbīj *adj* seedless, sterile

নির্বোধ nirbodh *adj* dull, stupid, foolish

নির্ভর nirbhôr *n* support, reliance

নির্ভর করা nirbhôr kɔra *vb* rely on, depend on

নির্ভাবনা nirbhabna *n* carefreeness

নির্ভীক nirbhīk *adj* fearless, dauntless

নির্ভুল nirbhul *adj* accurate, error-free

নির্মম nirmɔm *adj* merciless, ruthless

নির্মল nirmɔl *adj* immaculate, spotless

নির্মাণ nirmaṇ *n* manufacture

নির্মূল nirmūl *adj* eradicated

নির্যাস niryas *n* essence, extract, juice

নিলজ্জ nirlɔjjô *adj* shameless, brazen

নিলিপ্ত nirliptô *adj* unconcerned, aloof

নিলম্বন nilɔmbôn *n* adjournment, suspension

নিলয় nilɔy̌ *n* ventricle, receptacle

নিলাম nilam *n* auction

নিশপিশ niśpiś *onom* itching, irritating

নিশপিশ করা niśpiś kɔra *vb* fidget

নিশা niśa, নিশি niśi *n* night

নিশাগম niśagôm *n* nightfall, evening

নিশান niśan *n* flag, standard, sign, mark

নিশিত niśit *adj* sharp, keen, whetted

নিশুতি niśuti *adv* late night, at an advanced hour

নিশ্চয় niścɔy̌ *n* conviction, certainty; *adj* certain, convinced, sure; *int* of course

নিশ্চল niścɔl *adj* stationary, motionless

নিশ্চিত niścitô, niścit *adj* certain, sure, convinced

নিশ্চিন্ত niścintô *adj* carefree, troublefree, unperturbed

নিশ্চেষ্ট niśceṣṭô *adj* lazy, unenterprising, lethargic

নিষিদ্ধ niṣiddhô *adj* forbidden, prohibited

নিষেধ niṣedh *n* prohibition, ban

নিষ্কম্প niṣkɔmpô *adj* calm, firm, unshaking

নিষ্কর niṣkɔr *adj* tax-free; rent-free

নিষ্কর্মা niṣkɔrma *adj* good for nothing, lazy, worthless

নিষ্কাম niṣkam *adj* platonic

নিষ্কাশন করা niṣkaśôn kɔra *vb* extract, remove

নিষ্কৃতি niṣkr̥ti *n* acquittal, release

নিষ্ঠা niṣṭha *n* attachment, devotion, firm faith

নিষ্ঠুর niṣṭhur *adj* cruel, merciless, heartless

নিষ্পত্তি niṣpôtti *n* resolution, settlement, decision

নিষ্ফল niṣphɔl *adj* fruitless, futile, vain

নিসর্গ nisɔrgô *n* nature, creation, cosmos

নিসাড় nisaṛ *adj* unconscious, senseless

নিস্তব্ধ nistɔbdhô *adj* silent, still

নিস্তার nistar *n* deliverance, salvation

নিস্তেজ nistej *adj* weak, feeble, listless

নিহত nihɔtô *adj* killed, slain, murdered

নিহিত nihitô *adj* placed, laid, dormant

নীচ nīc *adj* low, low-lying, deep

নীড় nīṛ *n* nest, resting place

নীতি nīti *n* policy, ethics, morals

নীর nīr *n* water, liquid

নীরক্ত nīrɔktô *adj* bloodless, lifeless

নীরব nīrɔb *adj* silent, noiseless, soundless

নীরস nīrɔs *adj* sapless, dry, dried-up

নীল nīl *adj* blue

নীহার nīhar *n* snow

নীহারিকা nīharika *n* nebula

নুন nun *n* salt

নূপুর nūpur *n* ankle bells

নৃত্য nr̥tyô *n* dance

নৃবিদ্যা nr̥bidya *n* anthropology

নৃশংস nr̥śɔm̐sô *adj* barbarous, ferocious

নেই nei *vb* is not *denotes absence*

নেওয়া neoŷa *n* take

নেংটা næm̐ṭa *adj* naked

নেকড়া nækṛa *n* rag

নেকড়ে nekṛe *n* wolf

নেটা næṭa *adj* left-handed

নেড়া næṛa *adj* shaven-headed, shorn

নেতা neta *n* leader, director

নেতানো netano, নেতিয়ে যাওয়া netiŷe yaoŷa *vb* droop, go soft, go soggy

নেপালি nepali *adj* Nepali, Nepalese

নেবা neba, নিবা niba *vb* go out (fire), be extinguished, die down

নেবানো nebano, নিবানো nibano *vb* extinguish, put out (fire)

নেয়ে neŷe *n* boatman

নেশা neśa *n* intoxication, addiction

নেশা করা neśa kɔra *vb* get drunk/high

নেহাই nehai *n* anvil

নেহাত nehat *adv* necessarily, perforce

নৈকট্য noikôṭyô *n* nearness, proximity

নৈতিক noitik *adj* moral, ethical

নোংরা nomra *adj* dirty, filthy; ugly

নোঙর noṅôr *n* anchor

নোট noṭ *n* banknote

নোড়া noṛa *n* pestle

নোনতা nonta, নোনা nona *adj* salty

নৌকা nouka *(Bd)*, নৌকো nouko *n* boat

ন্যস্ত nyæstô *adj* entrusted, committed

ন্যাকা nyaka *(pron* næka*) adj* pretentious

ন্যাকামি nyakami *n* pretence, feigned ignorance

ন্যায় nyaŷ *n* justice, reasoning, logic

ন্যায্য nyayyô *(pron* næjjo*) adj* reasonable, logical

প p

পকেট pɔkeṭ n pocket

পক্ষ pôkṣô n side, flank, wing, team, faction

পক্ষপাত pôkṣôpat n preference, bias

পক্ষপাতী pôkṣôpatī adj biased, partial, prejudiced

পক্ষাঘাত pôkṣaghat n paralysis, palsy

পক্ষে pôkṣe pp for, on behalf of

পগার pɔgar n ditch, drain

পঙ্‌ক্তি pɔṅkti n line

পঙ্ক pɔṅkô n mud, clay, silt

পঙ্গু pôṅgu adj lame, crippled

পচা pɔca vb rot, decay, putrefy; adj rotten, spoiled

পছন্দ pɔchôndô n choice, liking, selection

পঞ্চ pɔñcô num five

পঞ্চাশ pɔñcaś num fifty

পঞ্জিকা pɔñjika n calendar, almanac

পট pɔṭ n cloth, canvas

পটকানো pɔṭkano vb knock down, fling to the ground

পটভূমি pɔṭôbhūmi n background

পটানো pɔṭano vb win over, seduce, lure

পটু pôṭu adj clever, adroit, skillful

পটোল pɔṭol n snake-bean

পঠন pɔṭhôn n study, recitation

পড়তি pôrti n fall, decline

পড়ন্ত pɔrôntô adj declining

পড়া pɔṛa vb fall, drop; read, study

পড়ানো pɔṛano vb teach, instruct

পড়াশোনা pɔṛaśona n education, study

পড়ে যাওয়া pôre yaoŷa vb fall down, collapse, deteriorate

পণ pɔṇ n stake, bet, wager

পণ নেওয়া pɔṇ neoŷa vb exact compulsory dowry; accept a bribe

পণ্ড pɔṇḍô adj futile, vain, useless

পণ্ডিত pôṇḍitô adj learned, erudite, versed, wise, experienced; pôṇḍit n scholar, pundit

পণ্য pôṇyô n article, merchandise, commodity, goods

পণ্যজীবী pôṇyôjībī n trader, salesman

পণ্য–বিনিময় pôṇyô–binimɔŷ n trade, commerce

পতঙ্গ pɔtôṅgô n grasshopper

পতন pɔtôn n decline, downfall, decay

পতাকা pɔtaka n flag, banner, standard

পতি pôti n master, husband, boss

পতিত pôtitô adj overcome, defeated

পত্তন pɔttôn n base, foundation

পত্র pɔtrô n letter, written document

পত্রিকা pôtrika n journal, magazine

পথ pɔth n path, way, course

পথিক pôthik n passer-by, traveller

পদ pɔd n foot, pace, verse; grammar: part of speech

পদবি pɔdôbi n surname, title

পদাবলী pɔdabôlī n anthology

পদার্থ pɔdarthô n matter, substance

পদার্থবিজ্ঞান pɔdarthôbijñan n physics

পদার্থবিদ্যা pɔdarthôbidya n physics

পদ্ধতি pɔddhôti n method, system

পদ্ম pɔdmô n lotus

পদ্মা pɔdma n the river Padma

পদ্য pɔdyô n verse, poetry

পনির pônir n cheese

পনের pônerô *num* fifteen

পন্থা pɔntha *n* way, manner

পবিত্র pôbitrô *adj* holy, sacred

পয় pɔŷ *n* luck, good fortune

পয়লা pɔŷla *n* first of the month

পয়সা pɔŷsa *n* currency, penny, 0.01 Taka

পর pɔr *adj* other, different, later, next, subsequent

পর pɔr, পরে pɔre *pp, adv* after, later, then

পরকাল pɔrôkal *n* afterlife

পরকীয় pɔrôkīŷô *adj* foreign, alien

পরগাছা pɔrgacha *n* parasite, parasitic plant

পরচর্চা pɔrôcɔrca *n* slander, gossip

পরচুল pɔrôcul *n* wig

পরজীবী pɔrôjībī *n* parasite

পরটা pɔrôṭa, পরোটা pɔrôṭa *n* thin fried bread

পরদা, পর্দা pɔrda *n* screen, curtain, veil

পরপর pɔrpɔr *adv* one after another, successively, consecutively

পরবর্তী pɔrôbɔrtī *adj* subsequent, next, following

পরম pɔrôm *adj* first, prime, supreme, highest, greatest

পরমাণু pɔrômanu *n* atom

পরম্পর pɔrômpɔr *adj* serial, successive

পরম্পরা pɔrômpɔra *n* succession, routine

পরশু pôrśu *n* day after tomorrow; day before yesterday

পরস্পর pɔrôspɔr *adj* reciprocal, mutual

পরহিত pɔrôhitô *n* philanthropy, benevolence

পরা pɔra *vb* wear, put on

পরাক্রম pɔrakrôm *n* strength, power, might

পরাগ pɔrag *n* pollen

পরাজয় pɔrajɔŷ *n* defeat

পরাজিত pɔrajitô *adj* defeated, conquered

পরানো pɔrano *vb* cause to wear, dress

পরামর্শ pɔramɔrśô *n* advice, consultation, counsel, conference

পরার্থ pɔrarthô *adj* altruistic

পরিকল্পনা pôrikɔlpôna *n* planning

পরিচয় pôricɔŷ *n* acquaintance, identity, familiarity, introduction

পরিচয় করিয়ে দেওয়া pôricɔŷ kôriŷe deoŷa *vb* introduce, make introductions

পরিচালক pôricalɔk *n* director, leader, administrator

পরিচালনা pôricalôna *n* management, direction, administration

পরিচিত pôricitô *adj* acquainted, familiar, known

পরিচ্ছেদ pôricched *n* division, section, chapter

পরিণত pôriṇɔtô *adj* ripe, mature, grown

পরিণাম pôriṇam *n* conclusion, last stage; future

পরিতাপ pôritap *n* lament, grief, remorse

পরিত্যাগ করা pôrityæg kɔra *vb* renounce, give up

পরিত্রাতা pôritrata *n* saviour

পরিতোষ pôritoṣ *n* satisfaction, pleasure

পরিদর্শক pôridɔrśôk *n* inspector, supervisor

পরিদর্শন pôridɔrśôn *n* inspection, supervision

পরিধি pôridhi *n* circumference, circle

পরিপাটি pôripaṭi *adj* tidy, orderly

পরিপালন pôripalôn *n* administration

পরিপ্রেক্ষিত pôripreksit *n* perspective

পরিবর্ত pôribɔrtô, পরিবর্তন pôribɔrtôn *n* change, alteration

পরিবর্তে pôribɔrte *pp* instead of, in place of

পরিবহণ pôribɔhôn *n* transport

পরিবার pôribar *n* family

পরিবেশ pôribeś *n* surroundings, environment

পরিভাষা pôribhaşa *n* terminology, metalanguage

পরিমাণ pôriman *n* amount, quantity

পরিমাপ pôrimap *n* measurement, weight

পরিমিত pôrimitô *adj* temperate, moderate, measured

পরিশেষ pôriśeṣ *n* remainder, last stage

পরিশেষে pôriśeṣe *adv* finally, at last

পরিশোধ pôriśodh *n* repayment, revenge

পরিশ্রম pôriśrôm *n* labor, toil, effort

পরিশ্রান্ত pôriśrantô *adj* exhausted, worn out

পরিষ্কার pôriṣkar *adj* clean, tidy, neat

পরিসংখ্যান pôrisɔṁkhyan *n* statistics

পরিসমাপ্ত pôrisɔmaptô *adj* finished, concluded

পরিসর pôrisɔr *n* extent, limit, boundary

পরিস্ফুট pôrisphuṭô *adj* manifest, obvious, well-developed

পরিহাস pôrihas *n* joke, mockery, ridicule

পরীক্ষা pôrīkṣa *n* examination, test, trial

পরীক্ষামূলক pôrīkṣamūlôk *adj* experimental

পরে pɔre *pp, adv* after, afterwards, then, later

পরোক্ষ pɔrokṣô *adj* circumstantial, indirect

পর্ণাঙ্গ pɔrṇaṅgô *n* fern

পর্বত pɔrbôt *n* mountain, hill

পর্যন্ত pôryôntô *pp, adv* until, as long as, even

পর্যায় pɔryaŷ *n* period, succession, generation

পলক pɔlôk *n* wink, blink

পলকহীন pɔlôkhīn *adj* steadfast, unblinking

পলকা pɔlôka, pɔlka *adj* brittle, fragile, precarious

পলায়ন pɔlaŷôn *n* act of fleeing, escape

পলি pôli *n* silt, alluvium

পলিতা pôlita (Bd), পলতে pôlte (WB) *n* wick

পল্টন pɔlṭôn *n* platoon, armed force

পল্লীগ্রাম pôllīgram *n* habitation, hamlet, settlement, village

পশম pɔśôm *n* wool, fur

পশু pôśu *n* animal, beast

পশুশিকার pôśuśikar *n* hunting

পশ্চাৎ pɔścat *adv* after, later, at the back

পশ্চিম pôścim *n* west

পসরা pɔsra *n* wares, merchandise

পসারী pɔsarī *n* shopkeeper, trader

পা pa *n* leg; foot

পাইকার paikar *n* wholesaler

পাইকারী paikarī *n* wholesale trading

পাউডার pauḍar *n* powder

পাউরুটি pauruṭi *n* European bread

পাওনা paona *n* earnings, income, claim

পাওয়া paoŷa *vb* receive, get, obtain

পাঁক pāk *n* slime, silt

পাঁচ pāc *num* five

পাঁচফোড়ন pācphoṛon *n* five spice (cumin, black cumin, aniseed, fenugreek, parsley)

পাঁচিল pācil *n* wall

পাঁজর pājôr *(Bd)*, পাঁজরা pājra *(WB)* n ribs, thorax

পাঁজা pāja *n* kiln, brick-kiln

পাঁজি pāji *n* almanac, calendar

পাক pak *n* act of cooking; rotation, circular motion, twisting

পাকা paka *vb* ripen, mature; *adj* ripe, mature, permanent, experienced, seasoned

পাকাপাকি করা pakapaki kɔra *vb* finalize, settle

পাকানো pakano *vb* cook

পাকানো pakano *vb* involve in, engage in; twist, complicate

পাখা pakha *n* wing, fan, sail

পাখি pakhi *n* bird

পাগড়ি pagṛi *n* turban

পাগল pagôl *adj* mad, crazy, insane; *n* lunatic, fool

পাগলা pagla *(m)*, পাগলী paglī *(f)* n lunatic, fool

পাগলামি paglami *n* madness, eccentricity

পাছা pacha *n* hip, loins, buttocks

পাছে pache *conj* lest, unless

পাজি paji *adj* mischievous, naughty

পাঞ্জাবী pañjabī *n* Punjabi; loose shirt

পাট paṭ *n* jute

পাটাতন paṭatɔn *n* deck, floor, platform

পাটি paṭi *n* mat

পাঠ paṭh *n* reading, perusal, study

পাঠক paṭhôk *n* reader

পাঠানো paṭhano *vb* send, dispatch

পাড় par *n* bank, shore, margin

পাড়া para *vb* lay out, spread; lay (eggs); pluck; *n* neighborhood, locality

পাড়ি pari *n* width, expanse, crossing over, distance

পাণ্ডিত্য panḍityô *n* erudition, learning

পাণ্ডুলিপি panḍulipi *n* manuscript

পাত pat *n* shedding, dropping; sheet, leaf

পাতলা patla *adj* thin, slender, fine, diluted, delicate

পাতা pata *n* leaf, page, lid; *vb* spread, lay out, prepare

পাতাল রেল patal rel *n* subway

পাতি pati *adj* small, unimportant, commonplace

পাত্তা patta *n* information, news, importance

পাত্তা না দেওয়া patta na deoŷa *vb* slight, make light of

পাত্র patrô *n* vessel, pot, container; partner, bridegroom

পাথর pathôr *n* stone, rock

পাদ pad *n* foot; leg; pace

পাদরি padri *n* Christian priest

পান pan *n* betel-leaf

পান pan *n* act of drinking

পানি pani *n* water

পানিবসন্ত panibɔsôntô *n* chicken-pox

পানীয় panīŷô *adj* drinkable

পান্তা panta *adj* stale (*of food*)

পাপ pap *n* sin, lapse, vice

পাপড়ি papṛi *n* petal

পাপী papī *adj* sinful; *n* sinner

পায়খানা paŷkhana *n* lavatory, latrine; feces

পায়চারি paŷcari *n* walk, stroll

পায়জামা paŷjama *n* pajamas, loose trousers

পায়েস paŷes *n* rice pudding

পার par *n* bank, shore, border

পার হওয়া par hɔoŷa *vb* cross, pass over

পারদ parôd *n* mercury, quicksilver

পারদর্শিতা parôdôrśita *n* foresight

পারদর্শী parôdôrśī *adj* experienced, judicious, expert

পারমাণবিক parômaṇôbik *adj* atomic

পারা para *vb* be able to, can, may; *n* mercury; simile

পারিবারিক paribarik *adj* familial

পার্থক্য parthôkyô *n* difference, distinction

পার্বত্য parbôtyô *adj* mountainous, hilly

পার্শ্ব parśvô *n* side, flank, border

পাল pal *n* sail

পালং palôṁ *n* spinach

পালক palôk *n* wing, feather

পালক palôk *n* foster-parent, guardian

পালকি palki *n* palanquin

পাল্টা palṭa *adj* contrary, counter-

পাল্টানো palṭano *vb* alter, revoke, change

পাল্টা-পাল্টি palṭa-palṭi *n* exchange

পালন palôn *n* rearing, nursing, fostering, breeding

পালন করা palôn kɔra *vb* bring up, maintain, observe (fast), maintain, nourish, keep

পালা pala *n* turn, period, time; *vb* maintain, bring up

পালাক্রমে palakrôme *adv* by turns, in turns

পালানো palano *vb* flee, escape, run away

পালিত palitô *adj* tame, reared, fostered

পালিয়ে যাওয়া paliŷe yaoŷa *vb* flee

পালিত-পুত্র palitô-putrô *n* foster-child

পাল্লা palla *n* strip; scale, range

পাশ paś *n* side, flank, edge

পাশা paśa *n* die, dice

পাশাপাশি paśapaśi *adj* alongside, next to

পাশে paśe *pp* next to, near, alongside

পাষাণ paṣaṇ *n* stone; *adj* stone-hearted, unfeeling

পাস pas *n* pass, permission

পাস করা pas kɔra *vb* pass (an examination)

পাহাড় pahar *n* mountain, hill, rock

পাহাড়িয়া pahariŷa *n* mountain-dweller, highlander

পাহারা pahara *n* watch, guard

পিঁপড়া pīpṛa *(Bd)*, পিঁপড়ে pīpṛe *(WB)* *n* ant

পিচ pic *n* tar, asphalt

পিচকারি pickari, পিচকিরি pickiri *n* jet, spray

পিছন pichôn *n* back, backside

পিছনে pichône *pp* at the back, behind

পিছপা pichpa *adj* taken aback, recoiled

পিছলা pichla *(Bd)*, পিছলে pichle *(WB)* *adj* slippery, treacherous

পিছানো pichano *(Bd)*, পিছোনো pichono *(WB)* *vb* recoil, retreat, back out

পিছে piche *adv* at the back of, on the heels of

পিটপিটানি piṭpiṭani *n* peevishness, fastidiousness

পিটপিটে piṭpiṭe *adj* over-scrupulous

পিঠ piṭh *n* back (*of the torso*)

পিঠা piṭha *(Bd)*, পিঠে piṭhe *(WB) n* cake, sweet pie

পিতা pita *n* father

পিতামাতা pitamata *n* parents

পিত্ত pittô *n* gall, bile

পিন্ধা pindha *vb* wear, put on

পিপা pipa *(Bd)*, পিপে pipe *(WB) n* barrel, cask

পিপাসা pipasa *n* thirst, eager desire

পিয়াদা piẏada, পেয়াদা peẏada *n* bailiff

পিরিচ piric *n* saucer

পিশাচ pisac *n* ghoul, demon, fiend

পিষা piṣa *see* পেষা peṣa

পিসা pisa *n* uncle *(father's sister's husband)*

পিসি pisi *n* aunt *(father's sister)*

পীড়া pīra *n* pain, disease, suffering

পীড়াপীড়ি pīrapīri *n* insistence, force, pressure

পীলু pīlu *n* jade

পুঁজ pūj *n* pus

পুঁজি pūji *n* savings, capital

পুঁতি pūti *n* bead

পুঁথি pūthi *n* ancient manuscript

পুকুর pukur *n* lake, pond

পুঙ্খানুপুঙ্খ puṅkhanupuṅkhô *adj* thorough, scrupulous

পুড়া pura *see* পোড়া pora

পুণ্য puṇyô *n* virtue, piety

পুতুল putul *n* doll

পুত্র putrô *n* son

পুদিনা pudina *n* mint

পুনঃপুনঃ punḥôpunḥô *adv* repeatedly

পুনরাবৃত্তি punôrabr̥tti *n* recital, repetition

পুনর্বাসন punôrbasôn *n* rehabilitation

পুরস্কার purôskar *n* prize, reward

পুরা pura *see* পোরা pora

পুরা pura *(Bd)*, পুরো puro *(WB) adj* entire, whole, complete

পুরাতন puratôn *adj* old, out-of-date, derelict

পুরানো purano *(Bd)*, পুরোনো purono *(WB) vb* fill, fulfil, satisfy; *adj* old, ancient

পুরাপুরি purapuri *(Bd)*, পুরোপুরি puropuri *(WB) adj* complete, entire

পুরুষ puruṣ *n* man, male, person

পুরুষত্ব puruṣôtvô *n* masculinity, manliness

পুরুষপরম্পরা puruṣpɔrômpɔra *n* generation

পুরুষানুক্রমিক puruṣanôkrômik *adj* hereditary, traditional

পুরোহিত purohit *n* priest

পুল pul *n* bridge

পুলিশ puliś *n* police

পুষ্ট puṣṭô *adj* nourished, fed, cherished

পুষ্প puṣpô *n* flower, blossom

পুস্তক pustɔk *n* book

পূজা pūja *(Bd)*, পূজা pūjo *n* worship, prayer, devotion

পূজিত pūjitô *adj* worshipped, revered

পূরণ pūrôṇ *n* fulfilment, repletion

পূর্ণ pūrṇô *adj* full, complete, all

পূর্ণিমা pūrṇima *n* full moon

পূর্ব pūrbô *n* east; first, former

পূর্বতন pūrbôtɔnô *adj* former, previous

পূর্বদিক pūrbôdik *n* the east

পূর্বাধিকার pūrbadhikar *n* precedence, priority

পূর্বাবধি pūrbabôdhi *adv* from before, since the beginning

পূর্বে pūrbe *adv* formerly, previous

পৃথক pr̥thôk *adj* separate, different

পৃথিবী pṛthibī *n* earth

পৃষ্ঠা pṛṣṭha *n* page (of a book)

পেঁচ pæ̃c *n* twist, coil, screw

পেঁচানো pæcano *vb* twist, involve, entangle

পেঁপে pēpe *n* papaya

পেঁয়াজ pēỹaj, পিয়াজ piỹaj *n* onion

পেচক pecɔk *n* owl

পেছনে pechône *adv* at the back, behind

পেচ্ছাব pecchab *n* urine

পেট peṭ *n* stomach, belly; womb; inside, inmost part

পেটুক peṭuk *adj* greedy, gluttonous

পেনসিল pensil *n* pencil

পেয়ারা peỹara *n* guava

পেরনো perôno *vb* cross, transcend, get through

পেরেক perek *n* nail, pin, spike

পেশা peśa *n* profession, trade

পেশী peśi *n* muscle, tendon

পেষা peṣa, পিষা piṣa *vb* grind, crush, pound, pulverize

পোঁটলা põṭla *n* bundle, baggage

পোকা poka *n* insect, worm

পোক্ত poktô *adj* durable, lasting

পোড়া pora, পুড়া pura *vb* burn, be scorched

পোড়ানো porano, পুড়ানো purano *vb* set on fire, incinerate, burn, afflict

পোনা pona *n* fingerling, young fish

পোয়া poỹa *n* a quarter, a fourth

পোয়াতি poỹati *adj* pregnant

পোয়ানো poỹano, পোহানো pohano *vb* dawn; come to an end, expire

পোরা pora, পুরা pura *vb* fill, stuff, cram

পোলাও polao *n* special rice dish, pilau

পোশাক pośak *n* dress, garment

পোষ poṣ *n* taming, domestication

পোষা poṣa *adj* tame, domesticated

পোস্টাফিস poṣṭapis *n* post office

পোস্তদানা postôdana *n* poppyseed

পোহানো pohano *see* পোয়ানো

পৌঁছা põucha, পৌঁছানো põuchano *vb* arrive, reach, come

পৌত্তলিক pouttôlik *adj* pagan

পৌনঃপুনিক pounôḥpunik *adj* recurring, frequent

পৌনে poune *n* three quarters/fourths; a quarter to (clock)

পৌষ pouṣ *n ninth Bengali month*

প্যানপ্যান pyænpyæn *onom* whining, complaining

প্যান্ট pyænṭ *n* trousers, pants

প্রকট prôkôṭ *adj* evident, revealed

প্রকম্প prôkômpô *n* tremor, quake

প্রকল্প prôkôlpô *n* plan, project

প্রকাণ্ড prôkaṇḍô *adj* huge, enormous, great

প্রকার prôkar *n* kind, type, sort

প্রকাশ prôkaś *n* revelation, exposition, publication

প্রকাশ করা prôkaś kɔra *vb* reveal, disclose, publish

প্রকাশিত prôkaśitô *adj* published, revealed, exposed

প্রকৃত prôkṛtô *adj* real, genuine, true

প্রকৃতি prôkṛti *n* nature, instinct, habit

প্রকৃষ্ট prôkṛṣṭô *adj* best, excellent

প্রকোপ prôkop *n* severity, excess, anger

প্রক্রিয়া prôkriỹa *n* process, procedure

প্রগতি prôgôti *n* progress, advance

প্রগাঢ় prôgaṛhô *adj* thick, deep, dense

প্রগাঢ় করা prôgaṛhô kɔra *vb* intensify

প্রগাঢ়তা prôgaṛhôta *n* intensity, depth, excess

প্রচল prôcɔl *adj* fashionable, current

প্রচলন prôcɔlôn *n* usage, practice

প্রচলিত prôcôlitô *adj* current, customary

প্রচার prôcar *n* preaching, proclamation, publicity

প্রচুর prôcur *adj* plentiful, abundant, profuse

প্রচ্ছন্ন prôcchɔnnô *adj* hidden, covered, concealed

প্রজা prôja *n* progeny, descendant

প্রজাপতি prôjapôti *n* butterfly

প্রণত prônɔtô *adj* deferential

প্রণয় prônɔẏ *n* love, affection, attachment

প্রণয়ন prônɔẏôn *n* composition, compilation

প্রণাম prônam *n* deference, obeisance

প্রণেতা prôneta *n* composer, creator

প্রতারক prôtarôk *n* swindler, cheat, imposter

প্রতারণা prôtarôṇa *n* fraud, deceit, cheating

প্রতি prôti *pp* towards, regarding

প্রতিকার prôtikar *n* redress, remedy

প্রতিকূল prôtikūl *adj* adverse, hostile

প্রতিক্রিয়া prôtikriẏa *n* reaction, response, side effect

প্রতিজ্ঞা prôtijña *n* promise, vow

প্রতিদান prôtidan *n* gift, payment, exchange

প্রতিদিন prôtidin *adv* daily; *n* every day

প্রতিদ্বন্দ্বী prôtidvôndvī *n* rival

প্রতিধ্বনি prôtidhvôni *n* echo

প্রতিনিধি prôtinidhi *n* deputy, representative

প্রতিপালন prôtipalôn *n* upbringing, rearing, fostering

প্রতিফল prôtiphɔl *n* retribution, punishment

প্রতিবাদ prôtibad *n* protest, counter-plea

প্রতিবেদন prôtibedɔn *n* report

প্রতিভা prôtibha *n* keen intelligence, genius

প্রতিভার pôtobhar *n* counterbalance

প্রতিভূ prôtibhū *n* representative; hostage

প্রতিমা prôtima *n* icon, image, idol

প্রতিযোগিতা prôtiyogita *n* rivalry, competition

প্রতিযোগী prôtiyogī *adj* rivalling, competing

প্রতিরক্ষা prôtirôkṣa *n* defense

প্রতিরোধ prôtirodh *n* prevention, resistance

প্রতিশোধ prôtiśodh *n* revenge

প্রতিশ্রুতি prôtiśruti *n* pledge, promise

প্রতিষ্ঠা prôtiṣṭha *n* establishment, foundation

প্রতিষ্ঠান prôtiṣṭhan *n* institute, institution

প্রতিহত prôtihɔtô *adj* checked, prevented, repelled

প্রতিহিংসা prôtihiṁsa *n* revenge, retaliation

প্রতীক prôtīk *n* symbol, sign

প্রতীক্ষা prôtīkṣa *n* expectation, waiting

প্রতুল prôtul *n* abundance, prosperity, richness

প্রত্ন prôtnô *adj* old, ancient

প্রত্নতত্ত্ব prôtnôtɔttvô *n* archaeology

প্রত্যক্ষ prôtyôkṣô *adj* manifest, perceptible

প্রত্যঙ্গ prôtyɔṅgô *n* organ; limb

প্রত্যয় prôtyɔẏ *n* belief, trust

প্রত্যাখ্যান prôtyakhyan *n* refusal, rejection

প্রত্যাবর্তন prôtyabɔrtôn *n* reversal, return

প্রত্যাবর্তন করা prôtyabɔrtôn kɔra *vb* revert, return

প্রত্যেক prôtyek *adj* each, every

প্রথম prôthôm *adj* first, chief

প্রথমে prôthôme *adv* at first, in the beginning

প্রথা prôtha *n* fashion, usage, custom, practice

প্রদর্শন prôdɔrśôn *n* act of exhibiting

প্রদর্শনী prôdɔrśônī *n* exhibition, show

প্রদাহ prôdahô *n* inflammation, infection

প্রদীপ prôdīp *n* light, lamp

প্রদেশ prôdeś *n* province, district

প্রধান prôdhan *adj* main, chief, principal

প্রধানত prôdhanɔtô *adv* mainly, above all

প্রধানমন্ত্রী prôdhanmôntrī *n* prime minister

প্রফুল্ল prôphullô *adj* blooming, blossoming

প্রবণ prôbôṇ *adj* inclined, sloping

প্রবন্ধ prôbôndhô *n* essay

প্রবর্তক prôbɔrtôk *n* pioneer, founder

প্রবর্তন prôbɔrtôn *n* introduction, inauguration

প্রবল prôbɔl *adj* strong, powerful

প্রবাদ prôbad *n* proverb

প্রবাহ prôbahô *n* stream, current, flow

প্রবেশ prôbeś *n* entrance, admission

প্রভাত prôbhat *n* morning, daybreak

প্রভাব prôbhab *n* power, influence

প্রভু prôbhu *n* lord, master, god

প্রভেদ prôbhed *n* distinction, difference

প্রমত্ত prômɔttô *adj* inebriated, intoxicated

প্রমাণ prômaṇ *n* proof, evidence

প্রমাণ করা prômaṇ kɔra *vb* prove, demonstrate

প্রমাদ prômad *n* carelessness, error

প্রমোদ prômod *n* joy, delight

প্রয়াস prôŷas *n* effort, endeavor

প্রযুক্তিগত prôyuktigɔtô *adj* technical

প্রযুক্তিবিদ্যা prôyuktibidya *n* technology

প্রয়োগ prôŷog *n* employment, use, application

প্রয়োজন prôŷojɔn *n* necessity, need, purpose

প্রয়োজনীয় prôŷojônīŷô *adj* necessary, essential

প্ররোচনা prôrocôna *n* instigation, inducement

প্রলাপ prôlap *n* raving, incoherent utterance

প্রলেপ prôlep *n* coating, layer; ointment

প্রলোভন prôlobhôn *n* allurement, temptation

প্রশংসা prôśômsa *n* admiration, praise

প্রশমন prôśômôn *n* quelling, allayment

প্রশাসন prôśasôn *n* administration

প্রশ্ন prôśnô *n* question

প্রশ্রয় prôśrɔŷ *n* indulgence, latitude, pampering

প্রশ্রয় দেওয়া prôśrɔŷ deôŷa *vb* indulge, pamper

প্রসঙ্গ prôsɔṅgô *n* subject, topic

প্রসন্ন prôsɔnnô *adj* satisfied, pleased

প্রসাধন prôsadhôn *n* decoration; make-up

প্রসার prôsar *n* width, expanse, extent

প্রস্তর prôstɔr *n* rock, pebble; fossil

প্রস্তাব prôstab *n* proposal

প্রস্তুত prôstut *adj* ready, prepared

প্রস্থান prôsthan *n* departure, setting out

প্রস্রাব prôsrab *n* urine

প্রস্রাব করা prôsrab kɔra *vb* urinate

প্রহসন prôhôsôn *n* banter, joke

প্রাকৃতিক prakr̥tik *adj* natural, physical, inorganic

প্রাক্তন praktôn *adj* previous, former

প্রাচীন pracīn *adj* old, ancient, antique

প্রাণ praṇ *n* life, life-breath, everything that is held dear

প্রাণপণ praṇôpɔṇ *n* resolve, obstinacy

প্রাণী praṇī *n* creature, living being

প্রাণীবিদ্যা praṇībidya *n* zoology

প্রাথমিক prathômik *adj* initial, early, primary

প্রান্ত prantô *n* tip, end, extremity

প্রান্তিক prantik *adj* extreme, marginal, terminal

প্রাপ্ত praptô *adj* attained, received, acquired

প্রাপ্তিস্বীকার praptisvīkar *n* acknowledgement

প্রায় praŷ *adv* usually, often; like, almost, resembling

প্রার্থনা prarthôna *n* supplication, prayer

প্রাসাদ prasad *n* palace

প্রিয় priŷô *adj* dear, beloved, favorite

প্রিয়তম priŷôtɔmô *(m)*, প্রিয়তমা priŷôtɔma *(f) n* lover, beloved, darling

প্রীতি prīti *n* pleasure, delight, joy

প্রেত pret *n* goblin, ghoul, ghost

প্রেম prem *n* love, affection, devotion

প্রেমে পড়া preme pɔra *vb* fall in love

প্রেমিক premik *(m)*, প্রেমিকা premika *(f) n* lover

প্রেরণ prerôṇ *n* transmission, sending

প্রেরণা prerôṇa *n* urge, inspiration

প্রৌঢ় prôuṛhô *adj* middle-aged, elderly

প্লাবন plabôn *n* flood, deluge

ফ ph

ফকির phôkir *n* fakir, ascetic,
mendicant

ফক্কড়ি phôkkôṛi *n* trickery

ফচকে phôcke *adj* garrulous, flippant, saucy, frivolous

ফজলি phôjli *n* type of mango

ফটক phɔṭôk *n* gate, portico

ফটিক phôṭik *n* crystal, quartz

ফড়িং phôṛiṃ *n* grasshopper

ফড়ফড় phɔrphɔr *onom* fluttering,
flapping

ফতুর phôtur *adj* penniless, broke

ফন্দি phôndi *n* intrigue, scheme, plot

ফরসা phɔrsa *adj* fair-complexioned,
light-skinned

ফরাসী phɔrasī *adj* French

ফরিয়াদ phôriŷad *n* lawsuit

ফর্দ phɔrdô *n* list, inventory

ফল phɔl *n* fruit, result, effect

ফলতঃ phɔlôtôḥ, ফলে phɔle *adv*
consequently, indeed

ফলপ্রসূ phɔlôprôsū *adj* productive,
fertile

ফলন phɔlôn *n* outcome, result

ফলা phɔla *vb* bear fruit, grow fruit

ফলাফল phɔlaphɔl *n* consequences,
results, upshot

ফষ্টিনষ্টি phôṣṭinôṣṭi *n* banter,
witticism

ফসকানো phɔskano *vb* slip, miss
an opportunity

ফসল phɔsôl *n* harvest

ফাউ phau *n* extra, freebie

ফাঁক phãk *n* gap, chink, fissure

ফাঁকি phãki *n* deception, evasion

ফাঁকি দেওয়া phãki deoŷa *vb*
deceive, hoax, cheat

ফাঁকি মারা phãki mara *vb* play
truant

ফাঁদ phãd *n* trap, snare

ফাঁদে পড়া phãde pɔra *vb* be
trapped, fall into a trap

ফাঁপা phãpa *vb* swell, distend,
inflate

ফাঁস phãs *n* noose, slip-knot

ফাঁসি phãsi *n* death by hanging

ফাজলামি phajlami *n* flippancy,
talkativeness

ফাজিল phajil *adj* talkative, cheeky,
flippant

ফাটল phaṭôl *n* crack, fissure

ফাটা phaṭa *vb* crack, split, burst,
explode

ফাটানো phaṭano *vb* cause to explode

ফাড়া phaṛa *vb* tear, rend, cleave

ফানুস phanus *n* balloon

ফাল phal *n* plowshare, coulter

ফালতু phaltu *adj* extra, spare,
unnecessary

ফালা phala, ফালি phali *n* strip,
slice

ফালি করা phali kɔra *vb* split, slice

ফাল্গুন phalgun *n eleventh month
of Bengali calendar*

ফিকা phika *(Bd)*, ফিকে phike
(WB) adj dim, pale, insipid

ফিটফাট phiṭphaṭ *adj* spick and
span, neat and clean

ফিতা phita *(Bd)*, ফিতে phite *(WB)*
n tape, ribbon

ফিনকি phinki *n* spray, spurt

ফিরা phira *see* ফেরা phera

ফিরে phire *adj, adv* next, again,
afresh

ফিরে আসা phire asa, ফিরে যাওয়া
phire yaoŷa *vb* return

ফিসফিস phisphis *onom* whispering

ফুঁ phũ *n* whiff, blow, puff

ফুঁ দেওয়া phū deoŷa *vb* blow out, blow

ফুকর phukôr *n* hole, crevice, niche

ফুট phuṭ *n* bubble, effervescence

ফুটকি phuṭki *n* dot, speck

ফুটা phuṭa *see* ফোটা phoṭa

ফুটানি phuṭani *n* bragging, boasting, vanity

ফুটানো phuṭano, ফোটানো photano *vb* cause to bloom; boil

ফুটফুট phuṭphuṭ *onom* clear, transparent

ফুৎকার phuṭkar *n* whiff, puff

ফুরানো phurano *(Bd)*, ফুরোনো phurono *(WB)* *vb* terminate, conclude, finish

ফুর্তি phurti *n* enjoyment, delight, amusement

ফুল phul *n* flower, blossom

ফুলকপি phulkôpi *n* cauliflower

ফুলা phula *see* ফোলা phola

ফুসফুস phusphus *n* lungs

ফুসলানো phuslano*(Bd)*, ফুসলোনো phuslono *(WB)* *vb* instigate, entice, seduce

ফেঁকড়ি phēkṛi *n* twig

ফেকাশে phækaśe *adj* pale, wan, anemic

ফেটানো phetano *vb* whisk, froth up

ফেনা phæna *n* froth, foam, lather

ফের pher *n* trouble, danger

ফের pher *adv* again

ফেরত pherôt *adj* returned, refused, back

ফেরা phera *(also* ফিরা phira*)* *vb* return, come back

ফেরি pheri *n* ferry

ফেরিওয়ালা pherioŷala *n* peddler, hawker

ফেল করা phel kɔra *vb* fail

ফেলনা phælna *adj* worthless, fit to be thrown away

ফেলা phæla *vb* throw, fling, cast, discard

ফেলে দেওয়া phele deoŷa *vb* throw away

ফেসাদ phesad *n* trouble, difficulty

ফোঁটা phõṭa *n* point, drop, globular mark

ফোঁপানো phõpano, ফুঁপানো phū-pano *vb* sob, whimper

ফোঁস phõs *int* sigh of grief, angry growl, snarl

ফোটা phoṭa, ফুটা phuṭa *vb* bloom, blossom

ফোড়া phoṛa *n* abscess, furuncle, boil

ফোন phon *n* telephone

ফোয়ারা phoŷara *n* fountain, shower

ফোলা phola, ফুলা phula *vb* swell, be distended, be puffed; flourish

ফোসকা phoska *n* blister

ফ্ল্যাট phlyaṭ *n* flat, apartment

ব b

বই bôi *n* book; *pp, adv* except, without, nothing but

বই কি bôi ki *adv* of course, naturally

বউ bôu *n* bride, young wife, wife

বউদি, বৌদি bôudi *n* sister-in-law *(elder brother's wife)*

বওয়া bɔoya *vb* endure, suffer, carry

বংশ bɔmśô *n* family, clan

বংশ তালিকা bɔmśô talika *n* family tree

বঁটি bõṭi *n* large curved knife

বকবক bɔkbɔk *n* prattle, excessive talking

বকশিশ bôkśiś *n* alms, bakhsheesh

বকা bɔka *vb* scold, tell off

বকাবকি bɔkabôki *n* altercation, dispute

বক্তা bɔkta *n* speaker, lecturer

বক্তৃতা bôktr̥ta *n* speech, lecture

বক্র bɔkrô *adj* fraudulent; bent, crooked

বক্রোক্তি bɔkrokti *n* sarcasm

বগল bɔgôl *n* armpit

বঙ্গ bɔṅgô *n* Bengal

বচন bɔcôn *n* speech, utterance

বছর bɔchôr *n* year

বজায় bɔjaŷ *adj* intact, in place

বজ্র bɔjrô *n* thunder

বজ্রপাত bɔjrôpat *n* thunderbolt

বঞ্চনা bɔñcôna *n* deception, deceit

বট bɔṭ *n* banyan tree

বটে bôṭe *adv* just so, true, indeed

বড় bɔrô *adj* big, large

বড় একটা না bɔrô ekṭa na *adv* hardly, not much, rarely

বড় কথা bɔrô kɔtha *n* main thing, important matter

বড়দিন bɔrôdin *n* Christmas

বড়াই bɔrai *n* bragging, boasting

বড়ি bôri *n* pill, tablet

বণিক bônik *n* trader, merchant

বৎস bɔtsô *n* child; darling

বদ bɔd *adj* bad, evil, wicked

বদমাইশ bɔdmaiś *adj* mischievous, wicked

বদহজম bɔdhɔjôm *n* indigestion, dyspepsia

বদল bɔdôl *n* exchange, change, substitution

বদলানো bɔdlano *vb* change, exchange

বদলে bɔdôle *pp* instead of, in place of

বদ্ধ bɔddhô *adj* bound, fastened, tied

বধূ bôdhu *n* bride, young wife

বন bôn *n* forest, wood, jungle

বনা bɔna *vb* get on together, be on good terms

বনাম bɔnam *pp* versus

বনিয়াদ bôniŷad *n* foundation, base

বন্দনা bɔndôna *n* praise, worship, adoration

বন্দর bɔndôr *n* port, harbor

বন্দী bôndī *n* prisoner, captive

বন্দুক bônduk *n* gun, musket, rifle

বন্ধ bɔndhô *n* tie, bond, bandage; *adj* shut, closed

বন্ধ করা bɔndhô kɔra *vb* close, shut, stop

বন্ধক bɔndhôk *n* mortgage, pawn, pledge

বন্ধন bɔndhôn *n* binding, tying, fastening

বন্ধনী bɔndhônī *n* bracket

বন্ধু bôndhu *n* friend

বন্যা bônya *n* flood, deluge

বপন bɔpôn *n* sowing, planting

বপু bôpu *n* body, figure, form

বমি bômi *n* vomit

বমি করা bômi kɔra *vb* vomit, be sick

বয়ন bɔŷôn *n* weaving, knitting

বয়স bɔŷôs *n* age

বয়সী bɔŷôsī, বয়স্ক bɔŷôskô *adj* adult, middle-aged

বয়াম bɔŷam *n* jar

বয়ে যাওয়া bôŷe yaoŷa *vb* not care, not give a damn

বর bɔr *n* husband, bridegroom

বরই bɔrôi *n* jujube

বরং bɔrôm *adv* rather, in preference

বরণ bɔrôn *n* welcome, reception

বরফ bɔrôph *n* ice

বরবটী bɔrbôṭī *n* green beans

বরাত bɔrat *n* fate, luck

বরাদ্দ bɔraddô *adj* fixed, allotted

বরাবর bɔrabɔr *adv* always, ever

বরাহ bɔrahô *n* boar, hog

বর্গ bɔrgô *n* class, set, collection

বর্গীয় bôrgīŷô *adj* generic, specific

বর্জন bɔrjôn *n* omission, exclusion, abandonment

বর্ণ bɔrnô *n* color; letter of the alphabet

বর্ণমালা bɔrnômala *n* alphabet

বর্ণনা bɔrnôna *n* description

বর্ণান্ধ bɔrnandô *adj* color-blind

বর্ণালি bɔrnali *n* spectrum

বর্তমান bɔrtôman *adj* present, current

বর্বরতা bɔrbôrôta *n* barbarism

বর্ষ bɔrsô *n* twelve-month period

বর্ষা bɔrsa *n* rain, rainfall; monsoon, rainy season

বল bɔl *n* strength, power, might; ball

বলবৎ bɔlôbɔṭ *adj* operative, intact

বলবান bɔlôban *adj* vigorous, strong, powerful

বলয় bɔlɔŷ *n* sphere, orbit

বলা bɔla *vb* speak, talk, say

বলাবলি bɔlabôli *n* conversation, discussion

বলি bôli *n* sacrifice; wrinkle

বলিষ্ঠ bôlisṭhô *adj* hardy, robust, sturdy

বলে bôle *conj* because of, as, on account of

বশ bɔś *n* command, will, authority

বশ করা bɔś kɔra *vb* hypnotize

বশত bɔśôtô *adv* on account of, owing to, because of

বসন্ত bɔsôntô *n* spring, springtime

বসবাস bɔsôbas *n* living; residence, dwelling

বসা bɔsa *vb* be seated, be installed, sit

বসানো bɔsano *vb* place, set down, cause to sit, set up, plant

বস্তা bɔsta *n* sack, large bag, bale

বস্তি bôsti *n* slum

বস্তু bôstu *n* substance, material

বস্তুত bôstutô *adv* in fact, indeed, really

বস্তুতত্ত্ব bôstutɔttvô *n* physics

বহন bɔhôn *n* carrying, bearing, suffering, enduring

বহু bôhu, বহুত bôhut *adj* many, numerous; *adv* very

বহুদূর bôhudūr *adv* very far, far-off

বহুভাষী bôhubhaṣī *adj* multilingual

বহুমূল্য bôhumūlyô *adj* costly, precious

বা ba *conj, adv* or, instead, whether

বাই bai *n* neurosis, mania

বাইবেল baibel *n* bible

বাইর bair, বাইরে baire *n, pp* outside, exterior, outside of, abroad, beyond

বাউল baul *n* Baul *(mystic minstrel)*

বাওয়া baoŷa *vb* steer, row

বাংলা baṁla *n* Bengali, Bangla

বাঃ bah *int expr* bravo, excellent

বাঁ bā *adj, n* left, the left side

বাঁক bāk *n* turn, bend

বাঁকা bāka *vb* bend, lean, incline; *adj* bent, uneven, curved

বাঁকানো bākano *vb* deflect, bend, cause to swerve, turn

বাঁচন bācôn *n* survival; act of living

বাঁচা bāca *vb* live, survive, be alive

বাঁচানো bācano *vb* save, rescue, revive

বাঁটা bāṭa *vb* distribute, divide

বাঁদর bādôr, বানর banôr *n* ape, monkey

বাঁধ bādh *n* dam; embankment

বাঁধা bādha *vb* tie, fasten, obstruct

বাঁধানো bādhano *vb* bind, enframe, dam up

বাঁশ bāś *n* bamboo

বাঁশি bāśi *n* flute, pipe

বাক bak *n* speech, voice, language

বাকি baki *adj* remaining, outstanding

বাক্য bakyô *n* sentence, statement

বাক্স baksô *n* box, chest, case

বাগড় bagôr, বাগড়া bagra *n* obstacle, hindrance

বাগান bagan *n* garden

বাগানো bagano *vb* manage, tame, master

বাঘ bagh *n* tiger

বাঙাল baṅal *adj* from East Bengal; rural

বাঙালি baṅali *n, adj* Bengali

বাচন bacôn *n* speaking, recitation

বাচনিক bacônik *adj* oral, verbal

বাচাল bacal *adj* talkative, garrulous

বাচ্চা bacca *n* child, baby

বাচ্য bacyô *adj* spoken, pronounced

বাছা bacha *vb* select, choose

বাছাই bachai *n* selection, choice

বাছুর bachur *n* calf

বাজা baja *vb* ring, strike (*clock*), sound; hurt

বাজানো bajano *vb* play (a musical instrument); strike

বাজার bajar *n* market, bazaar

বাজি baji *n* magic; juggling; fireworks

বাজে baje *adj* trashy, cheap, paltry

বাজে কথা baje kɔtha *n* nonsense

বাটা baṭa *vb* mash, grind

বাটালি baṭali *n* chisel

বাটি baṭi *n* small bowl

বাড় baṛ *n* growth

বাড়তি baṛti *n* growth, development; excess, surplus

বাড়া bara *vb* grow, increase, develop

বাড়ানো barano *vb* increase, augment, enhance, enlarge

বাড়াবাড়ি barabaṛi *n* excess, extremes, immoderation

বাড়ি baṛi *n* home, residence, village home

বাণী baṇī *n* message, maxim

বাত bat *n* rheumatism

বাতচক্র batɔkrô *n* windmill

বাতাস batas *n* wind, air, breeze

বাতি bati *n* lamp, light, candle

বাতিক batik *n* neurosis, mania

বাতিকগ্রস্ত batikgrôstô *adj* manic, neurotic

বাতিল batil *adj* cancelled, rejected

বাতুল batul *adj* childish

বাতুলতা batulɔta *n* childishness

বাৎসরিক baṯsôrik *adj* yearly, annual

বাদ bad *n* exception, exclusion, omission

বাদাম badam *n* nut, peanut

বাদামি badami *adj* brown

বাদে bade *pp* except, excluding; after

বাধা badha *n* obstacle, hindrance, impediment

বাধা দেওয়া badha deoẏa *vb* hinder, obstruct

বাধা পাওয়া badha paoẏa *vb* be obstructed, be opposed

বাধ্য badhyô *adj* obedient, docile, meek

বান ban *n* flood, deluge, tidal wave

বানর banôr *n* monkey, ape

বানান banan *n* spelling, orthography

বানানো banano *vb* prepare, create, build, get ready, devise

বান্ধবী bandhôbī *n* friend *(f)*

বাপ bap *n* father

বাপরে bapre *int expr* my goodness!, oh dear!

বাপু bapu *n* used in addressing one's father or one's son

বাবা baba *n* father

বাবু babu *suff* added to the name of a Hindu gentleman

বাবুর্চি baburci *n* cook, chef

বাম bam *adj* left; left-hand

বামন bamôn *n* dwarf

বামুন bamun *n* Brahmin

বায়ব baẏôb *adj* aerial, atmospheric

বায়ু baẏu *n* wind, breeze

বায়ুমণ্ডল baẏumɔṇḍôl *n* atmosphere

বার bar *n* day; fixed time

বার করা bar kɔra *vb* bring out

বার barô, বারো baro *num* twelve

বারণ barôn *n* resistance, prevention

বারোমাস baromas *n* twelve months, a year

বারি bari *n* water

বারুদ barud *n* gunpowder

বার্তা barta *n* information, message, news

বার্ষিক barṣik *adj* annual, yearly

বালক balôk *n* boy, male child

বালতি balti *n* bucket

বালি bali *n* sand, gravel

বালিকা balika *n* girl

বালিশ baliś *n* pillow, cushion

বাল্য balyô, বাল্যকাল balyôkal *n* childhood

বাষ্প baspô *n* vapor, steam

বাস bas *n* bus; habitation, settlement; *int expr* enough!

বাসনা basôna *n* wish, desire, longing

বাসভবন basbhɔbôn *n* house, residence

বাসা basa *n* house

বাসি basi *adj* stale, not fresh

বাসিন্দা basinda *n* inhabitant, resident

বাস্তব bastôb *adj* true, actual, real

বাস্তবতা bastôbɔta *n* reality

বাস্তু bastu *n* site, homestead

বাহন bahôn *n* vehicle, conveyance

বাহাদুর bahadur *adj* brave, bold, valiant

বাহানা bahana *n* excuse, pretence

বাহার bahar *n* beauty, glory, glamour

বাহারি bahari *adj* glamorous, beautiful

বাহিনী bahinī *n* army, division

বাহু bahu *n* arm

বাহুল্য bahulyô *n* excess, superfluity

বাহ্য bahyô (*pron* bajjho) *adj* outside, exterior

বিধা bīdha *see* বেঁধা bēdha

বিধানো bīdhano *see* বেঁধানো bēdhano

বিকট bikɔṭ *n* hideous, monstrous

বিকর্ষণ bikɔrṣôṇ *n* pull in the opposite direction, repulsion

বিকল bikɔl *adj* mutilated, maimed
বিকল্প bikɔlpô *n* substitute, alternative
বিকশিত bikôṣitô *adj* developed, manifest, expanded
বিকশিত করা bikôṣitô kɔra *vb* develop, display, exhibit
বিকানো bikano *(Bd)*, বিকোনো bikono *(WB)* *vb* sell, give away
বিকার bikar *n* perversion, deviation
বিকাল bikal *(Bd)*, বিকেল bikel *(WB)* *n* afternoon
বিকাশ bikaś *n* manifestation, development
বিকিরণ bikirôṇ *n* radiation
বিকৃত bikr̥tô *adj* perverted, corrupted
বিকৃতি bikr̥ti *n* perversion, corruption
বিক্রম bikrɔm *n* power, might
বিক্রয় bikrɔŷ, বিক্রি bikri *n* selling, sale
বিক্রিয়া bikriŷa *n* chemical reaction
বিক্ষিপ্ত bikṣiptô *adj* scattered, dispersed
বিক্ষোভ bikṣobh *n* mortification; grief; agitation
বিখ্যাত bikhyatô *adj* famous, renowned
বিগড়ানো bigrano *vb* corrupt, spoil
বিগত bigɔtô *adj* gone, departed
বিগ্রহ bigrôhô *n* image of a deity, idol
বিঘত bighɔt *n* span *(nine inches)*
বিঘা bigha *n measure of land (6400 square cubits)*
বিচক্ষণ bicɔkṣôn *adj* prudent, wise
বিচক্ষণতা bicɔkṣônôta *n* prudence, discretion
বিচরণ bicɔrôṇ *n* wandering, roaming, rambling

বিচলিত bicôlitô *adj* agitated, perturbed, excited
বিচার bicar *n* judgement, verdict, verification
বিচারক bicarôk *n* judge
বিচি bici, বীচ bīc *n* seed, stone
বিচিত্র bicitrô *adj* varied, colorful
বিচিত্রতা bicitrôta *n* variety, color
বিচ্ছিন্ন bicchinnô *adj* separated, torn apart
বিচ্ছেদ bicched *n* separation, divorce
বিছানা bichana *n* bed
বিজয় bijɔŷ *n* victory, triumph, conquest
বিজলি bijôli *n* lightning, electricity
বিজিত bijitô *adj* defeated, conquered
বিজ্ঞ bijñô *adj* learned, erudite
বিজ্ঞান bijñan *(pron* biggæn*) n* science
বিজ্ঞাপন bijñapôn *n* notice, advertisement
বিটকেল biṭkel *adj* hideous, monstrous, dreadful
বিড়বিড় birbir *onom* muttering, mumbling
বিড়াল biral, বেড়াল beral *n* cat
বিড়ি biri *n* indigenous cigarette
বিতরণ bitɔrôṇ *n* distribution
বিতর্ক bitɔrkô *n* debate, argument
বিত্ত bittô *n* wealth, riches
বিদগ্ধ bidɔgdhô *adj* intelligent; witty
বিদায় bidaŷ *n* farewell
বিদিত biditô *adj* known, understood
বিদীর্ণ bidīrṇô *adj* rent, torn, split
বিদূষক bidūṣôk *n* clown, jester
বিদেশ bideś *n* foreign country, abroad
বিদেশি bideśi *adj* foreign, alien
বিদ্ধ biddhô *adj* pierced, impaled, perforated

বিদ্বান bidvan *adj* learned, erudite

বিদ্বেষ bidveṣ *n* malice, envy, spite

বিদ্যা bidya *n* learning, scholarship, erudition

বিদ্যালয় bidyalɔẏ *n* academy, school

বিদ্যুৎ bidyut *n* electricity, lightning

বিদ্রোহ bidrohô *n* revolt, rebellion

বিদ্রোহী bidrohī *adj* rebellious, hostile

বিধবা bidhôba *n* widow

বিধাতা bidhata *n* God, providence, creator

বিধান bidhan *n* arrangement, prescription

বিধি bidhi *n* rule, regulation, precept

বিধেয় bidheŷô *adj* lawful, proper, right

বিনত binɔtô *adj* humble, submissive

বিনতি binôti *n* modesty, politeness

বিনয় binɔŷ *n* modesty, mildness

বিনষ্ট binɔṣṭô *adj* destroyed

বিনা bina *pp* without, except

বিনাশ binaś *n* loss, annihilation

বিনিময় binimɔŷ *n* exchange, barter, trade

বিন্দু bindu *n* drop

বিন্যাস binyas *n* arrangement, disposition

বিপক্ষ bipɔkṣô *n* opponent, enemy, rival

বিপজ্জনক bipɔjjɔnôk *adj* dangerous

বিপত্তি bipôtti *n* adversity, danger

বিপদ bipɔd *n* danger, hazard

বিপন্ন bipɔnnô *adj* endangered, at risk, embarrassed

বিপরীত bipôrīt *adj* opposite, contrary

বিপর্যয় bipɔryɔŷ *n* upheaval, inversion, disruption

বিপাক bipak *n* distress, trouble

বিপুল bipul *adj* large, big, huge

বিপ্লব biplɔb *n* revolution, revolt

বিপ্লবী biplɔbī *n* revolutionary

বিফল biphɔl *adj* fruitless, useless

বিবরণ bibɔrôṇ *n* explanation, comment

বিবর্ণ bibɔrṇô *adj* pale, washed-out

বিবর্তন bibɔrtôn *n* rotation

বিবশ bibɔś *adj* benumbed, stupefied

বিবাগী bibagī *adj* self-renouncing, stoical

বিবাদ bibad *n* strife, quarrel

বিবাহ bibahô *n* marriage, wedding

বিবাহিত bibahitô *adj* married

বিবি bibi *n* lady, wife *(Muslim)*

বিবেক bibek *n* conscience, discretion

বিবেচক bibecôk *adj* discriminating, judicious, thoughtful

বিবেচনা bibecôna *n* consideration, judgement

বিভক্তি bibhôkti *n gram* declension, inflection, case-ending

বিভব bibhɔb *n* omnipresence

বিভাগ bibhag *n* division, section

বিভাজন bibhajôn *n* division, partition

বিভিন্ন bibhinnô *adj* various, diverse

বিভেদ bibhed *n* breaking asunder, splitting apart

বিভ্রম bibhrôm *n* illusion, delusion

বিভ্রান্ত bibhrantô *adj* confused, bewildered

বিমত bimɔt *n* different opinion, dissent

বিমল bimɔl *adj* clear, transparent; pristine, pure

বিমর্ষ bimɔrṣô *adj* sad, morose

বিমা bima *n* insurance

বিমান biman *n* aircraft, airplane

বিমানবন্দর bimanbɔndôr *n* airport

বিমুখ bimukh *adj* adverse, hostile

বিমুগ্ধ bimugdhô *adj* mesmerised, charmed

বিমোহিত bimohitô *adj* enchanted, charmed

বিম্ব bimbô *n* bubble; image

বিযুক্ত biyuktô *adj* disjointed, detached, separated

বিয়োগ biŷog *n* subtraction

বিরক্ত birôktô *adj* annoyed, angry, vexed

বিরক্তি birôkti *n* annoyance, irritation

বিরচিত birôcitô *adj* written, composed

বিরত birɔtô *adj* ceased, ended, discontinued

বিরতি birôti *n* desistance, abstention

বিরল birɔl *adj* rare, scarce, scanty

বিরস birɔs *adj* juiceless, sapless, dry

বিরহ birɔhô *n* parting, separation

বিরহিত birôhitô *adj* deprived, destitute

বিরাট biraṭ *adj* enormous, vast, huge

বিরাম biram *n* abstention, cessation

বিরুদ্ধ biruddhô *adj* adverse, unfavorable

বিরুদ্ধে biruddhe *pp* against, in opposition to

বিরোধ birodh *n* enmity, hostility

বিল bil *n* marsh, flood-plain

বিল bil *n* bill

বিলকুল bilkul *adj* complete, thorough, outright

বিলম্ব bilɔmbô *n* delay, lateness

বিলাত bilat *(Bd)*, বিলেত bilet *(WB) n* foreign country; Europe; England

বিলাতি bilati *adj* foreign

বিলানো bilano, বিলিয়ে দেওয়া biliŷe deoŷa *vb* distribute, give away

বিলাস bilas *n* luxury, indulgence

বিলাসী bilasī *adj* luxurious, self-indulgent

বিলি bili *n* distribution

বিশ biś *num* twenty

বিশদ biśôd *adj* clear, evident, lucid

বিশারদ biśarɔd *adj* experienced, skilled

বিশাল biśal *adj* huge, enormous, immense

বিশিষ্ট biśiṣṭô *adj* distinguished, prominent, excellent

বিশুদ্ধ biśuddhô *adj* pure, holy, sacred

বিশৃঙ্খল biśṙṅkhɔl *adj* disorderly, wild, unruly

বিশেষ biśeṣ *n* kind, sort, type; *adj* special, particular

বিশেষজ্ঞ biśeṣɔjñô *n* expert, specialist

বিশেষত biśeṣɔtô *adv* especially, particularly

বিশেষণ biśeṣɔṇ *n* adjective

বিশেষ্য biśeṣyô *n* noun

বিশ্ব biśvô *n* world, universe, earth

বিশ্বজনীয় biśvôjônīŷô *adj* universal, all-pervasive

বিশ্বস্ত biśvɔstô *adj* trusted, faithful

বিশ্বাস biśvas *n* belief, trust, faith

বিশ্বাসী biśvasī *adj* trustworthy, loyal, faithful

বিশ্রাম biśram *n* rest, repose, break

বিশ্রী biśrī *adj* hideous, monstrous, ugly

বিশ্লেষণ biśleṣôṇ *n* analysis, dissolution

বিষ biṣ *n* poison, venom

বিষণ্ণ biṣɔṇṇô *adj* sad, dejected, despondent

বিষণ্ণতা biṣɔṇṇôta *n* sadness, depression

বিষম biṣɔm *adj* severe, unbearable, terrible

বিষয় biṣɔŷ *n* subject, topic

বিষাক্ত biṣaktô *adj* poisonous

বিষুব biṣub *n* equinox

বিষুবরেখা biṣubrekha *n* equator

বিসর্জন bisɔrjôn *n* sacrifice

বিস্তর bistɔr *adj* many, much, extensive

বিস্তার bistar *n* expanse, expansion

বিস্তৃত bistr̥tô *adj* extensive, detailed

বিস্ফোরণ bisphorôn *n* explosion

বিস্বাদ bisvad *adj* tasteless, flat, unsavory

বিস্ময় bismɔŷ *n* wonder, surprise, amazement

বিস্মরণ bismɔrôṇ *n* forgetting, oblivion

বিহিত bihitô *adj* prescribed; just proper

বীজ bīj *n* grain, seed

বীজগণিত bījgôṇit *n* algebra

বীণা bīna *n* lute, vina, lyre

বীথি bīthi *n* row, line, avenue

বীভৎস bībhɔtsô *adj* loathsome, horrible

বীর bīr *n* hero

বীরত্ব bīrɔtvô *n* heroism, bravery

বুক buk *n* chest

বুট buṭ *n* chickpea; gram; boots

বুড়া bura *(Bd)*, বুড়ো buṛo *(WB)* *adj* old, elderly *(for people)*

বুড়ি buri *n* old woman

বুদ্ধ buddhô *n* Buddha; *adj* enlightened, awakened

বুদ্ধি buddhi *n* wisdom, reason, understanding

বুদ্ধিমান buddhiman *(m)*, বুদ্ধিমতী buddhimôtī *(f) adj* intelligent, wise *(m, f)*

বুদ্বুদ budbud *n* bubble

বুধবার budhbar *n* Wednesday

বুনা buna *see* বোনা bona

বুভুক্ষা bubhūkṣa *n* hunger, appetite, desire

বুরুজ buruj *n* bastion, turret, tower

বুলবুল bulbul *n* nightingale

বুলানো bulano *(Bd)*, বুলোনো bulono *(WB) vb* caress, stroke

বৃক্ক br̥kkô *n* kidney

বৃত্ত br̥ttô *n* circle, sphere

বৃত্তি br̥tti *n* faculty, profession, scholarship

বৃথা br̥tha *adj* futile, in vain

বৃদ্ধ br̥ddhô *adj* old, ancient

বৃদ্ধাঙ্গুলি br̥ddhaṅguli *n* thumb; big toe

বৃদ্ধি br̥ddhi *n* growth, increase

বৃন্ত br̥ntô *n* stalk

বৃশ্চিক br̥ścik *n* scorpion

বৃষ br̥ṣô *n* bull, ox

বৃষ্টি br̥ṣṭi *n* rain

বৃহৎ br̥hɔt *adj* huge, big, large

বৃহস্পতিবার br̥hôspôtibar *n* Thursday

বেআইন beain *n* lawlessness

বেইমান beiman *adj* perfidious, treacherous

বেঁধা bēdha, বিঁধা bīdha *vb* be pierced, be perforated

বেঁধানো bēdhano, বিঁধানো bīdhano *vb* pierce, prick

বেকায়দা bekaŷda *adj* awkward

বেকার bekar *adj* unemployed

বেকারি bekari *n* unemployment

বেখাপ্পা bekhappa *adj* unfitting, inappropriate

বেগ beg *n* speed, velocity

বেগুন begun *n* eggplant, aubergine

বেগুনি beguni *adj* violet, purple

বেচা bæca *vb* sell

বেচারা becara *(m)*, বেচারি becari *(f) n* helpless, poor, miserable

বেজায় bejaẏ *adj* excessive, tremendous

বেজি beji *n* mongoose

বেজুত bejut *n* disadvantage

বেড় ber *n* circumference, girth

বেড়া bæra *n* fence, railing

বেড়ানো bærano *vb* walk, go out, visit

বেড়ি beri *n* shackle, fetter, chain

বেণি beni *n* braid of hair, plait

বেত bet *n* cane, rattan, reed

বেতন betɔn *n* salary, wages

বেতার betar *n* radio

বেদনা bedôna *n* pain, ache

বেদানা bedana *n* pomegranate

বেদী bedī *n* altar, pulpit

বেদে bede *n* Gypsy

বেনামি benami *adj* anonymous

বেনিয়ম beniẏôm *n* illegality, lawlessness, violation

বেপার bæpar *n* trade

বেপারী bæparī *n* trader

বেপরোয়া bepɔroẏa *adj* reckless

বেমালুম bemalum *adj* unobtrusive; *adv* imperceptibly

বেয়ারা beẏara *n* orderly, bearer, carrier

বেল bel *n* wood apple *(fruit)*; bell

বেলচা belca *n* shovel

বেলনা bælna *n* cylinder

বেলা bæla *n* hour, time of day

বেশ beś *adj, adv* quite, nice, fine

বেশি beśi *adj, adv* much, too much, many

বেশ্যা beśya *n* prostitute, whore

বেসরকারি besɔrkari *adj* non-governmental, private, unofficial

বেসামাল besamal *adj* erratic, unbalanced

বেহায়া behaẏa *adj* shameless, brazen

বেহালা behala *n* violin

বৈকাল boikal *n* afternoon

বৈচিত্র্য boicitryô *n* variety, diversity

বৈজ্ঞানিক boijñanik *adj* scientific

বৈতানিক boitanik *adj* sacrificial

বৈদিক boidik *adj* Vedic

বৈধ boidhô *adj* lawful, legal, just

বৈবাহিক boibahik *adj* matrimonial

বৈভাষিক boibhaṣik *adj* multilingual

বৈরিতা boirita *n* hostility

বৈশাখ boiśakh *n first Bengali month (mid-April to mid-May)*

বৈশিষ্ট্য boiśiṣṭyô *n* distinction, speciality

বোকা boka *adj* foolish, stupid

বোকামি bokami *n* foolishness, stupidity

বোজা boja *vb* shut, close

বোঝা bojha *vb* understand; *n* burden

বোঝানো bojhano *vb* explain; comfort

বোতল botôl *n* bottle

বোতাম botam *n* button

বোধ bodh *n* understanding, sense

বোধ হয় bodh hɔẏ *adv* perhaps

বোন bon *n* sister *(younger)*

বোনা bona, বুনা buna *vb* weave, knit, sow

বোবা boba *adj* dumb, speechless, mute

বোমা boma *n* bomb

বোয়াল boẏal *n* large fish, catfish

বোরখা borkha *n* hood, cape

বোল bol *n* speech, word

বোলতা bolta *n* wasp

বৌ bou *n* wife; daughter-in-law

ব্যক্ত byktô (*pron* bækto) *adj* expressed, revealed, uttered

ব্যক্ত করা byktô kɔra (*pron* bækto kɔra) *vb* disclose, utter, reveal

ব্যক্তি bykti (*pron* bekti) *n* person, man

ব্যক্তিগত byktigɔtô (*pron* bektigɔto) *adj* private, personal

ব্যঞ্জনবর্ণ byñjɔnbɔrṇô (*pron* bænjonbɔrno) *n* consonant

ব্যতিক্রম bytikrôm (*pron* betikrom) *n* exception

ব্যতিরেকে bytireke (*pron* betireke) *pp* excluding, besides

ব্যতিত bytitô (*pron* betito) *pp* except, without

ব্যথা bytha (*pron* bætha) *n* pain, ache

ব্যবধান bybôdhan (*pron* bæbodhan) *n* distance, remoteness

ব্যবসা bybsa (*pron* bæbsa) *n* business, trade, commerce

ব্যবস্থা bybôstha (*pron* bæbostha) *n* arrangement, preparation

ব্যবহার bybôhar (*pron* bæbohar) *n* behavior, use

ব্যবহারিক bybôharik (*pron* bæboharik) *adj* useful, handy

ব্যভিচার bybhicar (*pron* bæbhicar) *n* adultery, infidelity

ব্যয় byŷ (*pron* bæy) *n* expenditure, expense

ব্যর্থ byrthô (*pron* bærtho) *adj* futile, vain, useless

ব্যস্ত bystô (*pron* bæsto) *adj* busy, eager, anxious

ব্যস্ততা bystôta (*pron* bæstota) *n* preoccupation; hurry, hustle

ব্যাংক byænk *n* bank

ব্যাকরণ byækrônô *n* grammar

ব্যাকুল byækul *adj* anxious, agitated

ব্যাখ্যা byækhya *n* explanation, exposition

ব্যাঘাত byæghat *n* obstacle, impediment

ব্যাঙ byæṅ *n* frog, toad

ব্যাধি byædhi *n* disease, ailment, disorder

ব্যাপক byæpɔk *n* extensive, pervading, widespread

ব্যাপার byæpar *n* matter, affair, trade

ব্যাপারী byæparī *n* trader, merchant

ব্যাপী byæpī *suff* pervading, extending

ব্যাপ্ত byæptô *adj* pervaded, spread through

ব্যামো byæmo *n* illness, disease

ব্যায়াম byæŷam *n* exercise, gymnastics

ব্যাস byæs *n* diameter, expanse

ব্যাসার্ধ byæsardhô *n* radius

ব্রাহ্মণ brahmôṇ *n* Brahman

ব্রিজ brij *n* bridge

ব্রিটিশ briṭiś *n* British

ব্লাউজ blauj *n* blouse

ভ bh

ভক্ত bhɔktô *adj* devoted, reverent

ভক্তি bhôkti *n* devotion, worship

ভক্ষ bhɔkṣô *n* food, eating

ভগবান bhɔgôban *n* God *(Hindu)*

ভগ্ন bhɔgnô *adj* broken, fractured

ভঙ্গ bhɔṅgô *n* rupture, violation, breaking

ভঙ্গী bhôṅgi *n* style, posture

ভজা bhɔja *vb* worship

ভটভট bhɔṭbhɔṭ *onom* gurgling

ভড় bhɔr *n* large freight ship

ভড়ক bhɔṛôk *n* ostentation, display

ভণ্ড bhɔṇḍô *adj* deceitful, hypocritical

ভণ্ডামি bhɔṇḍami *n* hypocrisy, pretense

ভদ্র bhɔdrô *adj* gentle, polite, mannerly

ভদ্রতা bhɔdrôta *n* courtesy, refinement

ভদ্রলোক bhɔdrôlok *n* gentleman

ভনভন করা bhɔnbhɔn kɔra *vb* buzz, hum

ভব bhɔbô *n* the earth, universe

ভবঘুরে bhɔbôghure *n* vagabond, tramp

ভবন bhɔbôn *n* house, residence

ভবিষ্যৎ bhôbiṣyôt *n* future

ভয় bhɔŷ *n* fear, dread, terror

ভয়ঙ্কর bhɔŷôṅkɔr *adj* frightening, scary

ভর bhɔr *n* mass, weight

ভরণ bhɔrôṇ *n* filling, stuffing

ভরসা bhɔrsa *n* confidence, trust, faith

ভরা bhɔra *vb* be filled, be loaded

ভরানো bhɔrano *vb* fill, fill up, load

ভর্তি bhôrti *adj* filled, enrolled

ভাই bhai *n* brother *(younger)*

ভাংতি bhaṁti *n* small coins, change

ভাঁজা bhãja, ভাঁজ করা bhãj kɔra *vb* fold, plait

ভাগ bhag *n* partition, division

ভাগ করা bhag kɔra *vb* share, divide out

ভাগাভাগি bhagabhagi *n* reciprocity, mutuality

ভাগিনা bhagina *(Bd)*, ভাগ্নে bhagne *(WB) n* nephew *(sister's son)*

ভাগিনী bhaginī *(Bd)*, ভাগ্নী bhagnī *(WB) n* niece *(sister's daughter)*

ভাগী bhagī *n* shareholder

ভাগ্য bhagyô *n* fortune, luck

ভাগ্যবান bhagyôban *adj* fortunate, lucky

ভাঙন bhaṅôn *n* breach, rift

ভাঙা bhaṅa *vb* break, crumble, fracture; *adj* broken

ভাজা bhaja *vb* fry; roast

ভাজি bhaji *adj* fried; roasted

ভাড়া bhaṛa *n* rent, hire; fare

ভাণ্ডার bhaṇḍar *n* store, repository, treasury

ভাত bhat *n* cooked rice

ভান bhan *n* pretense, pretext

ভান করা bhan kɔra *vb* pretend, feign

ভানা bhana *vb* husk, grind, mill

ভাব bhab *n* mood, nature, feeling, substance, manner

ভাবগত bhabôgɔtô *adj* abstract, related to thought

ভাবনা bhabna *n* thought, worry

ভাবপ্রকাশ bhabprôkaś *n* emotional expression

ভাবপ্রবণ bhabôprôbôṇ *adj* sentimental, emotional

ভাবলেশ bhableś, ভাবালেশ bhabaleś *n* excitement, emotion

ভাবা bhaba *vb* think, worry, contemplate

ভাবুক bhabuk *adj* thoughtful, imaginative

ভার bhar *n* weight, gravity, burden, pressure

ভারত bharôt *n* India

ভারতীয় bharôtīŷô *adj* Indian

ভারী bharī *adj* heavy, weighty

ভাল bhalô, ভালো bhalo *adj* good, excellent, nice

ভালবাসা bhalôbasa *n* affection, love

ভাশুর bhaśur *n* brother-in-law *(husband's elder brother)*

ভাষা bhaṣa *n* language, speech

ভাষাতত্ত্ব bhaṣatɔttvô *n* linguistics

ভাষিত bhaṣitô *adj* spoken, said, uttered

ভাসা bhasa *vb* float, drift, swim

ভাস্কর bhaskɔr *n* sculptor

ভিক্ষা bhikṣa *n* begging, soliciting

ভিক্ষা করা bhikṣa kɔra *vb* beg, collect alms

ভিক্ষুক bhikṣuk *n* beggar *(m)*

ভিখারি bhikhari *n* beggar *(f)*

ভিজা bhija *(Bd)*, ভিজে bhije *(WB)* *adj* wet, soaked

ভিজানো bhijano *see* ভেজানো bhejano

ভিটা bhiṭa *(Bd)*, ভিটে bhiṭe *n* homestead, home-ground

ভিড় bhiṛ *n* crowd, throng

ভিতর bhitôr *n* inside, interior

ভিত্তি bhitti *n* foundation, base, ground

ভিন্ন bhinnô *adj* other, different, separate

ভিরমি bhirmi *n* dizziness, faintness

ভিসা bhisa *n* visa

ভীত bhītô *adj* frightened, alarmed, afraid

ভীরু bhīru *adj* timid, cowardly

ভীরুতা bhīruta *n* cowardice

ভীষণ bhīṣôṇ *adj* terrible, severe, awful

ভুঁড়ি bhūṛi *n* pot-belly

ভুক্ত bhuktô *adj* eaten; enjoyed; suffered

ভুট্টা bhuṭṭa *n* maize, corn

ভুবন bhubɔn *n* universe, world, earth

ভুল bhul *n* mistake, error, omission

ভুলা bhula *see* ভোলা bhola

ভুলে যাওয়া bhule yaôŷa *vb* forget

ভুসি bhusi *n* chaff, husk, bran

ভূ bhū *n* earth, world

ভূগোল bhūgol *n* geography

ভূচিত্র bhūcitrô *n* map

ভূত bhūt *n* ghost, spirit

ভূতত্ত্ব bhūtɔttvô *n* geology

ভূমি bhūmi *n* earth, land, soil

ভূমিকম্প bhūmikɔmpô *n* earthquake

ভূমিকা bhūmika *n* preface, preamble

ভূষণ bhūṣôṇ *n* embellishment, ornament

ভেংচি bhemci *n* grimace, grin

ভেঙ্গে পড়া bheṅe pɔra *vb* have a break-down

ভেজানো bhejano, ভিজানো bhijano soak, make wet

ভেজাল bhejal *n* adulteration, trouble

ভেড়া bhæra *n* sheep, ram

ভেদ bhed *n* difference, division, split

ভেদাভেদ bhedabhed *n* discrimination

ভেবা bhæba *adj* confounded, bewildered

ভেলকি bhelki *n* magic, juggling

ভেলা bhæla *n* raft, float

ভেস্তে bheste *adj* spoiled, upset, foiled

ভোঁতা bhõta *adj* blunt, dull

ভোগ bhog *n* enjoyment; suffering; appropriation

ভোগা bhoga *vb* suffer, undergo, sustain

ভোগান্তি bhoganti *n* extreme suffering

ভোজ bhoj *n* feast, banquet, meal

ভোজবাজি bhojbaji *n* juggling; hocus-pocus

ভোট bhoṭ *n* vote, election

ভোমরা bhomra *n* bumblebee

ভোর bhor *n* dawn, daybreak

ভোলা bhola, ভুলা bhula *vb* forget, omit

ভৌগোলিক bhougolik *adj* geographical

ভ্যাবা bhyæba *adj* confounded, bewildered

ভ্রমণ bhrômôṇ *n* travel, journey

ভ্রমণকারী bhrômôṇkarī *n* tourist

ভ্রাতা bhrata *n* brother

ভ্রান্ত bhrantô *adj* mistaken, erroneous

ভ্রান্তি bhranti *n* error, mistake

ভ্রূ bhru, ভ্রূ bhrū *n* eyebrow

ম m

মই môi *n* ladder

মকদ্দমা môkôddɔma *n* lawsuit, case

মকাই mɔkai *n* maize, sweet corn

মক্কেল mɔkkel *n* client (of an attorney/advocate)

মক্তব mɔktôb *n* Muslim primary school

মখমল mɔkhmɔl *n* velvet

মগ mɔg *n* mug

মগজ mɔgôj *n* brain, intelligence

মঙ্গল môṅgôl *n* benefit, welfare, good

মঙ্গলবার môṅgôlbar *n* Tuesday

মচকানো mɔckano *vb* sprain, twist (ankle etc)

মচমচ mɔcmɔc *onom* creaking sound

মজবুত môjbut *adj* firm, hard, stiff

মজা mɔja *vb* drown, lose oneself in; *n* pleasure, fun, enjoyment

মজাদার mɔjadar *adj* funny, amusing, tasty

মজুদ môjud *adj* stored, hoarded, ready

মজুর môjur *n* laborer, workman

মজ্জা mɔjja *n* bone marrow

মঞ্চ mɔñcô *n* stage, platform

মঞ্জুর môñjur *adj* sanctioned, approved, granted, permitted

মটকি môṭki *n* barrel, casket

মটকানো mɔṭkano *vb* twist, snap, break, crack

মটর mɔṭôr *n* pea

মঠ mɔṭh *n* monastery

মড়া mɔra *n* corpse, dead body

মণি môṇi *n* gem, jewel

মণ্ডপ mɔṇḍôp *n* pavillion, roof-terrace

মণ্ডল mɔṇḍôl *n* globe, sphere, circle

মত mɔt *n* view, opinion

মত mɔtô, মতন mɔtôn *pp* like, as, according to

মতভেদ mɔtôbhed *n* disagreement

মতলব mɔtlôb *n* intention, purpose, design

মৎস্য mɔtsyô *n* fish

মতামত mɔtamɔt *n* opinions, arguments, discussion, hypotheses

মতি môti *n* intellect, mentality, attention, memory

মতিগতি môtigôti *n* intention, design

মতিভ্রম môtibhrôm *n* delusion, hallucination

মতিস্থির motisthir *adj* sane, lucid, rational

মদ mɔd *n* alcohol, wine, spirits

মধু môdhu *n* honey

মধু môdhu, মধুর môdhur *adj* sweet, enchanting, pleasant

মধ্য môdhyô *n* middle, center, inside

মধ্যপন্থী môdhyôpônthī *adj* moderate

মধ্যরেখা môdhyôrekha *n* meridian

মধ্যস্থতা môdhyôsthôta *n* mediation

মধ্যে môdhye *pp* in between, within, inside, in the center

মন mɔn *n measure of weight (about 37 kilograms)*

মন mɔn *n* heart, mind, thought, feeling, attention, interest, mood

মন দেওয়া môn deoẏa *vb* concentrate

মনে করা mône kɔra *vb* think, consider, regard, contemplate, mind

মনে পড়া mône pɔra *vb* recollect, have on one's mind

মনে রাখা mône rakha *vb* remember, keep in mind

মনের কথা môner kɔtha *n* true feelings, secret thoughts

মনের মানুষ môner manuṣ *n* kindred spirit, soulmate

মনের মিল môner mil *n* empathy, accord, agreement

মন–মরা môn–mɔra *adj* disheartened, melancholy, sad

মনস্তত্ত্ব mônôstôttvô *n* psychology

মনস্থ করা mônôsthô kɔra *vb* intend, resolve

মনিব্যাগ mônibyæg *n* purse, wallet

মনীষী mônīṣī *adj* wise, intelligent

মনুষ্য mônuṣyô *n* mankind, humanity

মনোজ mônoj *adj* mental

মনোজ্ঞ mônojñô *adj* pleasing, lovely, beautiful

মনোনয়ন mônonɔyôn *n* choice, selection

মনোবিদ্যা mônobidya *n* psychology

মনোভঙ্গ mônobhɔngô *n* dejection, despondency

মনোভাব mônobhab *n* attitude, disposition

মনোমধ্যে mônomôdhye *adv* inwardly, secretly

মনোযোগ mônoyog *n* attention, concentration

মনোরম mônorɔm *adj* delightful, pleasant

মন্তব্য mɔntôbyô *n* remark, comment

মন্ত্র mɔntrô *n* mantra, spell; counsel, advice

মন্ত্রী môntrī *n* minister

মন্থর mɔnthôr *adj* slack, sluggish

মন্দ môndô *adj* bad, evil, wicked

মন্দির môndir *n* temple *(Hindu)*

মন্দ্র mɔndrô *n* bass; *adj* low *(of sound)*, deep, rumbling

মমতা mɔmota *n* love, affection

ময়দা mɔŷda *n* flour

ময়দান mɔŷdan *n* open road; plain; parade

ময়লা mɔŷla *n* refuse, litter, rubbish; *adj* dirty, filthy, soiled

ময়ূর môŷur *n* peacock

মর mɔr *adj* mortal, perishable, transient

মরণ mɔrôṇ *n* death

মরা mɔra *vb* die, pass away

মরামাস mɔramas *n* dandruff

মরাল mɔral *n* flamingo; swan; gander

মরিচ môric *n* pepper, chili

মরিচা môrica *(Bd)*, মর্চে môrce *(WB) n* rust

মরীচিকা môrīcika *n* mirage

মরু môru, মরুভূমি môrubhūmi *n* wilderness, desert

মরুদ্যান môrudyæn *n* oasis

মরে যাওয়া môre yaoŷa *vb* die

মর্জি môrji *n* fancy, whim, caprice

মর্দন mɔrdôn *n* massage, thrashing, pounding, kneading

মর্ম mɔrmô *n* heart, inmost feelings

মর্মর mɔrmɔr *n* marble

মর্মার্থ mɔrmarthô *n* gist, inner significance

মর্মাহত mɔrmahɔtô *adj* mortified, deeply hurt

মর্যাদা môryada *n* dignity, honor, respect

মলম mɔlôm *n* ointment, balm

মলমল mɔlmɔl *n* muslin

মলা mɔla *vb* thresh, knead, massage

মলাট mɔlaṭ *n* book cover

মলাশয় mɔlaśɔŷ *n* colon

মলিন môlin *adj* glum, dark, over-cast

মল্ল mɔllô *n* wrestler; athlete

মশলা mɔśla, মসলা mɔsla *n* spice, seasoning

মশা mɔśa *n* mosquito

মশারি mɔśari *n* mosquito net

মসজিদ môsjid *n* mosque

মসনদ mɔsnɔd *n* throne

মসুর môsur, মসুরি môsuri *n* kind of lentils

মসৃণ môsṛṇ (*pron* mosrin) *adj* smooth, sleek, even

মস্ত mɔstô *adj* high, tall, lofty

মস্তক mɔstôk *n* head, cranium, skull

মস্তিষ্ক môstiṣkô *n* brain

মহড়া mɔhôṛa *n* rehearsal, practice

মহৎ mɔhôṯ *adj* noble, sublime

মহল mɔhôl *n* palace, mansion

মহলা mɔhôla *n* rehearsal, practice

মহল্লা mɔhôlla *n* district, area

মহা mɔha *adj* great, main, chief

মহাকাশ mɔhakaś *n* outer space

মহাকাশচারী mɔhakaścarī *n* astronaut

মহামন্ত্রী mɔhamôntrī *n* prime minister

মহাশয় mɔhaśɔŷ *n address* Sir, Mister (*Hindu*)

মহিমা môhima *n* greatness, glory, divine grace

মহিলা môhila *n* woman, lady

মহিষ môhiṣ *n* water buffalo

মহী môhī *n* earth, ground, soil

মহীয়ান môhīŷan *adj* noble, exalted, majestic

মা ma *n* mother

মাইনা maina, মাইনে maine *n* monthly wages

মাইনে দেওয়া maine deôŷa *vb* pay heed, take notice

মাংস maṁsô *n* meat

মাকড়সা makôṛsa *n* spider

মাকু maku *n* shuttle

মাখন makhôn *n* butter

মাখা makha *vb* smear, dab, mix

মাগনা magna *adj* obtained by begging, free

মাগা maga *vb* beg, ask for, solicit

মাঙ্গলিক maṅgôlik *adj* auspicious, propitious (*Hindu*)

মাচা maca *n* platform, scaffold

মাছ mach *n* fish

মাছি machi *n* fly

মাজা maja *vb* scour, scrub, cleanse

মাঝ majh *n* middle, center, interior

মাঝখানে majhkhane *adv* in the middle, inside

মাঝামাঝি majhamajhi *adj* middle, central

মাঝি majhi *n* boatman

মাঝে majhe *pp* in between, in the middle

মাটি maṭi *n* earth, clay, soil, ground

মাটি দেওয়া maṭi deôŷa *vb* bury, inter

মাঠ maṭh *n* field, open land

মাড় maṛ *n* starch

মাড়া maṛa, মাড়ানো maṛano *vb* pound, thresh, tread

মাত mat *n* checkmate, defeat

মাতব্বর matôbbôr *n* leader, headman

মাতলামি matlami *n* revelry, drunkenness

মাতাপিতা matapita *n* parents

মাতাল matal *adj* intoxicated, drunken

মাতুল matul *n* maternal uncle

মাতৃভাষা matṛbhaṣa *n* mother tongue

মাতোয়ারা matoŷara *adj* rapt, besotted

মাত্র matrô *adv* only, merely, just

মাত্রা matra *n* amount, measure, degree

মাথা matha *n* head, top, summit

মাথা খারাপ matha kharap *adj* crazy, mad

মাথা ঘামানো matha ghamano *vb* think hard, worry

মাথা ধরা matha dhɔra *vb* have a headache

মাথা ব্যথা matha bytha *n* headache

মাদক madôk *adj* intoxicating, drugging; *n* intoxicant

মাদুর madur *n* mat, grass mat

মাদুলি maduli *n* amulet

মাধুর্য madhuryô *n* sweetness, pleasantness, beauty

মাধ্যম madhyôm *n* medium

মাধ্যমিক madhyômik *adj* middle, medium

মাধ্যাকর্ষণ madhyakɔrṣôṇ *n* gravity, gravitation

মানচিত্র mancitrô *n* map, chart

মাননীয় manônîŷô *adj* respected, honorable

মানব manôb *n* mankind

মানবজাতি manôbjati *n* mankind, the human race

মানবতা manôbɔta *n* humanity

মানমন্দির manmôndir *n* observatory

মানসিক manôsik *n* mental, imaginary

মানহানি manhani *n* defamation, libel

মানা mana *vb* honor, respect; observe

মানানো manano *vb* fit, suit, compromise

মানী manî *adj* honored, respected, respectable

মানুষ manuṣ *n* human being, person

মানে mane *n* meaning, import

মান্য manyô *n* honor, respect

মাপ map, মাফ maph *n* pardon, excuse

মাপ map *n* measure, dimension

মাপা mapa *vb* weigh, measure, survey

মামলা mamla *n* lawsuit, case, process

মামা mama *n* uncle *(mother's brother)*

মামুলি mamuli *adj* hackneyed, trite

মায়া maŷa *n* illusion, infatuation, pity, compassion

মায়াবি maŷabi *adj* deceitful, enchanting, infatuating

মায়ামমতা maŷamɔmôta *n* love and affection

মায়াময় maŷamɔŷ *adj* illusory, treacherous

মার mar *n* beating, striking

মারা mara *vb* hit, strike; kill

মারামারি maramari *n* scuffle, fight, affray

মারা যাওয়া mara yaoŷa *vb* die

মার্কিন markin *adj* American

মাল mal *n* merchandise, wares

মালপত্র malpɔtrô *n* baggage, luggage

মালঞ্চ malôñcô *n* flower garden

মালা mala *n* garland; necklace

মালিক malik *n* owner, proprietor

মালিশ maliś *n* massage

মাস mas *n* month

মাসি masi *n* aunt *(mother's sister, Hindu)*

মাসিক masik *adj* monthly

মাসুল masul *n* duty, customs, compensation

মাস্তুল mastul *n* mast (of a ship)

মাহাত্ম্য mahatmyô *n* high-mindedness, nobility, excellence

মিছরি michri *n* sugar candy

মিছিল michil *n* procession

মিট করা miṭ kɔra *vb* settle, balance

মিটমাট miṭmaṭ *n* compromise, settlement

মিটা miṭa *see* মেটা meṭa

মিটানো miṭano, মেটানো meṭano *vb* accomplish, finish, settle, compromise

মিঠা miṭha *adj* sweet, delicious, palatable

মিত mitô *adj* temperate, moderate

মিতব্যয়িতা mitôbyæ̂yita *n* frugality, thriftiness

মিতাচার mitacar *n* temperance, abstemiousness

মিত্র mitrô *n* friend

মিথ্যা mithya *(Bd)*, মিথ্যে mithye *(WB) n* lie, untruth

মিথ্যা কথা mithya kɔtha *n* lie, falsehood

মিথ্যা কথা বলা mithya kɔtha bɔla *vb* tell a lie

মিথ্যাচার mithyacar *n* hypocrisy, falsehood, treachery

মিথ্যাবাদী mithyabadī *n* liar

মিথ্যুক mithyuk *n* liar

মিনতি minôti *n* entreaty, request

মিনমিনে minmine *adj* faint-hearted, timid

মিনা mina *n* enamel

মিনার minar *n* tower

মিনিট miniṭ *n* minute

মিয়ানো miẏano *(Bd)*, মিয়োনো miẏono *(WB) vb* droop, go soggy, lose crispness

মিল mil *n* likeness, similarity

মিলন milôn *n* unity, coming together, meeting

মিলন করা milôn kɔra *vb* unite, have sexual intercourse

মিলা mila *see* মেলা mela

মিলিত militô *adj* combined, joined

মিশন miśôn *n* mission

মিশা miśa *see* মেশা meśa

মিশানো miśano *vb* mix, blend, join, unite

মিশুক miśuk *adj* sociable, friendly

মিশ্র miśrô *adj* blended, mixed

মিষ্টি miṣṭi *n* sweetmeat; *adj* sweet

মিস্ত্রি mistri *n* carpenter; mechanic

মিহি mihi *adj* refined, subtle

মীমাংসা mīimamsa *n* solution, reconciliation

মুকাবিলা mukabila, মোকাবিলা mokabila *n* settlement; confrontation

মুকাবিলা করা mukabila kɔra *vb* face, confront

মুকুট mukuṭ *n* crown, diadem

মুকুল mukul *n* bud, blossom

মুক্ত muktô *adj* free, liberated

মুক্তা mukta *(Bd)*, মুক্তো mukto *(WB) n* pearl

মুক্তি mukti *n* freedom, liberation

মুখ mukh *n* face

মুখের কথা mukher kɔtha *n* empty phrase, pretence

মুখবন্ধ mukhôbɔndhô *n* preface

মুখর mukhɔr *adj* garrulous, talkative

মুখস্থ mukhôstô *adj* memorized by heart

মুখামুখি mukhamukhi *(Bd)*, মুখোমুখি mukhomukhi *(WB) adv* face-to-face

মুগুর mugur *n* mallet, club, cudgel

মুগ্ধ mugdhô *adj* fascinated, entranced

মুগ্ধ করা mugdhô kɔra *vb* fascinate

মুচকানো muckano *vb* sprain, twist, injure

মুচকে হাসা mucke hasa *vb* smirk, grin

মুছা mucha *see* মোছা mocha

মুঠ muṭh *n* handful, fist

মুড়া mura *see* মোড়া mora

মুড়ি muri *n* parched rice; snack

মুতা muta *see* মোতা mota

মুদা muda *see* মোদা moda

মুদি mudi *n* grocer

মুদ্দত muddôtô *n* deadline

মুদ্রণ mudrɔṇ *n* printing, stamping, impression

মুদ্রা mudra *n* coin; seal; stamp

মুদ্রাকর mudrakɔr *n* printer

মুনশি munśi *n* clerk, secretary, scribe

মুনাফা munapha *n* profit, gain

মুনি muni *n* sage, hermit, ascetic

মুরগি murgi *n* chicken, hen

মুলতবি multôbi *adj* postponed, adjourned

মুলা mula, মূলা mūla *n* radish

মুশকিল muśkil *n* problem, difficulty

মুষ্টি muṣṭi *n* handful; palm of the hand

মুসলমান musôlman *n* Muslim

মুসুরি musuri *n* kind of lentils

মুহূর্ত muhūrtô *n* moment, point in time

মূর্খ mūrkhô *adj* foolish, stupid, ignorant

মূর্ছা mūrcha *n* fainting fit, swoon

মূর্ছারোগ mūrcharog *n* epilepsy

মূর্ত mūrtô *adj* concrete, material

মূর্তি mūrti *n* statue; appearance; shape

মূল mūl *n* root, bulb

মূলগত mūlôgɔtô *adj* fundamental, basic

মূলা mūla *n* radish

মূল্য mūlyô *n* value, worth, cost

মূল্যবান mūlyôban *adj* precious, valuable

মূল্যায়ন mūlyaŷôn *n* assessment

মূল্যহীন mūlyôhīn *adj* worthless, valueless

মৃগ mŕgô *n* deer, stag, antelope

মৃগয়া mŕgɔŷa *n* hunting for deer, game-hunting

মৃগী mŕgī *n* doe

মৃগী –রোগ mŕgī-rog *n* epilepsy

মৃত mŕtô *adj* dead, deceased, lifeless

মৃত্যু mŕtyu *n* death

মৃত্যুকাল mŕtyukal *n* moment of death

মৃত্যুদণ্ড mŕtyudɔṇḍô *n* death penalty, capital punishment

মৃদু mŕdu *adj* soft, supple, delicate

মেকি meki *adj* counterfeit, fake

মেঘ megh *n* cloud

মেঘলা meghla *adj* cloudy, overcast

মেছতা mechta *n* freckles

মেজ mej, মেজো mejo *adj* second-born, middle

মেজাজ mejaj *n* temperament, mood

মেজে meje, মেঝে mejhe *n* floor

মেটা meṭa, মিটা miṭa *vb* be accomplished, be finished

মেথর mæthôr *n* scavenger, sweeper

মেদ med *n* fat; marrow

মেধা medha *n* intellect, power, memory

মেনিমুখো menimukhô *adj* bashful, shy

মেয়াদ meŷad *n* appointed time, time limit

মেয়ে meye *n* girl; daughter

মেরামত করা meramɔt kɔra *vb* repair, mend

মেরু meru *n* pole, axis

মেরুদণ্ড merudɔɳɖô *n* spine, backbone

মেলা mela (*also* মিলা mila) *vb* mix, combine, fit together

মেলা mæla *adj* manifold, plenty, numerous; *n* fair; *vb* open

মেলামেশা melameśa, মিলামিশা milamiśa *n* social contact, familiarity, intimate association

মেলামেশা করা melameśa kɔra *vb* mix freely

মেশা meśa, মিশা miśa *vb* mingle, be mixed, be blended together

মেশিন meśin *n* machine

মেসো meso *n* uncle (*mother's sister's husband, Hindu*)

মেহনত mehônɔt *n* physical labor, toil

মেহমান mehôman *n* guest

মেহেদি mehedi *n* henna

মৈত্র moitrô *n* friendship, alliance

মোক্ষ mokṣô *n* salvation, release, nirvana

মোক্ষম mokṣôm *adj* unfailing, irrefutable

মোচ moc *n* nib (of pen), moustache

মোচড়ানো mocṛano *vb* twist, wrench

মোছা mocha, মুছা mucha *vb* wipe, mop, swab

মোজা moja *n* socks

মোট moṭ *n* total, sum total

মোটা moṭa *adj* fat, corpulent, bulky

মোটামুটি moṭamuṭi *adv* more or less, roughly

মোটে moṭe *adv* altogether, in total

মোড় moṛ *n* bend, turn

মোড়া mora *n* wicker stool; *vb* (*also* মুড়া mura) wrap, enfold, cover

মোড়ক morôk *n* package, parcel

মোতা mota, মুতা muta *vb* urinate

মোদা moda, মুদা muda *vb* close, shut

মোম mom *n* wax, beeswax

মোমবাতি mombati *n* candle

মোয়া moŷa *n* ball of sweet parched rice; sweet

মোরগ morôg *n* cock, fowl

মোলায়েম molaŷem *adj* smooth, suave

মোহ mohô *n* illusion, fascination, obsession

মোহনীয় mohônīŷô *adj* fascinating

মৌখিক moukhik *adj* verbal, oral

মৌচাক moucak *n* beehive

মৌমাছি moumachi *n* bee, honeybee

মৌলিক moulik *adj* basic, fundamental, primary

মৌসুম mousum *n* season, fixed time

ম্যাপ myæp *n* map

ম্যালেরিয়া myæleriŷa *n* malaria

ম্লান mlan *adj* dim, pale, wan

য y

যকৃৎ yôkṛt *n* liver

যখন yɔkhôn *conj* when

যত yɔtô *conj* as much as, until

যতক্ষণ yɔtôkṣɔṇ *conj* as long as

যতি yôti *n* punctuation

যত্ন yɔtnô *n* care, attention

যথা yɔtha *adv* for instance, namely

যথাযথ yɔthayɔthô *adj* accurate, right, correct

যথার্থ yɔtharthô *adj* accurate, right, correct

যথেষ্ট yɔtheṣṭô *adj* sufficient, enough

যদি yôdi *conj* if, in case

যন্ত্র yɔntrô *n* device, tool, instrument

যন্ত্রণা yɔntrôṇa *n* pain, torture

যব yɔb *n* barley

যমজ yɔmôj *n* twin

যমুনা yômuna *n* Jamuna *(river)*

যশ yɔś *n* fame, renown

যষ্টি yôṣṭi *n* stick, staff, rod

যা ya *pr* that

যাওয়া yaoŷa *vb* go, move, proceed, advance, leave

যাচাই yacai *n* estimate

যাচাই করা yacai kɔra *vb* estimate, guess

যাচানো yacano *vb* evaluate, determine

যাজক yajôk *n* priest, clergyman

যাতায়াত yataŷat *n* traffic, coming and going

যাতে yate *conj* so that

যাত্রা yatra *n* journey

যাত্রী yatrī *n* passenger

যান yan *n* vehicle, carriage

যানবাহন yanbahôn *n* transport

যান্ত্রিক yantrik *adj* mechanical

যাবৎ yabôt *conj* until, as long as

যাবতীয় yabôtīŷô *adv* all in all, whatever

যায়–যায় yaŷ-yaŷ *adj* almost exhausted, almost finished

যাযাবর yayabɔr *n* nomad, Gypsy

যুক্ত yuktô *adj* joined, connected, compound, united

যুক্তি yukti *n* connection, reason, logic, argument

যুক্তিহীন yuktihīn *adj* irrational, unreasonable

যুগ yug *n* era, epoch

যুগল yugɔl *n* yoke, brace; pair

যুঝা yujha *see* যোঝা yojha

যুদ্ধ yuddhô *n* war, fight, battle

যুদ্ধবিরতি yuddhôbirôti *n* truce, ceasefire, armistice

যুবক yubɔk *n* youth, young man

যুবতি yubôti *n* young girl

যুবাকাল yubakal *n* youth

যূথ yūth *n* flock, herd

যে ye *pr, conj* that, which, the one who

যেন yænô *conj* so that

যেমন yæmôn *adv* as, like, for instance; *conj* as if

যেহেতু yehetu *conj* because, since, as

যোগ yog *n* union, blending, mixture, connection; addition

যোগ করা yog kɔra *vb* unite, mix, blend, add

যোগাড় yogaṛ *n* procurement, obtaining, collecting

যোগানো yogano *vb* supply, purvey

যোগাযোগ yogayog *n* contact, association

যোগ্য yogyô *adj* suitable, worthy, fit, deserving

যোগ্যতা yogyôta *n* eligibility,
  worthiness
যোজন yoyôn *n* mixing; application;
  employment
যোজনা yojôna *n* planning
যোঝা yojha, যুঝা yujha *vb* struggle,
  contend with
যোদ্ধা yoddha *n* warrior, fighter
যোনি yoni *n* vagina
যৌতুক youtuk *n* dowry
যৌন younô *adj* sexual
যৌবন youbôn *n* youth

র r

রওনা rɔona *n* departure

রওয়া rɔôya *vb* be, remain

রকম rɔkôm *n* sort, kind, manner, variety

রক্ত rɔktô *n* blood

রক্ত পড়া rɔktô pɔṛa *vb* bleed

রক্তরস rɔktôrɔs *n* plasma

রক্তস্রাব rɔktôsrab *n* hemorrhage

রক্তাক্ত rɔktaktô *adj* blood-stained

রক্তিম rôktim *adj* red, crimson

রক্ষা rôkṣa *n* protection, defense

রক্ষা করা rôkṣa kɔra *vb* protect, save, guard

রক্ষিত rôkṣitô *adj* protected, guarded

রঙ rɔṅ, রং rɔṁ (*pron* rɔng) *n* color, hue; dye; paint

রঙ্গ rɔṅgô *n* joke, fun, frolic

রঙ্গ করা rɔṅgô kɔra *vb* make fun of, joke

রঙিন rôṅin, রঙ্গিন rôṅgin *adj* colored, dyed, variegated

রচনা rɔcôna *n* composition, structure

রচয়িতা rɔcôŷita *n* composer, maker, builder

রজন rɔjôn *n* resin

রজনীগন্ধা rɔjônīgɔndha *n* tuberose

রজোবন্ধ rɔjobɔndhô *n* menopause

রজ্জু rôjju *n* rope

রটন rɔṭôn, রটনা rɔṭôna *n* circulation; announcement; rumor

রটানো rɔṭano *vb* circulate, spread

রণ rɔṇ *n* battle, war

রণনীতি rɔṇônīti *n* strategy, tactics

রত্ন rɔtnô *n* jewel

রত্নাবলী rɔtnabôlī *n* gems

রথ rɔth *n* chariot

রদ rɔd *adj* nullified, revoked

রপ্ত rɔptô *adj* accustomed, acclimatized

রপ্তানি rɔptani *n* export

রফা rɔpha *n* settlement, compromise

রবার rɔbar *n* rubber

রবি rôbi *n* sun

রবিবার rôbibar *n* Sunday

রমনী rɔmônī *n* woman; wife

রমনীয় rɔmônīŷô *adj* delightful, beautiful

রশি rôśi *n* rope, cord

রস rɔs *n* juice, liquid; flavor

রসকষ rɔskɔṣ *n* charm, sweetness

রসগ্রহণ rɔsôgrôhôṇ *n* appreciation, taste

রসানো rɔsano *vb* add spice, add interest

রসায়ন rɔsaŷôn *n* elixir; chemistry

রসাল rɔsalô *adj* succulent, juicy, tasty

রসিক rôsik *adj* witty, humorous

রসুন rôsun *n* garlic

রহস্য rɔhôsyô *n* mystery, riddle

রহিত rôhitô *adj* lacking, devoid of, bereft

রাই rai *n* mustard

রাংতা raṁta *n* tinsel, tinfoil

রাঁধা rādha *vb* cook

রাক্ষস rakṣôs *n* glutton, greedy person; Rakshasa *(demon)*

রাখা rakha *vb* place, put, keep

রাখাল rakhal *n* cowherd, herdsman

রাগ rag *n* anger, passion, rage

রাগ করা rag kɔra *vb* be angry, get angry

রাগানো ragano *vb* enrage, make angry

রাগী ragī *adj* quick-tempered, hotheaded

রাজকন্যা rajkɔnya *n* princess

রাজ করা raj kɔra *vb* rule over

রাজকুমারী rajkumarī *n* princess

রাজত্ব rajôtvô *n* kingdom, reign, rule

রাজধানী rajdhanī *n* capital, capital city

রাজনীতি rajnīti *n* politics

রাজনৈতিক rajnoitik *adj* political

রাজপুত্র rajputrô *n* prince, crown prince

রাজবাড়ি rajbaṛi *n* palace

রাজহাঁস rajhās *n* goose; swan

রাজা raja *n* king

রাজি raji *adj* in agreement, consenting

রাজ্য rajyô *n* kingdom, reign, rule, territory

রাত rat *n* night

রাত্রি ratri *n* night, night-time

রানী ranī *n* queen

রান্না করা ranna kɔra *vb* cook

রান্নাঘর rannaghɔr *n* kitchen

রামধনু ramdhônu *n* rainbow

রায় raŷ *n* judgement, verdict

রাশি raśi *n* heap, pile

রাষ্ট্র raṣṭrô *n* state, country, kingdom

রাষ্ট্রপতি raṣṭrôpôti *n* president, head of state

রাসায়নিক rasaŷônik *adj* chemical, of chemistry

রাস্তা rasta *n* road, way

রাহাজানি rahajani *n* highway robbery

রিক্ত riktô *adj* deprived, poor, empty

রিকশা rikśa *n* rickshaw

রিপু ripu *n* enemy, adversary

রিফু riphu *n* darning, sowing

রিমঝিম rimjhim *onom* pattering (*rain*)

রীতি rīti *n* method, mode, custom, rule, convention

রীতিমত rītimɔtô *adv* regularly, properly, downright

রুইতন ruitɔn *n* diamonds (*in cards*)

রুক্ষ rukṣô *adj* rough, harsh, rude

রুচি ruci *n* taste, inclination, liking

রুটি ruṭi *n* bread

রুদ্ধ ruddhô *adj* shut, closed, bolted

রুমাল rumal *n* handkerchief

রুষ্ট ruṣṭô *adj* angry, enraged, furious

রূপ rūp *n* form, figure, shape; beauty; kind, sort

রূপকথা rūpkɔtha *n* folk-legend, tale

রূপা rūpa *(Bd)*, রূপো rupo *(WB) n* silver

রূপান্তর rūpantôr *n* transformation, metamorphosis

রূপায়ণ rūpaŷôṇ *n* embodiment; narration; impersonation

রেওয়াজ reoŷaj *n* custom, usage, practice

রেখা rekha *n* line, row, stripe

রেখাকার rekhakar *adj* linear

রেখাগণিত rekhagôṇit *n* geometry

রেণু reṇu *n* dust, pollen, powder

রেলগাড়ি relgaṛi *n* train

রেশ reś *n* trace, vestige

রেশম reśɔm *n* silk

রেহাই rehai *n* exemption, escape, acquittal

রোগ rog *n* illness, disease

রোগা roga *adj* thin, delicate, slim

রোগা–পাতলা roga–patla *adj* slim, thin, delicate

রোগী rogī *n* patient

রোজ roj *adj* daily, everyday

রোজা roja *n* fasting, fasting during the month of Ramadan

রোদ rod *n* sun; sunshine

রোধ rodh *n* obstruction, blockade

রোপন ropôn *n* plantation; act of sowing

রোম rom *n* bodyhair

রোমন্থন romônthôn *n* rumination

রোমশ romôś *adj* hairy, woolly, furry

রোশনাই rośnai *n* illumination, lustre

রোষ roṣ *n* anger, wrath, rage

রৌদ্র roudrô *n* sun; sunshine

ল।

লওয়া lɔôŷa *vb* take, take hold of, catch, seize

লকলকে lɔklɔke *onom* dangling, lolling; flashing

লক্ষ lôkṣô *num* a hundred thousand

লক্ষণ lôkṣôn *n* sign, mark, indication, symptom, characteristic

লক্ষিত lôkṣitô *adj* noticed, seen, observed

লক্ষ্মী lôkṣmi (*pron* lokkhi) *adj* well-behaved, good-natured, sweet

লক্ষ্মীছাড়া lôkṣmichara *adj* good-for-nothing

লক্ষ্য lôkṣyô *n* target, aim, intention; look, glance

লক্ষ্য করা lôkṣyô kɔra *vb* notice, observe; intend, aim at

লক্ষ্য রাখা lôkṣyô rakha *vb* keep watch, keep an eye on

লগ্নি lôgni *n* investment

লঘিষ্ঠ lôghiṣṭhô *adj* lightest, smallest, minimum

লঘু lôghu *adj* light, small, easy

লঘুকরণ lôghukɔrôn *n* reduction, simplification

লঘুচিত্ত lôghucittô *adj* lighthearted, flippant, frivolous

লঘুজ্ঞান lôghujñan (*pron* loghugæn) *n* disregard, slight

লঙ্কা lɔṅka *n* capsicum; green chilli

লঙ্গ lɔṅgô, লবঙ্গ lɔbôṅgô *n* clove

লজ্জা lɔjja *n* embarrassment, shame, diffidence

লজ্জিত lôjjitô *adj* embarrassed, ashamed

লটকানো lɔṭkano *vb* hang, hang up, post

লড়া lɔra *vb* fight, wrestle, contend

লড়াই lɔrai *n* fight, wrestle

লতা lɔta *n* creeper

লবণ lɔbôn *n* salt

লব্ধ lɔbdhô *adj* obtained, earned, acquired, gained

লভ্য lɔbhyô *adj* obtainable

লম্পট lɔmpɔṭ *adj* lascivious, licentious

লম্বা lɔmba *adj* long, tall, lengthy

লম্বালম্বি lɔmbalômbi *adv* lengthways

লয় lɔŷ *n* merging, fusion; ruin

ললনা lɔlôna *n* woman, lady

ললাট lɔlaṭ *n* temple, forehead; luck

ললিত lôlitô *adj* beautiful, pleasant, charming

লসিকা lôsika *n* lymph

লাইন lain *n* line, system, queue

লাউ lau *n* bottle-gourd

লাখ lakh *num* one hundred thousand

লাগসই lagsôi *adj* appropriate, fitting

লাগা laga *vb* contact, touch, be attached to, stick; begin, start; feel, need

লাগাড় lagar *n* continuity, stretch

লাগানো lagano *vb* plant, attach, apply, employ, engage

লাগাম lagam *n* bridle, reins

লাঘব laghôb *n* decrease, reduction, relief

লাঙ্গল laṅgôl *n* plow, plowshare

লাজুক lajuk *adj* shy, bashful

লাঞ্ছনা lañchôna *n* reproach, reprimand

লাট laṭ *adj* crumpled, awkward, awry, ruffled

লাটাই laṭai *n* reel, spool

লাঠি laṭhi *n* stick, staff

লাথি lathi *n* kick

লাথি দেওয়া lathi deoŷa, লাথি মারা lathi mara *vb* kick

লাপাত্তা lapatta *(Bd) adj* vanished, traceless

লাফ laph *n* leap, jump, skip

লাভ labh *n* profit, gain, income

লাম্পট্য lampôṭyô *n* lasciviousness, debauchery

লায়েক laŷek *adj* grown-up, competent, over-confident

লাল lal *adj* red

লালসা lalôsa *n* greed, desire, lust

লালা lala *n* saliva, spittle

লালিত্য lalityô *n* beauty, charm

লাশ laś *n* human body, corpse

লিকলিকে liklike *adj* slender, thin

লিখা likha *see* লেখা lekha

লিখিত likhitô *adj* written, composed

লিঙ্গ liṅgô *n* sex, gender; penis

লিচু licu *n* lychee

লিপি lipi *n* manuscript; letter, epistle

লিপিকার lipikar *n* copyist, scribe

লিপিবিদ্যা lipibidya *n* calligraphy

লিপ্ত liptô *adj* involved in, engaged in

লীলা līla *n* pleasure, dalliance, frolic

লুকাচুরি lukacuri *(Bd)*, লুকোচুরি lukocuri *(WB) n* hide-and-seek

লুকানো lukano *(Bd)*, লুকোনো lukono *(WB) vb* hide

লুকিয়ে রাখা lukiŷe rakha *vb* keep hidden, conceal

লুঙ্গি luṅgi *n* lungi, long loincloth

লুচি luci *n* sweet fried bread

লুচ্চা lucca *adj* lewd, vulgar

লুট luṭ *n* plunder, robbery, loot

লুপ্ত luptô *adj* extinct, defunct, hidden

লুব্ধ lubdhô *adj* greedy, avaricious; tempted

লেই lei *n* glue, paste

লেংটা læṁṭa *adj* naked, nude; destitute

লেংড়া læṁṛa *adj* lame

লেখক lekhɔk *n* writer

লেখা lekha, লিখা likha *vb* write

লেখাপড়া lekhapɔra *n* study, education

লেজ lej *n* tail

লেঠা læṭha *n* trouble, difficulty

লেনদেন lenden *n* transaction, exchange

লেপ lep *n* quilt

লেপটানো læpṭano *vb* wrap around oneself, huddle into

লেপন lepôn *n* coating, smearing

লেপা læpa *vb* coat, wash, smear

লেফাফা lephapha *n* envelope

লেবু lebu *n* lemon

লেলানো lælano *vb* incite, attack, set upon

লেশ leś *n* trace, shadow

লোক lok *n* person, human being

লোকগণনা lokgɔṇôna *n* census

লোকগীতি lokôgīti *n* folksong

লোকজন lokjɔn *n* people

লোকপ্রিয় lokôpriŷô *adj* popular, favorite

লোকসংখ্যা lokôsɔṁkhya *n* population

লোকসান loksan *n* loss, harm, damage

লোকাচার lokacar *n* custom; usage

লোকান্তর lokantɔr *n* life beyond death, the hereafter

লোকায়ত lokaŷɔtô *adj* secular

লোকালয় lokalɔŷ *n* habitation, settlement

লোচন locôn *n* eye

লোটা loṭa *vb* plunder, rob, loot

লোনা lona *adj* salty, saline, salted

লোপ lop *n* abolition, destruction, disappearance

লোপ করা lop kɔra *vb* abolish, get rid of, vanish

লোফা lopha *vb* take hold of, catch

লোভ lobh *n* greed, covetousness, avarice

লোভ দেখানো lobh dækhano *vb* tempt, allure

লোভী lobhī *adj* greedy, easily tempted

লোম lom *n* bodyhair, fur

লোমশ lomôś *adj* hairy, hirsute

লোল lol *adj* restless, eager, loose

লোলচর্ম lolôcɔrmô *n* wrinkles, weathered skin

লোলুপ lolup *adj* greatly tempted, greedy

লোহা loha *n* iron

লৌকিক loukik *adj* social, public, secular, worldly, terrestrial

শ ś

শ śɔ, শত śɔtô *n* one hundred

শংসন śɔṁsôn, শংসা śɔṁsa *n* praise, compliment

শকট śɔkôṭ *n* vehicle, carriage, wagon

শকুন śôkun *n* vulture

শক্ত śɔktô *adj* strong, firm, hard

শক্তি śôkti *n* power, strength, vigor

শক্তিশালী śôktiśalī *adj* powerful, strong

শখ śɔkh *n* inclination, fancy; hobby

শঙ্কা śɔṅka *n* fear, dread, terror

শঙ্কু śôṅku *n* cone, wedge

শঙ্খ śɔṅkhô *n* conch shell

শজিনা śôjina, শজনে śɔjne *n* horseradish

শঠ śɔṭh *adj* deceitful

শতাংশ śɔtaṁśô *n* percent

শতাব্দ śɔtabdô *n* century

শত্রু śôtru *n* enemy, opponent

শত্রুতা śôtruta *n* enmity, hostility

শনাক্ত śɔnaktô *n* identification

শনিবার śônibar *n* Saturday

শপথ śɔpôth *n* oath, vow, promise

শপথ করা śɔpôth kɔra *vb* swear

শব śɔb, শবদেহ śɔbdehô *n* corpse

শব–চুল্লি śɔb-culli *n* crematorium

শব্দ śɔbdô *n* sound, word, noise

শব্দকোষ śɔbdôkoṣ *n* vocabulary, glossary

শব্দতত্ত্ব śɔbdôtɔttvô *n* philology

শব্দার্থ śɔbdarthô *n* meaning (of a word)

শব্দার্থতত্ত্ব śɔbdarthôtɔttvô *n* semantics

শম śɔmô *n* restraint, control

শমিত śômitô *adj* restrained, suppressed

শম্বুক śômbuk *n* snail

শয়তান śɔytan *n* devil, wicked person

শয়তানি śɔytani *n* wickedness

শয্যা śɔyya (*pron* shɔjja) *n* bed, bedding

শর śɔr *n* arrow, shaft

শরৎ śɔrôṯ *n* autumn

শরবত śɔrbôt *n* sweet drink, sherbet

শরম śɔrôm *n* shame, modesty

শরিফ śôriph *adj* magnanimous, high-minded

শরীর śôrīr *n* body

শর্ত śɔrtô *n* condition, stipulation

শলা śɔla, শল্য śɔlyô *n* skewer, probe, thorn

শশক śɔśôk *n* hare, rabbit

শশিকর śôśikɔr *n* moonlight, moonbeam

শশা śɔśa *n* cucumber

শস্ত্র śɔstrô *n* weapon, iron tool

শস্য śôsyô *n* corn, grain, cereal

শহর śɔhôr *n* town, city

শহীদ śôhīd *n* martyr

শহুরে śôhure *adj* urban

শাঁখ śākh *n* conch shell

শাঁস śās *n* kernel, pulp

শাক śak *n* spinach

শাকসবজি śaksôbji *n* green vegetables

শাখা śakha *n* branch, sect

শাড়ি śari *n* saree

শাদি śadi *n* marriage (*Muslim*)

শান śan, শানপাথর śanpathɔr *n* whetstone, grindstone

শান দেওয়া śan deoŷa *vb* excite, instigate, stimulate

শানা śana, শানানো śanano *vb* whet, sharpen

শান্ত śantô *adj* peaceful, quiet

শান্তি śanti *n* peace

শাপ śap *n* curse

শাপলা śapla *n* water lily

শাবাশ śabaś *int* bravo, well done

শামিয়ানা śamiŷana *n* awning, canopy

শামিল śamil *adj* included, annexed

শামুক śamuk *n* snail, shell, conch

শায়েস্তা śaŷesta *adj* subdued, chastened, broken, tamed

শারীরিক śarīrik *adj* bodily, physical

শার্ট śart *n* shirt

শাল śal *n* shawl

শালগম śalgɔm *n* turnip

শালা śala *n* brother-in-law *(wife's younger brother)*

শালি śali *n* autumnal paddy

শালিক śalik *n* small blackbird

শালী śalī *n* sister-in-law *(wife's younger sister)*

শালীন śalīn *adj* bashful, modest, shy

শালুক śaluk *n* stalk of the water lily

শাশুড়ী śaśuṛī *n* mother-in-law

শাসক śasɔk *n* subduer, ruler, governor

শাসন śasɔn *n* rule, chastisement, control

শাসানি śasani *n* threat

শাস্তি śasti *n* punishment, sentence

শাস্ত্র śastrɔ *n* scripture

শাহ্ śah *n* ruler, king, shah

শাহজাদা śahjada *n* prince, son of a shah

শিং śim *n* horn

শিকড় śikɔṛ *n* root

শিকনি śikni *n* nasal mucus

শিকল śikɔl *n* chain, fetters

শিকার śikar *n* hunting

শিকার করা śikar kɔra *vb* hunt

শিক্ষক śikṣɔk *n* teacher

শিক্ষা śikṣa *n* education, learning

শিক্ষানবিশ śikṣanôbiś *n* apprentice, novice

শিক্ষানবিশি śikṣanôbiśi *n* apprenticeship

শিক্ষিকা śikṣika *n* teacher *(fem)*

শিক্ষিত śikṣitô *adj* educated

শিখা śikha *n* point, crest

শিগ্‌গির śiggir *adj* quickly, fast

শিঙা śiṅa *n* trumpet

শিঙাড়া śiṅaṛa *n* stuffed vegetable pasty

শিথিল śithil *adj* loose, flabby, baggy

শিব śib *n* Shiva

শিবিকা śibika *n* palanquin, sedanchair

শিবির śibir *n* camp, tent

শিম śim *n* bean, kidney bean

শিমুল śimul *n* silk-cotton

শিয়াল śiŷal *(Bd)*, শেয়াল śeŷal *(WB) n* fox; jackal

শিরনাম śirônam *n* title, heading

শিরস্ত্র śirɔstrô *n* helmet

শিরা śira *n* vein; nerve; tendon

শিল śil *n* grinding stone

শিলা śila *n* stone, rock, hail

শিলাবৃষ্টি śilabṛiṣṭi *n* hailstorm

শিল্প śilpô *n* craft, artistry, art

শিল্পী śilpī *n* artist

শিশি śiśi *n* glass bottle

শিশির śiśir *n* dew, frost

শিশু śiśu *n* small infant, baby

শিষ্ট śiṣṭô *adj* gentle, courteous, polite

শিষ্টাচার śiṣṭacar *n* courtesy

শিষ্য śiṣyô *n* disciple, student

শিস śis *n* whistle, pipe

শিহরণ śihɔrôṇ *n* thrill, shiver

শীত śīt *n, adj* cold, chill

শীতকাল śītkal *n* winter

শীতল śītɔl *adj* cold, chilly

শীতাতপ śītatôp *n* air-conditioning

শুঁটকি śũṭki *n* kind of dried fish

শুঁঠ śũṭh *n* dried ginger

শুঁয়া śũŷa *(Bd)*, শুঁয়ো śũŷo *(WB) n* antenna, feeler

শুকনা śukna *(Bd)*, শুকনো śuknô *(WB) adj* dry

শুকানো śukano *(Bd)*, শনকোনো śukono *(WB) vb* dry

শুকিয়ে যাওয়া śukiŷe yaoŷa *vb* dry out, age

শুক্রবার śukrôbar *n* Friday

শুচি śuci *adj* clean, immaculate, pure

শুদ্ধ śuddhô *adj* flawless, clean, immaculate; genuine

শুধু śudhu *adj, adv* only, empty

শুভ śubhô *n* good, well-being

শুভসংবাদ śubhôsɔṅgbad *n* good news

শুভাশিস śubhaśis *n* congratulation, benediction

শুরু śuru *n* beginning, start

শুল্ক śulkô *n* customs, tax-duty

শূকর śūkôr *n* pig

শূন্য śūnyô *n* naught, zero, emptiness; *adj* empty, void

শূর śūr *adj* heroic, brave, valiant

শৃঙ্খল śrṅkhɔl *n* chain, fetters

শৃঙ্খলা śrṅkhɔla *n* discipline, control

শৃঙ্গ śrṅgô *n* horn, antler; peak

শৃঙ্গার śrṅgar *n* eroticism

শেখ śekh *n* sheikh

শেখা śekha *vb* learn, study

শেখানো śekhano *vb* teach

শেষ śeṣ *n* end, termination

শেষ পর্যন্ত śeṣ pôryôntô *adv* after all

শেষে śeṣe *adv* finally, ultimately

শৈত্য śoityô *n* cold, chill, frigidity

শৈথিল্য śoithilyô *n* looseness, slackness

শৈবাল śoibal *n* lichen, moss, algae

শৈশব śoiśɔb *n* infancy, childhood

শোক śok *n* mourning, grief

শোকগীতি śokgīti *n* elegy

শোকার্ত śokartô *adj* grief-stricken

শোণিত śoṇit *n* blood

শোধ śodh *n* compensation, repayment

শোধ করা śodh kɔra *vb* repay, pay back

শোধন śodhôn *n* purification, consecration

শোধরানো śodhrano *v* correct, rectify

শোধিত śodhitô *adj* purified, sanctified

শোনা śona *vb* hear, listen

শোনানো śonano *vb* cause to hear

শোভন śobhôn *adj* beautiful, lovely

শোভা śobha *n* beauty, glamor, splendor, brilliance

শোয়া śoŷa *vb* lie, lie down

শোয়ানো śoŷano *vb* lay down, cause to lie down

শোর śor *n* uproar, loud noise

শৌখিন śoukhin *adj* given to niceties/luxuries

শৌখিনতা śoukhinôta *n* daintiness

শৌচ śoucô *n* purity, sanctity

শৌর্য śouryô *n* valor, prowess, strength

শ্বশুর śvôśur *n* father-in-law

শ্বাস śvas *n* breath

শ্বাস নেওয়া śvas neoŷa *vb* breathe

শ্বাসক্রিয়া śvaskriŷa *n* breathing, respiration

শ্বাসনালী śvasnalī *n* windpipe, trachea

শ্বেত śvet *adj* white

শ্বেতকুষ্ঠ śvetkuṣṭhô *n* leucoderma, leprosy

শ্যাম śyæm *adj* dark-colored

শ্যেন śyen *n* falcon, bird of prey

শ্রদ্ধা śrôddha *n* respect, admiration

শ্রদ্ধেয় śrôddheŷô *adj* reverent, venerable

শ্রবণ śrôbôṇ *n* hearing, listening

শ্রম śrôm *n* labor, toil

শ্রমিক śrômik *n* laborer, workman

শ্রাদ্ধ śraddhô *n* obsequies, last rites

শ্রাদ্ধ করা śraddhô kɔra *vb* squander, spend extravagantly

শ্রাবণ śrabôṇ *n fourth Bengali month (July-August)*

শ্রী śrī *n* wealth, riches, affluence

শ্রুতি śruti *n* legend; holy writing, the Vedas

শ্রেণী śreṇī *n* class, line, range, series

শ্রেয় śreŷô *adj* preferable, better

শ্রেষ্ঠ śreṣṭhô *adj* greatest, best

শ্রেষ্ঠতা śreṣṭhôta *n* superiority

শ্রোণি śroṇi *n* pelvis, hips, loins

শীল śīl *adj* decent, polite

শ্লিষ্ট śliṣṭô *adj* embraced, clasped, entwined

শ্লেষ śleṣ *n* irony, joke, taunt

শ্লেষ্মা śleṣma *n* mucus, phlegm

শ্লোক ślok *n* verse, "sloka"

ষ ড়

ষট ṣɔṭ *pref* six
ষণ্ড ṣɔṇḍô *n* bull, eunuch
ষাঁড় ṣā̃ṛ *n* bull
ষাঁড়াষাঁড়ি ṣā̃ṛaṣā̃ṛi *n* bullfight
ষাট ṣaṭ *num* sixty
ষোল ṣolô *num* sixteen

সs

স sɔ *pref expressing*: junction, conjunction

সই sôi *n* signature

সওদা sɔoda *n* purchase, trade

সওয়া sɔoŷa *n* one and a quarter; *vb* suffer, tolerate

সওয়াল sɔoŷal *n* question, inquiry

সংক্রম sɔṁkrɔm *n* transit, transition

সংক্রান্ত sɔṁkrantô *adj, pp* concerning, relating to

সংক্রামক sɔṁkramôk *adj* infectious, contagious (*for other combinations with* সংক *see* সঙ্ক)

সংক্ষিপ্ত sɔṁkṣiptô *adj* abridged, summarized

সংক্ষেপ sɔṁkṣep *n* abbreviation, summary

সংখ্যা sɔṁkhya *n* number, numeral

সংগঠক sɔṁgɔṭhôk *n* organizer

সংগঠন sɔṁgɔṭhôn *n* organization

সংগঠিত sɔṁgôṭhitô *adj* organized

সংগোপন sɔṁgopôn *n* concealment, secrecy

সংগোপনে sɔṁgopône *adv* secretly

সংগ্রহ sɔṁgrôhô *n* collection, compilation

সংগ্রাম sɔṁgram *n* fight, struggle

সংগ্রাহক sɔṁgrahôk *n* collector, compiler (*for other combinations with* সংগ *see* সঙ্গ)

সংঘটন sɔṁghɔṭôn *n* occurrence, incident

সংঘর্ষ sɔṁghɔrṣô *n* friction

সংজ্ঞা sɔṁjña (*pron* shɔngga) *n* consciousness; connotation; definition

সংবরণ sɔṁbɔrôṇ *n* restraint, check

সংবর্ধনা sɔṁbɔrdhôna *n* reception, greeting

সংবর্ধিত sɔṁbôrdhitô *adj* raised; cherished

সংবহন sɔṁbɔhôn, সংবাহ sɔṁbahô *n* circulation, massage

সংবাদ sɔṁbad *n* news, information

সংবিধান sɔṁbidhan *n* arrangement, disposition

সংযত sɔṁyɔtô *adj* self-controlled, regulated

সংযম sɔṁyɔm *n* restraint, control

সংযমিত sɔṁyômitô *adj* restrained, controlled

সংযুক্ত sɔṁyuktô *adj* joined, linked, attached

সংযোগ sɔṁyog *n* connection, conjunction

সংরক্ষা sɔṁrôkṣa *n* conservation, preservation

সংলাপ sɔṁlap *n* dialogue, conversation

সংশয় sɔṁśɔŷ *n* doubt, uncertainty, hesitation, suspicion

সংশোধন sɔṁśodhôn *n* correction, purification

সংশ্রয় sɔṁśrɔŷ *n* conjunction, combination

সংসদ sɔṁsɔd *n* parliament, assembly

সংসার sɔṁsar *n* world; family

সংস্কার sɔṁskar *n* prejudice, superstition

সংস্কৃত sɔṁskr̥tô *n* Sanskrit

সংস্কৃতি sɔṁskr̥ti *n* culture

সংস্থা sɔṁstha *n* organization, society

সংস্থাপন sɔṁsthapôn *n* establishment, foundation

সংস্পর্শ sɔṁspɔrśô *n* close touch, contact

সংস্রব sɔṁsrɔb *n* association, contact

সংহরণ sɔṁhɔrôṇ *n* revocation, withdrawal, retraction

সংহার sɔṁhar *n* killing, slaughter

সকল sɔkôl *adj* entire, whole, all

সকাল sɔkal *n* morning; *adv* early

সকাশ sɔkaś *n* nearness, proximity

সক্ষম sɔkṣɔm *adj* competent, capable

সক্ষমতা sɔkṣômɔta *n* ability, capability

সখা sɔkha *n* companion, confidant

সখিতা sôkhita, সখ্য sôkhyô *n* friendship, companionship

সগোত্র sɔgotrô *adj* kindred, related

সঙ্কট sɔṅkɔṭ *n* crisis, danger

সঙ্কর sɔṅkɔr *n* half-caste, mongrel

সঙ্কলন sɔṅkɔlôn *n* collection, compilation

সঙ্কল্প sɔṅkɔlpô *n* determination, resolve

সঙ্কাশ sɔṅkaś *adj* like, similar to, resembling

সঙ্কুচিত sɔṅkucitô *adj* curtailed, reduced, contracted

সঙ্কেত sɔṅket *n* signal, hint

সঙ্কেত দেওয়া sɔṅket deôŷa *vb* indicate, signal

সঙ্কোচ sɔṅkoc *n* hesitation, diffidence

সঙ্গত sɔṅgɔtô *adj* consistent, reasonable

সঙ্গতি sɔṅgôti *n* propriety

সঙ্গম sɔṅgɔm *n* confluence, union

সঙ্গামী sɔṅgamī *adj* concurrent

সঙ্গী sôṅgī *n* companion

সঙ্গীত sôṅgīt *n* music, song

সঙ্গে sɔṅge *pp* with

সচকিত sɔcôkitô *adj* startled, alarmed

সচল sɔcɔl *adj* moving, mobile

সচিত্র sɔcitrô *adj* illustrated

সচেতন sɔcetɔn *adj* animate, sentient

সচ্ছল sɔcchɔl *adj* well-to-do

সজনী sɔjônī *n* sweetheart

সজল sɔjɔl *adj* watery; tearful

সজাগ sɔjag *adj* wakeful, vigilant

সজীব sɔjīb *adj* invigorated, alive, fresh

সজীবতা sɔjībɔta *n* rejuvenation, refreshment

সজোরে sɔjore *adv* violently, forcefully

সজ্জা sɔjja *n* dress; decoration

সঞ্চয় sɔñcɔŷ *n* gathering, collection, savings, accumulation

সঞ্চরণ sɔñcɔrôṇ *n* movement, circulation

সঞ্চার sɔñcar *n* transition, motion

সটকানো sɔṭkano *vb* decamp, escape

সটান sɔṭan *adj* at full length, prostrate

সঠিক sɔṭhik *adj* correct, accurate

সড়ক sɔrôk *n* highway

সড়কি sôrki *n* spear, lance

সৎ sɔṯ *adj* honest, virtuous, good; *pref* step- *as in* সৎছেলে sɔṯchele *n* stepson *etc*

সতত sɔtôtô *adv* always, ever

সততা sɔtôta *n* honesty, integrity

সতর্ক sɔtɔrkô *adj* careful, cautious

সতীর্থ sɔtīrthô *n* classmate

সতেজ sɔtej *adj* vigorous, energetic

সতেরো sɔterô *num* seventeen

সত্তম sɔttôm *adj* most virtuous

সত্তর sôttôr *num* seventy

সত্তা sɔtta *n* existence, being, reality

সত্ত্ব sɔttvô *n* existence, essence, nature, energy

সত্ত্বেও sɔttveo *pp* despite, in spite of

সত্য sôtyô *n* truth, validity, reality; *adj* true, real, genuine, valid

সত্যবাদী sôtyôbadī *adj* truthful

সত্যি sôtyi *a* true, actual

সত্যিকার sôtyikar *adj* honest, genuine

সদকা sɔdôka *n* alms, sacrifice

সদন sɔdôn *n* dwelling, residence

সদয় sɔdɔy *adj* kind, merciful

সদর sɔdôr *n, adj* headquarters; principal, chief

সদর্থ sɔdɔrthô *n* true meaning, correct meaning

সদর্প sɔdɔrpô *adj* arrogant, haughty

সদস্য sɔdôsyô *n* member

সদা sɔda *adj* always, ever

সদৃশ sɔdŕśô *adj* resembling, similar

সদ্য sôdyô *adv* immediately, at once

সনদ sɔnôd *n* charter, certificate, testimonial

সনাতন sɔnatɔn *adj* eternal, perpetual

সন্তত sɔntɔtô *adj* stretched, extended

সন্ততি sɔntôti *n* lineage, progeny

সন্তপ্ত sɔntɔptô *adj* distressed, afflicted

সন্তর্পণে sɔntɔrpɔne *adv* cautiously, carefully

সন্তান sɔntan *n* offspring

সন্তাপ sɔntap *n* heat, glow, fire

সন্তুষ্ট sɔntuṣṭô *adj* satisfied, content

সন্তোষ sɔntoṣ *n* satisfaction, contentment

সন্ত্রাস sɔntras *n* terror, terrorism

সন্ত্রাসী sɔntrasī *n* terrorist

সন্দর্ভ sɔndɔrbhô *n* dissertation, essay; musical composition

সন্দিগ্ধ sôndigdhô *adj* suspicious, doubtful

সন্দেশ sɔndeś *n* sweetmeat

সন্দেহ sɔndehô *n* doubt, suspicion

সন্ধান sɔndhan *n* research, pursuit, discovery

সন্ধান-সূত্র sɔndhan-sūtrô *n* clue, trail

সন্ধি sôndhi *n* union, covenant, treaty

সন্ধ্যা sôndhya *n* evening, twilight

সন্নিধান sɔnnidhan *n* juxtaposition, nearness

সন্ন্যাসী sônnyasī *n* ascetic, devotee

সপক্ষ sɔpôkṣô *n* supporter; co-worker

সপক্ষে sɔpôkṣe *adj* in favor of, in support of

সপ্তাহ sɔptahô, সপ্তা sɔpta *n* week

সফর sɔphôr *n* trip, tour

সফল sɔphɔl *adj* fruitful, successful

সফলতা sɔphɔlôta *n* success, result

সব sɔb *adj* all, every, whole

সবজি sôbji *n* vegetables

সবল sɔbɔl *adj* powerful, strong

সবাই sɔbai *n* everybody

সবুজ sôbuj *adj* green

সবুর sôbur *n* patience; delay

সবে sɔbe *adv* in all, all told

সভা sɔbha *n* assembly, council

সভ্য sôbhyô *adj* courteous, polite

সভ্যতা sôbhyôta *n* civility, politeness; culture, civilization

সম sɔmô *adj* equal, equivalent, similar

সমকক্ষ sɔmôkôkṣô *adj* even, equal, balanced

সমকাম sɔmôkam *n* homosexuality

সমকাল sɔmôkal *adj* contemporary, simultaneous

সমগ্র sɔmôgrô *adj* whole, entire, all

সমজাতীয় sɔmôjatīyô *adj* homogenous

সমঝদার sɔmôjhdar *adj* sympathetic

সমতল sɔmôtɔl *adj* even, level, flat

সমতা sɔmôta *n* equality, similarity, levelness

সমদর্শী sɔmôdôrśī *adj* impartial, fair-minded

সমদুঃখী sɔmôduḥkhī *adj* sympathetic, understanding

সমধিক sɔmôdhik *adj* great, excessive, exceeding

সমন্বয় sɔmônvɔŷ *n* consistency, synthesis

সমন্বয় করা sɔmônvɔŷ kɔra *vb* coordinate, synthesize

সমবয়সী sɔmôbɔŷôsī *n, adj* contemporary

সমবর্তন sɔmôbôrtôn *n* polarization

সমবায় sɔmôbaŷ *n* co-operative

সমবাহু sɔmôbahu *adj* equilateral

সমবেত sɔmôbetô *adj* assembled, collected

সমব্যথা sɔmôbytha *n* sympathy, fellow-feeling

সমভাব sɔmôbhab *n* intuition; similarity

সমভূমি sɔmôbhūmi *adj* level, flat, plain

সমমূল্য sɔmômūlyô *n* equivalent

সময় sômôŷ *n* time

সময় কাটানো sômôŷ kaṭano *vb* spend time

সমর sɔmôr *n* war, battle

সমর্থ sɔmôrthô *adj* capable, able

সমর্থন sɔmôrthôn *n* support, help

সমস্ত sômôstô *adj* complete, all, whole

সমস্যা sɔmôsya *n* problem, dilemma

সমাকলন sɔmakɔlôn *n* integration

সমাগত sɔmagɔtô *adj* assembled, gathered

সমাজ sɔmaj *n* society, community

সমাধান sɔmadhan *n* solution, settlement, conclusion, decision

সমাধি sɔmadhi *n* trance, meditation

সমান sɔman *n* even, straight, equal

সমান–সমান sɔman-sɔman *adj* evenly, fairly, balanced

সমান্তর sɔmantôr *adj* equidistant

সমান্তরাল sɔmantôral *adj* parallel

সমাপ্ত sɔmaptô *adj* completed, finished

সমাবেশ sɔmabeś *n* assembly

সমায়ত sɔmaŷɔtô *adj* rectangular

সমালোচক sɔmalocôk *n* critic

সমালোচনা sɔmalocôna *n* criticism, review

সমাস sɔmas *n* compound

সমাহার sɔmahar *n* collection, combination

সমাহিত sɔmahitô *adj* engrossed, occupied

সমিতি sômiti *n* association, society

সমীক্ষা sômīkṣa *n* investigation, research

সমীপ sômīp *n* proximity, nearness

সমীরণ sômīrɔṇ *n* breeze, air, wind

সমীহ sômīhô *n* regard, respect

সমুদ্র sômudrô *n* ocean, sea

সমূহ sômūhô *n* assemblage

সমৃদ্ধ sômṙddhô *adj* enriched, rewarded

সম্পত্তি sɔmpôtti *n* property, wealth, riches

সম্পর্ক sɔmpɔrkô *n* relationship, connection

সম্পর্কে sɔmpɔrke *pp* concerning, about

সম্পাদক sɔmpadôk *n* editor; secretary

সম্পাদন sɔmpadôn *n* performance, accomplishment; editing

সম্পূর্ণ sɔmpūrṇô *adv* completely, wholly

সম্প্রতি sɔmprôti *adv* recently, lately

সম্প্রদান sɔmprôdan *n* act of giving, bestowal

সম্প্রদায় sɔmprôdaŷ *n* community, sect

সম্বন্ধ sɔmbɔndhô *n* concern; relationship

সম্বন্ধে sɔmbɔndhe *pp* concerning, about

সম্ভব sɔmbhɔb *adj* probable, likely

সম্ভাবনা sɔmbhabôna *n* probability, likelihood

সম্ভাষণ sɔmbhaṣôṇ *n* greeting, exchange

সম্মত sɔmmɔtô *adj* consenting, in agreement, willing

সম্মান sɔmman *n* respect, deference, reverence

সম্মেলন sɔmmelɔn *n* assembly, gathering

সরকার sɔrkar *n* government

সরকারি sɔrkari *adj* governmental, public

সরদি, সর্দি sôrdi *n* catarrh, cold, flu

সরল sɔrôl *adj* honest, candid, simple

সরা sɔra *vb* move, stir, step aside

সরানো sɔrano *vb* move, remove, shift

সরাসরি sɔrasôri *adj* straight, direct, candid

সরিষা sôriṣa *n* mustard

সরিসৃপ sôrisṛp (*pron* shorisrip) *n* reptile

সরু sôru *adj* narrow, delicate, thin

সর্ব sɔrbô *adj* whole, entire, complete

সর্বত sɔrbôtô *adv* entirely, wholly

সর্বদা sɔrbôda *adv* always, ever

সর্বনাম sɔrbônam *n* pronoun

সর্বনাশ sɔrbônaś *n* disaster, ruin

সর্বশেষ sɔrbôśeṣ *adj* final, ultimate

সর্বসাধারণ sɔrbôsadharôn *n* the public, the common people

সর্বাপেক্ষা sɔrbapekṣa *adv* of all, beyond all, above all

সস্তা sɔsta *adj* cheap

সহ sɔhô *pp* with

সহকারী sɔhôkarī *n* co-worker, assistant

সহজ sɔhôj *adj* easy, simple, innate

সহজে sɔhôje *adv* easily

সহন sɔhôn *n* tolerance, endurance

সহবাস sɔhôbas *n* cohabitation; sexual intercourse

সহানুভূতি sɔhanubhūti *n* sympathy, compassion

সহায় sɔhaŷ *n* helper, assistant

সহ্য sôhyô (*pron* shojjho) *n* tolerance, endurance

সহ্য করা sôhyô kɔra (*pron* shojjho kɔra) *vb* tolerate, suffer, endure

সাইকেল saikel *n* bicycle

সাইজ saij *n* size

সাউকারি saukari *n* assumed self-importance

সাউকারি করা saukari kɔra *vb* throw one's weight around

সাংঘাতিক saṁghaṭik *adj* terrible, fatal, dangerous

সাংবাদিক saṁbadik *n* journalist

সাংসারিক saṁsarik *adj* domestic, familial

সাংস্কৃতিক saṁskṛtik *adj* cultural

সাঁওতাল saotal *n* Santal (*tribe*)

সাঁড়াশি sāraśi *n* pincers, tongs

সাঁতরানো sātrano *vb* swim

সাঁতার sātar *n* swimming

সাঁতার কাটা sātar kaṭa *vb* swim

সাক্ষাৎ saksat *n* meeting

সাক্ষী saksi *n* witness

সাগর sagôr *n* sea, ocean

সাগু sagu *n* sago

সাজ-গোজ saj-goj *n* make-up

সাজা saja *vb* be dressed, be decorated; *n* punishment

সাজা দেওয়া saha deoŷa *vb* punish

সাজানো sajano *vb* dress, decorate, embellish

সাড়া sara *n* response, reaction

সাড়া দেওয়া sara deoŷa *vb* react, respond

সাড়ে sare *adj* half past; plus one half

সাথি sathi *n* companion

সাদর sadôr *adj* cordial

সাদরে sadôre *adv* cordially

সাদা sada *adj* white

সাদা-সিধে sada-sidhe *adj* honest, straight, unostentatious

সাধ sadh *n* desire, longing

সাধন sadhôn *n* endeavor, accomplishment

সাধনা sadhôna *n* worship, adoration; practice

সাধারণ sadharôn *adj* usual, ordinary, common

সাধারণত sadharɔṇôtô *adv* usually, generally

সাধু sadhu *n* saint

সাধ্য sadhyô *n* ability, capability

সাধ্যাতীত sadhyatītô *adj* beyond the range of one's capability

সান্ত্বনা santvôna *n* consolation, solace

সাপ sap *n* snake

সাপ্তাহিক saptahik *adj* weekly

সাফ saph *adj* empty, clean, clear

সাবধান sabdhan *adj* cautious, careful

সাবধানতা sabdhanôta *n* caution, care, heed

সাবান saban *n* soap

সাবালক sabalôk *n, adj* adult

সামঞ্জস্য samôñjɔsyô *n* consistency, harmony, symmetry

সামনাসামনি samnasamni *adv* face-to-face

সামনে samne *pp* in front of, facing

সাময়িক samôŷik *adj* periodical, temporary

সামরিক samôrik *adj* military, war-related

সামলানো samlano *vb* manage, check, guard

সামাজিক samajik *adj* social, formal, public

সামান্য samanyô *adj* little, trifling, unimportant

সামুদ্রিক samudrik *adj* marine, oceanic

সাম্প্রদায়িক samprôdaŷik *adj* communal

সাম্যবাদ samyôbad *n* communism

সাম্যবাদী samyôbadī *n* communist

সাম্রাজ্য samrajyô *n* empire

সায়া saŷa *n* petticoat

সার sar *n* marrow, essence, extract, compost

সারস sarôs *n* stork

সারগর্ভ sargɔrbhô *adj* substantial

সারা sara *vb* finish, accomplish; be cured; *adj* whole, entire, all

সারাংশ saraṁśô *n* gist, summary, abstract

সারানো sarano *vb* mend, repair, heal

সারি sari *n* row, line

সার্কাস sarkas *n* circus

সার্থ sarthô *adj* significant, meaningful

সার্থক sarthôk *adj* succesful, effective

সাল sal *n* era

সালগম salgɔm *n* turnip

সালিশি saliśi *n* arbitration

সাহস sahôs *n* courage, boldness, bravery

সাহায্য sahayyô *n* help, assistance, aid, support

সাহায্য করা sahayyô kɔra *vb* help, support

সাহিত্য sahityô *n* literature

সাহেব saheb *n address for a European gentleman*, Sir, Mr.

সিংহ simhô *n* lion

সিঁড়ি sĩṛi *n* stairs, staircase

সিঁধেল চোর sĩdhel cor *n* burglar, intruder, petty thief

সিকি siki *n* quarter, fourth part

সিক্ত siktô *adj* moist, wet

সিগারেট sigareṭ *n* cigarette

সিদ্ধ siddhô, সেদ্ধ seddhô *adj* boiled; realized, fulfilled; expert

সিদ্ধ করা siddhô kɔra, সেদ্ধ করা siddhô kɔra *vb* boil, cook

সিদ্ধান্ত siddhantô *n* decision, conclusion

সিদ্ধান্ত নেওয়া siddhantô neoŷa *vb* decide, resolve

সিদ্ধি siddhi *n* accomplishment, attainment, salvation

সিধা sidha *(Bd)*, সিধে sidhe *(WB) adj* straight, direct

সিনেমা sinema *n* cinema

সিন্দুক sinduk *n* chest, safe

সিরিশ siriś *n* glue

সিরিশ কাগজ siriś kagôj *n* sandpaper

সির্কা sirka *n* vinegar

সীমা sīma *n* limit, border, boundary

সীমানা sīmana *n* edge, border

সীমিত sīmitô *adj* limited

সীমাহীন sīmahīn *adj* boundless, infinite

সীস sīs *n* lead (*in a pencil*)

সুই sui, সুঁচ sũc *n* needle

সুখ sukh *n* happiness, ease, comfort

সুখবর sukhɔbôr *n* good news

সুখী sukhī *adj* happy, comfortable

সুগন্ধ sugɔndhô *n* fragrance, aroma

সুগোল sugol *adj* round, plump

সুজি suji *n* semolina

সুড়সুড়ি suṛsuṛi *onom* tickling, titillating

সুতরাং sutôram *conj* so, hence, consequently

সুতা suta *(Bd)*, সুতো suto *(WB) n* thread, yarn, cotton-thread

সুতি suti *n* cotton

সুদ sud *n* interest (on loans), usury

সুদখোর sudkhor *n* usurer

সুধা sudha *n* nectar, ambrosia

সুধা ঢালা sudha ḍhala *vb* flatter, charm

সুনাম sunam *n* reputation, fame

সুন্দর sundôr *adj* beautiful, pleasing, nice

সুন্দরী sundôrī *n* beautiful female

সুপারি supari *n* betel-nut

সুপারিশ supariś *n* recommendation

সুপারিশ করা supariś kɔra *vb* recommend

সুপ্ত suptô *adj* latent, dormant

সুপ্রভাত suprôbhat *int* good morning

সুফল suphɔl *n* success

সুবিচার subicar *n* fair judgement

সুবিধা subidha *(Bd)*, সুবিধে subidhe *(WB) n* advantage, convenience

সুবুদ্ধি subuddhi *n* prudence, wisdom

সুমেরু sumeru *n* North Pole

সুযোগ suyog *n* chance, opportunity

সুর sur *n* voice, tone, pitch

সুরকি surki *n* brick-dust

সুরঙ্গ surôṁgô *n* tunnel

সুরাহা suraha *n* solution, remedy

সুলভ sulɔbh *adj* easily available, cheap

সুশিক্ষিত suśikṣitô *adj* well-educated, well-trained

সুশীল suśīl *adj* good-natured, well-behaved

সুশৃঙ্খলা suśṙṅkhɔla *n* orderly, well-managed

সুষম suṣɔmô *adj* balanced

সুষ্ঠু suṣṭhu *adj* immaculate; smooth

সুসংবাদ susɔṁbad *n* good news

সুসময় susɔmôý *n* auspicious time

সুস্থ susthô *adj* sound, healthy, well

সুস্থিত susthitô *adj* stable, well-placed

সুস্পষ্ট suspɔṣṭô *adj* clear, evident, explicit

সুস্বাদু susvadu *adj* tasty, delicious

সূক্ষ্ম sūkṣmô *(pron* shukkho) *adj* fine, thin, delicate

সূচনা sūcôna *n* beginning, preface, commencement

সূচি sūci *n* index, table of contents

সূচিত sūcitô *adj* indicated, hinted, communicated

সূত্র sūtrô *n* thread, link, connection

সূর্য sūryô *n* sun

সূর্যগ্রহণ sūryôgrôhôṇ *n* solar eclipse

সূর্যাস্ত sūryasto *n* sunset

সূর্যোদয় sūryodɔý *n* sunrise

সৃষ্টি sṙṣṭi *n* creation

সৃষ্টি করা sṙṣṭi kɔra *vb* create

সে se *pr* he, she *(ord)*, that

সেই sei *pr* that

সেঁতসেঁতে sæ̃tsæ̃te *adj* damp

সেকরা sækra *n* goldsmith

সেকাল sekal *n* the past

সেকেলে sekele *adj* antiquated, old-fashioned

সেখান sekhan *n* there, that place

সেচন secôn *n* irrigation

সেতু setu *n* bridge

সেনা sena *n* army, troops

সেনা নিবাস sena nibas *n* cantonment

সেবক sebôk *n* nurse, attendant *(m)*

সেবা seba *n* care, serving, nursing

সেবিকা sebika *n* nurse, attendant *(f)*

সের ser *n* seer *(Indian weight)*

সেরা sera *adj* excellent, best

সেরে ফেলা sere phæla *vb* finish, complete

সেরেফ sereph *adv* merely, only

সেলাই selai *n* needlework

সেলাই করা selai kɔra *vb* sew, stitch

সেলাম selam *n* Muslim greeting, salaam

সৈকত soikɔt *n* seashore, beach

সৈনিক soinik *n* soldier, fighter

সোজা soja *adj* straight, honest, upright

সোনা sona *n* gold

সোপান sopan *n* flight of stairs, steps

সোমবার sombar *n* Monday

সোহাগ sohag *n* caress, affection

সৌজন্য soujônyô *n* courtesy, politeness

সৌন্দর্য soundôryô *n* beauty, grace, elegance

সৌভাগ্য soubhagyô *n* good fortune, prosperity

সৌম্য soumyô *adj* dignified

সৌর sourô *adj* solar

স্কন্ধ skɔndhô *n* part, division, installment; shoulder, neck

স্কুল skul *n* school

স্তন stɔn *n* breasts, mammary glands

স্তব stɔb *n* hymn; eulogy

স্তবক stɔbôk *n* stanza, chapter

স্তব্ধ stɔbdhô *adj* stunned, dazed

স্তম্ভ stombhô *n* pillar, column

স্তম্ভিত stômbhitô *adj* stupefied, astounded

স্তর stor *n* layer

স্ত্রী strī *n* wife

স্ত্রীলোক strīlok *n* woman, womenfolk

স্থল sthol *n* place, site

স্থলভাগ stolôbhag *n* plot, piece of land

স্থান sthan *n* place, region, locality

স্থাপত্য sthapotyô *n* architecture

স্থাপন sthapôn *n* establishment, setting up, installation

স্থায়ী sthaŷī *adj* lasting, enduring

স্থিতি sthiti *n* location

স্থিতিস্থাপকতা sthitisthapokôta *n* elasticity, spring

স্থির sthir *adj* motionless, calm, still, stationary

স্থূল sthulô *adj* fat, corpulent

স্নাত snatô *adj* bathed, cleansed

স্নান snan *n* bath, bathing, ablutions

স্নায়ু snaŷu *n* nerve

স্নিগ্ধ snigdhô *adj* affectionate, cordial

স্নেহ snehô *n* love, affection, tenderness

স্পর্ধা spordha *n* audacity, courage

স্পর্শ sporśô *n* touch, contact

স্পষ্ট spoṣṭô *adj* clear, evident, explicit

স্পষ্টবাদী spoṣṭôbadī *adj* outspoken, frank

স্ফটিক sphoṭik *n* crystal, quartz

স্ফীত sphītô *adj* swollen, bloated

স্ফুলিঙ্গ sphuliṅgô *n* spark

স্ফূর্ত sphūrtô *adj* manifest, revealed

স্ফোটক sphoṭôk *n* boil, abscess

স্বকীয় svokīŷô *adj* personal, of one's own

স্বগতোক্তি svogôtokti *n* soliloquy

স্বচ্ছ svocchô *adj* transparent, lucid, clear

স্বচ্ছন্দে svocchonde *adv* freely, easily

স্বজন svojon *n* kinsman

স্বতঃস্ফূর্ত svothôsphūrtô *adj* spontaneous

স্বতন্ত্র svotontrô *adj* independent, free

স্বত্ব svotvô *n* ownership; right

স্বপ্ন svopnô *n* dream

স্বপ্ন দেখা svopnô dækha *vb* dream

স্ববশ svobôś *adj* controlled

স্বভাব svobhab *n* characteristic, nature

স্বভাবত svobhabotô *adv* naturally, by nature

স্বয়ং svoŷôṁ *pr* oneself, personally

স্বয়ংসিদ্ধ svoŷôṁsiddhô *adj* self-evident, obvious

স্বর svor *n* tone, voice, tune

স্বরবর্ণ svorôborṇô *n* vowel

স্বর্গ svorgô *n* heaven, bliss

স্বর্গীয় svôrgīŷô *adj* heavenly, divine

স্বর্ণ svorṇô *n* gold

স্বল্প svolpô *adj* scant, meager

স্বস্তি svôsti *n* relief, comfort

স্বাগত svagotô, স্বাগতম svagotôm *n* welcome

স্বাদ svad *n* taste, flavor

স্বাদু svadu *adj* tasty, sweet, savory

স্বাধীন svadhīn *adj* independent, free

স্বাধীনতা svadhīnôta *n* independence

স্বাভাবিক svabhabik *adj* natural, characteristic, normal, usual

স্বামী svamī *n* husband; lord

স্বার্থ svarthô *n* self-interest, egoism

স্বার্থপর svarthôpor *adj* selfish

স্বাস্থ্য svasthyô *n* health; hygiene; happiness

স্বীকার svīkar, স্বীকারোক্তি svīkarokti
n confession, admission

স্বীকার করা svīkar kɔra *vb* confess,
admit, acquiesce

স্বীকৃত svīkŕtô *adj* acknowledged,
admitted

স্বেচ্ছা sveccha *n* free will, self-will

স্বেচ্ছাচারী svecchacarī *adj* willful,
wayward, wanton

স্মরণ smɔrôṇ (*pron* shɔron) *n*
recollection, remembrance

স্মরণশক্তি smɔrôṇśôkti *n* memory,
faculty of remembering

স্মারকলিপি smarôklipi *n* memo-
randum, reminder

স্মৃতি smŕti (*pron* sriti) *n* memory,
reminiscence, recollection

স্মৃতিকথা smŕtikɔtha *n* memoirs

স্মৃতিচারণ smŕticarôṇ *n*
reminiscence

স্মৃতিচিহ্ন smŕticihnô *n* memento

স্মৃতিমন্দির smŕtimôndir *n*
mausoleum

স্রোত srot *n* current, flow (of water)

হ h

হইচই hôicôi *n* loud uproar, hulla-
baloo, ruckus

হইতে hôite *pp* from, since

হওয়া hɔoẏa *vb* be, become, come
into existence, happen, occur

হকচকানো hɔkcɔkano *vb* be non-
plussed, be taken aback

হজম hɔjôm *n* digestion

হজম করা hɔjôm kɔra *vb* digest;
misappropriate

হটা hɔṭa *vb* retreat, withdraw

হটানো hɔṭano *vb* defeat, cause to
retreat

হঠকারী hɔṭhôkarī *adj* impetuous,
rash

হঠাৎ hɔṭhaṯ *adv* suddenly

হড়কানো hɔṛkano *vb* slip, tumble

হত hɔtô *adj* killed, slain

হতবাক hɔtôbak *n* amazement,
surprise

হতভাগ্য hɔtôbhagyô *adj* unfortunate, wretched

হতাশ hɔtaś *adj* dejected, crestfallen

হতাশা hɔtaśa *n* despondence,
dejection

হত্যা hɔtya *n* killing, slaughter

হত্যাকারী hɔtyakarī *n* killer,
murderer

হদিস hôdis *n* information, trace, clue

হনহনিয়ে hɔnhɔniẏe *adv* hurriedly,
hastily

হন্তদন্ত hɔntôdɔntô *adj* fussy, rushed

হবু hôbu *adj* would-be, to-be

হযবরল hɔyôbɔrôl *n* gibberish

হয়তো hɔẏto *adv* presumably,
perhaps

হয়রান করা hɔŷran kɔra *vb* harrass,
exasperate

হয়ে যাওয়া hôŷe yaoẏa *vb* become,
be finished

হরণ hɔrôṇ *n* robbing, plunder

হরতাল hɔrtal *n* strike

হরফ hɔrôph *n* letter of the alphabet, character, type

হরিণ hôriṇ *n* deer, stag

হরেক hɔrek *adj* diverse, various

হর্ষ hɔrṣô *n* joy, delight, pleasure

হলদে hôlde, হলুদ hôlud *adj* yellow

হলফ hɔlôph *n* oath

হল্লা hɔlla *n* uproar, tumult

হস্ত hɔstô *n* hand

হস্তক্ষেপ hɔstôkṣep *n* interference,
meddling

হস্তশিল্প hɔstôśilpô *n* handicraft,
handiwork

হা ha *int expr* grief, suffering

হাই hai *n* yawn

হাই তোলা hai tola *vb* yawn

হাউই haui *n* rocket, fireworks

হাউমাউ haumau *n* complaint,
uproar

হাওয়া haoẏa *n* air, wind, breeze

হাঁ করা hā kɔra *vb* stare open-
mouthed

হাঁকাহাঁকি hākahāki *n* uproar, loud
noise

হাঁচা hāca *vb* sneeze

হাঁচি hāci *n* sneeze

হাঁটা hāṭa *vb* walk

হাঁটু hāṭu *n* knee

হাঁড়ি hāṛi *n* big cooking-pot

হাঁপ hāp *n* labored breathing, panting

হাঁপানি hāpani *n* asthma

হাঁস hās *n* duck

হাকিম hakim *n* magistrate, judge

হাঙ্গামা haṅgama *n* disturbance, riot

হাজা haja *vb* rot, be spoiled

হাজার hajar *num* thousand
হাজির hajir *adj* present
হাট haṭ *n* market (*weekly*)
হাড় haṛ *n* bone
হাড্ডি haḍḍi *n* bone
হাত hat *n* hand
হাত–কষা hat-kɔṣa *adj* stingy, ungenerous
হাত–খরচ hat-khɔrôc *n* pocket money
হাত–ছানি hat-chani *n* beckoning
হাতড়ানো hatṛano *vb* appropriate, grab
হাত–তালি hat-tali *n* applause
হাত–মোজা hat-moja *n* gloves
হাতল hatôl *n* handle
হাতি hati *n* elephant
হাতুড়ি haturi *n* hammer
হাতুড়িয়া haturiɏa (*Bd*), হাতুড়ে hatuṛe (*WB*) *n* quack, charlatan
হানা hana *vb* strike, attack
হানি hani *n* destruction, loss, damage
হানিকর hanikɔr *adj* harmful, destructive
হাবা haba *adj* dumb, dull-witted
হাম ham *n* measles
হামলা hamla *n* attack, assault
হামা hama, হামাগুড়ি hamaguri *n* crawling
হামাগুড়ি দেওয়া hamaguri deoɏa *vb* crawl
হামেশা hameśa *adv* incessantly, always
হায় haɏ *int expr* regret, remorse, alas
হার har *n* defeat; necklace
হার মানা har mana *vb* admit defeat
হারা hara *vb* be defeated, lose
হারানো harano *vb* lose, misplace
হারাম haram *adj* unclean, unholy, forbidden

হাল hal *n* plow; helmet; rudder; condition, state, climate, fashion
হালকা halka *adj* light, easy, mild
হালচাল halcal *n* customs, behavior, demeanor
হালাল halal *n* Halal (*pure as prescribed by Muslim law*)
হাসা hasa *vb* laugh, smile
হাসি hasi *n* smile, laughter
হাসিখুশি hasikhuśi *n* liveliness, gaiety
হাহাকার hahakar *n* lamentation, desolation
হিংসা hiṁsa *n* malice, envy, jealousy; violence
হিংস্র hiṁsrô *adj* cruel, violent
হিজিবিজি hijibiji *adj* illegible, scrawling
হিত hitô *n* benefit, good, welfare
হিন্দু hindu *n* Hindu
হিম him *n* frost, snow; winter
হিম–দংশ him-dɔṁśô *n* frostbite
হিমশিম hiṁśim *n* exhaustion, fatigue
হিমানী-সম্প্রপাত himanī-sɔmprôpat *n* avalanche
হিমায়ক himaɏôk *n* refrigerator
হিমালয় himalɵɏ *n* Himalayas
হিসাব hisab (*Bd*), হিসেব hiseb (*WB*) *n* counting, accounting, reckoning, calculation
হিসাব করা hisab kɔra *vb* calculate
হিসাবনবিশ hisabnôbiś *n* accountant
হিসাব–পরীক্ষা hisab-pôrīkṣa *n* audit
হিসাবী hisabī *adj* frugal, economical, prudent
হীন hīn *suff* without, devoid of
হীন করা hīnô kɔra *vb* debase, humiliate
হীনতা hīnôta *n* meanness; humiliation

হীনমনা hīnômôna *adj* ungenerous, mean

হীরা hīra *(Bd)*, হীরে hīre *(WB)* *n* diamond

হুঁশ hūś *n* consciousness, sensibility

হুকুম hukum *n* order, command, injunction

হুবহু hubôhu *adv* exactly

হুমকি humki *n* threat, intimidation

হুমড়ি humṛi *n* stumbling

হুরি huri *n* fairy

হুল hul *n* antenna (*of insects*)

হৃদয় hṙdɔŷ *n* heart, mind

হৃদয়ঙ্গম করা hṙdɔŷɔṅgôm kɔra *n* internalize, feel deeply

হৃদয়-ভেদী hṙdɔŷ-bhedī *adj* pathetic, heartbreaking

হেঁচকা hæ̈cka *n* tug, pull

হেঁচকি hæ̈cki *n* hiccup

হেঁটে যাওয়া hēṭe yaoŷa *vb* walk

হেতু hetu *n* reason, cause, origin

হেন hænô *adj*, *adv* such, suchlike

হেন–তেন hænô-tænô *adv* etcetera, and so on

হেনস্তা hænôsta *n* humiliation

হেমন্ত hemôntô *n* autumn

হেরফের herpher *n* alteration, modification

হেলা hæla *vb* lean, slant; *n* slight, neglect, disdain

হেলাফেলা hælaphæla *n* contempt, disrespect, neglect

হোঁচট hõcôṭ *n* stumble

হোটেল hoṭel *n* hotel

হ্যাঁ hyæ̈ *int* yes

হ্রস্ব hrɔsvô *adj* short, small, dwarfish

হ্রাস hras *n* decrease, shortening

ENGLISH-BANGLA
DICTIONARY

West Bengal variations of words are given in the Bangla – English dictionary. In this section they are indicated in the first instance only, eg. a typical entry reads:

account *n (bookkeeping)* হিসাব hisab *(Bd)*, হিসেব hiseb *(WB)*; *(description)* বিবরণ bibôrôṇ
accountant *n* হিসাবরক্ষক hisabrôkṣôk
accounting *n* হিসাব করা hisab kɔra

Readers should apply the variations to subsequent occurrences of the word.

As in the Bangla – English dictionary, only basic numbers and basic (nominative) pronoun forms are given. Complete lists of these can be found at the back of the book.

A

a, an *det* একটা ækṭa

abandon *vb* ত্যাগ করা tyæg kɔra, ছাড়া chara

abbreviate *vb* সংক্ষিপ্ত করা sɔṁkṣiptô kɔra

abbreviation *n* সংক্ষেপ sɔṁkṣep

abdomen *n* পেট peṭ

ability *n* ক্ষমতা kṣɔmôta

able *adj* সমর্থ sɔmôrthô, দক্ষ dôkṣô; *vb (be ~ to)* পারা para

abnormal *adj (unusual)* অস্বাভাবিক ɔsvabhabik; *(paranormal)* অলৌকিক ɔloukik

aboard *adv* জাহাজে উঠে jahaje uṭhe

abode *n* আলয় alɔŷ

abolish *vb* লোপ করা lop kɔra

abolition *n* লোপ lop

abortion *n* গর্ভপাত gɔrbhôpat, গর্ভনাশ gɔrbhônaś

about *adv (approximately)* মোটামুটি moṭamuṭi; *pp (concerning)* সম্বন্ধে sɔmbôndhe

above *pp* উপর upôr

above all *adv* সবচেয়ে sɔbceŷe

abroad *adj* বিলাতি bilati, বিদেশে bideśe

absence *n* অনুপস্থিতি ɔnupôsthiti, না থাকা na thaka

absent *adj* অনুপস্থিত ɔnupôsthit

absentminded *adj* অন্যমনস্ক ɔnyômônôskô

absolute *adj* চরম cɔrôm

absolutely *adv* একেবারে ækebare

absorb *vb (take in)* গিলে ফেলা gile phæla; *(be engaged in)* লেগে থাকা lege thaka

abstract *adj (not concrete)* ভাববাচক bhabbacôk; *(theoretical)*

আনুমানিক anumanik; *vb (extract)* নিষ্কাশন করা niṣkaśôn kɔra; *(summarize)* সংক্ষিপ্ত করা sɔṁkṣiptô kɔra

absurd *adj (strange)* অদ্ভুত ôdbhut; *(unlikely)* অসম্ভব ɔsɔmbhɔb; *(ridiculous)* হাস্যকর hasyôkɔr

abundance *n* প্রাচুর্য pracuryô

abundant *adj* প্রচুর prôcur

abuse *vb* গালাগালি দেওয়া galagali deôŷa, অপব্যবহার করা ɔpôby- bôhar kɔra *(pron* ɔpobæbohar kɔra)

abusive *adj* অপব্যবহারমূলক ɔpôbybôharmulôk *(pron* ɔpobæboharmulok)

academic *adj* বিদ্যাবান bidyaban, শিক্ষাগত śikṣagtô

academy *n* একাডেমি ækaḍemi, পরিষৎ pôriṣɔt

accelerate *vb* দ্রুততর করা drutôtɔrô kɔra

accent *n* স্বরভঙ্গি svɔrbhôṅgi

accept *vb* গ্রহণ করা grôhôṇ kɔra

acceptance *n* গ্রহণ grôhôṇ

access *n* প্রবেশ prôbeś

accident *n* দুর্ঘটনা dūrghɔṭona, একসিডেন্ট æksiḍenṭ

accidental *adj* ভুল করে bhul kôre

accommodate *vb* স্থান দেওয়া sthan deôŷa

accommodation *n* থাকার স্থান thakar sthan, আবাস abas

accompany *vb* সঙ্গে যাওয়া sɔṅge yaôŷa

accomplice *n* সহযোগী sɔhôyogī

accomplish *vb* সম্পূর্ণ করা sɔm- pūrṇô kɔra

accomplishment *n* সম্পাদন sɔmpadôn

according to *pp* অনুযায়ী ônuyaŷī

account *n* *(bookkeeping)* হিসাব hisab *(Bd)*, হিসেব hiseb *(WB)*; *(description)* বিবরণ bibôrôṇ

accountant *n* হিসাবরক্ষক hisabrôkṣôk

accounting *n* হিসাব করা hisab kɔra

accumulate *vb* জমা করা jɔma kɔra, জমানো jɔmano

accurate *adj* ঠিক ṭhik, সঠিক sɔṭhik

accusation *n* নালিশ naliś, নিন্দা ninda

accuse *vb* নালিশ করা naliś kɔra, নিন্দা করা ninda kɔra

accused *(defendant) n* আসামি asami

accustom, be accustomed to *adj* অভ্যাস হওয়া ôbhyas hɔɔŷa

ace *n* তাসের টেক্কা taser ṭekka

ache *n* বেদনা bedôna, ব্যথা bytha *(pron* bæætha); *vb* ব্যথা করা bytha kɔra *(pron* bæætha kɔra)

achieve *vb* সাধন করা sadhôn kɔra

achievement *n* সাধন sadhôn, কসরত kɔsrɔt

acid *adj* অম্ল ɔmlô

acidity *n* অম্লতা ɔmlôta

acknowledge *n* স্বীকার করা svīkar kɔra

acknowledgement *n* প্রাপ্তিস্বীকার praptisvīkar

acoustics *n* স্বনবিদ্যা svɔnbidya

acquaint *vb* পরিচয় দেওয়া pôricɔŷ deoŷa

acquaintance *n* পরিচয় pôricɔŷ

acquire *vb* পাওয়া paoŷa

acquisition *n* অর্জন ɔrjôn, আহরণ ahôrôṇ

acre *n* *(measurement)* তিন বিঘা tin bigha; *(field)* জমি jômi

across *pp, adv* পার par

act *n* *(part of a drama)* নটকের অংশ naṭôker ɔṁśô; *(something done)* কাজ kaj, কর্ম kɔrmô; *vb* *(behave)* আচরণ করা acôrôṇ kɔra; *(perform)* অভিনয় করা ôbhinɔŷ kɔra

action *n* কাজ kaj

active *adj* চালু calu, সজীব sɔjīb, কাজের kajer

activity *n* *(endeavor)* তৎপরতা tɔtpɔrôta, কাজ kaj; *(business)* ব্যস্ততা bystôta *(pron* bæstota)

actor *n* অভিনেতা ôbhineta

actual *adj* বাস্তব bastôb

actually *adv* আসলে asôle

acute *adj* *(severe)* বিষম biṣôm; *(precise)* প্রখর prôkhɔr

A.D. *(Anno Domini) abbr* খ্রীষ্টাব্দ khrīṣṭabdô

adapt *vb* উপযোগী করা upôyogī kɔra

adaptability *n* উপযোগিতা upôyogita

add *vb* যোগ করা yog kɔra, সঙ্কলন করা sɔṅkɔlôn kɔra

addiction *n* নেশা neśa

addition *n* সঙ্কলন sɔṅkɔlôn

additional *adj* অতিরিক্ত ôtiriktô, বাড়তি barti, বেশি beśi

address *n* ঠিকানা ṭhikana

adequate *adj* পর্যাপ্ত pôryaptô, যথেষ্ট yɔtheṣṭô

adhere *vb* *(stick)* লাগিয়ে থাকা lagiŷe thaka; *(comply)* মেনে চলা mene cɔla

adhesive *adj* আঠালো aṭhalo

adjacent *adj* কাছে kache, নিকট nikɔṭ

adjective *n* বিশেষণ biśeṣôṇ

adjoin *vb* সংযুক্ত করা sɔṁyuktô kɔra

adjust *vb* সমন্বয়ন করা sɔmônvɔŷôn kɔra

adjustment *n* সমন্বয়ন sɔmônvɔŷôn

administer *vb* পরিচালনা করা pôricalôna kɔra

administration *n* পরিচালনা pôri-calôna, প্রশাসন prôśasôn

administrative *adj* প্রশাসনিক prôśasônik

admirable *adj* প্রশংসনীয় prôśôṁsônîŷô

admiral *n* সেনাধ্যক্ষ senadhyôkṣô

admiration *n* শ্রদ্ধা śrôddha

admire *vb* শ্রদ্ধা করা śrôddha kɔra

admission *n* (entrance) প্রবেশ prôbeś; (confession) স্বীকার svîkar

admit *vb* স্বীকার করা svîkar kɔra

adolescent *n* যুবক yubɔk (m), যুবতী yubôtî (f)

adopt *vb* (take, accept) অবলম্বন করা ɔbôlômbôn kɔra; (a child) আপন করে নেওয়া apôn kôre neoŷa, আশ্রয় দেওয়া aśrôŷ deôŷa

adopted *adj* আশ্রিত aśrito

adoption *n* দত্তক গ্রহণ dɔttôk grôhôṇ

adoration *n* ভক্তি bhôkti

adore *vb* ভক্তি করা bhôkti kɔra

adult *adj* সাবালক sabalôk

adultery *n* ব্যাভিচার byæbhicar

advance *n* আগমন agômôn, অগ্রগতি ôgrôgôti; *vb* এগোনো egono

advantage *n* সুবিধা subidha, উপকার upôkar

adventure *n* বিপজ্জনক কাজ bipôjjɔnôk kaj

adventurous *adj* দুঃসাহসী duhsahôsî

adverb *n* ক্রিয়ার বিশেষণ kriŷar biśeṣôṇ

adversary *n* শত্রু śôtru

adverse *adj* বিরুদ্ধ biruddhô

advertise *vb* ঘোষণা করা ghoṣôṇa kɔra, প্রচার করা prôcar kɔra

advertisement *n* বিজ্ঞাপন bijñapôn

advice *n* উপদেশ upôdeś, পরামর্শ pɔramɔrśô

advise *vb* উপদেশ দেওয়া upôdeś deôŷa

adviser *n* উপদেষ্টা upôdeṣṭa

advocate *n* অধিবক্তা ôdhibôkta, উকিল ukil

affair *n* (matter) ব্যাপার byæpar; (romance) প্রেমের সম্পর্ক premer sɔmpɔrkô

affect *vb* প্রভাবিত করা prôbhabitô kɔra

affection *n* স্নেহ snehô, আদর adôr

affectionate *adj* স্নেহশীল snehôśîl

affirm *vb* রাজি হওয়া raji hɔoŷa, ঠিক করা ṭhik kɔra

affirmation *n* প্রতিজ্ঞা prôtijña, সত্যাপন sɔtyapôn

afflict *vb* কষ্ট দেওয়া kôṣṭô deôŷa

affliction *n* কষ্ট, ক্লেশ kɔṣṭô, kleś

affluence *n* প্রাচুর্য pracuryô

afford *vb* যোগানো yogano

afraid *adj* ভীত bhîtô, ভয়প্রাপ্ত bhɔŷpraptô; *vb* (be ~) ভয় করা bhɔŷ kɔra

African *n* আফ্রিকান aphrikan

after *adv*, *pp* পর, পরে pɔr, pɔre

afternoon *n* বিকাল bikal (Bd), বিলেক bikel (WB)

afterwards *conj* তারপরে tarpɔre

again *adv* আবার abar

against *pp* বিরুদ্ধে biruddhe

age *n (years of one's life)* বয়স
bɔŷɔs; *(period of time)* যুগ yug

agenda *n* বিষয়সূচী biṣɔŷsūcī

agent *n (representative)* প্রতিনিধি
prôtinidhi; *(broker)* দালাল dalal

aggravate *vb* ক্রুদ্ধ করা kruddhô
kɔra, বিরক্ত করা birôktô kɔra

aggressive *adj* আক্রমণপ্রবণ
akrômôṇprôbôṇ

agile *adj* চঞ্চল cɔñcɔl

agitate *vb* আলোড়ন করা alorôn
kɔra

agitated *adj* আন্দোলিত andolitô

agitation *n (emotion)* আবেগ abeg;
(political movement) আন্দোলন
andolôn

ago *adv* আগে age

agony *n* বেদনা bedôna, যন্ত্রণা
ŷɔntrôṇa

agree *vb* রাজি হওয়া raji hɔoŷa

agreeable *adj* মনোজ্ঞ mônojñô

agreement *n* চুক্তি cukti

agricultural *adj* কৃষিজ kṛṣijô

agriculture *n (science)* কৃষিবিদ্যা
kṛṣibidya; *(farming)* চাষ caṣ, কৃষি
kṛṣi

ahead *adv* সামনে samne, সোজা soja

aid *n* সাহায্য sahayyô

aim *n (goal, target)* তাক tak, লক্ষ্য
lôkṣyô; *(purpose)* উদ্দেশ্য uddesyô

air *n* হাওয়া haoŷa, বাতাস batas

air-conditioning *n* শীতাতপ-নিয়ন্ত্রণ
śītatɔp-niŷôntrôṇ, এ-সি e-si

air force *n* বিমানবাহিনী biman-
bahinī

airmail *n* বিমান-ডাক biman-ḍak

airplane *n* বিমান biman

airport *n* বিমানবন্দর bimanbɔndôr

aisle *n* গলি gôli

alarm *n* বিপদ bipɔd

alarm clock *n* ঘুম ভাঙানোর ঘড়ি
ghum bhaṅanor ghôṛi

alcohol *n* মদ mɔd

alcoholic *adj* মদো môdo

alcove *n* ঘরের কোনা ghɔrer kona

ale *n* তেতো মদ teto mɔd, বিয়ার
biŷar

alert *adj* চটপটে cɔṭpɔṭe, সতর্ক
sɔtɔrkô

alien *adj* বিদেশি bideśi

align *vb* সমান করা sɔman kɔra

alike *adj* একই eki, একরকম
ækrɔkôm

alive *adj* জীবিত jībitô

all *adj* সব sɔb, সকল sɔkôl, সমস্ত
sɔmɔstô

allergy *n* এলার্জি ælarji

alley *n* গলি gôli

alliance *n* সম্বন্ধ sɔmbɔndhô

allow *vb* অনুমতি দেওয়া ônumôti
deoŷa, দেওয়া deoŷa

ally *n* সহায় sɔhaŷ, সঙ্গি sôṅgi

almond *n* কাগজি বাদাম kagôji
badam

almost *adv* প্রায় praŷ

alms *n* ভিক্ষা bhikṣa

alone *adj* একা eka

alongside *adv* পাশাপাশি paśapaśi

aloud *adv* জোরে jore

alphabet *n* বর্ণমালা bɔrṇômala

already *adv* ইতিমধ্যে itimôdhye

also *adv* ও o, আরও aro

altar *n* পূজাবেদী pūjabedī

alter *vb* পালটানো palṭano, পরিবর্তন
করা pôribɔrtôn kɔra

alteration *n* অদল-বদল ɔdôl-bɔdôl,
পরিবর্তন pôribɔrtôn

alternative *n* বিকল্প bikɔlpô

although *conj* যদিও yôdio

altitude *n* উচ্চতা uccôta, চড়াই cɔrai

altogether *adv* সম্পূর্ণ sɔmpūrṇô, একেবারে ekebare, সব মিলিয়ে sɔb miliŷe

always *adv* সব সময় sɔb sômôŷ, চিরদিন cirôdin

amateur *n* অপেশাদার ব্যক্তি ɔpeśadar bykti (*pron* ɔpeshadar bekti)

amazement *n* বিস্ময় bismɔŷ, অবাক ɔbak

amazing *adj* আশ্চর্য aścôryô

ambassador *n* দূত dūt

ambiguous *n* দ্ব্যর্থক dvyærthôk

ambition *n* উচ্চাকাঙ্ক্ষা uccakaṅkṣa

ambitious *adj* উচ্চাভিলাষী uccabhilaṣī

ambulance *n* এম্বুলেন্স embulens

amendment *n* সংশোধন sɔṁsodhôn

American *adj* মার্কিন markin

amid *pp* মধ্যে môddhe

amnesty *n* রাজ-ক্ষমা raj-kṣma

among *pp* মধ্যে môddhe, মাঝে majhe

amount *n* পরিমাণ pôrimaṇ

ample *adj* প্রচুর prôcur

amplification *n* সম্প্রসারণ sɔmprôsarôṇ

amputate *vb* অঙ্গচ্ছেদ করা ɔṅgôcched kɔra

amputation *n* অঙ্গচ্ছেদন ɔṅgôcched

amulet *n* মাদুলি maduli

amusement *n* আমোদ-প্রমোদ amod-prômod

analogy *n* সাদৃশ্য sadŕśyô

analysis *n* বিশ্লেষণ biśleṣɔṇ

analyze *vb* বিশ্লেষণ করা biśleṣɔṇ kɔra

anarchy *n* অরাজকতা ɔrajôkɔta

anatomy *n* শারীরস্থান śarīrôsthan

ancestor *n* পূর্বপুরুষ pūrbôpuruṣ

anchor *n* নঙ্গর nôṅgôr

ancient *adj* প্রত্ন prôtnô, প্রাচীন pracīn

and *conj* আর ar, ও o, এবং ebɔṁ

anecdote *n* কাহিনী kahinī, গল্প gɔlpô

anemia *n* রক্তের অভাব rɔkter ɔbhab

anesthesia *n* অবেদন ɔbedɔn

angel *n* দেবদূত debdūt, স্বর্গদূত svɔrgôdūt

anger *n* রাগ rag, ক্রোধ krodh

angle *n* কোণ koṇ

angry *adj* রাগী ragī, ক্রুদ্ধ kruddhô

anguish *n* মনঃকষ্ট mônôḥkɔṣṭô

animal *n* পশু pôśu, জীবজন্ত jībjôntu, জন্তু-জানোয়ার jôntu-janoŷar

animate *adj* প্রফুল্ল prôphullô, সচেতন sɔcetɔn

aniseed *n* মৌরি môuri

ankle *n* গোড়ালি gorali

annex *n* সংযোগ sɔṁyog

annihilation *n* অত্যয় ôtyɔŷ, ধ্বংস dhvɔṁsô

announce *vb* ঘোষণা করা ghoṣôṇa kɔra

announcement *n* ঘোষণা ghoṣôṇa

annoy *vb* বিরক্ত করা birôktô kɔra

annoyance *n* বিরক্তি birôkti

annual *adj* বার্ষিক barṣik

annul *vb* বাতিল করা batil kɔra

anomaly *n* অনিয়ম ɔniŷôm

anonymous *adj* বেনামি benami

another *adj* অন্য ônyô, ভিন্ন bhinnô

answer *n* উত্তর uttôr, জবাব jɔbab;
vb উত্তর দেওয়া uttôr deôýa, জবাব
দেওয়া jɔbab deôýa

ant *n* পিঁপড়া pīpṛa *(Bd)*, পিঁপড়ে
pīpṛe *(WB)*

antenna *n* শুঁয়া śūýa *(Bd)*, শুঁয়ো
śūýo *(WB)*

anticipate *vb* প্রত্যাশা করা prôtyaśa
kɔra

anticipation *n* প্রত্যাশা prôtyaśa

antique *adj* প্রাচীনকালের pracīnkaler

antiseptic *adj* পচন-নিবারক
pɔcôn-nibarôk

anxiety *n* দুশ্চিন্তা duścinta

anxious *adj* উদ্বিগ্ন udbignô, চিন্তিত
cintitô

any *adj* (যে) কোনও (ye) kono

anybody, anyone *n* (যে) কেউ (ye)
keu

anything *n* (যে) কোনও কিছু (ye)
kono kichu

anytime *adv* (যে) কোনও সময় (ye)
kono sômôý

anywhere *adv* (যে) কোনও স্থানে
(ye) kono sthane, (যে) কোনও
জায়গায় (ye) kono jaýgaý

apart *adv* আলাদা alada, পৃথক
pṙthɔk

apartment *n* ফ্ল্যাট phlyæṭ

apathetic *adj* উদাসীন udasīn

apathy *n* অনীহা ɔnīha

apologize *vb* দুঃখ প্রকাশ করা
duḥkhô prôkaś kɔra

apology *n* *(expression of regret)*
দুঃখ প্রকাশ duḥkhô prôkaś; *(excuse)* ওজর ojɔr, অজুহাত ôjuhat

apparatus *n* যন্ত্রপাতি yɔntrôpati

apparel *n* পরিচ্ছদ pôricchɔd

apparent *adj* স্পষ্ট spɔṣṭô

apparition *n* ছায়ামূর্তি chaýamūrti

appeal *n* অনুরোধ ônurodh

appear *vb* হাজির হওয়া hajir hɔôýa

appearance *n* *(being present)*
উপস্থিতি upôsthiti, বিকাশ bikaś;
(look) চেহারা cehara

appease *vb* মেটানো meṭano

appetite *n* *(inclination)* প্রবৃত্তি
prôbṙtti; *(hunger)* খিদা khida *(Bd)*,
খিদে khide *(WB)*

applaud *vb* *(praise)* প্রশংসা করা
prôśômsa kɔra; *(clap)* তালি
দেওয়া tali deôýa

applause *n* প্রশংসা prôśômsa

apple *n* আপেল apel

appliance *n* যন্ত্র yɔntrô

application *n* *(use)* প্রয়োগ prôýog;
(request) দরখাস্ত dɔrkhastô

apply *vb* *(use)* লাগানো lagano;
(request) দরখাস্ত করা dɔrkhastô
kɔra

appoint *vb* *(employ)* লাগানো
lagano; *(fix)* নির্দিষ্ট করা nirdiṣṭô
kɔra

appointment *n* নিয়োগ niýog

appraisal *n* বিচার bicar

appreciate *vb* ভাল লাগা bhalô
laga, রসগ্রহণ করা rɔsgrôhôn kɔra

appreciation *n* রসগ্রহণ rɔsgrôhôn

apprentice *n* শিক্ষার্থী śikṣarthī
(pron shikkharthi)

approach *vb* কাছে আসা kache asa;
n অভিগমন ôbhigɔmôn

appropriate *adj* উপযুক্ত upôyuktô

approval *n* অনুমোদন ônumodôn

approve *vb* সমর্থন করা sɔmôrthôn
kɔra, অনুমোদন করা ônumodôn
kɔra

approximately *adv* মোটামুটি moțamuți, কমবেশি kɔmbeśi

April *n* এপ্রিল মাস epril mas

apt *adj* উপযুক্ত upôyukto, যোগ্য yogyô

aptitude *n* ঝোঁক jhŏk

aquatic *adj* জলীয় jôlīẏô

Arab *n* আরববাসী arôbbasī

Arabic *adj* আরবী arbī

arable *adj* কৃষ্য kŗṣyô

arbitrary *adj* ইচ্ছামত icchamɔto

arbitration *n* সালিসি salisi

arch *n* খিলান khilan

archaeological *adj* প্রত্নতাত্ত্বিক prôtnôtattvik

archaeology *n* প্রত্নবিদ্যা prôtnôbidya, প্রত্নতত্ত্ব prôtnôtɔttvô

architect *n* স্থপতি sthɔpôti

architecture *n* স্থাপত্য sthapôtyô

archive *n* দলিল–পত্রাদি dôlil-pôtradi

arctic *adj* সুমেরু sumeru

area *n* এলাকা elaka

argue *vb* তর্ক করা tɔrkô kɔra

argument *n* তর্ক tɔrkô

arise *vb* ওঠা oțha

aristocracy *n* অভিজাতবর্গ ôbhijat-bɔrgô, আভিজাত্য abhijatyô

arithmetic *n* অঙ্ক ɔṅkô

arm *n* হাত hat, বাহু bahu

armpit *n* বগল bɔgôl

army *n* বাহিনী bahinī, সেনা sena

aroma *n* ঘ্রাণ ghraṇ, সুগন্ধ sugɔndhô

around *adv* চারদিকে cardike

arrange *vb (put in order)* সাজানো sajano; *(make arrangements)* ব্যবস্থা করা bybôstha kɔra (*pron* bæbostha kɔra)

arrangement *n* ব্যবস্থা, bybôstha (*pron* bæbostha)

arrest *vb* বন্দী করা bôndī kɔra

arrival *n* আগমন agômôn

arrive *vb* পৌছানো pŏuchano

arrogance *n* অহংকার ɔhôṁkar, ধৃষ্টতা dhŗṣțôta

arrogant *adj* সদর্প sɔdɔrpô, অহংকারী ɔhôṁkarī

arrow *n* তীর tīr

art *n* শিল্প śilpô

artery *n* ধমনি dhɔmôni, শিরা śira

article *n (item)* দফা dɔpha, পণ্য pôṇyô; *(piece of writing)* প্রবন্ধ prôbɔndhô

artificial *adj* কৃত্রিম kŗtrim, নকল nɔkôl

artist *n* শিল্পী śilpī

artistic *adj* শৈল্পিক śoilpik

as *adv* যেমন yæmôn; *pp* মত mɔtô

as if *conj* যেন yænô

ascetic *n* সন্ন্যাসী sɔnnyasī, তাপস tapôs, যোগী yogī

ash *n* ছাই chai

ashamed *adj* লজ্জিত lôjjitô

aside from *pp* ছাড়া chara

ask *vb (question)* জিজ্ঞাসা করা ji-jñasa kɔra; *(request)* চাওয়া caoẏa

asleep *adj* ঘুমন্ত ghumɔntô, নিদ্রিত nidritô

aspect *n* চেহারা cehara, আকৃতি akŗti

asphalt *n* পিচ pic

assault *n* আক্রমণ akrômôṇ, আঘাত aghat; *vb* মারা mara, আক্রমণ করা akrômôṇ kɔra

assemble *vb* জমা করা jɔma kɔra

assembly *n* সভা sɔbha, সম্মেলন sɔmmelôn

assert *vb* নিশ্চয় করে বলা niścɔy kôre bɔla

assertion *n* উক্তি ukti

assessment *n* মূল্যায়ন mulyayôn

assign *vb* নিদিষ্ট করা nirdiṣṭô kɔra

assimilate *vb* হজম করা hɔjôm kɔra

assist *vb* সাহায্য করা sahayyô kɔra

assistance *n* সাহায্য sahayyô

assistant *n* সহায় sɔhay, সহকারী sɔhôkarī

associate *vb* মেলামেশা করা melameśa kɔra

association *n* সমিতি sômiti, সংঘ sɔṁghô

assume *vb (take on)* গ্রহণ করা grôhôn kɔra; *(suppose)* মনে করা mône kɔra, আঁচ করা ãc kɔra

assumption *n* ধারণা dharôna

assure *vb* নিশ্চিত করে বলা niścitô kôre bɔla

assurance *n* নিশ্চয়তা niścɔyôta

asthma *n* হাঁপানি hãpani

astonish *vb* স্তম্ভিত করা stômbhitô kɔra

astonished *adj* স্তম্ভিত stômbhitô

astray *adv* বিপথে bipɔthe

astringent *adj* তিতা tita, তেঁতো teto

astrologer *n* জ্যোতিষী jyotiṣī

astrology *n* জ্যোতিষ jyotiṣ

astronaut *n* মহাকাশচারী mɔhakaścarī

astronomy *n* জ্যোতির্বিদ্যা jyotibidya

astute *adj* চালাক calak

asylum *n* আশ্রয়স্থান aśrɔŷsthan

at *pp* মধ্যে môdhye, কাছে kache

atheism *n* নাস্তিকতা nastikôta

atheist *n* নাস্তিক nastik

athlete *n* মল্ল mɔllô

athletics *n* শরীরচর্চা śôrīrcɔrca, খেলাধুলা khæladhula *(Bd)*, খেলাধুলো khæladhulo *(WB)*

atmosphere *n* বায়ুমণ্ডল baŷumɔṇḍôl

atom *n* পরমাণু pɔrômaṇu

attach *vb* লাগা laga, লাগানো lagano

attack *n* আক্রমণ akrômôn, হামলা hamla; *vb* আক্রমণ করা akrômôn kɔra

attempt *n* চেষ্টা ceṣṭa; *vb* চেষ্টা করা ceṣṭa kɔra

attend *vb (look after)* সেবা করা seba kɔra; *(be present)* উপস্থিত হওয়া upôsthit hɔoŷa

attendance *n* উপস্থিতি upôsthiti

attendant *n* সেবক sebɔk *(m)*, সেবিকা sebika *(f)*

attention *n* মনোযোগ mônoyog

attentive *adj* অবহিত ɔbôhitô, মনোযোগী mônoyogī

attic *n* চিলে ঘর cile ghɔr, চিলে কোঠা cile koṭha

attitude *n* মনোভাব mônobhab

attorney *n* প্রতিনিধি prôtinidhi

attract *vb* টানা ṭana, আকর্ষণ করা akôrṣôn kɔra

attraction *n* টান ṭan, আকর্ষণ akôrṣôn

attractive *adj* সুন্দর sundôr

attribute *n* বিশেষণ biśeṣɔn

aubergine *n* বেগুন begun

auction *n* নিলাম nilam

audience *n* উপস্থিত ব্যক্তি upôsthit byekti

auditor *n (examiner)* পরীক্ষক pôrīkṣɔk

augment *vb* বাড়ানো baṛano

August *n* আগষ্ট মাস agôṣṭ mas

aunt *n (mother's sister)* খালা khala *Muslim*, মাসি masi *Hindu*; *(father's sister)* ফুফু phuphu *Muslim*, পিসি pisi *Hindu*; *(mother's*

brother's wife) মামি mami
Muslim, মামি mami *Hindu*;
(*father's older brother's wife*) বড়
চাচি bɔrô caci *Muslim*, জেঠি jethi,
জেঠিমা jethima *Hindu*; (*father's
younger brother's wife*) চাচি caci
Muslim, কাকি kaki, কাকিমা
kakima *Hindu*

auspicious *adj* মাঙ্গলিক maṅgôlik

authentic *adj* সত্য sôtyô, খাঁটি
khāṭi

author *n* লেখক lekhɔk

authority *n* (*power*) ক্ষমতা kṣɔmota;
(*government*) শাসক śasôk;
(*weight, importance*) গুরুত্ব gurutvô; (*influence*) প্রভাব prôbhab

authorization *n* প্রাধিকার pradhikar,
অনুমোদন ônumodôn

authorize *vb* প্রাধিকার দেওয়া
pradhikar deoŷa, অনুমোদন করা
ônumodôn kɔra

automatic *adj* এমনি emni, স্বয়ংক্রিয়
svɔyôṁkriyô

automobile *n* গাড়ি gaṛi

autonomous *adj* স্বশাসিত svɔśasitô

autopsy *n* শবদেহ-পরীক্ষা śɔbdehô-
pôrīkṣa, পোস্ট মর্টেম posṭ môrṭem

autumn *n* হেমন্ত hemôntô

auxiliary *adj* সহায়ক sɔhayôk

availability *n* পাওয়ার সম্ভাবনা
paoŷar sɔmbhabôna

available *adj* পাওয়া প্রাপ্ত paoŷa
praptô, পাওয়া যায় paoŷa yaŷ

avalanche *n* হিমানী –সম্প্রপাত
himanī–sɔmprôpat

avenue *n* রাজপথ rajpɔth

average *n* গড় gɔṛ

avoid *vb* এড়ানো eṛano, এড়িয়ে
যাওয়া eṛiŷe yaoŷa

awake *vb* জাগা jaga

award *n* পুরস্কার purôskar

aware *adj* সতর্ক sɔtɔrkô, সচেতন
sɔcetôn; *vb* (be ~) সতর্ক থাকা
sɔtɔrkô thaka

away *adv* দূরে dūre

awful *adj* জঘন্য jɔghônyô

awkward *adj* অস্বস্তিকর ɔsvôstikɔr

axe *n* কুড়াল kuṛal *(Bd)*, কুড়োল
kuṛol

axis *n* অক্ষরেখা ɔkṣôrekha

axle *n* চক্রনাভি cɔkrônabhi

B

baby *n* শিশু śiśu, বাচ্চা bacca

back *n* পিছন pichôn, পেছন pechôn; *(of the body)* পিঠ piṭh

backbone *n* মেরুদণ্ড merudôṇḍô

backward *adv* অনুন্নত ɔnunnɔtô; *(direction)* পিছন দিকে pichôn dike

bacteria *n* জীবাণু jībaṇu

bad *adj* খারাপ kharap, মন্দ môndô, বদ bɔd

badge *n* তকমা tɔkma

badly *adv* কুভাবে kubhabe, মন্দভাবে môndôbhabe

bag *n* থলি thôli

baggage *n* মালপত্র malpɔtrô

bail *n* জামিন jamin

bailiff *n* পেয়াদা peyada

bait *n* প্রলোভন prôlobhôn, টোপ ṭop,

bake *vb* সেকা sæka, বানানো banano

baker *n* রুটিওয়ালা ruṭioŷala

balance *n* সমতা sɔmôta

balanced *adj* সুষম suṣɔmô

balcony *n* ঝুল-বারান্দা jhul-baranda

bald *adj* টাকমাথা ṭakmatha, টেকো ṭeko

ball *n* বল bɔl

balloon *n* ফানুস phanus

bamboo *n* বাঁশ bãś

banana *n* কলা kɔla

band *n* বন্ধনী bɔndhônī

bandage *n* পটি pôṭi

bangle *n* বালা bala, চুড়ি cuṛi

bank *n (financial institution)* ব্যাংক byæṁk; *(side of a river)* পাড় paṛ

banner *n* ব্যানার byanar (*pron* bænar)

banquet *n* ভোজ bhoj

banter *n* ফষ্টিনষ্টি phôṣṭinôṣṭi, প্রহসন prôhôsôn

banyan tree *n* বটগাছ bɔṭgach

baptism *n* অভিসিঞ্চন ôbhisiñcôn

bar *n (metal piece)* ডাণ্ডা ḍaṇḍa; *(place for drinking)* পানশালা pansala; *vb* আটকানো aṭkano

barbarian *adj* অসভ্য ɔsôbhyô, অমার্জিত ɔmarjitô

barber *n* নাপিত napit

bare *adj* উলঙ্গ ulɔṅgô, নগ্ন nɔgnô

barefoot *adj* খালি পায়ে khali paye

bargain *vb* দামাদামি করা damadami kɔra, দরদাম করা dɔrdam kɔra

bark *n (of a tree)* ছাল chal; *(of a dog)* কুকুরের ডাক kukurer ḍak

barley *n* যব yɔb

barometer *n* ব্যারোমিটার byæromiṭar

barrack *n* সেনানিবাস senanibas

barrel *n* পিপা pipa (*Bd*), পিপে pipe (*WB*), মটকা mɔṭka

barren *adj* বন্ধ্যা bɔndhya

barrier *n* বাধা badha

base *n (bottom, root)* তল tɔl, গোড়া goṛa; *adj* নীচু nīcu, মূল্যহীন mūlyôhīn

basement *n* নিচতলা nictɔla

basic *adj* মৌলিক moulik

basil *n* তুলসী tulsī

basin *n* বাটি baṭi, গামলা gamla

basis *n* ভিত্তি bhitti, বনিয়াদ bôniyad

basket *n* টুকরি ṭukri, ঝুড়ি jhuṛi

bass *n, adj* মন্দ্র mɔndrô, খাদ khad

bat *n (animal)* বাদুড় baduṛ; *(stick)* ব্যাট byæṭ

batch *n* দল dɔl, গাদা gada, গোছা gocha

bath *n* গোসল gosôl, স্নান snan

bathe *vb* স্নান করা snan kɔra, গোসল করা gosôl kɔra, গা ধোয়া ga dhoẏa

bathroom *n* স্নানঘর snanghɔr, গোসলখানা gosôlkhana, বাথরুম bathrum

batter *vb* আঘাত করা aghat kɔra

battery *n* ব্যাটারি byæṭari

battle *n* যুদ্ধ yuddhô, লড়াই lɔrai

bay *n* উপসাগর upôsagôr

bayleaf *n* তেজপাতা tejpata

B.C. *abbr* খ্রীষ্টপূর্ব khrīṣṭôpūrbô

be *vb (become, occur, happen)* হওয়া hɔẏa; *(exist)* আছ্- ach-

beach *n* সমুদ্রতীর sômudrôtīr, তট tɔṭ

beak *n* পাখির ঠোঁট pakhir ṭhõṭ

beam *n (wooden plank)* কড়িকাঠ kôṛikaṭh; *(ray of light)* অংশু ôṁśu

bean *n* শিম śim, বরবটি bɔrbôṭi

bear *n* ভালুক bhaluk; *vb* সহ্য করা sôhyô kɔra *(pron* sojjho kɔra*)*

beard *n* দাড়ি daṛi

bearing *n* অবস্থান ɔbôsthan

beast *n* পশু pôśu

beat *n* তাল tal; *vb* মারা mara

beautiful *adj* সুন্দর sundôr, শোভন śobhôn

beauty *n* সৌন্দর্য soundôryô, লালিত্য lalityô, ছিরি chiri

because *conj* কারণ karôṇ, যেহেতু yehetu, বলে bôle

become *vb* হওয়া hɔẏa

bed *n* বিছানা bichana

bedroom *n* শোবার ঘর śobar ghɔr

bedstead *n* চৌকি couki, খাট khaṭ

bee *n* মৌমাছি moumachi

beef *n* গরুর মাংস gôrur maṁsô

beer *n* তেতো মদ teto mɔd, বিয়ার biyar

beetle *n* গুবরে পোকা gubre poka

before *pp* আগে age

beg *vb* ভিক্ষা করা bhikṣa kɔra

beggar *n* ভিক্ষুক bhikṣuk, ভিখারি bhikhari

begin *vb* আরম্ভ হওয়া arômbhô hɔẏa, আরম্ভ করা arômbhô kɔra

beginning *n* আরম্ভ arômbhô, গোড়া gora, শুরু śuru

behalf of *pp* (on ~) পক্ষে pôkṣe

behave *vb* আচরণ করা acôrôṇ kɔra, ব্যবহার করা bybôhar kɔra *(pron* bæbohar kɔra*)*

behavior *n* আচরণ acôrôṇ, ব্যবহার bybôhar *(pron* bæbohar*)*, হালচাল halcal

behind *pp* পিছনে pichône *(Bd)*, পেছনে pechône *(WB)*, পিছে piche

being *n* অস্তিত্ব ɔstitvô

belief *n* বিশ্বাস biśvas

believe *vb* বিশ্বাস করা biśvas kɔra

belittle *vb* তুচ্ছ করা tucchô kɔra

bell *n* ঘণ্টা ghɔṇṭa, বেল bel

belly *n* পেট peṭ

belong *vb* অংশী হওয়া ɔṁśī hɔẏa

belonging *n* নিজের জিনিস nijer jinis

beloved *adj* আদুরে adure

below *pp* নিচে nice

belt *n* বেল্ট belṭ

bench *n* বেঞ্চি beñci, টুল ṭul

bend *n* ঝোঁক jhõk; *vb* বাঁকানো bākano

beneath *pp* নিচে nice, নিম্নে nimne

beneficial *adj* উপকারী upôkarī, হিতকর hitôkɔr

benefit *n* উপকার upôkar, সুবিধা

subidha *(Bd)*, সুবিধে subidhe *(WB)*; *(profit)* লাভ labh

Bengal *n* বাংলাদেশ baṁladeś, বঙ্গদেশ bôṅgôdeś

Bengali *adj* বাঙালি baṅali; *n* বাংলা baṁla

benign *adj* হিতকর hitôkɔr, প্রসন্ন prôsɔnnô

bent *adj* *(bowed)* নত nɔtô; *(uneven, crooked)* বাঁকা bāka

berry *n* জাম jam

beside *pp* পাশে paśe

besides *adv, conj* তা ছাড়া ta chaṛa

besiege *vb* অবরোধ করা ɔbôrodh kɔra

best *adj* সেরা sera, শ্রেষ্ঠ śreṣṭhô

bet *n* বাজি baji, জুয়া juẏa *(Bd)*, জুয়ো juẏo *(WB)*; *vb* জুয়া খেলা juẏa khæla

betel-leaf *n* পান pan

betel-nut *n* সুপারি supari

betray *vb* ছলনা করা chɔlôna kɔra, ঠকানো ṭhɔkano

better *adj* আরও ভাল aro bhalô

between *n* মাঝে majhe, মধ্যে môdhye

beverage *n* পানীয় panīẏô

beware *int* সাবধান *(adj)* sabdhan

bewilder *vb* বিভ্রান্ত করা bibhrantô kɔra

beyond *pp* বাইরে baire, অতিক্রমে ôtikrôme

bias *n* পক্ষপাত pôkṣôpat

Bible *n* বাইবেল baibel

bicker *vb* খেঁচাখেঁচি করা khẽcakhẽci kɔra

bicycle *n* সাইকেল saikel

big *adj* বড় bɔrô

bilingual *adj* দুভাষী dubhaṣī *(Bd)*,

দোভাষী dobhaṣī *(WB)*, দ্বিভাষিক dvibhaṣik

bill *n* *(account of money)* টাকার হিসাব ṭakar hisab, বিল bil; *(document)* দলিল dôlil

bin *n* *(container)* পাত্র patrô; *(garbage container)* ময়লার বালতি mɔẏlar balti

bind *vb* বাঁধানো bādhano

biography *n* জীবনী jībônī, জীবন-কথা jībôn-kɔtha

biological *adj* জীবতাত্ত্বিক jībtattvik

biology *n* জীবতত্ত্ব jībtɔttvô

bird *n* পাখি pakhi

birth *n* জন্ম jɔnmô

birthday *n* জন্মদিন jɔnmôdin

biscuit *n* বিস্কুট biskuṭ

bisexual *adj* উভলিঙ্গ ubhôliṅgô

bit *n, adv* টুকরা ṭukra, কিছু kichu, একটু ekṭu

bite *n* কামড় kamɔr; *vb* কামড় দেওয়া kamôr deoẏa, কামড়ানো kamrano

bitter *adj* তেতো teto, তিতা tita

black *adj* কালো kalo

blackberry *n* কালোজাম kalojam

bladder *n* মূত্রাশয় mūtraśɔẏ

blade *n* ফলক phɔlôk

blame *vb* দোষ দেওয়া doṣ deoẏa, নিন্দা করা ninda kɔra *(Bd)*, নিন্দে করা ninde kɔra *(WB)*

blanket *n* কম্বল kɔmbôl

blast *n* ঝাপটা jhapṭa; *vb* ফাটা phaṭa

blaze *n* আলোক alok

bleak *adj* জীবশূন্য jībśūnyô, নিরানন্দ niranɔndô

bleed *vb* রক্ত পড়া rɔktô pɔra

bless *vb* আশীর্বাদ করা aśīrbad kɔra

blessing *n* আশীর্বাদ aśīrbad

blind *adj* অন্ধ ɔndhô

blindness *n* অন্ধতা ɔndhôta

blink *vb* চোখ পিটপিট করা cokh piṭpiṭ kɔra

blister *n* ফোস্কা phoska

block *n* কুঁদা kũda; *vb* বাধা দেওয়া badha deoŷa, আটকানো aṭkano

blond *adj* সোনালি চুলের sonali culer

blood *n* রক্ত rɔktô

bloom *vb* ফোটা phoṭa

blooming *adj* প্রফুল্ল prôphullô

blossom *n* ফুল phul

blouse *n* ব্লাউজ blauj

blow *n* আঘাত aghaṭ, চোট coṭ; *vb* ফু দেওয়া phu deoŷa

blue *adj* নীল nīl

bluff *n* ধাপ্পা dhappa

blunt *adj* ভোঁতা bhõta

blush *vb* লজ্জা পাওয়া lɔjja paoŷa

board *n* তক্তা tɔkta

boast *vb* তড়পানো tɔrpano

boat *n* নৌকা nouka, নৌকো nouko, তরী tôrī

bodily *adj* শারীরিক śarīrik, দৈহিক doihik

body *n* গা ga, শরীর śôrīr, দেহ dehô

boil *n* স্ফোট sphoṭ; *vb* সিদ্ধ করা siddhô kɔra (*Bd*), সেদ্ধ করা sed-dhô kɔra (*WB*), ফোটা phoṭa

bold *adj* সাহসী sahôsī

bolt *n* ছিটকিনি chiṭkini, খিল khil

bomb *n* বোমা boma

bone *n* হাড় haṛ, হাড্ডি haḍḍi

bone marrow *n* মজ্জা mɔjja

book *n* বই bôi, গ্রন্থ grônthô, পুস্তক pustɔk

bookcase *n* বইয়ের আলমারি bôiŷer almari

bookmark *n* পুস্তক চিহ্ন pustɔk cinhô

bookstore *n* বইয়ের দোকান bôiŷer dokan

boot *n* বুটজুতা buṭjuta (*Bd*), বুটজুতো buṭjuto (*WB*)

border *n* কিনারা kinara, সীমা sīma

born *adj* জাত jat, জন্মিত jɔnmitô

borrow *vb* ধার করা dhar kɔra

boss *n* মনিব mônib, বস bɔs, মালিক malik

botany *n* উদ্ভিদ-বিদ্যা udbhid-bidya

both *adj* উভয় ubhɔŷ, দুজন dujɔn

bother *vb* জ্বালানো jvalano

bottle *n* বোতল botôl

bottle-gourd *n* লাউ lau

bottom *n* তল tɔl, ভিত্তি bhitti

bounce *vb* লাফিয়ে ওঠা laphiŷe oṭha

bound *adj* নিবদ্ধ nibɔddhô

boundary *n* সীমানা sīmana

boundless *adj* অসীম ɔsīm, বিশাল biśal

bountiful *adj* উদার udar, দানী danī

bow *n* (*arc*) ধনু dhônu; (*musical*) ছিলা chila, ধনুক dhônuk; *vb* (*bend*) নত করা nɔtô kɔra

bowels *n* অন্ত্র ɔntrô

bowl *n* বাটি baṭi

box *n* বাক্স, বাক্স baksô

boxing *n* মুষ্টিযুদ্ধ muṣṭiyuddhô

boy *n* ছেলে chele, বালক balôk, খোকা khoka

boyfriend *n* ছেলে বন্ধু chele bôndhu, প্রেমিক premik

bracelet *n* বালা bala

bracket *n* বন্ধনী bɔndhônī

brag *vb* বড়াই করা bɔrai kɔra

braid *n* বেণি beni

brain *n* মস্তিষ্ক môstiskô, মেধা medha

brake *n* ব্রেক brek

bramble *n* ডালপালা ḍalpala

branch *n* *(of a tree)* ডাল ḍal; *(division)* বিভাগ bibhag

brass *n* পিতল pitôl

brave *adj* সাহসী sahôsī

bread *n* রুটি ruṭi, চাপাটি capaṭi

break *vb* ভাঙ্গা bhaṅga, ভাঙ্গানো bhaṅgano; *n (rest)* বিশ্রাম biśram; *(split)* বিভেদ bibhed

breakdown (have a ~) *vb* ভেঙে পড়া bheṅe pɔra

breakfast *n* নাস্তা nasta

breast *n* বুক buk, স্তন stɔn

breath *n* নিঃশ্বাস niḥśvas

breathe *vb* নিঃশ্বাস নেওয়া niḥśvas neoẏa

breed *vb* পালন করা palôn kɔra

breeze *n* নরম বাতাস nɔrôm batas, হালকা হাওয়া halka haoẏa

bribe *n* ঘুষ ghuṣ; *vb* ঘুষ দেওয়া ghuṣ deoẏa

brick *n* ইট iṭ

bride *n* বধূ bôdhu, নতুন বউ nôtun bôu

bridegroom *n* বর bɔr

bridge *n* পুল pul, ব্রিজ brij

brief *adj* সংক্ষিপ্ত sɔṁkṣiptô

bright *adj* উজ্জ্বল ujjvɔl

brilliant *adj (shiny)* উজ্জ্বল ujjvɔl; *(clever)* মেধাবী medhabī

bring *vb* আনা ana, নিয়ে আসা niẏe asa

British *adj* ব্রিটিশ briṭiś

brittle *adj* ঠুনকো ṭhunkô

broad *adj* চওড়া cɔora

broadcast *n* প্রচার prôcar

broken *adj* ভাঙ্গা bhaṅga

broker *n* দালাল dalal

bronchitis *n* ফুসফুসের রোগ phusphuser rog

bronze *n* তামা tama

broom *n* ঝাড়ু jharu

broth *n* ঝোল jhol

brother *n (general and younger)* ভাই bhai; *(older)* দাদা dada

brow *n* ভ্রূ bhru, ভুরু bhuru

brown *adj* বাদামি badami

brush *vb* ঝাড়া jhara, ঝাড়ু দেওয়া jharu deoẏa; *n (thicket)* ঝোপ jhop; *(paintbrush)* কুঁচি kūci; *(hairbrush)* ব্রাশ braś

brutal *adj* নিষ্ঠুর niṣṭhur

bubble *n* বিম্ব bimbô

bucket *n* বালতি balti

budget *n* আয়ব্যয়ক aŷbyŷôk *(pron* aybæyok)

buffalo *n* মহিষ môhiṣ

bug *n* পোকা poka

build *vb (establish)* স্থাপন করা sthapôn kɔra, তৈরি করা toiri kɔra; *(erect a building)* গড়া gɔra, গড়িয়ে তোলা gôriẏe tola

building *n* ঘর ghɔr, বাড়ি baṛi, দালান dalan

bulb *n (flower)* ফুল phul; *(light)* বাল্ব balb

bullet *n* গুলি guli

bulletin *n* ঘোষণা ghoṣôṇa

bully *vb* দাবড়ানো dabṛano, ভয় দেখানো bhoẏ dækhano

bumblebee *n* ভোমরা bhomra

bunch, bundle *n* গোছ goch, তোড়া toṛa

burden *n* বোঝা bojha, ভার bhar

bureaucracy *n* আমলাতন্ত্র amlatɔntrô

bureaucratic *adj* আমলাতান্ত্রিক amlatantrik

burglar *n* চোর cor, সিঁধেল চোর sĩdhel cor

burn *vb* পোড়া poṛa, পোড়ানো poṛano

burning *n* দাহ dahô

burst *vb* ফোটা phoṭa, ভেঙ্গে যাওয়া bheṅge yaoŷa

bury *vb* মাটি দেওয়া maṭi deoŷa, কবর দেওয়া kɔbôr deoŷa

bus *n* বাস bas

bush *n* ছোট গাছ choṭô gach

business *n* ব্যবসা bybsa (*pron* bæbsha)

busy *adj* ব্যস্ত bystô (*pron* bæsto)

but *adv*, *conj* কিন্তু kintu, তবে tɔbe, ছাড়া chaṛa

butcher *n* কসাই kɔsai

butter *n* মাখন makhôn

butterfly *n* প্রজাপতি prôjapôti

buttocks *n* পাছা pacha

button *n* বোতাম botam

buttonhole *n* বোতামের ঘর botamer ghɔr

buy *vb* কেনা kena

buyer *n* বেপারি bæpari, বণিক bônik

buzz *vb* ভনভন করা bhɔnbhɔn kɔra

by *pp* (*near*) কাছে kache; (*at the side of*) পাশে paśe; (*from*) থেকে theke; (*within a time*) মধ্যে môddhe

by now *adv* এতক্ষণে etôkṣône

C

cabbage *n* বাঁধাকপি bādhakôpi

cabin *n* কুটির kuṭir

cabinet *n* (chest of drawers) আলমারি almari; (group of ministers) মন্ত্রিপরিষৎ môntripôriṣôt

cable *n* তারের দড়ি tarer dôṛi

café *n* কফিখানা kôphikhana

cage *n* খাঁচা khāca

cajole *vb* চুমরানো cumrano

cake *n* পিঠা piṭha (Bd), পিঠে piṭhe (WB), কেক kek

calcium *n* চুন cun

calculate *vb* হিসাব করা hisab kɔra (Bd), হিসেব করা hisab kɔra (WB)

calculation *n* হিসাব hisab (Bd), হিসেব hiseb (WB)

calendar *n* পঞ্জিকা pônjika

calf *n* বাছুর bachur

call *vb* ডাকা ḍaka; *n* ডাক ḍak

call off *vb* বাতিল করা batil kɔra

calm *adj* শান্ত śantô

camel *n* উট uṭ

camera *n* ক্যামেরা kyæmera

camp *n* শিবির śibir

campaign *n* অভিযান ôbhiyan

can *vb* পারা para

canal *n* খাল khal

cancel *vb* বাতিল করা batil kɔra

cancer *n* ক্যানসার kyænsar, কর্কট রোগ kɔrkôṭ rog

candid *adj* খোলাখুলি kholakhuli

candidate *n* উমেদার umedar

candle *n* মোমবাতি mombati

candy *n* মিছরি michri

cane *n* বেত bet

cannon *n* কামান kaman

canoe *n* ডোঙা ḍoṅa

canopy *n* শামিয়ানা śamiŷana

canteen *n* ক্যানটিন kyæntin

canvas *n* ক্যানভাস kyænbhas

cap *n* টুপি ṭupi

capability *n* ক্ষমতা kṣɔmôta, দক্ষতা dɔkṣôta

capable *adj* সক্ষম sɔkṣɔm

capacity *n* ধরবার ক্ষমতা dhɔrbar kṣɔmôta

cape *n* অন্তরীপ ɔntôrîp

capital *n* (main city) রাজধানী rajdhanî; (money) পুঁজি pūji; *adj* প্রধান prôdhan

capitalism *n* পুঁজিবাদ pūjibad

caprice *n* খেয়ালি kheŷali, খামখেয়ালি khamkheŷali

capsicum *n* মিষ্টি লঙ্কা miṣṭi lɔṅka

capsule *n* বড়ি bôṛi

captain *n* অধ্যক্ষ ɔdhyôkṣô

captive *n* বন্দী bôndî

car *n* গাড়ি gaṛi

car rental *n* গাড়ি-ভাড়া gaṛi-bhaṛa

card *n* (stiff paper) কার্ড karḍ; (for games) তাস tas

cardamon *n* এলাচ elac

cardboard *n* কার্ডবোর্ড karḍbôrḍ

care *n* (attention) যত্ন yɔtnô; (caution) সাবধান sabdhan

careful *adj* সতর্ক sɔtɔrkô

carefully *adv* সতর্পণে sɔntɔrpôṇe, সতর্কভাবে sɔtɔrkôbhabe

careless *adj* অসাবধানে ɔsabdhane

carelessness *n* অসাবধানতা ɔsabdhanôta

caress *vb* আদর করা adôr kɔra, হাত বুলানো hat bulano

caretaker *n* অবধায়ক ɔbôdhaŷôk

carpenter *n* মিস্ত্রি mistri

carriage *n* বহন bɔhôn

carrot *n* গাজর gajôr

carry *vb* নেওয়া neoẏa, কোলে নেওয়া kole neoẏa

cart *n* ঠেলাগাড়ি ṭhælagaṛi

cartilage *n* তরুণাস্তি tôruṇasti

carton *n* কার্ডবোর্ডের বাক্স kardbôrḍer baksô

cartoon *n* ব্যঙ্গচিত্র byṅgôcitrô (*pron* bænggocitro)

carve *vb* খোদাই করা khodai kɔra

carving *n* খোদাই khodai

case *n* (*container*) খাপ khap; (*precedent, example*) নজির nôjir

cash *n* (*ready money*) নগদ টাকা nɔgôd ṭaka; (*fund*) তহবিল tɔhôbil

cask *n* পিপা pipa (*Bd*), পিপে pipe (*WB*)

cast *vb* (*throw*) ফেলা phæla; *n* (*mold*) ছাঁচ chãc

castle *n* দুর্গ durgô

casual *adj* সাময়িক samôẏik

casually *adv* এমনি emni

cat *n* বিড়াল biṛal, বেড়াল beṛal

catalog *n* তালিকা talika

cataract *n* ছানি chani

catastrophe *n* সর্বনাশ sɔrbônaś

catch *vb* ধরা dhɔra

cathedral *n* প্রধান গির্জা prôdhan girja

Catholic *adj* রোমান ক্যাথলিক roman kyæthôlik

cattle *n* গবাদি gɔbadi

cauldron *n* কড়াই kɔṛai

cauliflower *n* ফুলকপি phulkôpi

cause *vb* ঘটানো ghɔṭano; *n* কারণ karôṇ

caution *n* সাবধানতা sabdhanôta; *vb* সাবধান করা sabdhan kɔra

cautious *adj* সাবধান sabdhan

cautiously *adv* সন্তর্পণে sɔntɔrpôṇe

cave *n* গুহা guha

cease *vb* থামা thama, শেষ হওয়া śeṣ hɔoẏa

ceaseless *adj* অবিরাম ɔbiram

cedar *n* দেবদারু গাছ debdaru gach

ceiling *n* ছাদ chad

celebrate *vb* পালন করা palôn kɔra

celebration *n* অনুষ্ঠান ônusthan

celibacy *n* কৌমার্য koumaryô

cell *n* জীবকোষ jībkoṣ

cell phone *n* মোবাইল mobail

cellar *n* নিচতলা nictɔla

cement *n* সিমেন্ট simenṭ

cemetery *n* কবরস্থান kɔbôrsthan

census *n* লোকগণনা lokgɔṇôna

center *n* কেন্দ্র kendrô, মধ্য môdhyô

central *adj* কেন্দ্রীয় kendrīẏô, মধ্যে môdhye

century *n* শতাব্দ śɔtabdô

ceramics *n* মৃৎশিল্প mṛṭśilpô

cereal *n* গম gɔm

ceremony *n* উৎসব uṭsɔb

certain *adj* নিশ্চিত niścit, niścitô

certificate *n* সনদ sɔnôd, প্রমাণ পত্র prômaṇ pɔtrô

certify *vb* সাক্ষ্য দেওয়া sakṣyô deoẏa

chaff *n* ভুসি bhusi

chain *n* (*necklace*) মালা mala; (*fetter*) শিকল śikɔl

chair *n* চেয়ার ceẏar

chalk *n* খড়ি khôri

challenge *n* আহ্বান ahvan (*pron* ahovan)

chamber *n* কক্ষ kôkṣô

chameleon *n* গিরগিটি girgiṭi

champion *n* বীরপুরুষ bīrpuruṣ, জয়ী jɔŷī

chance *n (opportunity)* সুযোগ suyog; *(luck)* ভাগ্য bhagyô, কপাল kɔpal; *(risk)* ঝুঁকি jhūki

chancellor *n* আচার্য acaryô

change *n (alteration)* পরিবর্তন pôribɔrtôn; *(loose coins)* খুচরা khucra; *vb* বদলানো bɔdlano

changeable *adj* পরিবর্তনীয় pôribɔrtônīŷô

channel *n* প্রণালি prônali

chaos *n* অব্যবস্থা ɔbybôstha *(pron* ɔbæbostha)

chapel *n* প্রার্থনাকক্ষ prarthôna kôkṣô

chapter *n* অধ্যায় ôdhyaŷ

character *n* চরিত্র côritrô

characteristic *n* বৈশিষ্ট্য boiśiṣṭyô; *adj* চারিত্রিক caritrik

charge *n* দাবি dabi

charity *n (kindness)* দয়া dɔŷa, কৃপা kr̥pa; *(generosity)* দানশীলতা danśīlôta

charm *n* আকর্ষণশক্তি akôrṣôṇśôkti

charming *adj* মনোরম mônorɔm, আকর্ষণীয় akôrṣôṇīŷô

chart *n* মানচিত্র mancitrô

charter *n* সনদ sɔnôd

chase *vb (hunt)* শিকার করা śikar kɔra; *(drive away)* তাড়ানো taṛano

chasm *n* ফাঁক phãk

chaste *adj* নির্মল nirmôl

chat *vb* গল্প করা gɔlpô kɔra; *n* খোশগল্প khośgɔlpô

chatter *n (of birds)* কিচিরমিচির kicirmicir; *(of humans)* বকবক bɔkbɔk

cheap *adj* সস্তা sɔsta

cheat *vb* ঠকা ṭhɔka, ঠকানো ṭhɔkano

check *vb (restrain)* বাধা দেওয়া badha deôŷa; *(prevent)* প্রতিহত করা prôtihɔtô kɔra; *(verify)* পরীক্ষা করা pôrīkṣa kɔra; *n (money order)* চেক cek

checkmate *n* মাত mat

cheek *n* গাল gal

cheese *n* পনির pônir

cheetah *n* চিতাবাঘ citabagh

chemical *adj* রাসায়নিক rasaŷônik

chemistry *n* রসায়ন rɔsaŷôn

cherish *vb* মমতা করা mɔmôta kɔra

chess *n* দাবাখেলা dabakhæla

chest *n (front of the body)* বুক buk; *(box)* সিন্দুক sinduk

chew *vb* চিবানো cibano, চেবানো cebano

chick *n* পাখির ছানা pakhir chana

chicken *n* মুর্গি murgi

chief *n (leader)* নেতা neta; *adj (main)* প্রধান prôdhan

child *n* বাচ্চা bacca

childhood *n* ছোটবেলা choṭôbela, শৈশব śoiśɔb

childish *adj* ছেবলা chæbla, বাচাল bacal

chill *n* ঠাণ্ডা ṭhaṇḍa

chilli *n* কাঁচা মরিচ kãca môric *(Bd)*, কাঁচা লঙ্কা kãca lɔṅka

chimney *n* চিমনি cimni

chin *n* চিবুক cibuk

china *n* চীনামাটির cīnamaṭir

China *n* চীন cīn

Chinese *n, adj* চীনা cīna

chip *n* ছিলকা chilka

chisel *n* বাটালি baṭali

chocolate *n* চকলেট cɔkleṭ

choice *n* পছন্দ pɔchôndô

choir *n* গীতের দল gīter dɔl

choke *vb* শ্বাসরোধ হওয়া śvasrodh hɔoŷa

cholera *n* ওলাওঠা olaoṭha

choose *vb* পছন্দ করা pɔchôndô kɔra, বেছে নেওয়া beche neoŷa

chop *vb* কুচানো kucano

chorus *n* গায়কদল gaŷôkdɔl

christen *vb* বাপ্তিস্ম দেওয়া baptismô deoŷa

Christian *n, adj* খ্রিষ্টান khriṣṭan

Christianity *n* খ্রিষ্ট ধর্ম khriṣṭô dhɔrmô

Christmas *n* বড়দিন bɔṛôdin

chronic *adj* অনেক দিনের ɔnek diner

church *n* গির্জা girja

churn *vb* মন্থন করা mɔnthôn kɔra

chutney *n* আচার acar, চাটনি caṭni

cigar *n* চুরুট curuṭ

cigarette *n* সিগারেট sigareṭ, বিড়ি biri

cinder *n* অঙ্গার ɔngar

cinema *n* সিনেমা sinema

cinnamon *n* দারচিনি darcini

circle *n* বৃত্ত bṛttô, পরিধি pôridhi

circuit *n* পরিসীমা pôrisīma

circulate *vb (move around)* ঘোরা ghora; *(spread)* রটা rɔṭa, রটানো rɔṭano

circulation *n* রটন rɔṭôn

circumference *n* পরিধি-রেখা pôridhi-rekha

circumstance *n (surroundings)* পরিবেশ pôribeś; *(condition)* অবস্থা ɔbôstha

circumstantial *adj* পরোক্ষ pɔrokṣô

circus *n* সার্কাস sarkas

cite *vb* উল্লেখ করা ullekh kɔra

citizen *n* অধিবাসী ôdhibasī, নাগরিক nagôrik

city *n* শহর śɔhôr

civil *adj* ভদ্র bhɔdrô

civilization *n* সভ্যতা sɔbhyôta

claim *n* দাবি dabi; *vb* দাবি করা dabi kɔra

clan *n* গোত্র gotrô

clap *vb* হাত তালি দেওয়া hat tali deoŷa

clarity *n* স্পষ্টতা spɔṣṭôta

clash *n (conflict)* দ্বন্দ্ব dvɔndvô; *(loud noise)* ঝঙ্কার jhɔnkar

clasp *vb* জড়ানো jɔrano

class *n (category)* শ্রেণী śrenī; *(division in schools)* ক্লাস klas

classify *vb* শ্রেণীভাগ করা śrenībhag kɔra

claw *n* পশুপাখির নখ pôśupakhir nôkh

clay *n* কাদামাটি kadamaṭi

clean *adj* পরিষ্কার pôriṣkar; *vb* পরিষ্কার করা pôriṣkar kɔra

clear *adj (distinctive)* স্পষ্ট spɔṣṭô; *(spotless)* বিমল bimɔl; *vb* সরানো sɔrano

clergyman *n* যাজক yajôk

clerk *n* কেরানি kerani

clever *adj (knowledgeable)* জ্ঞানী jñanī *(pron* gænī); *(ingenious)* দক্ষ dôkṣô; *(cunning)* চালাক calak

client *n* খরিদ্দার khôriddar

cliff *n* খাড়াই kharai

climate *n* আবহাওয়া abhaoŷa

climax *n* পরিণতি pôrinôti

climb *vb* চড়া cɔra, ওঠা oṭha

cling *vb* লেগে থাকা lege thaka

clinic *n* হাসপাতাল haspatal

clip *vb* ছাঁটা chãṭa

clock *n* ঘড়ি ghôri

close *adj, adv (near)* কাছাকাছি kachakachi; *vb (shut)* বন্ধ করা

bɔndhô kɔra; *(finish)* শেষ করা
śeṣ kɔra

closed *adj* বন্ধ bɔndhô

closet *n* ছোট ঘর chɔṭô ghɔr

cloth *n* কাপড় kapɔṛ

clothe *vb* কাপড় পরা kapɔṛ pɔra

clothes *n* পোশাক pośak, কাপড়–
চোপড় kapɔṛ-copɔṛ

clothing *n* কাপড়–চোপড় kapɔṛ-
copɔṛ

cloud *n* মেঘ megh

cloudy *adj* মেঘাচ্ছন্ন meghacchɔnnô,
মেঘলা meghla

clove *n* লবঙ্গ lɔbôṅgô

clown *n* ক্লাউন klaun, বিদূষক
biduṣôk

club *n (stick)* গদা gɔda, ঠেঙ্গা
ṭhæṅga; *(association)* সমিতি
sômiti

clue *n* সন্ধানসূত্র sɔndhansūtrô, খেই
khei

clump *n* ঢেলা ḍhæla

cluster *n* গুচ্ছ gucchô

clutch *vb* ধরে রাখা dhôre rakha; *n*
খপ্পর khɔppôr

coach *n (bus)* বাস bas

coal *n* কয়লা kɔyla

coarse *adj* মোটা moṭa

coarse cotton (khadi) *n* খদ্দর
khɔddôr

coarse flour *n* আটা aṭa

coast *n* উপকূল upôkūl

coat *n (clothing)* কোট koṭ; *(layer)*
লেপন lepôn

cobweb *n* মাকড়সার জাল makôrsar
jal

cock *n* মোরগ morôg

cockroach *n* তেলাপোকা telapoka
(Bd), আরশোলা arśola *(WB)*

cocoa *n* কোকো koko

coconut *n* নারিকেল narikel, নারকেল
narkel

coddle *n* প্রশ্রয় দেওয়া prôśrɔẏ deoẏa

code *n* সঙ্কেত sɔṅket

coffee *n* কফি kôphi

coffin *n* শবাধার śɔbadhar

coil *n* পেঁচ, প্যাঁচ pæc

coin *n* মুদ্রা mudra

coincide *vb* মিলে যাওয়া mile yaoẏa,
সংঘটিত হওয়া sɔṃghôṭitô hɔoẏa

coincidence *n* সংঘটন sɔṃghôṭôn,
সমাপতন sɔmapɔtôn

coincidental *adj* কাকতালীয়
kaktalīyô

cold *adj* ঠাণ্ডা ṭhaṇḍa, শীতল śītôl;
n (low temperature) শীত śīt, ঠাণ্ডা
ṭhaṇḍa; *(infection)* সর্দি sôrdi

collaboration *n* সহযোগ sɔhôyog

collapse *n* পতন pɔtôn; *vb* পড়ে
যাওয়া pôre yaoẏa

collect *vb* সংগ্রহ করা sɔṃgrôhô
kɔra

collection *n* সঞ্চয় sɔñcɔẏ, সংগ্রহ
sɔṃgrôhô

college *n* কলেজ kɔlej

collide *vb* ধাক্কা খাওয়া dhakka
khaoẏa

collision *n* ধাক্কা dhakka

colon *n* মলাশয় mɔlaśɔẏ

colonel *n* কর্নেল kɔrnel

colony *n* উপনিবেশ upônibeś

color *n* রঙ rɔṅ

column *n* স্তম্ভ stɔmbhô

comb *n* চিরুনি ciruni

combination *n (linking)* সংযোগ
sɔṃyog; *(mixture)* মিশ্র miśrô

combine *vb* মেশানো meśano

come *vb* আসা asa

comedy *n* হাস্যরসের নাটক hasyôrôser naṭôk

comfort *n (relaxation)* আরাম aram; *(relief)* স্বস্তি svôsti; *(consolation)* সান্ত্বনা santvôna; *vb* সান্ত্বনা দেওয়া santvôna deoÿa

comfortable *adj* আরামদায়ক aramdaÿôk

comic *adj* রসিক rôsik

comma *n* কমা kôma

command *n (order)* আদেশ adeś, হুকুম hukum; *(authority)* বশ bôś

commence *vb* আরম্ভ করা arômbhô kôra

comment *vb* মন্তব্য করা môntôbyô kôra; *n* মন্তব্য môntôbyô, মতামত môtamôt

commerce *n (trade)* পণ্য-বিনিময় pônÿô-binimôÿ; *(social exchange)* সংসর্গ sôṁsôrgô

commercial *n* বিজ্ঞাপন bijñapôn; *adj* ব্যবসায়িক byæbsaÿik

commission *n* কর্মভার kôrmôbhar

committee *n* সমিতি sômiti

common *adj* সাধারণ sadharôṇ

communal *adj* সাম্প্রদায়িক samprôdaÿik

communicate *vb* যোগাযোগ রাখা yogayog rakha

communication *n* যোগাযোগ yogayog

communion *n* অংশগ্রহণ ôṁśôgrôhôṇ

communism *n* সাম্যবাদ samyôbad

communist *n* সাম্যবাদী samyôbadī

compact *adj* ঘন ghônô

companion *n* সঙ্গী sôṅgī

companionship *n* সঙ্গীত্ব sôṅgītvô

company *n (social contact)* সংসর্গ sôṁsôrgô; *(business)* কোম্পানি kompani

compare *vb* তুলনা করা tulôna kôra

comparison *n* তুলনা tulôna

compartment *n* বিভাগ bibhag, কামরা kamra

compass *n* কম্পাস kômpas

compassion *n* সহানুভূতি sôhanubhūti

compatible *adj* সুসংগত susôṁgtô

compensation *n* খেসারত khesarôt, শোধ śodh

compete *vb* জুঝা jujha, প্রতিযোগিতা করা prôtiyogita kôra

competence *n* দক্ষতা dôkṣôta

competent *adj* দক্ষ dôkṣô

competition *n* প্রতিযোগিতা prôtiyogita

competitive *adj* প্রতিযোগিতাপূর্ণ prôtiyogitapūrṇô

complain *vb* অভিযোগ করা ôbhiyog kôra, নালিশ করা naliś kôra

complaint *n* অভিযোগ ôbhiyog, নালিশ naliś

complete *vb* সম্পূর্ণ করা sômpūrṇô kôra; *adj (whole)* সম্পূর্ণ sômpūrṇô, পুরা pura, পুরো puro; *(finished)* সমাপ্ত sômaptô

completely *adv* একেবারে ækebare, সম্পূর্ণভাবে sômpūrṇôbhabe

complex *adj* জটিল jôṭil

complexion *n* চেহারা cehara

complicate *vb* পেঁচানো pæcano

complicated *adj* জটিল jôṭil

compliment *n* প্রশংসা prôśôṁsa

comply *vb* সম্মত হওয়া sômmôtô hôoÿa

compose *vb* রচনা করা rôcôna kôra

composition *n* রচনা rôcôna

composure *n* ধীরস্বভাব dhīrsvɔbhab

compound *adj* যৌগিক yougik

comprehensive *adj* ব্যাপক byæpôk

compromise *n* মিটমাট miṭmaṭ, আপস-মীমাংসা apôs-mīmaṁsa; *vb* মিটমাট করা miṭmaṭ kɔra

computer *n* কম্পিউটার kɔmpiuṭar

conceal *vb* লুকিয়ে রাখা lukiŷe rakha

conceit *n* আত্মগৌরব atmôgourôb

concentrate *vb* মনোযোগ দেওয়া mônoyog deoŷa

concentration *n* মনোযোগ mônoyog

concept *n* ধারণা dharôṇa

concern *n* (worry) উদ্বেগ udbeg; (matter) ব্যাপার byæpar, সম্বন্ধ sɔmbɔndhô

concert *n* জলসা jɔlsa, কনসার্ট kɔnsarṭ

concession *n* (bestowal) অর্পণ ɔrpôṇ; (admission) স্বীকার svīkar

conch *n* শাঁখ śākh

concise *adj* সংক্ষিপ্ত sɔṁkṣiptô

conclusion *n* পরিণাম pôriṇam, পরিণতি pôrinôti

concrete *adj* মূর্ত mūrtô

condemn *vb* দোষ দেওয়া doṣ deoŷa, নিন্দা করা ninda kɔra

condition *n* (situation) অবস্থা ɔbôstha; (stipulation) শর্ত śɔrtô

condolence *n* শোকপ্রকাশ śokprôkaś

condom *n* কন্ডম kɔnḍôm

condominium *n* ফ্ল্যাট phlyaṭ

conduct *n* আচরণ acôrôṇ, ব্যবহার bybôhar (pron bæbohar), চালচলন calcɔlôn

cone *n* শঙ্কু śôṅku

confess *vb* স্বীকার করা svīkar kɔra

confession *n* স্বীকার svīkar

confidence *n* আস্থা astha, ভরসা bhɔrsa

confirm *vb* বলবৎ করা bɔlôbɔt kɔra

confirmation *n* অনুমোদন ônumodôn

conflict *n* দ্বন্দ্ব dvɔndvô, বিরোধ birodh

confused *adj* দিশেহারা diśehara

confusion *n* বিভ্রান্তি bibhranti

congratulate *vb* অভিনন্দন জানানো ôbhinɔndôn janano

congratulations *n* অভিনন্দন ôbhinɔndôn

congress *n* সভা sɔbha

conjecture *n* আন্দাজ andaj, আঁচ āc

conjunction *n* যোগ yog

connect *vb* যুক্ত করা yuktô kɔra

connection *n* সংযোগ sɔṁyog

conquer *vb* জয় করা jɔŷ kɔra

conscience *n* বিবেক bibek

conscientious *adj* বিবেচক bibecɔk

conscious *adj* (aware) জ্ঞাত jñætô; (deliberate) সচেতন sɔcetôn

consent *n* অনুমোদন ônumodôn; *vb* রাজি হওয়া raji hɔoŷa

consequence *n* ফলাফল phɔlaphɔl

conservation *n* সংরক্ষণ sɔṁrôkṣôn

conserve *vb* রক্ষা করা rôkṣa kɔra

consider *vb* বিবেচনা করা bibecôna kɔra

considerate *adj* বিবেচক bibecɔk

consideration *n* বিবেচনা bibecôna

consist of *vb* গঠিত হওয়া gôṭhitô hɔoŷa

consistency *n* (texture) সার sar; (steadiness) ধ্রুবতা dhrubôta

consolation *n* সান্ত্বনা santvôna

console *vb* সান্ত্বনা দেওয়া santvôna deoŷa

consonant *n* ব্যঞ্জনবর্ণ byñjônbɔrṇô (pron bænjonbɔrno)

conspiracy *n* ষড়যন্ত্র ṣɔṛyɔntrô

constant *adj* স্থির sthir

constellation *n* (*cluster of stars*) তারকামণ্ডলী tarôkamɔṇḍôlī; (*gathering*) সমাবেশ sɔmabeś

constipation *n* শক্ত পায়খানা śɔktô paykhana, বদহজম bɔdhɔjôm

constitute *vb* স্থাপন করা sthapôn kɔra

constitution *n* শাসনতন্ত্র śasôntɔntrô, প্রথা prôtha

construct *vb* গড়া gɔṛa, গঠন করা gɔṭhôn kɔra

construction *n* গঠন gɔṭhôn

consul *n* রাষ্ট্রদূত raṣṭrôdūt

consulate *n* দূতাবাস dūtabas

consult *vb* পরামর্শ করা pɔramɔrśô kɔra

consultant *n* পরামর্শদাতা pɔramɔrśôdata

consume *vb* খাওয়া khaoŷa

consumer *n* ক্রেতা kreta

consumption *n* (*wasting disease*) ক্ষয়রোগ kṣɔŷrog; (*eating*) খাওয়া khaoŷa

contact *n* যোগাযোগ yogayog

contagious *adj* সংক্রামক sɔṁkramôk

contain *vb* ধরা dhɔra

container *n* পাত্র patrô

contaminate *vb* সংক্রামিত করা sɔṁkramitô kɔra

contemporary *adj* (*of the same period*) সমকালীন sɔmôkalīn; (*modern*) আধুনিক adhunik

contempt *n* হেলা hæla, হেলাফেলা hælaphæla

contend *vb* চেষ্টা করা ceṣṭa kɔra

contend with *vb* প্রতিযোগিতা করা prôtôyogita kɔra

content *adj* সন্তুষ্ট sɔntuṣṭô

contest *vb* যুঝা yujha; *n* প্রতিযোগিতা prôtiyogita

continent *n* মহাদেশ mɔhadeś

continue *vb* চালিয়ে যাওয়া caliye yaoŷa

continuous *adj* অবিরাম ɔbiram, একটানা æktana

continuously *adv* এক নাগাড়ে æk nagaṛe

contraception *n* গর্ভনিরোধ gɔrbhônirodh

contract *n* চুক্তি cukti

contrary *adj* বিপরীত bipôrīt

contrast *n* প্রতিতুলনা prôtitulôna, বৈপরীত্য boipôrītyô

contribute *vb* দেওয়া deoŷa

contribution *n* দান dan

control *vb* নিয়ন্ত্রণ করা niyɔntrôṇ kɔra; *n* (*check*) নিয়ন্ত্রণ niyɔntrôṇ; (*rule*) শাসন śasôn

controller *n* শাসক śasôk

convenience *n* সুবিধা subidha (*Bd*), সুবিধে subidhe (*WB*)

convenient *adj* সুবিধাজনক subidhajɔnôk

convention *n* প্রথা prôtha

conventional *adj* স্বাভাবিক svabhabik

conversation *n* আলাপ alap, কথাবার্তা kɔthabarta

convert *vb* বদলানো bɔdlano

conviction *n* নিশ্চয়তা niścɔŷôta

convince *vb* প্ররোচিত করা prôrocita kɔra, রাজি করানো raji kɔrano

cook *vb* রান্না করা ranna kɔra; *n* বাবুর্চি baburci (*Bd*), রাঁধুনি rādhuni (*WB*)

cooker *n (stove)* চুলা cula *(Bd)*, চুলো culo *(WB)*

cookie *n* বিস্কুট biskuṭ

cooking *n* রান্না ranna, পাক pak

cool *adj* শীতল śītɔl; *vb* জুড়ানো jurano

cooperation *vb* সহযোগিতা sɔhôyogita

cooperative *n* সমবায় sɔmôbaŷ

coordinate *vb* সমন্বয় করা sɔmônvɔŷ kɔra

cope *vb* সামলানো samlano

copious *adj* প্রচুর prôcur

copper *n* তামা tama

copy *n (transcript)* নকল nɔkôl; *(duplicate)* প্রতিমূর্তি prôtimūrti

copyright *n* গ্রন্থস্বত্ব grônthôsvɔtvô

coral *n* প্রবাল prôbal

cordial *adj* আন্তরিক antôrik, সাদর sadôr

cordially *adv* সাদরে sadôre

core *n (pulp, kernel)* শাঁস śãs; *(heart, center)* অন্তর ɔntôr, মর্ম mɔrmô

coriander *n* ধনিয়া dhôniya *(Bd)*, ধনে dhône *(WB)*

cork *n* ছিপি chipi

corn *n (grain)* শস্য śôsyô; *(maize)* ভুট্টা bhuṭṭa

corner *n* কোণ koṇ

corporation *n* নিগম nigɔm

corpse *n* শব śɔb, মড়া mɔra

correct *adj* ঠিক ṭhik, সঠিক sɔṭhik; *vb* ঠিক করা ṭhik kɔra, সংশোধন করা sɔṁśodhôn kɔra

correction *n* সংশোধন sɔṁśodhôn

correspond *vb* মানানো manano

correspondence *n* চিঠিপত্র ciṭhipɔtrô

correspondent *n* সাংবাদিক sɑṁbadik

corridor *n* দরদালান dɔrdalan

corrode *vb* জারা jara, নষ্ট হওয়া nɔṣṭô hɔoŷa

corrupt *adj (defiled)* বিকৃত bikr̥tô; *(rotten)* পচা pɔca

corruption *n (decay)* বিকৃতি bikr̥ti; *(bribery)* ঘুষ ghuṣ, দুর্নীতি durnīti

cosmos *n* বিশ্ব biśvô

cost *n (price)* দাম dam; *(expense)* খরচ khɔrôc

costly *adj* দামি dami, বহুমূল্য bôhumūlyô

cot *n* খাট khaṭ, চৌকি couki

cottage *n* কুটির kuṭir

cotton *n (raw material)* তুলা tula *(Bd)*, তুলো tulo *(WB)*; *(cloth)* সুতি suti

couch *n* বিছানা bichana

cough *vb* কাশা kaśa; *n* কাশি kaśi

council *n* পরিষৎ pôriṣɔṯ

counsel *n* পরামর্শ pɔramɔrśô, উপদেশ upôdeś

count *vb* গোনা gona

counter *n* কাউন্টার kaunṭar

counter-balance *n* প্রতিভার prôtibhar

counterfeit *n, adj* জাল jal, মেকি meki

countless *adj* অসংখ্য ɔsɔṁkhyô

country *n* দেশ deś

county *n* জেলা jela

couple *n* জোড়া jora

courage *n* সাহস sahôs

courageous *adj* সাহসী sahôsī, তেজী tejī

course *n* গতিপথ gôtipɔth; *adv* **(of ~)** নিশ্চয় niścɔŷ, অবশ্য ɔbôśyô

court *n* আদালত adalɔt

courteous *adj* সভ্য sôbhyô, শিষ্ট śiṣṭô

courtesy *n* শিষ্টাচার śiṣṭacar

courtyard *n* উঠান uṭhan *(Bd)*, উঠোন uṭhon

cousin *n* ভাই bhai *(m)*, বোন bon *(f)*

cover *n* *(lid)* ঢাকনা ḍhakna; *(case, shell)* খোল khol; *vb* ঢাকা ḍhaka

cow *n* গরু gôru

cow dung *n* গোবর gobɔr

coward *n* কাপুরুষ kapuruṣ

cowardice *n* ভীরুতা bhīruta

cowshed *n* গোয়াল goŷal

coy *adj* লাজুক lajuk

crab *n* কাঁকড়া kākṛa

crack *n* ফাটল phaṭɔl, চিড় ciṛ; *vb* ফাটা phaṭa

cradle *n* দোলনা dolna

craft *n* *(art)* শিল্প śilpô; *(dexterity)* দক্ষতা dôkṣôta

craftsman *n* কারিগর karigɔr, শিল্পী śilpī

crafty *adj* চতুর côtur

cramp *n* খিল khil

crane *n* সারস sarôs

crash *vb* ভেঙে যাওয়া bheṅe yaoŷa

crater *n* আগ্নেয়গিরির মুখ agneŷô-girir mukh

crawl *vb* হামাগুড়ি দেওয়া hamaguṛi deoŷa

crazy *adj* পাগল pagôl

cream *n* নবনী nɔbônī, ক্রিম krim

crease *n* ভাঁজ bhāj

create *vb* সৃষ্টি করা sṛṣṭi kɔra

creation *n* সৃষ্টি sṛṣṭi

creature *n* প্রাণী praṇī

credible *adj* বিশ্বাসযোগ্য biśvasyogyô

credit *n* পাওনা paona

creditor *n* পাওনাদার paonadar

credulous *adj* বিশ্বাসী biśvasī

creed *n* ধর্মবিশ্বাস dhɔrmôbiśvas

creep *vb* চুপিসারে চলা cupisare cɔla

creeper *n* লতাগাছ lɔtagach

crematorium *n* শব-চুল্লি śɔb-culli, শ্মাশান śmaśan

crest *n* চূড়া cūṛa *(Bd)*, চূড়ো cūṛo *(WB)*

crew *n* ক্রু kru

cricket *n* ক্রিকেট krikeṭ

crime *n* অপরাধ ɔpôradh

criminal *n* অপরাধী ɔpôradhī

crippled *adj* পঙ্গু pôṅgu

crisis *n* সঙ্কট sɔṅkɔṭ

critic *n* সমালোচক sɔmalocɔk

criticism *n* *(review)* সমালোচনা sɔmalocôna; *(attack)* আক্রমণ akrômôṇ

criticize *vb* নিন্দা করা ninda kɔra *(Bd)*, নিন্দে করা ninde kɔra *(WB)*

crocodile *n* কুমির kumir

crooked *adj* বাঁকা bāka

crop *n* ফসল phɔsôl

cross *n* ক্রুশ kruś; *vb* পার হওয়া par hɔoŷa *(Bd)*, পেরোনো perono *(WB)*

cross-examination *n* জেরা jera

cross-eyed *adj* টেরা ṭera

crossroads *n* চৌরাস্তা courasta

crosswise *adj* আড়া-আড়ি aṛa-aṛi

crossword *n* শব্দের ধাঁধা śɔbder dhādha

crouch *vb* গুটিসুটি হয়ে বসা guṭisuṭi hoŷe bɔsa

crow *n* কাক kak

crowd *n* ভিড় bhiṛ

crowded *adj* জমজমাট jɔmjɔmaṭ, জনাকীর্ণ jɔnakīrṇô

crown *n* মুকুট mukuṭ

crude *adj* অশোধিত ɔśodhitô

cruel *adj* নিষ্ঠুর niṣṭhur, উগ্র ugrô

cruise *vb* ঘোরা ghora, ঘুরে বেড়ানো ghure beṛano; *n* প্রমোদভ্রমণ prômodbhrômôn

crumb *n* ছোট টুকরা chotô ṭukra

crumble *vb* ধূলিষাৎ হওয়া dhūliṣaṭ hɔôỷa

crunch *n* কচকচানি kɔckɔcani

crush *vb* চূর্ণ করা cūrṇô kɔra

crust *n* খোলা khola

crutch *n* যষ্ঠি yôṣṭhi

cry *vb* (*weep*) কাঁদা kãda, কান্নাকাটি করা kannakaṭi kɔra; (*shout*) চিৎকার করা ciṭkar kɔra, চেঁচামেচি করা cẽcameci kɔra

crystal *n* স্ফটিক sphôṭik

cube *n* ঘনক্ষেত্র ghɔnôkṣetrô

cubic *adj* ঘানিক ghanik

cuckoo *n* কোকিল kokil

cucumber *n* শসা śɔsa

cult *n* তন্ত্র tɔntrô

cultivate *vb* (*farm*) চাষ করা caṣ kɔra; (*keep active*) অনুশীলন করা ônuśīlôn kɔra

cultivation *n* চাষ caṣ, আবাদ abad

cultural *adj* সাংস্কৃতিক saṁskr̥tik

culture *n* সংস্কৃতি sɔṁskr̥ti

cup *n* কাপ kap, পেয়ালা peẏala

cupboard *n* আলমারি almari

curb *vb* (*harness*) সাজ লাগানো saj lagano; (*suppress*) দমন করা dɔmôn kɔra; (*reduce*) কমানো kɔmano

curd *n* দই dôi

cure *n* আরোগ্য arogyô

curious *adj* উৎসুক uṭsuk, কৌতূহলী koutūhôlī

curl *n* কুন্তল kuntôl

curly *adj* কোঁকড়া kõkra

currency *n* চালু টাকা calu ṭaka

current *n* (*electricity*) বিদ্যুৎ bidyut; (*flow*) স্রোত srot; *adj* বর্তমান bɔrtôman, চলতি côlti

curry *n* তরকারি tɔrkari

curse *n* অভিশাপ ôbhiśap

curtain *n* পরদা, পর্দা pɔrda

curve *n* বাঁক bãk, ঘোঁজ ghõj

cushion *n* বালিশ baliś

custard *n* ডিমের পায়েস ḍimer payes

custody *n* অভিরক্ষা ôbhirôkṣa

custom *n* অভ্যাস ôbhyas

customer *n* খরিদ্দার khôriddar

customs *n* শুল্ক śulkô

cut *vb* কাটা kaṭa

cycle *n* (*wheel*, *circle*) চক্র cɔkrô; (*recurring period of time*) যুগাবর্ত yugabɔrtô; (*bicycle*) সাইকেল saikel

cyclone *n* ঘূর্ণিঝড় ghurṇijhɔr

cylinder *n* বেলনা belna (*Bd*), বেলন belôn (*WB*)

cynic *n* বিশৃনিন্দক biśvônindôk

cynicism *n* বিশৃনিন্দাবাদ biśvônindabad

D

dad(dy) *n* বাবা baba, আব্বা abba

dagger *n* ছোরা chora

daily *adj* রোজ roj, দৈনিক doinik

dam *n* বাঁধ bādh

damage *n* ক্ষতি kṣôti

damn *vb (curse)* অভিশাপ দেওয়া ôbhiśap deôŷa

damp *adj* ভিজা bhija, ভেজা bheja, সেঁতসেঁতে sæ̃tsẽte

dampen *vb* ভিজানো bhijano, ভেজানো bhejano

dance *n* নাচ nac; *vb* নাচা naca, নাচ করা nac kɔra

danger *n* বিপদ bipɔd

dangerous *adj* বিপজ্জনক bipɔjjɔnôk

dare *vb* সাহস করা sahôs kɔra

daring *adj (fearless)* সাহসী sahôsī; *(reckless)* ডানপিটে ḍanpiṭe

dark *adj* আঁধার ādhar, অন্ধকার ɔndhôkar

darkness *n* অন্ধকার ɔndhôkar

darn *vb* রিফু করা riphu kɔra

dash *vb* ছুটে যাওয়া chuṭe yaoŷa, দৌড়ে যাওয়া douṛe yaoŷa

data *n* উপাত্ত upattô

date *n (calendar day)* তারিখ tarikh; *(fruit)* খেজুর khejur

daughter *n* মেয়ে meye, কন্যা kônya

daughter-in-law *n* ছেলের বউ cheler bôu, বউমা bôuma

dawn *n* ভোর bhor

day *n* দিন din, দিবস dibɔs

day after tomorrow *n* আগামী পরশু agamī pôrśu

day before yesterday *n* গত পরশু gɔto pôrśu

dead *adj* মরা mɔra, মৃত mr̥tô

deadline *n* সময়সীমা sômôŷsīma, মুদ্দত muddɔtô

deaf *adj* কালা kala

deal *vb (behave)* আচরণ করা acôrôṇ kɔra; *(distribute)* বিলি করা bili kɔra; *(do business)* কেনাবেচা করা kenabeca kɔra; *n (amount)* পরিমাণ pôrimaṇ; *(agreement)* চুক্তি cukti

dealer *n* ব্যবসায়ী byæbsayī

dear *adj (beloved)* প্রিয় priŷô; *(expensive)* দামী damī

death *n* মরণ mɔrôṇ, মৃত্যু mr̥tyu *(pron* mritu*)*

debate *n* আলোচনা alocôna, বিতর্ক bitɔrkô

debit *n* খরচের হিসাব khɔrôcer hisab

debt *n* ঋণ r̥ṇ *(pron* rin*)*, দেনা dena

decade *n* দশক dɔśôk

decay *n* ক্ষয় kṣɔŷ, পতন pɔtôn; *vb* ক্ষয় হওয়া kṣɔŷ hɔoŷa, নষ্ট হওয়া nɔṣṭô hɔoŷa

deceit *n* ফাঁকি phāki, ছলনা chɔlôna

deceive *vb* ফাঁকি দেওয়া phāki deôŷa, ঠকানো ṭhɔkano

December *n* ডিসেম্বর মাস ḍisembôr mas

decent *adj (decorous)* শোভন śobhôn; *(suitable)* উপযুক্ত upôyuktô

deception *n* ফাঁকি phāki, ছলচাতুরী chɔlcaturī

decide *vb* সিদ্ধান্ত করা siddhantô kɔra, মনঃস্থির করা mônôḥsthir kɔra

decimal *adj* দশমিক dɔśômik

decision *n* সিদ্ধান্ত siddhantô

decisive *adj* চূড়ান্ত cūṛantô

deck *n* পাটাতন paṭatôn

declaration *n* ঘোষণা ghoṣôṇa

declare *vb* ঘোষণা করা ghoṣôṇa kɔra

decline *vb* পতন হওয়া pɔtôn hɔoŷa, ক্ষয় হওয়া kṣɔŷ hɔoŷa; *n* পতন pɔtôn

declining *adj* পড়ন্ত pɔrôntô

decorate *vb* সাজানো sajano

decoration *n* সজ্জা sɔjja

decrease *vb* কমা kɔma, কমানো kɔmano; *n* কমতি kômti

dedicate *vb* উৎসর্গ করা uṯsɔrgô kɔra

dedication *n* উৎসর্গ uṯsɔrgô

deduction *n* অনুমান ônuman

deed *n* কাজ kaj, ক্রিয়া kriŷa

deem *vb* বিচার করা bicar kɔra

deep *adj* গভীর gôbhīr

deer *n* হরিণ hôriṇ

default *n* অনুপস্থিতিতে ônupôsthitite

defeat *n* হার har, পরাজয় pɔrajɔŷ

defect *n* ক্রটি truṭi, দোষ, doṣ

defend *vb* (*protect*) রক্ষা করা rôkṣa kɔra; (*fight off*) প্রতিহত করা prôtihɔtô kɔra

defendant *n* আসামী asamī

defense *n* প্রতিরক্ষা prôtirôkṣa

defer *vb* পিছিয়ে দেওয়া pichiye deoŷa, মুলতবি করা multôbi kɔra

deference *n* শ্রদ্ধা śrɔddha

deficiency *n* কমতি kômti, অভাব ɔbhab

deficient *adj* কম kɔm

define *vb* স্থির করা sthir kɔra

definite *adj* নিশ্চিত niścitô, যথাযথ yɔthayɔth

definition *n* সংজ্ঞা sɔṁjña

deflate *vb* হ্রাস করা hras kɔra

defy *vb* অবাধ্য হওয়া ɔbadhyô hɔoŷa

degree *n* (*measure*) মাপ map, পরিমাণ pôrimaṇ; (*educational*) ডিগ্রি ḍigri

dehydrated *adj* জলের অভাবে jɔler ɔbhabe

dejection *n* বিষাদ biṣad, হতাশ hɔtaś

delay *n* দেরি deri

delete *vb* বাদ দেওয়া bad deoŷa, মুছে ফেলা muche phæla

deliberate *adj* অভিপ্রেত ôbhipret, ইচ্ছা করে iccha kôre

delicate *adj* চিকন cikɔn, হালকা halka

delight *n* আনন্দ anôndô, উল্লাস ullas

delightful *adj* মনোরম mônorɔm

deliver *vb* (*set free*) উদ্ধার করা uddhar kɔra; (*bring*) পৌঁছে দেওয়া pôuche deoŷa

delivery *n* উদ্ধার uddhar

delusion *n* ভ্রান্তি bhranti

demand *n* দাবি dabi

democracy *n* গণতন্ত্র gɔṇôtɔntrô

democratic *adj* গণতান্ত্রিক gɔṇôtantrik

demolish *vb* ভেঙ্গে ফেলা bheṅge phæla, ধ্বংস করা dhvɔṁsô kɔra

demon *n* রাক্ষস rakṣôs

demonstrate *vb* প্রকাশ করা prôkaś kɔra

demonstration *n* মিছিল michil

denial *n* অস্বীকার ɔsvīkar

dense *adj* ঘন ghɔnô

density *n* ঘনতা ghɔnôta, ঘনত্ব ghɔnôtvô

dent *n* খাঁজ khāj

dental *adj* দন্ত্য dɔntyô

dentist *n* দাঁতের ডাক্তার dāter ḍaktar

deny *vb* অস্বীকার করা ɔsvīkar kɔra

depart vb রওনা দেওয়া rɔona deoŷa

department n বিভাগ bibhag

departure n রওনা rɔona, প্রস্থান prôsthan

depend vb নির্ভর করা nirbhɔr kɔra

dependent adj পরাধীন pôradhīn

deposit vb রাখা rakha, জমা করা jɔma kɔra

depot n গুদাম gudam, দপ্তর dɔptɔr, দফতর dɔphtɔr

depress vb বিষণ্ণ করা biṣɔnnô kɔra

depressed adj বিষণ্ণ biṣɔnnô, মন–মরা môn–mɔra

depression n বিষাদ biṣad, মনোভঙ্গ mônôbhɔṅgô

deprive vb কেড়ে নেওয়া keṛe neoŷa, বঞ্চিত করা bɔncitô kɔra

depth n গভীরতা gôbhirɔta

deputy n প্রতিনিধি prôtinidhi, উপ upô

derive vb উৎপত্তি নির্ণয় করা utpôtti nirṇɔŷ kɔra

descend vb নামা nama

descent n অবতরণ ɔbôtɔrôṇ

describe vb বর্ণনা করা bɔrṇôna kɔra

description n বর্ণনা bɔrṇôna

desert n মরুভূমি môrubhūmi; vb ছেড়ে যাওয়া cheṛe yaoŷa, ত্যাগ করা tyæg kɔra

deserve vb যোগ্য হওয়া yogyô hɔoŷa

design n নকশা nɔkśa

designate vb নিযুক্ত করা niyuktô kɔra

designer n পরিকল্পক pôrikɔlpôk

desirable adj কাম্য kamyô, মনোরম mônorɔm

desire n কামনা kamôna, বাসনা basôna; vb চাওয়া caoŷa, কামনা করা kamôna kɔra

desk n লেখার টেবিল lekhar ṭebil

despair n হতাশা hɔtaśa; vb হতাশ হওয়া hɔtaś hɔoŷa

despise vb অবজ্ঞা করা ɔbɔjña kɔra, ঘৃণা করা ghṛṇa kɔra (pron ghrina kɔra)

despite conj সত্ত্বেও sɔttveo

destiny n ভাগ্য bhagyô, নিয়তি niyôti

destroy vb ধ্বংস করা dhvɔṁsô kɔra, নষ্ট করা nɔṣṭô kɔra

destruction n ধ্বংস dhvɔṁsô, বিনাশ binaś

detach vb খুলে দেওয়া khule deoŷa

detain vb আটকে রাখা aṭke rakha

detect vb আবিষ্কার করা abiṣkar kɔra

detective n গোয়েন্দা goŷenda

detergent n সাবান saban

determination n ইচ্ছাশক্তি icchaśôkti

determine vb নিদিষ্ট করা nirdiṣṭô kɔra

determined adj নির্ধারিত nirdharitô

develop vb উন্নতি করা unnôti kɔra

development n (progress) অগ্রগতি ɔgrôgôti; (improvement) উন্নতি unnôti

deviation n বিচ্যুতি bicyuti

device n (scheme) কৌশল kouśɔl, ফন্দি phôndi; (tool) যন্ত্র yɔntrô

devil n শয়তান śɔŷtan

devise vb পরিকল্পনা করা pôrikɔlpôna kɔra

devotion n উপাসনা upasɔna

devout adj ভক্ত bhɔktô

dew n শিশির śiśir

dexterity n কৌশল kouśôl

diabetes n বহুমূত্র রোগ bôhumūtrô rog

diabetic *adj* বহুমূত্রপীড়িত bôhumûtrôpîṛitô, ডায়াবেটিক ḍaŷabeṭik

diagnosis *n* নিদান nidan

diagonal *adj* তির্যক tiryɔk

dial *vb* ডায়েল করা ḍayel kɔra

dialect *n* উপভাষা upôbhaṣa

dialogue *n* সংলাপ sɔṁlap

diameter *n* ব্যাস byæs

diamond *n* হীরক hîrɔk

diarrhea *n* পাতলা পায়খানা patla paŷkhana, পেটের অসুখ peṭer ɔsukh

diary *n* দিনলিপি dinôlipi, ডায়েরি ḍaiyeri

dictate *vb* হুকুম করা hukum kɔra

dictator *n* একনায়ক ekônayôk

dictionary *n* অভিধান ôbhidhan

die *vb* মরা mɔra, মরে যাওয়া môre yaoŷa, মারা যাওয়া mara yaoŷa; *n* (*pl* **dice**) পাশা paśa, অক্ষ ɔkṣô

diesel *n* গাড়ির তেল gaṛir tel, ডিসেল ḍisel

diet *n* পথ্য pôthyô

differ *vb* ভিন্ন হওয়া bhinnô hɔoŷa

difference *n* পার্থক্য parthôkyô, তফাত tɔphat

different *adj* ভিন্ন bhinnô; (*various*) বিভিন্ন bibhinnô, নানা nana

difficult *adj* কঠিন kôṭhin, শক্ত śɔktô

difficulty *n* (*effort*) কষ্ট kɔṣṭô; (*problem*) সমস্যা sɔmôsya, মুশকিল muśkil; (*complexity*) জটিলতা jôṭilôta

dig *vb* খোঁড়া khõṛa

digest *vb* হজম করা hɔjôm kɔra

digestion *n* হজম hɔjôm, জারণ jaroṇ

dignified *adj* সম্মানিত sɔmmanitô

dignity *n* মর্যাদা môryada, সম্মান sɔmman

diligent *adj* যত্নশীল yɔtnôśîl

dim *adj* ফিকা phika (*Bd*), ফিকে phike (*WB*), ঝাপসা jhapsa, ম্লান mlan

dimension *n* মাপ map, মাত্রা matra

diminish *vb* কমা kɔma

dine *vb* খাওয়া khaoŷa, ভোজন করা bhojôn kɔra

dining room *n* খাবার ঘর khabar ghɔr

dinner *n* রাতের খাবার rater khabar, ভাত bhat

dip *vb* ডোবানো ḍobano

diplomat *n* দূত dût

diplomatic *adj* কূটনীতিক kûṭônîtik

direct *adj*, *adv* সোজা soja; *vb* পরিচালনা করা pôricalôna kɔra

direction *n* দিক dik

director *n* পরিচালক pôricalôk

directory *n* তালিকা talika

dirt *n* ময়লা mɔŷla, ধুলা dhula (*Bd*), ধুলো dhulo (*WB*)

dirty *adj* ময়লা mɔŷla, নোংরা nɔṁra

disability *n* অশক্তি ɔśôkti

disagree *vb* রাজি না হওয়া raji na hɔoŷa, মতভেদ হওয়া motobhed hɔoŷa

disagreement *n* অমিল ɔmil, মতভেদ mɔtbhed

disappear *vb* হাওয়া হয়ে যাওয়া haoŷa hôŷe yaoŷa, অদৃশ্য হওয়া ɔdŕśyô hɔoŷa

disappoint *vb* নিরাশ করা niraś kɔra

disappointed *adj* অসন্তুষ্ট ɔsɔntuṣṭô

disappointment *n* নৈরাশ্য noiraśyô

disaster *n* দুর্ঘটনা durghɔṭôna, সর্বনাশ śɔrbônaś

discipline n (order, system) নিয়ম niŷôm; (restraint) শৃঙ্খলা śṙṅkhɔla

discount n কমতি kômti, দস্তুরি dôsturi

discover vb খুঁজে পাওয়া khũje paoŷa, আবিষ্কার করা abiṣkar kɔra

discovery n আবিষ্কার abiṣkar

discreet adj বিবেচক bibecɔk

discretion n বিবেচনা bibecôna

discriminate vb প্রভেদ করা prôbhed kɔra

discriminate against vb অসম্মান করা ɔsɔmman kɔra

discuss vb আলোচনা করা alocôna kɔra

discussion n আলোচনা alocôna

disease n রোগ rog

disgrace n চুনকালি cunkali, লজ্জা lɔjja

disguise n ছদ্মবেশ chɔdmôbeś

disgust n ঘৃণা ghṙṇa

disgusting adj জঘন্য jɔghônyô

dish n বাটি baṭi, থালা thala

disheartened adj মন–মরা môn-mɔra, হতাশ hɔtaś

dishonest adj অসৎ ɔsɔṯ

disinfect vb নির্বীজ করা nirbīj kɔra

disinfectant n বীজঘ্ন bījɔghnô

disk n চাকতি cakti

dislike n অপছন্দ ɔpɔchôndô; vb অপছন্দ করা ɔpɔchôndô kɔra

dismiss vb (ignore) অবহেলা করা ɔbôhæla kɔra; (terminate employment) বিদায় করা bidaŷ kɔra

disobey vb না মানা na mana, অমান্য করা ɔmanyô kɔra

display vb প্রদর্শনী prôdɔrśônī

displease vb বিরক্ত করা birɔktô kɔra

dispose of vb ফেলে দেওয়া phele deoŷa

dispute n তর্ক tɔrkô

disregard vb অবহেলা করা ɔbôhæla kɔra

distance n দূর dūr

distant adj দূরে dūre

distill vb চোলাই করা colai kɔra

distinct adj (clear) স্পষ্ট spɔṣṭô; (separate) আলাদা alada

distinction n পার্থক্য parthôkyô, প্রভেদ prôbhed

distinguish vb আলাদা করা alada kɔra

distinguish oneself vb প্রসিদ্ধ হওয়া prôsiddhô hɔoŷa

distort vb বিকৃত করা bikṙtô kɔra

distract vb মনযোগ ভাঙ্গা mônôyog bhaṅga

distress n কষ্ট kɔṣṭô

distribute vb (share) ভাগ করা bhag kɔra; (spread out) ছড়িয়ে দেওয়া chôriŷe deoŷa

distribution n বিতরণ bitɔrôṇ

district n জেলা jela

distrust n সন্দেহ sɔndehô, অবিশ্বাস ɔbiśvas

disturb vb বিরক্ত করা birɔktô kɔra, জ্বালানো jvalano

disturbance n গোল gol

ditch n খাত khat

dive vb ডুবে যাওয়া ḍube yaoŷa

diverse adj নানা রকম nana rɔkôm

divide vb ভাগ করা bhag kɔra

division n বিভাগ bibhag

divorce n তালাক talak, বিচ্ছেদ bicched

divorced adj তালাকপ্রাপ্ত talakpraptô

dizziness n মাথা ঘোরা matha ghora

dizzy *adj* ঝিমঝিম jhimjhim

do *vb* করা kɔra

dock *n* ঘাট ghat

doctor *n* ডাক্তার ḍaktar

dog *n* কুকুর kukur

doll *n* পুতুল putul

dollar *n* ডলার ḍɔlar

dolphin *n* শুশুক śuśuk

domain *n* ক্ষেত্র kṣetrô

dome *n* গম্বুজ gômbuj

domestic *adj* ঘরোয়া ghɔroya

dominate *vb* শাসন করা śasôn kɔra

domination *n* শাসন śasôn

donate *vb* দান করা dan kɔra

donation *n* দান dan

donkey *n* গাধা gadha

door *n* দরজা dɔrja

doorman *n* দারোয়ান daroyan

dose *n* সেব্য মাত্রা sebyô matra

dot *n* বিন্দু bindu

double *adj* জোড়া jora, ডবল ḍɔbôl

doubt *n* সন্দেহ sɔndehô

doubtful *adj* অনিশ্চিত ɔniścitô

dough *n* ময়দার তাল mɔŷdar tal

dove *n* কবুতর kôbutôr

down *n* নরম পালক nɔrôm palôk;
adv নিচে nice

downright *adv* রীতিমত rītimɔtô

dozen (twelve) *n* বার barô, ডজন
ḍɔjôn

draft *n* ছকা chɔka, খসড়া khɔsṛa

drag *vb* টানা ṭana

drain *n* নর্দমা nɔrdôma; *vb* নিষ্কাশন
করা niṣkaśôn kɔra

drama *n* নাটক naṭôk

draw *vb* আঁকা ãka

drawer *n* দেরাজ deraj

drawing *n* ছবি chôbi

dread *n* আতঙ্ক atɔṅkô

dream *n* স্বপ্ন svɔpnô

dreary *adj* একঘেয়ে ækgheye

dregs *n* তলানি tɔlani

dress *n* ফ্রক phrɔk, পোশাক pośak;
vb পরানো pɔrano

drift *vb* ভাসা bhasa, ভেসে যাওয়া
bhese yaoŷa

drill *n* তুরপুন turpun; *vb* তুরপুন
দিয়ে ছিদ্র করা turpun diŷe chidrô
kɔra

drink *vb* খাওয়া khaoŷa, পান করা
pan kɔra; *n* পানীয় panīŷô

drive *vb* চালানো calano

driver *n* চালক calôk

drizzle *vb* গুড়ি গুড়ি বৃষ্টি guṛi guṛi
bṛṣṭi

drop *n* বিন্দু bindu; *vb* পড়ে যাওয়া
pôṛe yaoŷa

drown *vb* ডুবে মরা ḍube mɔra

drug *n* ওষুধ oṣudh

drum *n* তবলা tɔbla, ঢোল ḍhol

drunk *adj* নেশা neśa

dry *vb* শুকানো śukano; *adj* শুকনা
śukna *(Bd)*, শুকনো śukno *(WB)*

duck *n* হাঁস hãs

due *adj* দেনা dena, উচিত ucit

dull *adj* (*not clever*) নির্বোধ nirbodh,
মূর্খ mūrkhô; (*overcast*) মেঘলা
meghla;(*monotonous*) একঘেয়ে
ækgheye; (*blunt*) ভোঁতা bhõta

dumb *adj* বোবা boba

dung *n* গোবর gobôr

durable *adj* টেকসই ṭeksôi, মজবুত
mɔjbut

during *pp* ধরে dhôre

dusk *n* সন্ধ্যা sɔndhya *(Bd)*, সন্ধ্যে
sɔndhye *(WB)*

dust *n* ধুলা dhula *(Bd)*, ধুলো dhulo
(WB), ধুলি dhuli

dusty *adj* ধূলিময় dhūlimɔŷ
duty *n* কর্তব্য kɔrtôbyô
dwarf *n* বামন bamôn
dwell *vb* বাস করা bas kɔra
dwelling *n* নিবাস nibas
dye *n* রং rɔṁ
dynamic *adj* প্রবল prôbɔl
dysentry *n* আমাশা amaśa

E

each *adj* প্রত্যেক prôtyek

eager *adj* উৎসুক uṭsuk

eagle *n* ঈগল পাখি īgôl pakhi

ear *n* কান kan

earache *n* কানের ব্যথা kaner bytha (*pron* kaner bæitha)

early *adv* সকালে sɔkale, তাড়াতাড়ি ṭaraṭari

earn *vb* কামানো kamano, উপার্জন করা uparjôn kɔra

earnest *adj* আন্তরিক antôrik

earnings *n* উপার্জিত টাকা uparjitô ṭaka, মাইনে maine

earring *n* কানের ফুল kaner phul (*Bd*), কানের দুল kaner dul (*WB*)

earth *n* (*world*) পৃথিবী pṛthibī, দুনিয়া duniya; (*soil*) মাটি maṭi

earthquake *n* ভূমিকম্প bhūmikɔmpô

east *adj* পূর্ব pūrbô

eastern *adj* পূর্বদিকে pūrbôdike

easy *adj* সহজ sɔhôj

eat *vb* খাওয়া khaoŷa

eccentric *adj* খামখেয়ালী khamkheyalī

echo *n* প্রতিধ্বনি prôtidhvôni, অনুনাদ ônunad

economical *adj* আর্থিক arthik, অর্থনৈতিক ɔrthônoitik

economist *n* অর্থবিজ্ঞানী ɔrthôbijñanī

economy *n* অর্থনীতি ɔrthônīti

edge *n* কিনারা kinara, ধার dhar

edible *adj* খাওয়ার যোগ্য khaoŷar yogyô

edit *vb* সম্পাদন করা sɔmpadôn kɔra

edition *n* সংস্করণ sɔṁskɔrôṇ

editor *n* সম্পাদক sɔmpadôk

educate *vb* শিক্ষা দেওয়া śikṣa deoŷa

education *n* শিক্ষা śikṣa

eel *n* বান মাছ ban mach

effect *n* ফল phɔl

effective *adj* সফল sɔphɔl

effort *n* চেষ্টা ceṣṭa, প্রয়াস prôŷas

egg *n* ডিম ḍim

eggplant *n* বেগুন begun

Egypt *n* মিশর miśôr

Egyptian *adj* মিশরী miśôrī

eight *num* আট aṭ

eighteen *num* আঠার aṭharô

eighth *num* অষ্টম ɔṣṭôm

eighty *num* আশি aśi

either ... or *conj* হয় ... না হয় hɔŷ ... na hɔŷ

elastic *adj* স্থিতিস্থাপক sthitisthapôk

elbow *n* কনুই kônui

elderly *adj* প্রৌঢ় prourhô

elect *vb* (*vote for*) নির্বাচন করা nirbacôn kɔra; (*choose*) পছন্দ করা pɔchôndô kɔra, বেছে নেওয়া beche neoŷa

electric *adj* বৈদ্যুতিক boidyutik

electricity *n* বিদ্যুৎ bidyut

elegance *n* ছিরি chiri

elegant *adj* মার্জিত marjitô

elegy *n* শোকগীতি śokgīti

element *n* পদার্থ pɔdarthô

elementary *adj* প্রাথমিক prathômik

elephant *n* হাতি hati

elevate *vb* তোলা tola

elevator *n* লিফট lipht

eleven *num* এগার ægarô

eleventh *num* একাদশ ekadɔś

eliminate *vb* বাদ দেওয়া bad deoŷa

else *adv* আরও aro

e-mail *n* ইমেল imel

embark *vb* জাহাজে ওঠা jahaje oṭha

embarrass *vb* বিব্রত করা bibrôtô kɔra, লজ্জা দেওয়া lɔjja deoŷa

embassy *n* দূতাবাস dūtabas

embezzlement *n* চাঁদাবাজি cãdabaji

emblem *n* প্রতীক prôtīk

embrace *vb* জড়িয়ে ধরা jôṛiŷe dhɔra; *n* আলিঙ্গন aliṅgôn

embroidery *n* কশিদা kôśida, সূচিশিল্প sūciśilpô

emerge *vb* (come out) নির্গত হওয়া nirgɔtô hɔoŷa; (be revealed) প্রকাশ হওয়া prôkaś hɔoŷa

emergency *n* জরুরি অবস্থা jôruri ɔbôstha, বিপদ bipɔd

emigrant *n* পরবাসী pɔrôbasī

emit *vb* নিঃসরণ করা niḥsɔrôṇ kɔra

emotion *n* অনুভূতি ônubhūti, আবেগ abeg

emperor *n* সম্রাট sɔmraṭ

emphasis *n* জোর jor, ঝোঁক jhõk

emphasize *vb* জোর দেওয়া jor deoŷa

empire *n* সাম্রাজ্য samrajyô

employ *vb* কাজে লাগানো kaje lagano

employer *n* মনিব mônib

employment *n* চাকরি cakri, প্রয়োগ prôŷog

empty *adj* খালি khali

enable *vb* সমর্থ করা sɔmôrthô kɔra

enamel *n* মিনা mina (Bd), মিনে mine (WB)

encircle *vb* ঘিরে রাখা ghire rakha

enclose *vb* ভিতরে রাখা bhitôre rakha (Bd), ভেতরে রাখা bhetôre rakha (WB)

enclosure *n* ঘেরাও gherao

encounter *n* সাক্ষাৎ sakṣat

encourage *vb* উৎসাহ দেওয়া utsahô deoŷa

encyclopedia *n* জ্ঞানকোষ jñænkoṣ

end *n* শেষ śeṣ, ইতি iti

ending *n* সমাপ্তি sɔmapti

endorse *vb* সমর্থন করা sɔmôrthôn kɔra

endurance *n* সহ্য sôhyô (pron sojjho)

endure *vb* সহ্য করা sôhyô kɔra (pron sojjho kɔra)

enemy *n* শত্রু śôtru

energetic *adj* শক্তিপূর্ণ śôktipūrṇô

energy *n* শক্তি śôkti

engagement *n* (employment) নিয়োগ niŷog; (betrothal) বিবাহের বাগদান bibaher bagdan

engine *n* ইঞ্জিন iñjin

engineer *n* যান্ত্রিক yantrik, ইঞ্জিনিয়ার iñjiniŷar

English *n* ইংরেজ imrej; *adj* ইংরেজি imreji

engrave *vb* খুদাই করা khudai kɔra, খোদাই করা khodai kɔra

engraving *n* খুদাই khudai, খোদাই khodai

enjoy *vb* ভাল লাগা bhalô laga, পছন্দ করা pɔchôndô kɔra

enjoyment *n* আমোদ amod, উপভোগ upôbhog

enlarge *vb* বাড়ানো baṛano

enormous *adj* বিশাল biśal, প্রকাণ্ড prôkaṇḍo

enough *adv* যথেষ্ট yɔtheṣṭô

enquire *vb* জিজ্ঞাসা jijñasa, জিজ্ঞেস করা jijñes kɔra

enroll *vb* ভর্তি হওয়া bhôrti hɔoŷa

ensure *vb* নিশ্চিত করা niścit kɔra

entangle *vb* পেঁচানো *(also* প্যাচানো*)* pæ̃cano

enter *vb* ঢোকা ḍhoka, প্রবেশ করা prôbeś kɔra

enterprise *n* প্রচেষ্টা prôceṣṭa

entertain *vb* আমোদিত করা amoditô kɔra

entertainment *n* আমোদ-প্রমোদ amod-prômod

enthusiasm *n* আগ্রহ agrôhô, উল্লাস ullas

entire *adj* পুরা pura *(Bd)*, পুরো purô *(WB)*, সমস্ত sɔmɔstô, সম্পূর্ণ sɔmpūrṇô

entrance *n* প্রবেশ prôbeś

entrust *vb* ভার দেওয়া bhar deoŷa

envelope *n* খাম kham

envious *adj* হিংসুক hiṁsuk

environment *n* পরিবেশ pôribeś

envy *n* হিংসা hiṁsa *(Bd)*, হিংসে hiṁse *(WB)*

epidemic *n* মহামারী mɔhamarī

epilepsy *n* মৃগীরোগ mr̥gīrog

equal *adj* সমান sɔman

equality *n* সমতা sɔmôta

equator *n* নিরক্ষ nirôkṣô

equip *vb* সজ্জিত করা sôjjitô kɔra

equipment *n* উপকরণ upôkɔrôṇ

equity *n* ন্যায় nyaŷ

equivalent *adj* সমতুল sɔmôtul

era *n* যুগ yug

erase *vb* মুছে ফেলা muche phæla

erect *vb (build)* স্থাপন করা sthapôn kɔra; *(put upright)* খাড়া khaṛa

erotic *adj* কামদ kamôd, কামুক kamuk

erratic *adj (arbitrary)* খেয়ালী kheŷalī; *(confused)* বিভ্রান্ত bibhrantô

error *n* ভুল bhul

escalator *n* চলা সিঁড়ি cɔla sĩṛi

escape *vb* পালানো palano, পালিয়ে যাওয়া paliŷe yaoŷa

escort *vb* সঙ্গে যাওয়া sɔṅge yaoŷa

especially *adv* বিশেষভাবে biśeṣbhabe

esplanade *n* ময়দান mɔŷdan

essay *n* প্রবন্ধ prôbɔndhô

essence *n* নির্যাস niryas, আরক arôk

essential *adj* অপরিহার্য ɔpôriharyô

establish *vb* স্থাপন করা sthapôn kɔra

estate *n* সম্পত্তি sɔmpôtti

estimate *vb (guess)* অনুমান করা ônuman kɔra, আন্দাজ করা andaj kɔra; *(judge value)* যাচানো yacano

etcetera (etc.) *n* ইত্যাদি ityadi

eternal *adj* অনাদি ɔnadi, সনাতন sɔnatɔn, অমর ɔmɔr

eternity *n* অনন্তকাল ɔnɔntôkal

ethical *adj* নীতিমান nītiman

ethics *n* নীতিবিজ্ঞান nītibijñæn

ethnology *n* জাতিতত্ত্ব jatitɔttvô

Europe *n* ইউরোপ iurop

European *adj* ইউরোপীয় iuropīŷô

evacuate *vb* খালি করা khali kɔra, অপসারণ করা ɔpôsarôṇ kɔra

evacuation *n* অপসারণ ɔpôsarôṇ

evaluation *n* নির্ধারণ nirdharôṇ, নির্ণয় nirṇôŷ

even *adj (level)* সমান sɔman; *(balanced)* সমকক্ষ sɔmôkɔkṣô; *adv* এমনকি emônki

evening *n* সন্ধ্যা sɔndhya *(Bd)*, সন্ধ্যে sondhye *(WB)*

event *n* ঘটনা ghɔṭona

ever *adv* কখনও kɔkhôno

every *adj* প্রতি prôti, প্রত্যেক prôtyek

everybody, everyone *n* সবাই sɔbai, সকলে sɔkôle

everything *n* সব কিছু sɔb kichu

everywhere *adv* সব জায়গায় sɔb jaŷgaŷ, সবখানে sɔbkhane

evidence *n* প্রমাণ prômaṇ

evident *adj* সুস্পষ্ট suspɔṣṭô, প্রকট prôkɔṭ

evil *adj* মন্দ mɔndô

exact *adj* ঠিক ṭhik, ঠিকঠাক ṭhikṭhak

exaggerate *vb* বাড়িয়ে বলা bariŷe bɔla

exaggeration *n* অতিবাদ ôtibad

examination *n* পরীক্ষা pôrīkṣa

examine *vb* পরীক্ষা করা pôrīkṣa kɔra

example *n* উদাহরণ udahɔrôṇ, দৃষ্টান্ত dṛṣṭantô

excavation *n* খনন khɔnôn

exceed *vb* বেশি হওয়া beśi hɔoŷa

excellent *adj* সেরা sera, চমৎকার cɔmôṭkar

except *pp* ছাড়া chara, বাদে bade

exception *n* ব্যতিক্রম bytikrôm

excess *n* অতিরিক্ততা ôtiriktôta, বাড়তি barti

excessive *adj* অতিরিক্ত ôtiriktô, বেশি beśi

exchange *vb* বদল করা bɔdôl kɔra

excite *vb* উত্তেজিত করা uttejitô kɔra

excitement *n* উত্তেজনা uttejôna

exclude *vb* বাদ দেওয়া bad deoŷa

excuse *n* ছুতা chuta *(Bd)*, ছুতো chuto *(WB)*, অজুহাত ôjuhat; *vb* ক্ষমা করা kṣɔma kɔra, মাফ করা maph kɔra

execute *vb* সম্পাদন করা sɔmpadôn kɔra

executive *n* নিষ্পাদক niṣpadôk

exempt *vb* রেহাই দেওয়া rehai deoŷa

exemption *n* রেহাই rehai, মুক্তি mukti

exercise *n* *(practice)* চর্চা cɔrca, অনুশীলন ônuśīlôn; *(sport)* ব্যায়াম byæŷam; *vb* চর্চা করা cɔrca kɔra

exhale *vb* নিঃশ্বাস ছাড়া niḥśvas chara

exhausted *adj* কাহিল kahil

exhibit *vb* প্রকাশ করা prôkaś kɔra

exhibition *n* প্রদর্শনী prôdɔrśônī

exile *n* নির্বাসন nirbasôn

exist *vb* আছ- ach-, থাকা thaka

existence *n* অস্তিত্ব ôstitvô

expand *vb* বিস্তার করা bistar kɔra, ছড়ানো chɔrano

expansion *n* পরিব্যাপ্তি pôribyæpti

expect *vb* আশা করা aśa kɔra

expectation *n* আশা aśa, প্রত্যাশা prôtyaśa

expedition *n* অভিযান ôbhiyan

expense *n* খরচ khɔrôc, ব্যয় byæŷ

expensive *adj* দামী damī

experience *n* অভিজ্ঞতা ôbhijñôta

expert *n* বিশেষজ্ঞ biśeṣɔjñô; *adj* দক্ষ dôkṣô

explain *vb* বোঝানো bojhano

explanation *n* কৈফিয়ত koiphiŷɔt, ব্যাখ্যা byækhya

explode *vb* ফাটা phaṭa

explore *vb* *(discover)* আবিস্কার করা abiskar kɔra; *(examine)* পরীক্ষা করা pôrīkṣa kɔra

explosion *n* বিস্ফোরণ bisphorôṇ

export *n* রপ্তানি rɔptani

expose *vb* দেখানো dækhano

exposure *n* প্রকাশ prôkaś

express *vb* প্রকাশ করা prôkaś kɔra

extend *vb* পরিব্যাপ্ত করা pôribyaptô kɔra

extension *n* ব্যাপ্তি byæpti

extensive *adj* বিস্তৃত bistr̥tô, ব্যাপক byæpôk

extent *n* বিস্তার bistar

external *adj* বাইরের bairer

extinct *adj* অবলুপ্ত ɔbôluptô

extinguish *vb* নিবানো nibano, নিভানো nibhano

extra *adj (leftover)* বাকি baki; *(superfluous)* বেশি beśi, অতিরিক্ত ôtiriktô

extract *vb* উৎপাটন করা uṭpaṭôn kɔra

extradite *vb* অর্পণ করা ɔrpôṇ kɔra

extraordinary *adj* অসাধারণ ɔshadharôṇ

extreme *adj* ভীষণ bhīṣôṇ, প্রচণ্ড prôcɔṇḍô, নিদারুণ nidaruṇ

extremely *adv* ভীষণভাবে bhīṣôṇ-bhabe, অত্যন্ত ôtyôntô

eye *n* চোখ cokh

eyebrow *n* ভ্রু bhru, ভুরু bhuru

eyelid *n* চোখের পাতা cokher pata

F

fabric *n* কাপড় kapôṛ

facade *n* চেহারা cehara

face *n* মুখ mukh

facial *adj* মুখের mukher

facilitate *vb* সুবিধা করে দেওয়া subidha kôre deoẏa

facility *n* সুবিধা subidha

fact *n* তথ্য tɔthyô, সত্য sôtyô

factory *n* কারখানা karkhana

factual *adj* তাথ্যিক tathyik

faculty *n* (aptitude) দক্ষতা dôkṣôta

fad *n* চাল cal

fade *vb* শুকিয়ে যাওয়া śukiẏe yaoẏa, ফিকে হয়ে যাওয়া phike hôẏe yaoẏa

fail *vb* ব্যর্থ হওয়া byærthô hɔoẏa; (~ an exam) ফেল করা phel kɔra

failure *n* ব্যর্থতা byærthota

faint *adj* (weak) দুর্বল durbɔl; (slight) অল্প ɔlpô, হালকা halka

fair *n* (exhibition) মেলা mela; *adj* (of light complexion) ফরসা phɔrsa; (good) শুভ śubhɔ; (just) ঠিক ṭhik, ভাল bhalɔ

fairy *n* পরী pɔrī

faith *n* আস্থা astha, বিশ্বাস biśvas, ভরসা bhɔrsa

faithful *adj* বিশ্বস্ত biśvɔstô

fall *vb* পড়া pɔṛa, পড়ে যাওয়া pôṛe yaoẏa; *n* (act of falling) পতন pɔtôn; (autumn) হেমন্তকাল hemôntôkal

false *adj* (mistaken) ভুল bhul; (fake) মেকি meki; (untrue) মিথ্যা mithya

falsify *vb* জাল করা jal kɔra

fame *n* খ্যাতি khyæti

familiar *adj* চেনা cena, পরিচিত pôricitô

family *n* পরিবার pôribar, সংসার sɔmsar

famine *n* অনাহার ɔnahar

famous *adj* বিখ্যাত bikhyatô

fan *n* পাখা pakha

fanatic *n* গোঁড়া gõṛa; *adj* ধর্মান্ধ dhɔrmandô

fancy *n* মর্জি môrji, খোশখেয়াল khôśkheẏal

far *adv* দূরে dūre

faraway *adj* অনেক দূরের ɔnek dūrer

fare *n* ভাড়া bhaṛa

farewell *n* বিদায় bidaẏ

farm *n* খামার khamar

farmer *n* চাষী caṣī, কৃষক kr̥ṣɔk

farsighted *adj* সুবিবেচক subibecôk

fascinate *vb* মুগ্ধ করা mugdhô kɔra

fascination *n* মুগ্ধ mugdhô, মোহ mohô

fashion *n* চাল cal, প্রথা prôtha

fashionable *adj* চলতি côlti

fast *adj, adv* (quickly) জোরে jore, দ্রুত drutô; *adj* (steady) অটল ɔṭɔl, স্থির sthir

fasten *vb* লাগানো lagano

fasting *n* না খেয়ে থাকা na kheẏe thaka, (for Ramadan) রোজা roja

fat *n* চর্বি côrbi, তেল tel; *adj* স্থূল sthulô, মোটা moṭa

fatal *adj* মারাত্মক maratmôk

father *n* বাবা baba, আব্বা abba, পিতা pita

father-in-law *n* শ্বশুর śvôśur

fathomless *adj* অতল ɔtɔl

fatigue *n* ক্লান্তি klanti

fatty *adj* তেলা tela, গোবদা gobda

faucet *n* ট্যাপ ṭyæp

fault *n (shortcoming)* ক্রটি truṭi, ভুল bhul; *(wrong-doing)* দোষ doṣ; *(offense)* অপরাধ ɔpôradh

faulty *adj* ভাঙা bhaṅga

favor *n* উপকার upôkar

favorite *adj* জনপ্রিয় jɔnôpriŷô

fax *n* ফ্যাক্স phyæks; *vb* ফ্যাক্স করা phyæks kɔra

fear *n* ভয় bhɔŷ, আতঙ্ক atôṅkô, ভীতি bhīti

feasible *adj* সম্ভব sɔmbhɔb

feast *n* উপভোগ upôbhog

feather *n* পালক palôk

February *n* ফেব্রুয়ারি মাস phebruŷari mas

feces *n* পায়খানা paŷkhana, গু gu

fee *n* বেতন betôn

feed *vb* খাওয়ানো khaoŷano

feel *vb (perceive)* লাগা laga, অনুভব করা ônubhɔb kɔra; *(realize)* টের পাওয়া ṭer paoŷa, বোধ করা bodh kɔra

feeling *n* অনুভূতি ônubhūti

feign *vb* ছদ্ম chɔdmô

fell *vb* কেটে ফেলা keṭe phæla

fellow *n* সঙ্গী sôṅgī

female *adj* স্ত্রীজাতীয় strījatīŷô

feminine *adj* মেয়েলি meŷeli

fence *n* বেড়া beṛa

fender *n* ঠেকনা ṭhekna

ferment *vb* গাঁজানো gāžano

fern *n* পর্ণাঙ্গ pɔrṇaṅgô

ferry *n* ফেরি pheri, খেয়া kheŷa

fertile *adj* উর্বর urbɔr

festival *n* উৎসব uṯsɔb

fetch *vb* আনা ana, নিয়ে আসা niŷe asa

fetter *n* বেড়ি beṛi

fever *n* জ্বর jvɔr

few *adj* অল্প ɔlpô কম kɔm; *(a ~)* কয়েক kɔŷek

fiber *n* আঁশ āś

fiction *n (story)* গল্প gɔlpô; *(novel)* উপন্যাস upônyas

fictitious *adj* কল্পিত kôlpitô

fiddle *n* বেহালা behala

fidget *vb* নিশপিশ করা niśpiś kɔra

field *n (piece of land)* মাঠ maṭh; *(area, bounds)* ক্ষেত্র kṣetrô

fierce *adj (violent)* উগ্র ugrô; *(strong)* প্রবল prôbɔl

fifteen *num* পনের pɔnerô

fifth *num* পঞ্চম pɔṅcôm

fifty *num* পঞ্চাশ pɔṅcaś

fig *n* ডুমুর ḍumur

fight *vb (struggle)* সংগ্রাম করা sɔṁgram kɔra; *(wrestle)* মারামারি করা maramari kɔra; *n* সংগ্রাম sɔṁgram, লড়াই lɔṛai

figure *n (shape)* রূপ rūp, গঠন gɔṭhôn; *(number)* সংখ্যা sɔṁkhya

file *n (folder)* ফাইল phail; *(rasp)* উকো ukô

fill *vb* ভরা bhɔra, ভরানো bhɔrano, ভর্তি করা bôrti kɔra

filled *adj* ভর্তি bhôrti

film *n (thin layer)* ছাল chal; *(motion picture)* চলচ্চিত্র cɔlôccitrô, ছবি chôbi; *(for a camera)* ফিল্ম film

filter *n* ফিল্টার philṭar

filthy *adj* নোংরা nomra

final *adj (last)* অন্তিম ôntim, শেষ śeṣ; *(decisive)* চূড়ান্ত cūṛantô

finalize *vb* পাকাপাকি করা pakapaki kɔra, নিশ্চিত করা niścit kɔra

finally *adv* অবশেষে ɔbôśeṣe

finance *n* অর্থ ɔrthô

financial *adj* আর্থিক arthik

find *vb* পাওয়া paoŷa

fine *n* জরিমানা jôrimana; *adj (delicate)* চিকন cikɔn; *(good)* ভাল bhalô; *adv (OK)* আচ্ছা accha

finger *n* আঙুল aṅgul

fingerling *n* পোনা মাছ pona mach

fingernail *n* নখ nɔkh

fingerprint *n* আঙুলের ছাপ aṅguler chap

finish *vb* সারা sara, শেষ করা śeṣ kɔra

fire *n* আগুন agun

firefly *n* জোনাকি jônaki

fireworks *n* আতশবাজি atôśbaji

firm *n* কোম্পানি kompani; *adj* মজবুত môjbut

first *adj, adv* প্রথম prôthôm

fish *n* মাছ mach

fish net *n* জাল jal

fisherman *n* জেলে jele

fishing *n* মাছ ধরা mach dhɔra

fist *n* কিল kil, মুষ্টি muṣṭi

fit *vb* মানানো manano; *n (attack of illness)* খিঁচুনি khĩcuni; *adj (suitable)* উপযুক্ত upôyuktô; *(healthy)* সুস্থ susthô

fitness *n (health)* স্বাস্থ্য svasthyô *(pron* shastho)

five *num* পাঁচ pāc

fix *vb (settle)* ঠিক করা ṭhik kɔra; *(repair)* মেরামত করা meramɔt kɔra; *(fasten)* আটকানো aṭkano

flabby *adj* থলথল thɔlthɔl

flag *n* পতাকা pɔtaka

flame *n* আগুনের ঝলক aguner jhɔlôk

flamingo *n* মরাল mɔral

flap *vb* ঝাপটানো jhaptano; *n* ঝাপটা jhapṭa

flash *n* ঝলক jhɔlôk

flat *adj* চেপটা *(also* চ্যাপটা) cæpṭa; *n* ফ্ল্যাট phlyæṭ

flatter *vb* তেল দেওয়া tel deoŷa, তোষামোদ করা toṣamod kɔra

flattery *n* তোষামোদ toṣamod

flavor *n* স্বাদ svad

flaw *n* ত্রুটি truṭi

flawless *adj* শুদ্ধ suddhô

flea *n* নীলমাছি nīlmachi

fleck *n* ছিটা–ফোঁটা chiṭa–phõṭa

flee *vb* পালানো palano

fleet *n* পোতবহর potbɔhôr

flesh *n* মাংস maṁsô

flight *n (act of fleeing)* পলায়ন pɔlaŷôn; *(act of flying)* ওড়া oṛa; *(plane journey)* বিমান যাত্রা biman yatra; *(set of stairs)* সোপান sopan

flippancy *n* ফাজলামি phajlami

flirt *vb* ছিনালি করা chinali kɔra *(Bd)*, ছেনালি করা chenali kɔra *(WB)*

float *vb* ভাসা bhasa

flock *n* ঝাঁক jhãk

flood *n* বন্যা bônya, বান ban

floor *n (area underfoot)* মেঝে mejhe; *(storey)* তলা tɔla, তালা tala

flop *n* বিফলতা biphɔlôta; *vb* হেলে পড়া hele pɔra

florist *n* ফুলওয়ালা phuloŷala

flour *n* ময়দা mɔŷda, আটা aṭa

flow *n* ধারা dhara, স্রোত srot; *vb* বওয়া bɔoŷa, বয়ে যাওয়া bôŷe yaoŷa

flower *n* ফুল phul

flu *n* সর্দিজ্বর sôrdijvɔr

fluent *adj (eloquent)* বাকপটু bakpôṭu; *(effortless)* সাবলীল sabôlīl

fluid *adj* তরল tɔrôl

flurry *n* হৈচৈ hoicoi

flush *n* তেজ tej

flute *n* বাঁশি bāśi

flutter *n* ফড়ফড় phɔrphɔr

fly *vb* ওড়া ɔra; *n* মাছি machi

foam *n* ফেনা phæna

focus *n (center)* কেন্দ্র kendrô; *(target, aim)* লক্ষ্য lôkṣyô

fog *n* কুয়াশা kuŷaśa

foggy *adj* কুয়াশাচ্ছন্ন kuŷaśacchɔnnô

fold *n* ভাঁজ bhāj

folder *n* কাগজের আধার kagôjer adhar, ফাইল fail

follow *vb* অনুসরণ করা ônusɔrôṇ kɔra, পিছনে যাওয়া pichône yaoŷa

following *adj* পরবর্তী pɔrôbôrtī

fond *adj* আশক্ত aśɔktô

food *n* খাবার khabar, আহার ahar, খাওয়া-দাওয়া khaoŷa-daoŷa

fool *n* বোকা boka

foolish *adj* বোকা boka, মূর্খ mūrkhô

foot *n* পা pa

football *n* ফুটবল phuṭbɔl

for *pp (for the benefit of)* জন্য jônyô, জন্যে jônye; *(on behalf of)* পক্ষে pôkṣe; *(lasting)* ধরে dhôre

for instance *adv* যেমন yæmôn

forbearance *n* তিতিক্ষা titikṣa

forbid *vb* নিষেধ করা niṣedh kɔra

forbidden *adj* নিষিদ্ধ niṣiddhô

force *n (strength)* জোর jor; *(oppression)* জুলুম julum

forceful *adj* জোরালো joralo

forecast *n* পূর্বানুমান pūrbanuman, পূর্বাভাস pūrbabhas

forehead *n* কপাল kɔpal

foreign *adj* বিদেশি bideśi

foreigner *n* বিদেশি bideśi

foresight *n* পারদর্শিতা pɔrôdôrśita

forest *n* বন bôn জঙ্গল jɔṅgôl

forever *adv* চিরদিন cirôdin, চিরকাল cirôkal

foreword *n* ভূমিকা bhūmika

forgery *n* জালিয়াতি jaliŷati

forget *vb* ভোলা bhola, ভুলে যাওয়া bhule yaoŷa

forgive *vb* ক্ষমা করা kṣɔma kɔra

forgiveness *n* ক্ষমা kṣɔma

fork *n* কাঁটা চামচ kāṭa camôc

form *n (shape)* রূপ rūp, আকার akar; *(structure)* গঠন gɔṭhôn

formal *adj* বিধিসম্মত bidhisɔmmtô

format *n* আয়তন aŷôtɔn

former *adj* আগের ager, প্রাক্তন praktôn

formula *n* বিধি bidhi

fortnight *n* দুই সপ্তাহ dui sɔptah

fortress *n* নগরদুর্গ nɔgôrdurgô

fortunate *adj* ভাগ্যবান bhagyôban *(m)*, ভাগ্যবতী bhagyôbôtī *(f)*

fortunately *adv* ভাগ্যিস bhagyis

fortune *n* ভাগ্য bhagyô

forty *num* চল্লিশ côlliś

forward *adv* অগ্রসর ɔgrôsɔr, সামনের দিকে samner dike

fossil *n* জীবাশ্ম jībaśmô

foster *vb* লালন-পালন করা lalôn-palôn kɔra

foul *adj* নোংরা nomra, জঘন্য jɔghônyô

found *vb* স্থাপন করা sthapôn kɔra

foundation *n* ভিত্তি bhitti, বনিয়াদ bôniŷad

founder *n* প্রতিষ্ঠাতা prôtiṣṭhata

fountain *n* ঝরনা jhɔrna, নির্ঝর nirjhɔr

four *num* চার car

fourteen *num* চৌদ্দ couddô

fourth *num* চতুর্থ côthurthô

fowl *n* বনের মুরগি bôner murgi

fox *n* শিয়াল śiŷal, শেয়াল śeŷal

fracture *n* ভঙ্গ bhɔṅgô; *vb* ভাঙা bhaṅga

fragile *adj* ভঙ্গুর bhôṅgur, পলকা pɔlka

fragment *n* টুকরো ṭukro

fragrance *n* সুগন্ধ sugɔndhô, ঘ্রাণ ghraṇ

frame *n* (*structure*) গঠন gɔṭhôn; (*scaffold*) ভারা bhara

framework *n* কাঠামো kaṭhamo

France *n* ফ্রান্সের দেশ phranser deś

frank *adj* অকপট ɔkɔpôt, সরল sɔrôl

frantic *adj* ক্ষিপ্ত kṣiptô

fraud *n* প্রতারণা protarôṇa, ছল chɔl

freckles *n* মেচেতা meceta

free *adj* স্বাধীন svadhīn, মুক্ত muktô

freedom *n* স্বাধীনতা svadhīnɔta, মুক্তি mukti

freely *adv* স্বচ্ছন্দে svɔcchɔnde

freeze *vb* (*become frozen*) বরফ হওয়া bɔrôph hɔŷa; (*put in freezer*) ফ্রিজ করা frij kɔra

freight *n* বাহিত মাল bahitô mal

French *adj* ফরাসি phɔrasi

frequent *adj* বারবার barbar

frequently *adv* প্রায়ই praŷi, হামেশা hameśa

fresh *adj* টাটকা ṭaṭka

Friday *n* শুক্রবার śukrôbar

fried *adj* ভাজি bhaji (*Bd*), ভাজা bhaja (*WB*)

friend *n* বন্ধু bôndhu (*m*), বান্ধবী bandhobī (*f*)

friendly *adj* মিশুক miśuk (*Bd*), মিশুকে miśuke (*WB*)

friendship *n* বন্ধুত্ব bôndhutvô, বন্ধুতা bôndhuta

fright *n* ভয় bhɔŷ, আতঙ্ক atôṅkô, ভীতি bhīti

frighten *vb* ভয় দেখানো bhɔŷ dækhano

frightening *adj* ভয়ঙ্কর bhɔŷôṅkɔr

frog *n* ব্যাঙ byæṅ

from *pp* থেকে theke

front *n* সামনে samne, মুখ mukh

front of (in ~) *pp* সামনে samne

frontier *n* সীমানা sīmana, সীমান্ত sīmantô

frost *n* হিম him

frostbite *n* হিম-দংশ him-dɔṁśô

frown *n* ভ্রূকুটি bhrukuṭi

frugal *adj* হিসাবি hisabi (*Bd*), হিসেবি hisebi (*WB*)

fruit *n* ফল phɔl

fruitful *adj* সফল sɔphôl, ফলপ্রসূ phɔlprôsū

fruition *n* উপভোগ upôbhog

fruitless *adj* নিস্ফল niṣphɔl

frustrate *vb* অসন্তুষ্ট করা ɔsɔntuṣṭô kɔra

frustrated *adj* আশাহত aśahɔtô, অসন্তুষ্ট ɔsɔntuṣṭô

frustration *n* আশাভঙ্গ aśabhɔṅgô

fry *vb* ভাজা bhaja

frying pan *n* চাটু caṭu

fuel *n* জ্বালানি jvalani; (*gas*) তেল tel

fugitive *n* পলাতক pɔlatɔk

fulfil *vb* (*make complete*) সম্পূর্ণ করা sɔmpūrṇô kɔra; (*satisfy*) তৃপ্ত করা tṛptô kɔra

full *adj (filled up)* ভরা bhɔra, ভর্তি bhôrti; *(whole)* পুরা pura, সারা sara; *(utmost)* চরম cɔrôm

full moon *n* পূর্ণিমা pūrṇima

fully *adv* সম্পূর্ণভাবে sɔmpūrṇôbhabe

fumes *n* ধুমা dhuma, ধোঁয়া dhõya

fun *n* ফুর্তি phurti, মজা mɔja

function *vb* চলা cɔla, কাজ করা kaj kɔra; *n (use)* ব্যবহার bybôhar *(pron* bæbohar); *(purpose)* কাজ kaj, ক্রিয়া kriŷa; *(ceremony)* অনুষ্ঠান ônuśṭhan

fund *n* তহবিল tɔhôbil, কোষ koṣ

fundamental *adj* মৌলিক moulik

funeral *n (burial)* মাটি দেওয়া maṭi deoŷa, *(Hindu)* শ্রাদ্ধ śraddhô

funeral procession *n* শবানুগমন śɔbanugɔmôn

fungus *n* ছাতা chata

funny *adj* মজাদার mɔjadar, রসিক rôsik

fur *n* পশম pɔśôm

furious *adj* রাগী ragī, ক্রুদ্ধ kruddhô

furnace *n* চুল্লি culli

furnish *vb* সাজানো sajano

furniture *n* আসবাব asbab

further *adj, adv (additional)* আরও aro, *(at a greater distance); adv* আরও দূরে aro dūre; *vb* অগ্রসর করা ɔgrôsôr kɔra

fury *n* রাগ rag, ক্রোধ krodh

fuss *n* হৈচৈ hôicôi, ব্যস্ততা bystôta *(pron* bæstota)

fussy *adj* হন্তদন্ত hɔntôdɔntô

futile *adj* ব্যর্থ byærthô, পণ্ড pɔṇḍô

future *n* ভবিষ্যৎ bhôbiṣyɔṯ; *adj* আগামী agamī

G

gadfly *n* গোমাছি gomachi

gain *n* লাভ labh; *vb* পাওয়া paôŷa, লাভ করা labh kɔra

galaxy *n* ছায়াপথ chaŷapɔth

gall *n* পিত্ত pittô

gallery *n* দরদালান dɔrdalan

gallon *n* গ্যালন gyælôn

gallop *n* ঘোড়ার ধাবন ghoɽar dhabôn

gambling *n* জুয়াখেলা juŷakhæla

game *n* (*entertainment*) খেলা khæla; (*wildlife*) শিকারের জন্তু śikarer jôntu

Ganges *n* গঙ্গা gɔnga

gap *n* ফাঁক phãk

garage *n* গ্যারেজ gyærej

garbage *n* ময়লা mɔŷla

garden *n* বাগান bagan

gardener *n* মালী malī

gargle *vb* মুখ ধোয়া mukh dhoŷa

garland *n* মালা mala

garlic *n* রসুন rôsun

garment *n* জামা jama, পোশাক pośak

garrulous *adj* বাচাল bacal

gas *n* গ্যাস gyæs

gate *n* গেট geṭ

gatekeeper *n* দারোয়ান daroŷan

gather *vb* কুড়ানো kuɽano (*Bd*), কুড়োনো kuɽono (*WB*), সংগ্রহ করা sɔṁgrôhô kɔra

gathering *n* সঞ্চয় sɔñcɔŷ

gauge *n* মাপনযন্ত্র mapônyɔntrô

gay *adj* (*exuberant*) হাসিখুশি hasikhuśi, প্রফুল্ল prôphullô; (*homosexual*) সমকামী sɔmôkamī

gear *n* সজ্জা sɔjja

gecko *n* টিকটিকি ṭikṭiki

gem *n* মণি môṇi, রত্ন rɔtnô

gender *n* লিঙ্গ liṅgô

general *adj* সাধারণ sadharôṇ, প্রধান prôdhan

generally *adv* সাধারণত sadharôṇtô, সব মিলে sɔb mile

generate *vb* উৎপাদন করা utpadôn kɔra

generation *n* পুরুষপরম্পরা puruṣpɔrôspɔra

generic *adj* বর্গীয় bôrgīŷô

generous *adj* দানশীল danśīl, উদার udar

genetic *adj* উৎপাদ্য utpadyô

genital *adj* যৌন youn

genitals *n* উপস্থ upôsthô

genius *n* প্রতিভা prôtibha

gentle *adj* নরম nɔrôm, ভদ্র bhɔdrô

gentleman *n* ভদ্রলোক bhɔdrôlok

genuine *adj* আসল asôl, সত্য sɔtyô

geography *n* ভূগোল bhūgol

geology *n* ভূতত্ত্ব bhūtɔttvô

geometry *n* জ্যামিতি jyæmiti

germ *n* জীবাণু jībaṇu

German *adj* জার্মান jarman

Germany *n* জার্মানি jarmani

gesticulate *vb* ঠারা ṭhara

gesture *n* ইশারা iśara, ইঙ্গিত iṅgit

get *vb* পাওয়া paôŷa

get down *vb* নামা nama, নেমে যাওয়া neme yaoŷa

get over *vb* ভাল হওয়া bhalô hɔoŷa

get up *vb* ওঠা oṭha, উঠে পড়া uṭhe pɔra

ghost *n* ভূত bhūt

giant *n* দৈত্য doityô

gift *n* দান dan, উপহার upôhar

giggle *vb* খিলখিল করে হাসা khilkhil kôre hasa

gin *n* জিন jin

girl *n* মেয়ে meŷe, বালিকা, balika

girlfriend *n* বান্ধবী bandhôbī, প্রেমিকা premika

give *vb* দেওয়া deoŷa

give back *vb* ফেরত দেওয়া pherôt deoŷa

give up *vb* ত্যাগ করা tyæg kɔra, ছেড়ে দেওয়া chere deoŷa

given *adj* দত্ত dɔttô

glad *adj* আনন্দিত anônditô

glamorous *adj* বাহারি bahari

glamour *n* চটক cɔṭôk, বাহার bahar

glance *n* পলক pɔlôk

gland *n* গ্রন্থি grônthi

glare *n (bright light)* উজ্জ্বলতা ujjvôlɔta; *(angry look)* জ্বলন্ত দৃষ্টি jvɔlôntô dṛṣṭi

glass *n (material)* কাচ kac; *(for drinking)* গেলাস gelas

glasses *n* চশমা cɔśma

glimpse *n* ক্ষণিক দৃষ্টি kṣôṇik dṛṣṭi

glitter *n* ঝকঝক jhɔkjhɔk

global *adj* বিশ্বব্যাপী biśvôbyæpī

globe *n (spherical body)* গোলক golôk; *(the world)* পৃথিবী pṛthibī, বিশ্ব biśvô

gloom *n* বিষণ্নতা biṣɔṇṇôta, অন্ধকার ɔndhôkar

gloomy *adj* বিষণ্ন biṣɔṇṇô

glory *n* গৌরব gourɔb

glove *n* দস্তানা dɔstana, হাত-মোজা hat-moja

glow *vb* জ্বলজ্বল করা jvɔljvɔl kɔra

glue *n* আঠা aṭha

go *vb* যাওয়া yaoŷa

go away *vb* চলে যাওয়া côle yaoŷa

go back *vb* ফিরে যাওয়া phire yaoŷa

go by *vb (of time)* কাটা kaṭa, পার হওয়া par hɔoŷa

go off *vb (of food)* নষ্ট হওয়া nɔṣṭô hɔoŷa

go on *vb (continue)* চালিয়ে যাওয়া caliŷe yaoŷa

go out *vb* বেরোনো berono

go under *vb (sink)* ডোবা ḍoba

go up *vb (increase)* বেড়ে যাওয়া bere yaoŷa

goal *n* তাক tak, লক্ষ্য lôkṣyô

goat *n* ছাগল chagôl

god *n* দেবতা debôta, ভগবান bhɔgôban, ঈশ্বর īśvɔr

goddess *n* দেবী debī

godfather *n* ধর্মপিতা dhɔrmôpita

godmother *n* ধর্মমা dhɔrmôma

gold *n* সোনা sona

golden *adj* সোনার sonar, সোনালি sonali

gone *adv* বিগত bigɔtô

good *n (welfare)* মঙ্গল môṅgôl; *adj* ভাল, bhalô, ভালো bhalo

good-bye *n* বিদায় bidaŷ

goodness *n* সততা sɔtôta

goods *n* মাল mal

goose *n* রাজহাঁস rajhãs

gospel *n* যীশুর বাণী yīśur baṇī

gossip *n* বাজে গুজব baje gujɔb, গল্পগুজব gɔlpôgujɔb; *vb* গল্পগুজব করা gɔlpôgujɔb kɔra

govern *vb (manage)* পরিচালনা করা pôricalôna kɔra; *(control)* শাসন করা śasôn kɔra

government *n (management)* শাসন śasôn, পরিচালনা pôricalôna; *(body of administration)* সরকার sɔrkar

governmental *adj* সরকারি sɔrkari

governor *n* পরিচালক pôricalôk

grace *n* কৃপা kṙpa

graceful *adj* লাবণ্যময় labɔṇyômɔŷ, সুন্দর sundôr

gracious *adj* সদয় sɔdɔŷ

grade *n (degree)* ক্রম krôm; *(class)* শ্রেণী śreni

gradual *adj* ক্রমশ krômôśô

graduate *vb* বি এ পাশ করা bi e paś kɔra

graft *vb* জোড়া দেওয়া jɔra deôŷa

grain *n* শস্য śɔsyô

gram *n* গ্রাম gram

grammar *n* ব্যাকরণ byækɔrôṇ

grand *adj* মহান mɔhan, চমৎকার cɔmôtkar

granddaughter *n* নাতনি natni

grandfather *n (paternal)* দাদা dada *(Muslim)*, ঠাকুরদা ṭhakurda *(Hindu)*; *(maternal)* নানা nana *(Muslim)*, দাদু dadu *(Hindu)*

grandmother *n (paternal)* দাদি dadi *(Muslim)*, ঠাকুরমা ṭhakurma *(Hindu)*; *(maternal)* নানি nani *(Muslim)*, দিদিমা didima *(Hindu)*

grandson *n* নাতি nati

grant *n* দান dan, অনুদান ônudan; *vb* দেওয়া deôŷa, অনুমতি দেওয়া ônumôti deôŷa

grape *n* আঙ্গুর ফল aṅgur phɔl

grapefruit *n* জামবুরা jambura *(Bd)*, বাতাবীলেবু batabīlebu *(WB)*

graph *n* চিত্র citrô

graphic *adj* স্পষ্ট spɔṣṭô

grasp *vb* ধরা dhɔra

grass *n* ঘাস ghas

grasshopper *n* ফড়িং phôṙiṁ

grateful *adj* কৃতজ্ঞ kṙtɔjñô

gratitude *n* কৃতজ্ঞতা kṙtɔjñôta

grave *n* কবর kɔbor, সমাধি sɔmadhi; *adj* গম্ভীর gômbhir

gravity *n (attraction)* অভিকর্ষ ôbhikɔrṣô; *(importance)* গুরুত্ব gurutvô

gray *adj* ধূসর রঙের dhūsôr rɔṅger, ছাই রং chai rɔṁ

grease *n* চর্বি côrbi

great *adj (big)* বড় bɔṙô, মস্ত mɔstô; *(excellent)* চমৎকার cɔmôtkar, দারুণ daruṇ

great-grandfather *n* প্রপিতামহ prôpitamɔhô

great-grandmother *n* প্রপিতামহী prôpitamôhī

greed *n* লোভ lobh

Greek *n* গ্রীক grīk

green *adj (color)* সবুজ sôbuj; *(inexperienced)* কাঁচা kāca

greet *vb* অভিবাদন করা ôbhibadôn kɔra, নমস্কার জানানো nɔmôskar janano

greeting *n* নমস্কার nɔmôskar *(Hindu)*; আদাব adab *(Muslim)*

grief *n* শোক śok, দুঃখ duḥkhô

grievance *n* নালিশের কারণ naliśer karôṇ

grieve *vb* দুঃখ করা duḥkhô kɔra, শোক করা śok kɔra

grill *vb* ঝাঁঝরিতে ভাজা jhā̃jhôrite bhaja

grimace *n* খিঁচুনি khī̃cuni; *vb* খিঁচানো khī̃cano

grind *vb* পিষা piṣa, পেষা peṣa

grip *vb* ধরা dhɔra

groan *n* আর্তনাদ artônad; *vb* উ –আ করা u-a kɔra

grocer *n* মুদি mudi

grocery *n* মুদিখানা mudikhana
groin *n* কুঁচকি kŭcki
ground *n (earth)* ভূমি bhūmi; *(foundation)* বনিয়াদ bôniŷad; *adj* পিষ্ট piṣṭô
group *n* দল dɔl
grow *vb* বাড়া baṛa, বড় হয়ে যাওয়া bɔṛô hôŷe yaoya
growl *vb* বিড়বিড় করা biṛbiṛ kɔra
grown-up *n* বয়স্ক bɔŷɔskô
growth *n (increase)* বাড়া baṛa, বৃদ্ধি bṙddhi; *(development)* উন্নতি unnôti
guarantee *n* জামিন jamin
guard *n* দারোয়ান daroŷan; *vb* পাহারা দেওয়া pahara deoŷa, রক্ষা করা rôkṣa kɔra
guardian *n* পালক palôk
guava *n* পেয়ারা peŷara
guerilla *n* বিদ্রোহী bidrohī
guess *n* অনুমান ônuman; *vb* আন্দাজ করা andaj kɔra
guest *n* অতিথি ôtithi, মেহমান mehôman

guidance *n* নির্দেশ nirdeś
guide *vb (advise)* উপদেশ দেওয়া upôdeś deoŷa; *n (leader)* চালক calôk, নেতা neta
guilt *n* দোষ doṣ, অপরাধ ɔpôradh
guilty *adj* দোষী doṣī, অপরাধী ɔpôradhī
guitar *n* গিটার giṭar
gulf *n* উপসাগর upôsagôr
gum *n* মাড়ি maṛi
gun *n* বন্দুক bônduk
gush *vb* প্রবাহিত হওয়া prôbahitô hɔoŷa
gust *n* ঝাপটা jhapṭa
gymnasium *n* ব্যায়ামাগার byæŷamagar
gymnastics *n* ব্যায়াম byæŷam
gynecologist *n* স্ত্রীরোগ-বিশেষজ্ঞ strīrog-biśeṣɔjñô
gynecology *n* স্ত্রীরোগতত্ত্ব strīrogtɔttvô
gypsy *n* বেদে bede

H

habit *n* অভ্যাস ɔbhyas *(Bd)*, অভ্যেস ɔbhyes

habitation *n* লোকালয় lokalɔŷ

hail *n* শিলাবৃষ্টি śilabr̥ṣṭi

hair *n (on the head)* চুল cul; *(on the body)* লোম lom

hairdresser *n* নাপিত napit

hairy *adj* লোমশ lomôś

half *n* অর্ধেক ɔrdhek, আধ adh, আধা adha

half-and-half *adv* আধা-আধি adha-adhi

half past *adv* সাড়ে saṛe

hall *n* হলঘর hɔlghɔr

halt *vb* থামা thama, থেমে যাওয়া theme yaoŷa, থামানো thamano

hammer *n* হাতুড়ি haturi

hamper *vb* বাধা দেওয়া badha deoŷa

hand *n* হাত hat

handbag *n* থলি thôli

handful *n* মুষ্টি muṣṭi

handicap *n* অসুবিধা ɔsubidha *(Bd)*, অসুবিধে ɔsubidhe *(WB)*

handicraft *n* হস্তশিল্প hɔstôśilpô

handkerchief *n* রুমাল rumal

handle *vb* সামলানো samlano; *n* হাতল hatôl

handsome *adj* সুন্দর sundôr, কমনীয় kɔmônîŷô

handy *adj (dexterous)* কুশলী kuśôlî; *(convenient)* সুবিধাজনক subidhajônôk

hang *vb* ঝোলা jhola, ঝোলানো jholano

hanger *n* কাপড়ের ফ্রেম kapôṛer phrem, আলনা alna

hanker *vb* কামনা করা kamôna kɔra

happen *vb* হওয়া hɔoŷa, ঘটা ghɔṭa

happiness *n* সুখ sukh

happy *adj* খুশি khuśi, সুখী sukhî

harass *vb* নাকাল করা nakal kɔra

harassment *n* নাকাল nakal

harbor *n* বন্দর bɔndôr

hard *adj (not soft)* শক্ত śɔktô; *(difficult)* কঠিন kôṭhin

harden *vb* শক্ত হওয়া śɔktô hɔoŷa, শক্ত করা śɔktô kɔra

hardly *adv* প্রায় ... না praŷ ... na

hardness *n* শক্তি śôkti

hardship *n* কষ্ট kɔṣṭô

hardware *n* লোহালক্কড় lohalɔkkôṛ

hardy *adj* বলিষ্ঠ bôliṣṭhô

hare *n* শশক śɔśôk

harm *n (disservice)* অপকার ɔpôkar; *(ruin)* ক্ষতি kṣôti, হানি hani

harmful *adj* হানিকর hanikɔr

harmless *adj* অক্ষত ɔkṣɔtô

harness *n* সাজ saj; *vb* সাজ পরানো saj pɔrano

harsh *adj (severe)* কড়া kɔṛa; *(angry)* কটমট kɔṭmɔṭ

harvest *n* ফসল phɔsôl

haste *n* তাড়া taṛa

hasty *adj* হড়বড় hɔṛbɔṛ

hat *n* টুপি ṭupi

hatch *vb (eggs)* ডিম পাড়া ḍim paṛa; *(to plot)* ফন্দি আঁটা phôndi ãṭa

hate *n* ঘৃণা ghr̥na

haul *vb* টানা ṭana

haunt *vb* বারবার আসা barbar asa

have *vb* আছ- ach-, অধিকারে রাখা ôdhikare rakha

haven *n* রেহাই rehai, আশ্রয় aśrɔŷ

hawk *n* বাজপাখি bajpakhi

hay *n* খড় khɔṛ

hazard *n* ঝুঁকি jhūki

haze *n* কুয়াশা kuɏaśa

hazy *adj* কুয়াশাছন্ন kuɏaśachɔnnô

he *pr* সে se, তিনি tini

head *n* মাথা matha

headache *n* মাথা ধরা matha dhɔra

heading *n* শিরনাম śirônam

headline *n* শিরনাম śirônam

headlouse *n* উকুন ukun

headquarters *n* সদর sɔdôr

headstrong *adj* জেদি jedi

heal *vb* সেরে যাওয়া sere yaoɏa;
অসুখ সারিয়ে দেওয়া ɔsukh sariɏe
deoɏa

health *n* স্বাস্থ্য svasthyô

healthy *adj* সুস্থ susthô

heap *n* রাশি raśi, গাদা gada

hear *vb* শোনা śona

hearing *n (sense)* শ্রবণশক্তি
śrôbôṇśôkti; *(presentation)* শুনানি
śunani

heart *n* মন mɔn, হৃদয় hṛdɔɏ

heartbeat *n* হৃৎস্পন্দন hṛtspɔndôn

heartbroken *adj* মনভাঙ্গা
mônbhaṅga

heartfelt *adj* আন্তরিক antôrik

heat *n* গরম gɔrôm উত্তাপ uttap; *vb*
গরম দেওয়া gɔrôm kɔra;

heating *n* উত্তাপন uttapôn

heaven *n* স্বর্গ svɔrgô

heavy *adj (weighty)* ভারী bharī;
(dark, glum) থমথম thɔmthɔm;
(grave) গম্ভীর gômbhīr

hedge *n* ঝোপ jhop

heel *n* গোড়ালি goṛali

height *n* উচ্চতা uccôta

heir *n* উত্তরাধিকারী uttôradhikarī

helicopter *n* হেলিকপ্টার helikɔpṭar

hell *n* নরক nɔrôk

helm *n* হাল hal

helmet *n* শিরস্ত্র śirôstrô

help *n (assistance)* সাহায্য sahayyô;
(favor) উপকার upôkar; *vb* সাহায্য
করা sahayyô kɔra

helper *n* সহায় sɔhay

helpful *adj* উপকারী upôkarī

helpless *adj* অসহায় ɔsɔhay

hem *n* সেলাই–দেওয়া পাড় selai–
deoɏa paṛ

hen *n* মুর্গি murgi

hence *conj* অতএব ɔtôeb

henna *n* মেহেদি mehedi

herb *n* উদ্ভিদ udbhid, ওষধি oṣôdhi

herd *n* পশুপাল pôśupal

here *adv* এখানে ekhane

hereby *adv* এতে ete

heritage *n* উত্তরাধিকার uttôradhikar

hermaphrodite *adj* হিজড়া hijra
(Bd), হিজড়ে hijṛe *(WB)*

hermit *n* সন্ন্যাসী sɔnnyasī

hero *n (courageous man)* বীর bīr;
(leading actor) নায়ক naɏôk, নেতা
neta

heroic *adj* বীর্যবান bīryôban

heroine *n (courageous woman)*
বীরনারী bīrnarī, *(leading actress)*
নায়িকা nayika

heroism *n* বীরত্ব bīrôtvô

hesitate *vb* ইতস্ততঃ করা itɔstɔtôḥ
kɔra

hesitation *n* দ্বিধা dvidha

heterosexual *adj* ইতর–রতি–প্রবণ
itɔr–rôti–prôbôṇ

hiccup *n* হেঁচকি hēcki

hidden *adj* গোপন gopôn

hide *vb* লুকানো lukano *(Bd)*,
লুকোনো lukono *(WB)*

hide-and-seek *n* লুকাচুরি lukacuri
(Bd), লুকোচুরি lukocuri

hideous *adj* বিকট bikôṭ

high *adj* উচ্চ uccô (Bd), উঁচু ũcu
(WB)

high-minded *adj* গুণী guṇī, উচ্চ
মনের uccô môner

highway *n* সড়ক sɔrôk

hill *n* পাহাড় pahaṛ

hilly *adj* পাহাড়ি pahaṛi

hinder *vb* বাধা দেওয়া badha deoẏa

Hindi *n* হিন্দি hindi

Hindu *n* হিন্দু hindu

hinge *n* কবজা kɔbja

hint *n* ইঙ্গিত iṅgit

hip *n* পাছা pacha

hippopotamus *n* জলহস্তী jɔlôhôstī

hire *vb* লাগানো lagano, ভাড়া করা
bhaṛa kɔra; *n* ভাড়া bhaṛa

historical *adj* ঐতিহাসিক oitihasik

history *n* ইতিহাস itihas

hit *vb* মারা mara, আঘাত করা aghat
kɔra

hoard *vb* মজুদ রাখা môjud rakha

hoax *n* ফাঁকি phāki

hobby *n* শখ śɔkh

hockey *n* হকি খেলা hôki khæla

hocus-pocus *n* ভোজবাজি bhojbaji

hodge-podge *n* জগাখিচুড়ি
jɔgakhicuṛi

hoe *n* নিড়ানি niṛani

hold *vb* (grasp) ধরা dhɔra; (keep)
ধরে রাখা dhôre rakha

hole *n* গর্ত gɔrtô

holiday *n* ছুটি chuṭi

hollow *adj* ফাঁপা phāpa

holy *adj* পবিত্র pôbitrô

holy place *n* তীর্থ tīrthô

holy scripture *n* ধর্মগ্রন্থ dhɔrmôgrônthô; (Hindu) শাস্ত্র śastrô

home *n* ঘর ghɔr, বাড়ি baṛi

homeland *n* স্বদেশ sʋɔdeś

homework *n* বাড়ির কাজ baṛir kaj

homosexual *adj* সমকামী
sɔmôkamī

honest *adj* (candid, simple) সৎ sɔt,
সরল sɔrôl; (truthful) সত্যিকার
sôtyikar

honesty *n* সততা sɔtôta

honey *n* মধু môdhu

honor *n* মর্যাদা mɔryada, সম্মান
sɔmman

honorable *adj* মাননীয় manônīẏô

honored *adj* মানী manī

hood *n* বোরখা borkha

hook *n* হুক huk

hookah *n* হুঁকা hũka (Bd), হুঁকো
hũko (WB)

hooligan *n* গুণ্ডা guṇḍa

hope *n* আশা aśa; *vb* আশা করা aśa
kɔra

hopeful *adj* আশাপূর্ণ aśapūrṇô

hopeless *adj* নিরাশ niraś

horizon *n* দিগন্ত digɔntô

horizontal *adj* সমতল sɔmôtɔl

horn *n* (of an animal) শিং śiṁ; (of
a car) হর্ন hɔrn

horrible *adj* বীভৎস bībhɔtsô

horror *n* (disgust) ঘৃণা ghṛṇa;
(terror, dread) আতঙ্ক atôṅkô

horse *n* ঘোড়া ghoṛa

hose *n* হোজ পাইপ hoj paip

hospitable *adj* আতিথেয় atitheẏô

hospital *n* হাসপাতাল haspatal

hospitality *n* অতিথিসেবা
ôtithiseba, আতিথেয়তা atitheẏôta

hostage *n* প্রতিভূ prôtibhū

hostel *n* হস্টেল hɔsṭel, নিবাস nibas

hostile *adj* বিদ্রোহ bidrohô

hot *adj (very warm)* গরম gɔrôm, তপ্ত tɔptô; *(spicy)* ঝাল jhal, মসলাদার mɔsladar; *(incensed, excited)* উদ্দীপ্ত uddīptô

hotel *n* হোটেল hoṭel

hour *n (sixty minutes)* ঘণ্টা ghɔnṭa; *(time of day)* বেলা bæla

house *n (building)* ঘর ghɔr; *(residence)* বাসভবন basbhɔbôn, বাসা basa, বাড়ি baṛi

household *n* পরিবার pôribar

housewife *n* গৃহিনী gr̥hinī, গিন্নি ginni

how *adv* কেমন kæmôn

however *adv* যে কোনও ভাবে ye kono bhabe; *conj* তৎসত্ত্বেও tɔtsɔttveo

hug *n* আলিঙ্গন aliṅgôn; *vb* জড়িয়ে ধরা jôriŷe dhɔra

huge *adj* প্রকাণ্ড prôkanḍô, বিশাল biśal

human *adj* মানবিক manôbik

humane *adj* দয়ালু dɔŷalu

humanity *n* মানবতা manôbɔta

humble *adj* বিনত binɔtô, নম্র nɔmrô

humid *adj* আর্দ্র ardrô, সেঁতসেঁতে sæ̃tsæ̃te

humidity *n* আর্দ্রতা ardrôta

humor *n (temperament)* মেজাজ mejaj; *(sense of the comic)* হাস্যরস hasyôrɔs

humorous *adj* রসিক rôsik

hump *n* কুঁজ kũj

hundred *num* একশ æksô, এক শত æk śɔtô

hunger *n* খিদা khida *(Bd)*, খিদে khide *(WB)*

hungry *adj* ক্ষুধিত kṣudhito, ক্ষুধার্ত kṣudhartô

hunt *vb* শিকার করা śikar kɔra

hunter *n* শিকারী śikarī

hurl *vb* নিক্ষেপ করা nikṣep kɔra, ছুঁড়ে ফেলা chũṛe phæla

hurry *vb* তাড়াতাড়ি করা taṛataṛi kɔra; *n* তাড়াহুড়া taṛahuṛa *(Bd)*, তাড়াহুড়ো taṛahuṛo *(WB)*

hurt *n* ব্যথা bytha *(pron* bætha*)*, বেদনা bedôna; *vb (experience pain)* ব্যথা করা bytha kɔra; *(inflict pain)* ব্যথা দেওয়া bytha deôŷa; *(damage)* ক্ষতি করা kṣôti kɔra; *(wound)* আহত করা ahɔtô kɔra

husband *n* স্বামী svamī

husk *n* তুষ tuṣ

hut *n* কুটির kuṭir

hydrogen *n* উদজান udjan

hygiene *n* স্বাস্থ্যবিধি svastyôbidhi

hymn *n* স্তবগান stɔbgan

hypnotize *vb* বশ করা bɔś kɔra

hypocrisy *n* মিথ্যাচার mithyacar, ভণ্ডামি bhɔnḍami

hypocritical *adj* দ্বিভাব dvibhab, ভণ্ড bhɔnḍô

I

I *pr* আমি ami

ice *n* বরফ bɔrôph

ice cream *n* আইস ক্রিম ais krim

icon *n* প্রতিমূর্তি prôtimūrti

icy *adj* হিমশীতল himśītôl

idea *n* ধারণা dharôṇa

ideal *n* আদর্শ adôrśô

identical *adj* একই eki, একরকম ӕkrɔkôm

identification *n* শনাক্ত śɔnaktô

identify *vb* শনাক্ত করা śɔnaktô kɔra

idiom *n* বাগধারা bagdhara

idiot *n* মূর্খ mūrkhô

idle *adj* কুঁড়ে kūṛe, অলস ɔlôs

idol *n* প্রতিমূর্তি prôtimūrti

if *conj* যদি yôdi

ignorance *n* অজ্ঞতা ɔjñôta

ignorant *adj* অজ্ঞ ɔjñô

ignore *vb* না দেখা na dӕkha, তুচ্ছ করা tucchô kɔra

ill *adj* অসুস্থ ɔsusthô

illegal *adj* বেআইনী beainī

illegible *adj* হিজিবিজি hijibiji

illiterate *adj* অনক্ষর ɔnɔkṣôr, অশিক্ষিত ɔśikṣitô

illness *n* অসুখ ɔsukh

illumination *n* রোশনাই rośnai

illusion *n* মোহ mohô, মায়া maya

illustrate *vb* ব্যাখ্যা করা byækhya kɔra

illustration *n* চিত্র citrô

image *n* ছবি chôbi

imagination *n* কল্পনা kɔlpôna

imaginative *adj* ভাবুক bhabuk, কল্পনাপ্রবণ kɔlpônaprôbôn

imagine *vb* কল্পনা করা kɔlpôna kɔra

imitate *vb* অনুকরণ করা ônukɔrôṇ kɔra

imitation *n* অনুকরণ ônukɔrôṇ; *adj* মেকি meki

immaculate *adj* নিখুঁত nikhūt

immature *adj* কাঁচা kāca

immeasurable *adj* অপরিমিত ɔpôrimitô

immediate *adj* তৎক্ষণাৎ tɔtkṣɔṇat

immediately *adv* সঙ্গে সঙ্গে sɔṅge sɔṅge, শিগ্গির śiggir, জলদি jôldi

immense *adj* বিশাল biśal, প্রকাণ্ড prôkaṇḍô

immigration *n* অভিবাসন ôbhibasôn

immoral *adj* নীতিহীন nītihīn, অসৎ ɔsɔt

immortal *adj* অমর ɔmɔr

impartial *adj* নিরপেক্ষ nirɔpekṣô

impasse *n* অচল অবস্থা ɔcɔl ɔbôstha

impatient *adj* অধীর ɔdhīr

imperfect *adj* অপূর্ণ ɔpūrnô

impetuous *adj* হঠকারি hɔṭhkari

implement *vb* লাগানো lagano

imply *vb* ইঙ্গিতে বলা iṅgite bɔla

impolite *adj* অবিনয়ী ôbinɔŷī, অভদ্র ɔbhɔdrô

import *n* আমদানি amdani; *vb* আমদানি করা amdani kɔra

importance *n* গুরুত্ব gurutvô

important *adj* গুরুত্বপূর্ণ gurutvô-pūrnô

impose *vb* বাধ্য করা badhyô kɔra

impossible *adj* অসম্ভব ɔsɔmbhɔb

impotent *adj* অক্ষম ɔkṣɔm

impractical *adj* অসাধ্য ɔsadhyô

impress *vb* ছাপ মারা chap mara, ছাপ দেওয়া chap deôŷa

impression *n* ছাপ chap
impressive *adj* চিত্তাকর্ষক cittakôrṣôk
imprint *vb* ছাপা chapa
imprison *vb* কয়েদ করা kôyed kôra, আটকিয়ে রাখা aṭkiye rakha
improper *adj* অনুচিত ônucit
improve *vb* উন্নতি করা unnôti kôra
improvement *n* উন্নতি unnôti
improvise *vb* উদ্ভাবন করা udbhabôn kôra
impulse *n* আবেগ abeg
in *pp* ভিতরে bhitôre
inability *n* অক্ষমতা ôkṣômôta
inaccessible *adj* অগম্য ôgômyô
inactive *adj* জড় jôṛ
inane *adj* অর্থহীন ôrthôhīn
inappropriate *adj* বেমানান bemanan
inauguration *n* অভিষেক ôbhiṣek, সূচনা sūcôna
inauspicious *adj* অকাল ôkal
incentive *n* উদ্দীপনা uddīpôna
incessant *adj* নিরবকাশ nirôbôkaś
inch *n* ইঞ্চি iñci
inclination *n* (*liking*) ছন্দ chôndô, ঝোঁক jhõk; (*leaning*) হেলা hæla
incline *n* চালু calu, উতরাই utôrai
include *vb* সঙ্গে নেওয়া sônge neoya, অন্তর্ভুক্ত করা ôntôrbhuktô kôra
income *n* আয় ay
incomparable *adj* অতুল ôtul, অনুপম ônupôm
incomplete *adj* অপূর্ণ ôpūrṇô
inconsiderate *adj* অবিবেচক ôbibecôk
inconvenience *n* অসুবিধা ôsubidha (*Bd*), অসুবিধে ôsubidhe (*WB*)
increase *vb* বাড়া baṛa, বাড়ানো baṛano

indecent *adj* অশ্লীল ôślīl
indeed *adv* সত্যি sôtyi; *int* তাই তো tai to
independence *n* স্বাধীনতা svadhīnôta
independent *adj* স্বাধীন svadhīn
index *n* তালিকা talika
India *n* ভারত bhârôt
Indian *adj* ভারতীয় bhârôtīyô
indicate *vb* (*mark*) সূচনা করা sūcôna kôra; (*hint*) ইঙ্গিত করা iṅgit kôra
indication *n* নির্দেশ nirdeś, ইঙ্গিত iṅgit
indifferent *adj* উদাসীন udasīn
indigestion *n* অপাক ôpak, বদহজম bôdhôjôm
indirect *adj* পরোক্ষ pôrokṣô
indiscreet *adj* অবিচক্ষণ ôbicôkṣôṇ
indistinct *adj* অস্পষ্ট ôspôṣṭô
individual *n* (*person*) ব্যক্তি bykti (*pron* bekti); *adj* (*single*) একক ækôk; (*personal*) ব্যক্তিগত byktigotô
indivisible *adj* অবিভাজ্য ôbibhajyô
indomitable *adj* অদম্য ôdômyô, অজেয় ôjeyô
indulgence *n* প্রশ্রয় prôśrôy̆
industrial *adj* শ্রমজ śrômôj
industrious *adj* ব্যস্ত bystô *pron* bæsto
industry *n* শ্রমশিল্প śrômôśilpô
inedible *adj* অখাদ্য ôkhadyô
inefficient *adj* অপটু ôpôṭu
inertia *n* জড়তা jôṛôta, অনীহা ônīha
inevitable *adj* অপরিহার্য ôpôriharyô
inexpensive *adj* সস্তা sôsta
infant *n* শিশু śiśu
infect *vb* সংক্রামিত করা sômkramitô kôra

infection *n* প্রদাহ prôdahô

infectious *adj* সংক্রামক sɔṁkramôk

inferior *adj* অবর ɔbɔr, হীন hīn

inferiority *n* হীনতা hīnôta

inferno *n* নরক nɔrôk

infertile *adj* নিষ্ফল nisphɔl

infinite *adj* অনন্ত ɔnɔntô, অসীম ɔsīm

inflamed *adj* রুক্ষ rukṣô, ক্রুদ্ধ kruddhô

inflammation *n* প্রদাহ prôdahô

inflation *n* স্ফীতি sphīti

influence *n* প্রভাব prôbhab, ক্ষমতা kṣɔmôta

inform *vb* জানানো janano

information *n* খবর khɔbôr, জ্ঞাপন jñapôn

infringe *vb* হস্তক্ষেপ করা hɔstôkṣep kɔra

ingenious *adj* কৌশলী kouśôlī

ingredient *n* উপাদান upadan

inhabit *vb* বাস করা bas kɔra

inhabitant *n* অধিবাসী ôdhibasī

inhale *vb* নিঃশ্বাস নেওয়া niḥśvas neôŷa

inherit *vb* উত্তরাধিকারী হওয়া uttôradhikarī hɔôŷa

inheritance *n* উত্তরাধিকার uttôradhikar

inhibition *n* বাধা badha

inhuman *adj* অমানুষিক ɔmanuṣik

initial *adj* প্রথম prôthôm

initiative *n* দীক্ষা dīkṣa

injection *n* ইনজেকশন injekśôn

injure *vb* অঘাত করা aghat kɔra

injured *adj* আহত ahôtô

injury *n* অপঘাত ɔpôghat

injustice *n* অবিচার ɔbicar

ink *n* কালি kali

inn *n* হোটেল hoṭel, সরাইখানা sɔraikhana

inner *adj* অন্তরে ɔntôre

innocent *adj* সরল sɔrôl, নির্দোষ nirdoṣ

inoculate *vb* টিকা দেওয়া ṭika deôŷa

inoculation *n* টিকা ṭika deôŷa

inquire *vb* প্রশ্ন করা prɔśnô kɔra, অনুসন্ধান করা ônusɔndhan kɔra

inquiry *n* প্রশ্ন prɔśnô, অনুসন্ধান ônusɔndhan

insane *adj* পাগল pagôl

insect *n* পোকা poka

insert *vb* ঢোকানো ḍhokano, ঢুকানো ḍhukano

inside *pp* ভিতরে bhitôre

insight *n* পরিজ্ঞান pôrijñæn

insist *vb* জেদ করা jed kɔra

insistence *n* জোরাজুরি jorajuri, জোরাজোরি jorajori

insomnia *n* অনিদ্রা ɔnidra

inspect *vb* পরিদর্শন করা pôridɔrśôn

inspection *n* পরিদর্শন pôridɔrśôn, পরীক্ষা pôrīkṣa

inspector *n* পরিদর্শক pôridɔrśôk

inspiration *n* প্রেরণা prerôṇa

inspire *vb* অনুপ্রাণিত করা ônupraṇitô kɔra

install *vb* প্রতিষ্ঠা করা prôtiṣṭha kɔra

installation *n* স্থাপন sthapôn

installment *n* দফা dɔpha

instance *n* নজির nôjir

instant *n* মুহূর্ত muhūrtô

instead *pp, adv* পরিবর্তে pôribôrte, বদলে bɔdôle

instigate *vb* ফুসলানো phuslano *(Bd)*, ফুসলোনো phuslono *(WB)*

instinct *n* সহজিয়া sɔhôjiŷa

institute *n* প্রতিষ্ঠান prôtiṣṭhan

instruct *vb* শিক্ষা দেওয়া śikṣa deoŷa

instruction *n* শিক্ষা śikṣa, নির্দেশ nirdeś

instrument *n (tool)* যন্ত্র yɔntrô; *(musical)* বাজনা bajna

insufferable *adj* অসহ্য ɔsôhyô *(pron* ɔshojjho)

insufficient *adj* কম kɔm, অপ্রাপ্ত ɔpraptô

insulate *vb* বিযুক্ত করা biyuktô kɔra

insult *n* অপমান ɔpɔman; *vb* অপমান করা ɔpôman kɔra

insurance *n* বিমা bima

insure *vb* বিমা করা bima kɔra

intact *adj* অটুট ɔṭuṭ

integrity *n (wholeness)* অখণ্ডতা ɔkhɔṇḍôta; *(sincerity)* সততা sɔtôta

intellect *n* মেধা medha

intelligence *n (knowledge)* জ্ঞান jñæn; *(wisdom)* বুদ্ধি buddhi

intelligent *adj (knowledgeable)* জ্ঞানী jñænī; *(wise)* বুদ্ধিমান buddhiman *(m)*, বুদ্ধিমতী buddhimôtī *(f)*

intend *vb* মনস্থ করা mônôsthô kɔra

intense *adj* প্রগাঢ় prôgaṛhô

intention *n* মতলব mɔtlôb, উদ্দেশ্য uddeśyô

intercourse *n (social contact)* যোগাযোগ yogayog; *(sexual union)* মিলন milɔn

interest *n* টান ṭan, গরজ gɔrôj, আগ্রহ agrôhô

interesting *adj* মজার mɔjar, চিত্তাকর্ষক cittakɔrṣôk

interfere *vb* হস্তক্ষেপ করা hɔstôkṣep kɔra

interference *n* অনধিকার চর্চা ɔnôdhikar cɔrca

interior *n* ভিতরে bhitôre, মধ্য môddhô

internal *adj* অন্তরে ɔntôre, আভ্যন্তরীণ abhyôntɔrīṇ

international *adj* আন্তর্জাতিক antôrjatik

interpreter *n* দোভাষী dobhaṣī, ভাষান্তরিক bhaṣastôrik

interrogation *n* জিজ্ঞাসাবাদ jijñasabad

interval *n* বিরাম biram

intervene *vb* হস্তক্ষেপ করা hɔstôkṣep kɔra

interview *n* সাক্ষাৎকার sakṣaṭkar

intestine *n* অন্ত্র ɔntrô

intimate *adj* ঘনিষ্ঠ ghôniṣṭhô, অন্তরঙ্গ ɔntôrɔṅgô

into *pp* দিকে dike

intricate *adj* জটিল jôṭil

introduce *vb (start)* আরম্ভ করা arɔmbhô kɔra; *(make acquainted)* পরিচয় করিয়ে দেওয়া pôricɔŷ kôriŷe deoŷa

introduction *n* পরিচয় pôricɔŷ

invade *vb* আক্রমণ করা akrômôṇ kɔra

invasion *n* আক্রমণ akrômôṇ

invent *vb* আবিষ্কার করা abiṣkar kɔra

invention *n* উদ্ভাবন udbhabôn, আবিষ্কার abiṣkar

inventory *n* তালিকা talika

investigate *vb* অনুসন্ধান করা ônusɔndhan kɔra

investigation *n* তদন্ত tɔdôntô

invisible *adj* অদৃশ্য ɔdṛśyô

invitation *n* দাওয়াত daoŷat, নিমন্ত্রণ nimɔntrôṇ

invite *vb* দাওয়াত দেওয়া daoŷat

deoŷa, নিমন্ত্রণ করা nimɔntrôṇ
kɔra

involve *vb* পেঁচানো pēcano

involved in *adj* লিপ্ত liptô

iron *n (metallic element)* লোহা
loha; *(appliance)* ইস্ত্রি istri

irony *n* শ্লেষ śleṣ, ব্যাজস্তুতি
byæjôstuti

irrelevant *adj* অবান্তর ɔbantôr

irresistible *adj* অনিবার্য ônibaryô

irresponsible *adj* দায়িত্বজ্ঞানহীন
daŷitvôjñænhīn

irrigate *vb* সেচ করা sec kɔra

irrigation *n* সেচন secɔn

Islam *n* ইসলাম ধর্ম islam dhɔrmô

Islamic *adj* মুসলিম muslim,
মুসলমান musôlman

island *n* দ্বীপ dvīp

isolate *vb* আলাদা রাখা alada
rakha, আলাদা করা alada kɔra

Israel *n* ইহুদির দেশ ihudir deś

Israeli *n* ইহুদি ihudi

issue *n (topic)* বিষয় biṣɔŷ; *(edition)*
সংস্করণ sɔṁskɔrôṇ; *(result)* ফল
phɔl; *(offspring)* সন্তান sɔntan

it *pr* তা ta

italics *n* হেলানো অক্ষর hælano
ɔkṣɔr

itch *n* চুলকানি culkani

item *n* জিনিস jinis, দফা dɔpha

ivory *n* হস্তিদন্ত hôstidɔntô, হাতির
দাঁত hatir dāt

ivy *n* লতা lɔta

J

jab *vb* খোঁচা মারা khŏca mara

jackal *n* শিয়াল śiŷal *(Bd)*, শেয়াল śeŷal *(WB)*

jackfruit *n* কাঁঠাল kāṭhal

jade *n* পীলু pīlu

jail *n* জেল jel, কারাগার karagar

jam *n* জেলি jeli; *vb* চেপে দেওয়া cepe deoŷa

Jamuna River *n* যমুনা yômuna

January *n* জানুয়ারি মাস januŷari mas

Japan *n* জাপান দেশ japan deś

Japanese *adj* জাপানি japani

jar *n* বয়াম bôŷam

jasmine *n* জুঁই jũi

jaw *n* চোয়াল coŷal

jealous *adj* হিংসুক hiṁsuk, হিংসুটে hiṁsuṭe

jealousy *n* হিংসা hiṁsa, ঈর্ষা īrṣa

jeans *n* জিনসের প্যান্ট jinser pyænṭ

jeer *n* টিটকারি ṭiṭkari

jerk *vb* ঝাঁকি jhāki

jet *n* পিচকারি pickari

jewel *n* মণি môni, রত্ন rôtnô

jewelry *n* গহনা gôhona, গয়না gôŷna

Jewish *adj* ইহুদি ihudi

jingle *vb* ঝিনিঝিনি শব্দ jhinijhini śôbdô

job *n* চাকরি cakri

jog *vb* ছোটা choṭa, ছুটা chuṭa

join *vb* সংযুক্ত করা sôṁyuktô kôra, লাগিয়ে দেওয়া lagiŷe deoŷa

joint *n* গিঁট gĩṭ

joist *n* কড়িকাঠ kôṙikaṭh

joke *n* তামাশা tamaśa, ইয়ারকি iŷarki; *vb* তামাশা করা tamaśa kôra

jolt *n* ধাক্কা dhakka

journal *n* পত্রিকা pôtrika

journalist *n* সাংবাদিক saṁbadik

journey *n* যাত্রা yatra, ভ্রমন bhrômôṇ

joy *n* আনন্দ anôndô

jubilee *n* জয়ন্তী jôŷôntī

judge *n* বিচারক bicarôk; *vb* বিচার করা bicar kôra

judgment *n* বিচার bicar, রায় raŷ

jug *n* জগ jôg

juice *n* রস rôs, জুস jus

jujube *n* বরই bôrôi *(Bd)*, কুল kul *(WB)*

July *n* জুলাই মাস julai mas

jumble *n* এলোমেলো elomelo

jump *n* লাফ laph; *vb* লাফানো laphano, লাফ দেওয়া laph deoŷa

junction *n* সংযোগ sôṁyog সন্ধি sôndhi

June *n* জুন মাস jun mas

jungle *n* জঙ্গল jôṅgôl

junior *adj* অবর ôbôr, ছোট choṭô

junk *n* জঞ্জাল jôñjal

jury *n* জুরি juri

just *adj (impartial)* নিরপেক্ষ nirôpekṣô; *(correct)* ঠিক ṭhik; *adv (only)* মাত্র matrô

justice *n* ন্যায় nyæy, ইনসাফ insaph *(Muslim)*

justification *n* ন্যায়ের ভাষ্য nyæŷer bhaṣyô

justify *(prove) vb* প্রমাণ করা prô-maṇ kôra

jute *n* পাট paṭ

juvenile *adj (of children)* কৈশোরক koisorôk; *(immature)* বাচ্চার মত baccar môtô

K

kangaroo *n* ক্যাঙ্গারু kyæṅgaru

kedgeree *n* খিচুরি khicuri

keel *n* জাহাজের তলা jahajer tɔla

keen *adj (sharp)* ধারাল dharalô; *(interested)* উৎসাহী uṭsahī

keep *vb (retain)* রাখা rakha; *(protect)* রক্ষা করা rɔkṣa kɔra; *(preserve)* জিয়ানো jiŷano *(Bd)*, জিয়োনো jiŷono *(WB)*

keep up *vb* চালিয়ে যাওয়া caliŷe yaoŷa

keeper *n* পালক palôk

kennel *n* কুকুরশালা kukurśala

kernel *n* বীজ bīj, আঁটি āṭi

kerosene *n* কেরোসিন kerosin, তেল tel

kettle *n* কেটলি keṭli

key *n* চাবি cabi

keyboard *n* কিবোর্ড kiborḍ

keyhole *n* চাবির ছিদ্র cabir chidrô

khaki *n* খাকি khaki

kick *vb* লাথি মারা laṭhi mara

kid *n (child)* বাচ্চা bacca, শিশু śiśu; *(young animal)* ছানা chana

kidnap *vb* অপহরণ করা ɔpôhɔrôṇ kɔra

kidney *n* মূত্রগ্রন্থি mutrôgrônthi, বৃক্ক bṙkkô

kill *vb* মেরে ফেলা mere phæla, হত্যা করা hɔtya kɔra

kilo(gram) *n* কিলো kilo, কেজি keji

kilometer *n* কিলোমিটার kilomiṭar

kind *n* রকম rɔkôm, ধরন dhɔrôn; *adj (sociable)* মিশুক miśuk; *(benevolent)* সদয় sɔdɔŷ, দয়ালু dɔŷalu

kindergarten *n* ছোটদের স্কুল choṭôder skul, নার্সারি narsari

kindle *vb* জ্বলা jvɔla, জ্বালানো jvalano

kindness *n* দয়া dɔŷa

king *n* রাজা raja

kingdom *n* রাজ্য rajyô

kinship *n* আত্মীয়তা atmīŷôta

kiosk *n* ছোট দোকান chɔṭo dokan

kiss *n* চুমু cumu; *vb* চুমু খাওয়া cumu khaoŷa

kit *n* জামাকাপড় jamakapôṙ

kitchen *n* রান্না ঘর ranna ghɔr

kite *n (bird of prey)* চিল পাখি cil pakhi; *(flying toy)* ঘুড়ি ghuṙi

kitten *n* বিড়ালের biṙaler *(also* বেড়ালের beṙaler*)*, বাচ্চা bacca

knapsack *n* ছোট ব্যাগ chɔṭo byæg

knead *vb* চটকানো cɔṭkano, মাখা makha

knee *n* হাঁটু hāṭu

kneel *vb* হাঁটু গাড়া hāṭu gara

knife *n* ছুরি churi, বঁটি bôṭi

knight *n* যোদ্ধা yoddha

knit *vb* বোনা bona

knob *n* আব ab, গাঁট gāṭ

knock *vb* টোকা দেওয়া ṭoka deoŷa, ধাক্কা দেওয়া dhakka deoŷa

knot *n* গিরা gira *(Bd)*, গিঁট gīṭ *(WB)*

know *vb* জানা jana, চেনা cena

knowledge *n (act of knowing)* জ্ঞান jñæn; *(learning)* বিদ্যা bidya; *(understanding)* বিচার –বুদ্ধি bicar–buddhi

knuckle *n* আঙুলের গাঁট aṅuler gāṭ

kohlrabi *n* ওলকপি olkôpi

Koran *n* কোরান koran

kosher *adj (according to Jewish dietary laws)* ইহুদিদের নিয়মমত খাবার ihudider niŷômmɔtô khabar; *(pure, clean)* খাঁটি khāṭi

L

label *n* লেবেল lebel

labor *n* *(hard work)* পরিশ্রম pôriśrôm; *(in childbirth)* প্রসব বেদনা prôsôb bedôna

laboratory *n* রস-শালা rôs-śala

laborer *n* মজুর môjur, জনমজুর jônmôjur

labyrinth *n* গোলক-ধাঁধা golôk-dhādha

lace *n* লেস les

lack *n* অভাব ôbhab

ladder *n* মই môi

ladle *n* হাতা hata, খুন্তি khunti

lady *n* ভদ্রমহিলা bhôdrômôhila, বিবি bibi *(Muslim)*

lag *vb* দেরি করা deri kôra

lake *n* পুকুর pukur

lamb *n* ভেড়ার বাচ্চা bheŗar bacca

lame *adj* পঙ্গু pôṅgu

lament *vb* খেদ করা khed kôra; *n* বিলাপ bilap

lamp *n* বাতি bati

land *n* জমি jômi

landing *n* অবতরণ ôbôtôrôṇ

landlord *n* বাড়িওয়ালা bariôŷala, মালিক malik

landowner *n* জমিদার jômidar

landscape *n* ভূচিত্র bhūcitrô

lane *n* গলি gôli

language *n* ভাষা bhaşa

lantern *n* হারিকেন hariken

lap *n* কোল kol

lapse *vb* তামাদি হওয়া tamadi hôôŷa

laptop *n* লেপটপ læptɔp

lard *n* চর্বি côrbi

large *adj* *(big)* বড় bɔrô; *(extensive)* বিশাল biśal, ব্যাপক byæpôk

lascivious *adj* লম্পট lɔmpɔṭ

laser *n* লেজার lejar

lassitude *n* অবসন্নতা ɔbôsɔnnôta, ঝিম jhim

last *vb* টেকা ṭeka, টিকা ṭika; *adj* *(previous)* গত gɔtô; *(final)* শেষ śeṣ, চূড়ান্ত cūŗantô

latch *n* খিল khil

late *adv* *(behind time)* দেরিতে derite; *adj* *(deceased)* প্রাক্তন praktôn

lately *adv* সম্প্রতি sɔmprôti

latent *adj* সুপ্ত suptô

lather *n* ফেনা phæna

Latin *n* ল্যাটিন lyæṭin

latitude *n* অক্ষাংশ ɔkṣaṁśô

latrine *n* পায়খানা paŷkhana

lattice *n* জাফরি japhri

laugh *vb* হাসা hasa

laughter *n* হাসি hasi

launch *n* প্রবৃত্তি prôbr̥tti, আরম্ভ arômbhô

laundry *n* ধোপাখানা dhopakhana

laundryman *n* ধোপা dhopa

lavatory *n* পায়খানা paŷkhana, বাথরুম bathrum

lavish *adj* বিলাসী bilasī

law *n* আইন ain

lawful *adj* বিধেয় bidheŷô

lawn *n* ঘাসের জমি ghaser jômi

lawsuit *n* মামলা mamla, মকদ্দমা môkôddôma

lawyer *n* উকিল ukil

laxative *n* রেচক recɔk

lay *vb* *(cause to lie down)* শোয়ানো śoŷano; *(place, establish)* স্থাপন করা sthapôn kɔra; *(put)* রাখা

rakha *(prepare)* পাতা pata;
(produce eggs) পাড়া paṛa

layer *n* স্তর stɔr

laziness *n* আলস্য alôsyô

lazy *adj* অলস ɔlôs, নিশ্চেষ্ট niścesṭô,
আলসে alse

lead *vb (go first)* আগে যাওয়া age
yaoŷa; *(conduct)* চালানো calano;
n সীস sīs, সীসা sīsa

leader *n* নেতা neta, নায়ক naŷôk

leadership *n* পরিচালনা pôricalôna

leaf *n* পাতা pata

leak *vb* ফুটা হওয়া phuṭa hɔoŷa; *n*
ফুটা phuṭa *(Bd)*, ফুটো phuṭo
(WB), ছিদ্র chidrô

lean *vb* হেলা hæla; *adj* রোগা roga

leap *vb* লাফানো laphano

leap over *vb* টপকানো ṭɔpkano

leap year *n* অধিবর্ষ ôdhibɔrṣô

learn *vb* শেখা śekha

learned *adj* বিজ্ঞ bijñô

learner *n* ছাত্র chatrô, শিক্ষার্থী
śikṣarthī *(pron shikkharthi)*

lease *n* ইজারা ijara

leash *n* দড়ি dôṛi

least *adj, adv* সবচেয়ে কম sɔbceŷe
kɔm; *adv* **(at ~)** অন্তত ɔntɔtô

leather *n* চামড়া camṛa

leave *vb (go away)* চলে যাওয়া côle
yaoŷa; *(give up)* ছেড়ে দেওয়া
cheṛe deoŷa; *(abandon)* ত্যাগ করা
tyæg kɔra, ছেড়ে যাওয়া cheṛe
yaoŷa; *n (holiday)* ছুটি chuṭi

leave out *vb* বাদ দেওয়া bad deoŷa

lecture *n* বক্তৃতা bôktṛta

ledge *n* সরু তাক sôru tak

left *adj (remaining)* বাকি baki; *(opposite of right)* বাঁ bā, বাম bam;
adv **(to the ~)** বাঁয়ে bãŷe, বামে

bame, বামদিকে bamdike, বাঁদিকে
bādike

left-handed *adj* ডেবড়া ḍebṛa, বাঁ
হাতের bā hater

left-wing *adj* বাঁ পন্থী bā pônthī,
বামপন্থা bampɔntha

leg *n* পা pa

legal *adj* বৈধ boidhô,

legality *n* বৈধতা boidhôta

legally *adj* আইনত ainɔtô

legend *n (fairy tale)* উপকথা
upôkɔtha; *(traditional story)*
লোক-কাহিনী lok-kahinī; *(text)*
লেখা lekha

legible *adj* স্পষ্ট spɔsṭô

legislation *n* আইন প্রণয়ন ain
prônɔŷôn

legitimate *adj (proper)* ঠিক ṭhik,
যথারীতি yɔtharīti; *(genuine)* আসল
asôl, ন্যায়সঙ্গত nyæŷsɔṅgôtô

leisure *n* অবসর ɔbôsɔr, অবকাশ
ɔbôkaś

lemon *n* লেবু lebu

lend *vb* ধার দেওয়া dhar deoŷa

length *n* লম্বাই lɔmbai

lengthen *vb* লম্বা করা lɔmba kɔra

lengthways *adv* লম্বালম্বি
lɔmbalômbi

lentil *n* ডাল dal

leprosy *n* কুষ্ঠরোগ kusṭhôrog

lesbian *n* সমকামী sɔmôkamī

less *adj, adv* কম kɔm

lesson *n* শিক্ষা śikṣa, পাঠ paṭh

let *vb (allow)* দেওয়া deoŷa; *(rent
out)* ভাড়া দেওয়া bhaṛa deoŷa

letter *n (of the alphabet)* অক্ষর
ɔkṣɔr; *(printed character)* হরফ
hɔrôph; *(written message)* চিঠি
ciṭhi, পত্র pɔtrô

lettuce *n* লেটুস leṭus

level *vb* সমান করা sɔman kɔra; *n* স্তর stɔr; *adj* সমতল sɔmôtɔl

lever *n* লিভার libhar

lewd *adj* লম্পট lɔmpɔṭ

liability *n* দায়িত্ব dayitvô

liable *adj* দায়ী dayī

liaison *n* লীলা līla

liar *n* মিথ্যুক mithyuk

libel *n* নিন্দা ninda

liberal *adj* উদার udar

liberalism *n* উদারনীতি udarnīti

liberty *n* (freedom) মুক্তি mukti; (independence) স্বাধীনতা svadhīnɔta

librarian *n* গ্রন্থাগারিক grônthagarik

library *n* গ্রন্থাগার grônthagar, লাইব্রেরি laibreri

license *n* অনুমতি ônumôti, লাইসেনস laisens

lick *vb* চাটা caṭa

lid *n* (eyelid) পাতা pata; (cover for a container) ঢাকনা ḍhakna

lie *n* মিথ্যা কথা mithya kɔtha (Bd), মিথ্যে কথা mithye kɔtha (WB); *vb* (make false statement) মিথ্যা কথা বলা mithya kɔtha bɔla; (lie down) শোয়া śoya;

lieutenant *n* সহকারী কর্নেল sɔhôkarī kôrnel

life *n* জীবন jībɔn, প্রাণ praṇ

lifeboat *n* জীবনতরী jībɔntôrī

lifeforce *n* প্রাণশক্তি praṇśôkti

lifeless *adj* নিস্তেজ nistej

lifestyle *n* হালচাল halcal

lifetime *n* জীবনকাল jībɔnkal

lift *vb* তোলা tola

light *n* আলো alo; *adj* (easy, mild, not heavy) হালকা halka; (bright) উজ্জ্বল ujjvôl

lighten *vb* উপশম করা upôśɔm kɔra

lighthearted *adj* হাসিখুশি hasikhuśi

lighthouse *n* লাইটহাউস laiṭhaus

lighting *n* প্রজ্বলন prôjvɔlôn

lightning *n* বিজলি bijli

like *pp* মত mɔtô; *vb* ভাল লাগা bhalô laga

likely *adv* সঢ়বত sɔmbhɔbɔtô

likeness *n* (image) প্রতিরূপ prôtirūp; (similarity) উপমা upôma

likewise *adv* একি রকম eki rɔkôm, সেই ভাবে sei bhabe

limb *n* অঙ্গ ɔṅgô

lime *n* (fruit) লেবু lebu; (mineral) চুন cun

limit *n* সীমা sīma

limp *vb* খোঁড়ানো khõṛano; *adj* নিস্তেজ nistej

line *n* (mathematical) রেখা rekha, লাইন lain; (row) সারি sari

linear *adj* রেখাকার rekhakar

linen *n* ক্ষৌম kṣoum

linger *vb* দেরি করা deri kɔra

linguist *n* ভাষাবিশেষজ্ঞ bhaṣabiśeṣɔjñô

linguistics *n* ভাষাতত্ত্ব bhaṣatɔttvô

link *n* গাঁট gãṭ, সংযোগ sɔṁyog; *vb* সংযুক্ত করা sɔṁyuktô kɔra

lion *n* সিংহ siṁhô

lip *n* ঠোঁট ṭhõṭ

liquid *adj* তরল tɔrôl

liquor *n* মদ mɔd

list *n* তালিকা talika

literary *adj* সাহিত্যিক sahityik

literature *n* সাহিত্য sahityô

litter *n* ময়লা mɔyla

little *adj* ছোট choṭô

live *vb* (exist) জীবিত থাকা jībitô thaka; (survive) বাঁচা bāca; (stay, *dwell)* থাকা thaka, বাস করা bas kɔra

lively *adj* প্রাণবন্ত prańbɔntô

liver *n* যকৃৎ yôkṛt

living room *n* বসার ঘর bɔsar ghɔr

lizard *n* টিকটিকি ṭikṭiki

load *n (burden)* বোঝা bojha; *(weight)* ভার bhar; *(freight)* মাল mal

loaf *n* গোটা রুটি gɔṭa ruṭi

loan *vb* ধার দেওয়া dhar deoẏa; *n* ঋণ ṛṇ *(pron* rin*)*, দেনা dena

loathe *vb* ঘৃণা করা ghṛṇa kɔra

loathsome *adj* বীভৎস bībhôtsô

lobster *n* গলদা চিংড়ি gɔlda ciṁri

local *adj* স্থানীয় sthanīẏô, আঞ্চলিক añcôlik

location *n* স্থিতি sthiti

lock *vb* তালা দেওয়া tala deoẏa; *n* তালা tala

locomotive *n* রেলগাড়ির ইঞ্জিন relgaṛir iñjin

locust *n* পঙ্গপাল pɔṅgôpal

lodger *n* ভাড়াটে bharaṭe

lodging *n* অস্থায়ী বাস ɔsthaẏī bas, ডেরা ḍera

loft *n* চিলে cile, চিলেকোঠা cilekoṭha

log *n* গুঁড়ি gūṛi

logic *n (science of reasoning)* ন্যায়–শাস্ত্র nyæ̃ŷôśastrô; *(reason, sense)* যুক্তি yukti

logical *adj* ন্যায়িক nyæ̃ŷik, ন্যায়সঙ্গত nyæ̃ŷsɔṅgôtô

loins *n* পাছা pacha

lone *adj* একাকী ækakī

loneliness *n* নিঃসঙ্গতা nihsɔṅgôta, একাকিত্ব ækakitvô

lonely *adj (feeling alone)* একা একা æka æka, নিঃসঙ্গ nihsɔṅgô; *(secluded)* নিরিবিলি niribili

long *adj* লম্বা lɔmba, দীর্ঘ dīrghô; *vb (aspire to)* আকাঙ্ক্ষা করা akaṅksa kɔra; *(desire)* কামনা করা kamôna kɔra

longitude *n* দ্রাঘিমা draghima

look *vb* তাকানো takano, দেখা dækha

look after *vb* দেখাশোনা করা dækhaśona kɔra

look back *vb* ফিরে তাকানো phire takano

look down on *vb* ছোট মনে করা choṭô mône kɔra

look for *vb* খোঁজা khõja

look forward to *vb* প্রত্যাশা করা prôtyaśa kɔra

look up to *vb* শ্রদ্ধা করা śrôddha kɔra

loom *n* তাঁত tãt

loop *n* ফাঁস phãs

loose *adj* ঢিলা ḍhila *(Bd)*, ঢিলে ḍhile *(WB)*, শিথিল śithil, আলগা alga

loosen *vb* খসা khɔsa, আলগা করা alga kɔra

loot *n* লুঠ luṭh

lord *n* প্রভু prôbhu

lose *vb (misplace)* হারা hara, হারানো harano; *(be defeated)* হেরে যাওয়া here yaoẏa

loss *(deficit)* *n* লোকসান lôksan; *(waste)* *n* বিনাশ binaś

lost *adj* হারানো harano

lot *n (piece of land)* জমি jômi; *(fate)* ভাগ্য bhagyô; *adj (great amount)* প্রচুর prôcur

lotus *n* জলপদ্ম jɔlpɔdmô, পদ্ম pɔdmô

loud *adj* জোরে jore

lounge *vb* এলানো elano, এলিয়ে বসা
eliẏe bɔsa; *n* বসার ঘর bɔsar ghɔr

love *vb* ভালবাসা bhalôbasa; *n (affection)* স্নেহ snehô, আদর adôr; *(passion)* প্রেম prem, ভালবাসা
bhalôbasa

lovely *adj* কমনীয় kɔmônīẏô

lover *n* প্রেমিক premik *(m)* প্রেমিকা
premika *(f)*

low *adj* নিচু nicu

loyal *adj* বিশ্বস্ত biśvôstô, আস্থাবান
asthaban

lucid *adj* স্বচ্ছ svɔcchô

luck *n* ভাগ্য bhagyô, কপাল kɔpal

lucky *adj* ভাগ্যবান bhagyôban

luggage *n* মালপত্র malpɔtrô

lull *vb* ঘুম পাড়ানো ghum paṛano;
n প্রশান্তি prôśanti

lump *n* ডেলা ḍela, দলা dɔla

lunar *adj* চান্দ্র candrô

lunatic *adj* পাগল pagôl

lunch *n* দুপুরের খাবার dupurer
khabar

lung *n* ফুসফুস phusphus

lungi (traditional garment) *n* লুঙ্গি
luṅgi

lure *n* প্রলোভন prôlobhôn

lust *n* লালসা lalôsa

luxurious *adj* বিলাসী bilasī

luxury *n* বিলাস bilas

M

machine *n* কল kɔl, যন্ত্র yɔntrô

machinery *n* যন্ত্র yɔntrô

mad *adj (insane)* পাগল pagôl; *(furious)* রাগী ragī

madam *n* ভদ্রমহিলা bhɔdrômôhila, মেম mem

magazine *n* পত্রিকা pôtrika

magic *n* জাদু jadu

magical *adj* জাদুময় jadumɔẏ

magician *n* জাদুকর jadukɔr

magistrate *n* শাসক śasôk, পরিচালক pôricalôk

magnet *n* চুম্বক cumbɔk

magnetic *adj* চুম্বকীয় cumbôkīẏô

magnificent *adj* চমৎকার cɔmôṯkar

magnify *vb* বাড়ানো baṛano

maid *n* ঝি jhi, কাজের মেয়ে kajer meẏe

mail *n* ডাক ḍak

main *adj* প্রধান prôdhan

mainland *n* মহাদেশ mɔhadeś

maintain *vb* অবলম্বন করা ɔbôlɔmbôn kɔra, রাখা rakha

maintenance *n* অবলম্বন ɔbôlɔmbôn

maize *n* ভুট্টা bhuṭṭa

majestic *adj* মহৎ mɔhôṯ

majesty *n* মহিমা môhima

major *adj* প্রধান prôdhan; *n* সেনাপতি senapôti

majority *n* অধিকাংশ ôdhikaṁśô, বেশির ভাগ beśir bhag

make *vb (do)* করা kɔra, বানানো banano; *(create)* সৃষ্টি করা sr̥ṣṭi kɔra

make up *vb* আবিষ্কার করা abiṣkar kɔra

maker *n* উৎপাদক uṯpadôk

make-up *n* সাজ-গোজ sajgoj

male *n* পুরুষ puruṣ

malignant *adj* ক্ষতিকর kṣôtikôr

mammal *n* স্তন্যপায়ী প্রাণী stɔnyô-payī praṇī

man *n (human being)* মানুষ manuṣ, লোক lok; *(male person)* পুরুষ puruṣ

manage *vb* সামলানো samlano

management *n* পরিচালনা pôricalôna

manager *n* পরিচালক pôricalôk, শাসক śasôk

maneuver *vb* অভিযান করা ôbhiyan kɔra

manhood *n* পুরুষত্ব puruṣɔtvô

manifold *adj* বহু bôhu

manipulate *vb* চালানো calano

mankind *n* মানবজাতি manôbjati

manner *n (style)* রীতিনীতি rītinīti; *(behavior)* ব্যবহার bybôhar

mansion *n* বাসভবন basbhɔbôn

manufacture *n* উৎপাদন uṯpadôn; *vb* উৎপাদন করা uṯpadôn kɔra

manure *n* সার sar

manuscript *n* পাণ্ডুলিপি paṇḍulipi

many *adj* অনেক ɔnek, বহু bôhu

map *n* মানচিত্র mancitrô, ম্যাপ myæp

marble *n (stone)* মর্মর mɔrmôr; *(toy)* গুলি guli

March *n* মার্চ মাস marc mas

margin *n* সীমা sīma

marine *adj* সামুদ্রিক samudrik; *n* নৌসেনা nousena

mark *n (target)* লক্ষ্য lôkṣyô, তাক tak; *(sign)* চিহ্ন cihnô *(pron* cinho); *(brand)* মার্কা marka

market *n* হাট haṭ, বাজার bajar

marketing *n* কেনা-বেচা kena-bæca

marmalade *n* কমলার আচার kɔmlar acar

marriage *n* বিয়ে biye, বিবাহ bibahô

married *adj* বিবাহিত bibahitô

marrow *n* মজ্জা mɔjja

marry *vb* বিয়ে করা biye kɔra, বিয়ে হওয়া biye hɔoýa

marsh *n* জলাজমি jɔlajômi, বিল bil

marshal *n* সেনাপতি senapôti

marvelous *adj* চমৎকার cɔmôṯkar

masculine *adj* পুংজাতীয় puṁjatīyô, পুংলিঙ্গ puṁliṅgô

mash *vb* বাটা baṭa

mask *n* মুখোশ mukhoś

mass *n* ভর bhɔr

massage *n* মালিশ maliś

massive *adj* বিরাট biraṭ

mast *n* মাস্তুল mastul

master *n* প্রভু prôbhu, মালিক malik

mastery *n* দক্ষতা dôkṣôta

mat *n* মাদুর madur

match *n* *(fire stick)* দেশলাই deśôlai, ম্যাচ myæc; *(equal)* জোড়া joṛa; *(game)* খেলা khæla

mate *n* সঙ্গী sôṅgī

material *adj* বস্তুগত bôstugɔtô, দৈহিক doihik; *n* কাপড় kapɔṛ

math *n* অঙ্ক ɔṅkô

mathematics *n* গণিতবিদ্যা gônitôbidya

matter *n* *(substance)* উপাদান upadan; *(affair)* ব্যাপার byæpar

mattress *n* তোশক tośôk

mature *vb* পাকানো pakano; *adj* পাকা paka

maturity *n* পরিপক্বতা pôripɔkkôta

maxim *n* নীতিবাক্য nītibakyô, বাণী banī

maximum *adj* *(highest)* চরম cɔrôm; *(to capacity)* ভরা bhɔra

may *vb* পারা para

May *n* মে মাস me mas

maybe *adv* হয়তো hɔýto, বোধ হয় bodh hɔý

mayor *n* নগরপাল nɔgôrpal

maze *n* গোলকধাঁধা golôkdhādha

meadow *n* ঘাসের মাঠ ghaser maṭh

meager *adj* পাতলা patla, অল্প ɔlpô

meal *n* খাবার khabar, আহার ahar

mean *vb* পদার্থ থাকা pɔdarthô thaka; *adj* *(intermediate)* মধ্য môdhyô; *(ungenerous)* হীনমনা hīnômôna

meaning *n* অর্থ ɔrthô, মানে mane

means *n* উপায় upay

meantime *n* মধ্যকাল môdhyôkal; *adv* *(in the ~)* ইতিমধ্যে itimôdhye

measles *n* হাম ham

measure *n* মাপ map

measurement *n* পরিমাণ pôriman

meat *n* মাংস maṁsô

mechanic *n* মিস্ত্রি mistri

mechanical *adj* যান্ত্রিক yantrik

medal *n* পদক pɔdôk

meddle *vb* হস্তক্ষেপ করা hɔstôkṣep kɔra, নাক গলানো nak gɔlano

mediate *vb* মধ্যস্থতা করা môdhyô-sthôta kɔra

mediation *n* মধ্যস্থতা môdhyôsthôta

medical *adj* চিকিৎসামূলক cikiṯsamulôk

medicine *n* *(science)* চিকিৎসাবিদ্যা cikiṯsabidya; *(treatment)* ওষুধ oṣudh

meditate *vb* ধ্যান করা dhyæn kɔra

meditation *n* ধ্যান dhyæn

medium *adj* মাধ্যম madhyôm

meet *vb* দেখা করা dækha kɔra

meeting *n* সভা sɔbha, অধিবেশন ôdhibeśôn

meeting-place *n* আড্ডা aḍḍa

mellow *adj* কোমল komôl

melody *n* সুর sur

melon *n* তরমুজ tôrmuj

melt *vb* গলা gɔla, গলানো gɔlano, গলে যাওয়া gôle yaoẏa

member *n* সদস্য sɔdôsyô

membrane *n* ঝিল্লী jhillī

memoir *n* জীবনী jībônī

memorize *vb* মুখস্থ করা mukhôsthô kɔra

memory *n* (*sense*) স্মরণশক্তি smɔrôṇśôkti; (*recollection*) স্মৃতি smṛti

menace *n* বিপদ bipɔd

mend *vb* ঠিক করা ṭhik kɔra, মেরামত করা meramôt kɔra

menopause *n* রজোবন্ধ rɔjobɔndhô

mental *adj* মানসিক manôsik

mentality *n* মনোভাব mônobhab

mention *vb* উল্লেখ করা ullekh kɔra

menu *n* খাদ্যতালিকা kadyôtalika

merchandise *n* মাল mal

merchant *n* বণিক bôṇik

merciful *adj* দয়ালু dɔyalu

merciless *adj* দয়াহীন dɔyahīn

mercy *n* দয়া dɔya, কৃপা kṛpa, ক্ষমা kṣɔma

merely *adv* শুধু śudhu, কেবল kebôl

merge *vb* মিলানো milano

merit *n* গুণ guṇ

merry *adj* ফুর্তিপূর্ণ phurtipūrṇô, খুশি khuśi

mesh *n* জালের বুনানি jaler bunani (*Bd*), জালের বুনুনি jaler bununi (*WB*)

mess *n* (*canteen*) মেস mes; (*muddle*) এলোমেলো elomelo

message *n* (*teaching*) বাণী baṇī; (*news*) সংবাদ sɔmbad, খবর khɔbôr

messenger *n* দূত dūt

metal *n* ধাতু dhatu

metaphysics *n* অধিবিদ্যা ôdhibidya

meter *n* (*unit of length*) মিটার miṭar; (*verse rhythm*) ছন্দ chɔndô

method *n* কায়দা kayda, পদ্ধতি pɔddhôti

methodical *adj* যথারীতি yɔtharīti

microphone *n* মাইক maik

microscope *n* অণুবীক্ষণ ôṇubīkṣôṇ

mid *adj* মাঝ majh, মধ্য môdhyô

midday *n* দুপুর dupur

middle *n* মধ্য môdhyô

Middle Ages *n* মধ্যযুগ môdhyôyug

middle-aged *adj* প্রৌঢ় prourhô

midnight *n* রাত বারটা rat barôṭa

midwife *n* দাই dai, ধাইমা dhaima

might *vb* পারা para; *n* ক্ষমতা kṣɔmôta, শক্তি śôkti

migraine *n* কঠিন মাথা ধরা kôṭhin matha dhɔra

migrate *vb* পরিযান করা pôriyan kɔra

mild *adj* (*light, not severe*) হালকা halka; (*soft*) কোমল komôl

mile *n* মাইল mail

militant *adj* সংগ্রামশীল sɔmgramśīl

military *n, adj* সৈনিক soinik, সেনা sena

milk *n* দুধ dudh

mill *n* জাঁতা jāta

miller *n* জাঁতাওয়ালা jätaoŷala

million *n* দশ লাখ dɔś lakh

mind *vb* মনে করা mône kɔra; *n (mentality, inclination, feeling)* মন môn; *(judgement)* বিবেচনা bibecôna; *(intellect)* মেধা medha; *(thought)* ভাব bhab; *(opinion)* মত mɔt

mindful *adj* বিবেচক bibecôk

mindless *adj* আনমনা anmôna

mine *n* খনি khôni

mineralogy *n* খনিজবিদ্যা khônijôbidya

mingle *vb* মেশানো meśano

minimum *adj* সবচেয়ে অল্প sɔbceye ɔlpô

mining *n* খনন khɔnôn

minister *n* মন্ত্রী môntrī

ministry *n* মন্ত্রিত্ব môntritvô

minor *adj (lesser)* অপ্রধান ɔprô-dhan; *n (under age person)* অপ্রাপ্তবয়স্ক ɔpraptôbɔŷôskô

minority *n* অপ্রধান অংশ ɔprôdhan ɔṁśô

mint *n* পুদিনা pudina

minus *pp* বাদে bade

minute *n* মিনিট miniṭ

miracle *n* অলৌকিক ঘটনা ɔloukik ghɔṭôna

miraculous *adj* অলৌকিক ɔloukik

mirage *n* মরীচিকা môrīcika

mire *n* পাঁক pāk

mirror *n* আয়না ayna

misadventure *n* দুর্ঘটনা durghɔṭôna

mischief *n* দুষ্টুমি duṣṭumi, ইতরামি itrami

mischievous *adj* দুষ্টু duṣṭu, পাজি paji

misdeed *n* অপকর্ম ɔpôkɔrmô

miser *n* কঞ্জুস kôñjus

miserly *adj* কৃপণ kṙpɔṇ, কঞ্জুস kôñjus

misery *n* দুর্দশা durdôśa

misfortune *n* দুর্ভাগ্য durbhagyô

misplace *vb* ভুল জায়গায় রাখা bhul jaygay rakha

miss *n (young girl)* কুমারী kumarī; *vb (omit)* বাদ দেওয়া bad deoŷa; *(feel absence of)* মনে লাগা mône laga, মনে পড়া mône pɔra

missile *n* ক্ষেপণাস্ত্র kṣepôṇastrô

mission *n (preaching)* ধর্মপ্রচার dhɔrmôprôcar; *(building)* মিশন miśôn

mist *n* কুয়াশা kuyaśa

mistake *n* ভুল bhul

mister (Mr.) *n* সাহেব saheb, স্যার syar

mistress (Mrs.) *n* মেমসাহেব mem-saheb, মেম mem

mistrust *vb* অনাস্থা ɔnastha, সন্দেহ sɔndehô

misunderstanding *n* ভুল বোঝা bhul bojha

mix *vb* মেশানো meśano

mixture *n* মিশ miś

moan *vb* উ-আ করা u-a kɔra

mobile *adj* জঙ্গম jɔṅgôm

mode *n* প্রকার prôkar

model *n* নকশা nɔkśa

modern *adj* আধুনিক adhunik

modest *adj* নম্র nɔmrô, বিনয়ী binôŷī

modesty *n* বিনয় binɔŷ, নম্রতা nɔmrota

modification *n* হেরফের herpher

modify *vb* হেরফের করা herpher kɔra

moist *adj* সেঁতসেঁতে sæ̃tsẽte

moisten vb ভিজানো bhijano (Bd), ভেজানো bhejano (WB)

moisture n আর্দ্রতা ardrôta

mold n ছাঁচ chāc (Bd), ছুঁচো chūco (WB)

mole n (muskrat) ছুঁচা chūca; (growth on skin) তিল til

moment n মুহূর্ত muhūrtô

monarch n রাজা raja

monarchy n রাজতন্ত্র rajtntrô

monastery n মঠ môṭh

Monday n সোমবার sombar

money n টাকা ṭaka

mongoose n বেজি beji

monk n সন্ন্যাসী sɔnnyasī

monkey n বানর banôr (Bd), বাঁদর bādôr (WB)

monopoly n একচেটিয়া অধিকার ekceṭiŷa ôdhikar

monotonous adj একঘেয়ে ekgheŷe

monsoon n বর্ষা bɔrṣa, বর্ষাকাল bɔrṣakal

monster n দৈত্য doityô

monstrous adj ভীষণ bhīṣôṇ

month n মাস mas

mood n (temperament) মেজাজ mejaj; (atmosphere) হালচাল halcal

moon n চাঁদ cād

moonlight n শশিকর śôśikɔr, চাঁদের আলো cāder alo

mop vb মোছা mocha, মুছা mucha

moral adj নৈতিক nôitik

morale n শৃঙ্খলা śṛṅkhɔla

more adj আরও aro

moreover conj তা ছাড়া ta chaṛa

morning n সকাল sɔkal

mortal adj মর mɔr

mortar n খল khɔl

mortgage n বন্ধক bɔndhôk

mosque n মসজিদ môsjid

mosquito n মশা mɔśa

mosquito net n মশারি mɔśari

most adj অধিকাংশ ôdhikaṁśô

moth n কাপড়-কাটা পোকা kapôr-kaṭa poka

mother n মা ma, আম্মা amma

mother-in-law n শাশুড়ি śaśuṛi

motion n চলন cɔlôn, গতি gôti

motivate vb প্রেরণা জাগানো prerôṇa jagano

motivation n ইচ্ছা iccha

motive n উদ্দেশ্য uddeśyô

motor n ইঞ্জিন iñjin

motorcycle n মোটর সাইকেল moṭôr saikel

mount vb চড়া cɔṛa

mountain n পর্বত pɔrbôt

mourn vb শোক করা śok kɔra

mourning n শোক śok

mouse n ইঁদুর īdur

mouth n মুখ mukh

move vb চলা cɔla, নড়া nɔṛa

movement n নড়াচড়া nɔṛacɔṛa

movie n চলচ্চিত্র cɔlôccitrô

moving adj (mobile) চঞ্চল cɔñcôl; (emotional) মর্মস্পর্শী mɔrmôspôrśī

much adj অনেক ɔnek

mucus n শ্লেষ্মা śleṣma

mud n কাদা kada

muffle vb মুড়িয়ে দেওয়া muṛiye deoŷa

muffler n মাফলার maphlar

mug n মগ mɔg

multiplication n গুণন guṇôn, গুণ guṇ

multiply vb পূরণ করা pūrôṇ kɔra, গুণ করা guṇ kɔra

mumble *vb* বিড়বিড় করে বলা biṛbiṛ
kôre bɔla

municipality *n* নগর পালিকা nɔgôr
palika

murder *n* খুন khun, হত্যা hɔtya

murderer *n* খুনী khunī, হত্যাকারী
hɔtyakarī

murmur *n* কলকল শব্দ kɔlkɔl
śɔbdô

muscle *n* পেশী peśī

muscular *adj* পেশীয় peśīyô,
পেশীবহুল peśībôhul

museum *n* জাদুঘর jadughɔr

mushroom *n* ছাতা chata

music *n* সঙ্গীত sôṅgīt

musician *n* সঙ্গীতকার sôṅgītôkar

Muslim *n* মুসলমান musôlman; *adj*
মুসলিম muslim

mussel *n* ঝিনুক jhinuk

must *vb* বাধ্য হওয়া badhyô hɔoŷa

mustache *n* গোঁফ gõph

mustard *n* সরিষা sôriṣa

mustard oil *n* সরিষার তেল sôriṣar
tel

musty *adj* বাসি basi

mute *adj (speech-impaired)* বোবা
boba; *(silent)* নীরব nīrɔb

mutiny *n* বিদ্রোহ bidrohô

mutton *n* খাসির মাংস khasir
maṁsô *(Bd)*, পাঁঠার মাংস pā̃thar
maṁsô *(WB)*

mutual *adj* পরস্পর pɔrôspɔr

myself *pr* নিজে nije

mystery *n* রহস্য rɔhôsyô

mystify *vb* বিমূঢ় করা bimūṛhô kɔra

myth *n* কাহিনী kahinī, শ্রুতি śruti

mythology *n* পুরাণ puraṇ

N

nag *vb* খুঁত ধরা khūt dhɔra

nail *n* পেরেক perek

naive *adj* সরল sɔrôl

naked *adj* নেংটা næṁṭa, উলঙ্গ ulɔṅgô

name *n* নাম nam

namely *adv* যেমন yæmôn, অর্থাৎ ɔrthat

nanny *n* আয়া aya

nap *n* ঘুম ghum

nape *n* ঘাড় ghar

narcotic *n* চেতনা-নাশক cetona-naśôk

narrate *vb* বর্ণনা করা bɔrṇôna kɔra

narration *n* কাহিনী kahinī

narrator *n* নিবেদক nibedôk

narrow *adj* সরু sôru

nasty *adj* বিছিরি bichiri, নোংরা noṁra

nation *n* জাতি jati

national *adj* জাতীয় jatīyô

nationalism *n* জাতীয়তাবাদ jatīyôtabad

nationality *n* জাতীয়তা jatīyôta

native *adj* দেশি deśi

natural *adj* (of nature) প্রাকৃতিক prakṙtik; (normal) স্বাভাবিক svabhabik

naturally *adv* স্বাভাবিকভাবে svabhabikbhabe

nature *n* (natural life) প্রকৃতি prôkṙti; (characteristic) স্বভাব svɔbhab; (disposition) শীল śīl

naught *adj* শূন্য śūnyô

naughty *adj* দুষ্টু duṣṭu

nausea *n* বমি bômi

nauseous *adj* বমির মত bômir mɔtô

navel *n* নাভি nabhi

navigate *vb* চালানো calano

navigation *n* চালনা calôna

navy *n* নৌবাহিনী noubahinī

near *adv, pp* কাছে kache

nearby *adv* কাছে kache

nearly *adv* প্রায় pray

nearsighted *adj* অদূরবদ্ধদৃষ্টি ɔdūrbɔddhôdṙṣṭi

neat *adj* যথাযথ yɔthayɔth, ফিটফাট phiṭphaṭ, ছিমছাম chimcham

necessary *adj* প্রয়োজনীয় prôyojônīyô

necessity *n* প্রয়োজন prôyojôn

neck *n* ঘাড় ghar

necklace *n* মালা mala

need *n* চাহিদা cahida, দরকার dɔrkar

needle *n* সুই sui *(Bd)*, সূঁচ sūc *(WB)*

needless *adj* অপ্রয়োজনীয় ɔprôyojônīyô

needy *adj* দুঃস্থ duḥsthô

negate *vb* অস্বীকার করা ɔsvīkar kɔra

negative *adj* নেতিবাচক netibacôk; *n* নেগেটিভ negeṭibh

neglect *vb* অবহেলা করা ɔbôhæla kɔra

negotiate *vb* (discuss) আলোচনা করা alocɔna kɔra; (bargain) দামাদামি করা damadami kɔra

negotiation *n* বিনিময় binimɔŷ, দরদাম dɔrdam

neighbor *n* প্রতিবেশী prôtibeśī

neighborhood *n* প্রতিবেশ prôtibeś, পাড়া paṛa

nephew *n* (brother's son) ভাইপো bhaipo; (sister's son) ভাগিনা bhagina *(Bd)*, ভাগ্নে bhagne *(WB)* nerve *n* স্নায়ু snaŷu

nervous *adj (relating to nerves)* স্নায়বিক snaŷôbik; *(restless)* অস্থির ɔsthir; *(worried)* উদ্বিগ্ন udbignô

nest *n* পাখির বাসা pakhir basa

net *n (fish net)* জাল jal; *(mosquito net)* মশারি mɔśari

network *n* সংযোগ sɔṁyog

neuralgia *n* স্নায়ুশূল snaŷuśūl

neurologist *n* স্নায়ুবিশেষজ্ঞ snayubiśeṣôjñô

neurosis *n* বাতিক batik

neurotic *adj* বাতিকগ্রস্ত batikgrôstô

neutral *adj* নিরপেক্ষ nirôpekṣô

neutrality *n* নিরপেক্ষতা nirôpekṣôta

never *adv* কখনও ... না kɔkhôno ... na

nevertheless *conj* তবুও tôbuo, তা সত্ত্বেও ta sɔttveo, তা হলেও ta hôleo

new *adj* নতুন nôtun

New Year *n* নববর্ষ nɔbôbɔrṣô

newborn *adj* নবজাতক nɔbôjatôk

news *n* খবর khɔbôr, সংবাদ sɔṁbad

newspaper *n* খবরের কাগজ khɔbôrer kagôj

next *adj* আগামী agamī, সামনের samner

next door *adv* পাশের বাড়ি paśer baṛi

nice *adj* মনোরম mɔnorɔm, ভাল bhalô

niche *n* কুলুঙ্গি kuluṅgi

nickname *n* ডাকনাম ḍaknam

niece *n (brother's daughter)* ভাইঝি bhaijhi; *(sister's daughter)* ভাগিনি bhagini *(Bd)*, ভাগ্নী bhagnī *(WB)*

night *n* রাত rat

nightmare *n* দুঃস্বপ্ন duḥsvɔpnô

nighttime *n* রাত্রি ratri

night-watch *n* রাতের পাহারা rater pahara

nimble *adj* তৎপর tɔtpɔr

nine *num* নয় nɔŷ

nineteen *num* উনিশ uniś

ninety *num* নব্বই nɔbbôi

ninth *num* নবম nɔbôm

nitrogen *n* নাইট্রোজেন naiṭrojen

no *adv* না na

noble *adj (of high birth)* অভিজাত ôbhijat; *(generous)* উদার udar, মহৎ mɔhôt

nobody *n* কেউ ... না keu ... na

noise *n* আওয়াজ aoŷaj, শব্দ śɔbdô

noisy *adj* হইচইপূর্ণ hôicôipūrṇô

nomad *n* যাযাবর yayabɔr

nominate *vb* প্রস্তাব করা prôstab kɔra

none *n (nobody)* কেউ ... না keu ... na; *(nothing)* কিছু ... না kichu ... na; *adv (not at all)* মোটেই ... না moṭei ... na

non-observance *n* অনিষ্ঠা ɔniṣṭha

non-plussed *adj* হকচকিয়ে hɔkcôkiŷe

nonsense *n* আজেবাজে ajebaje, আবোলতাবোল aboltabol

non-stop *adj* অবিরাম ɔbiram

noon *n* দুপুর dupur

norm *n* নিয়ম niŷôm

normal *adj (natural)* স্বাভাবিক svabhabik; *(regular)* নিয়মিত niŷômitô

normally *adv* সাধারণত sadharônɔtô

north *n* উত্তর uttôr

North Pole *n* সুমেরু sumeru

northern *adj* উত্তরের uttôrer

nose *n* নাক nak

nostril *n* নাকের গর্ত naker gɔrtô

not *adv* না na

notable *adj* বিশিষ্ট biśiṣṭô

note *vb (observe)* লক্ষ্য করা lɔkṣyô kɔra; *n (musical)* সুর sur

note down *vb* লিখে রাখা likhe rakha

notebook *n* খাতা khata

nothing *pr* কিছু ... না kichu ... na

notice *vb (be aware of)* টের পাওয়া ṭer paoŷa; *n (announcement)* ঘোষণা ghoṣôṇa

noticeable *adj* লক্ষণীয় lôkṣôṇīyô

notify *vb* জ্ঞাপন করা jñæpôn kɔra

notion *n* ধারণা dharôṇa

noun *n* বিশেষ্য biśeṣyô

nourish *vb* খাওয়ানো khaoŷano

nourishing *adj* পুষ্টিকর puṣṭikɔr

nourishment *n* পুষ্টি puṣṭi, খাবার khabar

novel *n* উপন্যাস upônyas

novelty *n* নতুনত্ব nôtunɔtvô

November *n* নভেম্বর মাস nôbhembôr mas

now *adv* এখন ækhôn, এক্ষণে ækṣôṇe

nowadays *adv* আজকাল ajkal

nowhere *adv* কোথাও ... না kothao ... na

noxious *adj* ক্ষতিকর kṣôtikɔr

nuance *n* সামান্য তফাত samanyô tɔphat

nuclear *adj* পারমাণবিক parmaṇôbik

nucleus *n* কেন্দ্র kendrô

nude *adj* নেংটা næṁṭa

nuisance *n* বিরক্তি birôkti

null *adj* শূন্য śūnyô

nullify *vb* বাতিল করা batil kɔra

numb *adj* অসাড় ɔsaṛ

number *n* সংখ্যা sɔṁkhya

numerous *adj* বহু bôhu, প্রচুর prôcur

nun *n* মঠবাসিনী môṭhbasinī, সিস্টার sisṭar

nurse *n* নার্স nars, সেবক sebɔk *(m.)* সেবিকা sebika *(f.)*

nursery *n* শিশুশালা śiśuśala

nursing *n* সেবা seba

nurture *n (up-bringing)* প্রতিপালন prôtipalôn; *(care)* যত্ন yɔtnô

nut *n* বাদাম badam

nutmeg *n* জায়ফল jaŷphɔl

nutrition *n* পুষ্টিবিধান puṣṭibidhan

nutritious *adj* পুষ্টিকর puṣṭikɔr

O

oak *n* ওক-গাছ ok-gach

oar *n* দাঁড় dāṛ

oat *n* জই jôi

oath *n* সপথ sɔpɔth

oatmeal *n* জইচূর্ণ jôicūrṇô

obdurate *adj* একগুঁয়ে ekgūye

obedience *n* বশ্যতা bɔśyôta, বাধ্যতা badhyôta

obedient *adj* বশ্য bɔśyô, অনুগত ônugôtô

obeisance *n* প্রণাম prôṇam

obey *vb* মানা mana, আদেশ পালন করা adeś palôn kɔra

object *n* বস্তু bôstu, জিনিস jinis

objection *n* আপত্তি apôtti

objective *n* লক্ষ্য lôkṣyô; *adj* নিরপেক্ষ nirôpekṣô

obligation *n* দায় day

oblige *vb* মানা mana, মেনে চলা mene cɔla

oblique *adj* তির্যক tiryôk

oblong *adj* লম্বা lɔmba

obscene *adj* অশ্লীল ɔślīl

obscenity *n* অশ্লীলতা ɔślīlôta

obscure *adj (dark)* অন্ধকার ɔndhôkar; *(hard to understand)* দুর্বোধ্য dūrbodhyô

observation *n* নজর nɔjôr

observatory *n* মানমন্দির manmôndir

observe *vb* লক্ষ্য করা lɔkṣyô kɔra, নজর রাখা nɔjôr rakha

obsolete *adj* সেকেলে sekele, প্রাচীন pracīn

obstacle *n* বাধা badha

obstetrics *n* ধাত্রীবিদ্যা dhatrībidya

obstinate *adj* গোঁয়ার gõyar, জেদী jedī

obstruct *vb* বাধা দেওয়া badha deoya, আটকানো aṭkano

obstruction *n* বাধা badha

obtain *vb* পাওয়া paoya

obtainable *adj* প্রাপ্য prapyô

obvious *adj* সুস্পষ্ট suspɔṣṭô

occasion *n* উপলক্ষ্য upôlôkṣyô

occasional *adj* সাময়িক samôyik

occasionally *adv* সময় সময় sômôy sômôy, মাঝে মাঝে majhe majhe

occult *adj* গুপ্ত guptô

occupation *n (possession)* দখল dɔkhôl; *(profession)* পেশা peśa

occupy *vb* দখল করা dɔkhôl kɔra

occur *vb* ঘটা ghɔṭa

occurrence *n* ঘটনা ghɔṭôna

ocean *n* সাগর sagôr, সমুদ্র sômudrô

o'clock *adv* বাজে baje

October *n* অক্টবর মাস ɔkṭôbôr mas

octopus *n* অক্টোপাস ɔkṭopas

odd *adj (of numbers)* বিষম biṣôm; *(single)* বিজোড় bijoṛ; *(strange)* অদ্ভুত ɔdbhut

odor *n* গন্ধ gɔndhô

odorless *adj* গন্ধহীন gɔndhôhīn

off *adj (spoiled, rotten)* নষ্ট nɔṣṭô; *(cancelled)* বাতিল batil

offend *vb* অপমান করা ɔpôman kɔra

offense *n* অপরাধ ɔpôradh

offensive *adj* বিরক্তিকর birôktikɔr

offer *n* প্রস্তাব prôstab

office *n* আপিস apis, অফিস ɔphis, দপ্তর dɔptôr

officer *n* সেনাপতি senapôti

official *adj* সরকারী sɔrkarī

offspring *n* সন্তান sɔntan

often *adv* প্রায়ই prayi

oil *n* তেল tel

oily *adj* তেলা tela

ointment *n* মলম mɔlôm

OK *adv* ঠিক আছে ṭhik ache

old *adj (of things)* পুরানো purano *(Bd)*, পুরোনো purono *(WB); (of people)* বুড়া buṛa *(m)*, বুড়ি buṛi *(f)*

old-fashioned *adj* সেকেলে sekele

olive *n* জলপাই jɔlpai

Olympics *n* ওলিম্পিক olimpik

omen *n* উপলক্ষণ upôlôkṣôṇ

omission *n* বাদ bad

omit *vb* বাদ দেওয়া bad deoẏa

on *pp* উপর upôr (*also* ওপর opôr)

once *adv* একবার ækbar; (at ~) সঙ্গে সঙ্গে sɔṅge sɔṅge, শিগগির śiggir

one *num* এক æk

one and a half *num* দেড় deṛ

one and a quarter *num* সওয়া sɔoẏa

oneself *pr* নিজ nij, আপন apôn

onion *n* পিঁয়াজ pĩyaj, পেঁয়াজ pẽyaj

only *adj* একমাত্র ekmatrô; *adv* শুধু śudhu, কেবল kebôl, মাত্র matrô

ooze *vb* চুয়ানো cuẏano

opaque *adj* অস্বচ্ছ ɔsvɔcchô

open *vb* খোলা khola; *adj* খোলা khola

opening *n* ফাটল phaṭôl

opera *n* গীতিনাট্য gītinaṭyô

operate *vb (handle)* চালানো calano; *(perform surgery)* অস্ত্রচিকিৎসা করা ɔstrôcikitsa kɔra

operation *n* অস্ত্রোপচার ɔstropôcar, অপারেশন ɔpareśôn

operator *n* চালক calôk

opinion *n* মত mɔt

opium *n* আফিম aphim

opponent *n* বিপক্ষ bipɔkṣô, শত্রু śôtru

opportunity *n* সুযোগ suyog

oppose *vb* বিরোধ করা birodh kɔra

opposite *adj* উল্টা ulṭa, বিপরীত bipôrīt

opposition *n* বিরোধ birodh

oppress *vb* চাপ দেওয়া cap deoẏa, অত্যাচার করা ɔtyacar kɔra

oppression *n* অত্যাচার ɔtyacar

oppressive *adj* ভারী bharī

optical *adj* চোখের cokher

optician *n* চক্ষুচিকিৎসক côkṣucikitsôk, চোখের ডাক্তার cokher ḍaktar

optimist *n* আশাবাদী aśabadī

optimistic *adj* আশাবাদী aśabadī

option *n* উপায় upaẏ

optional *adj* ঐচ্ছিক oicchik

or *conj* বা ba, অথবা ɔthôba

oral *adj* মৌখিক moukhik

orange *n, adj* কমলা kɔmla

orchard *n* ফলের বাগান phɔler bagan

order *n (command)* হুকুম hukum, আদেশ adeś; *(arrangement)* ব্যবস্থা bybôstha; *(system)* নিয়ম niẏôm; *(sequence)* অনুযায়িতা ônuyaẏîota; *vb (command)* আদেশ দেওয়া adeś deoẏa, হুকুম করা hukum kɔra, হুকুম দেওয়া hukum deoẏa

orderly *n* বেয়ারা beyara; *adj* ঠিকঠাক ṭhikṭhak

ordinary *adj* সাধারণ sadharôṇ, স্বাভাবিক svabhabik

ore *n* আকরিক akôrik

organ *n (part of the body)* প্রত্যঙ্গ prôtyɔṅgô; *(musical instrument)* অর্গান ɔrgan

organic *adj* জৈব joibô

organization *n (formation)* সংগঠন sɔṁgɔthôn; *(organized group)* সংস্থা sɔṁstha

organize *vb (make arrangements)*

ব্যবস্থা করা bybôstha kɔra; *(tidy up)* গুছানো guchano *(Bd)*, গুছোনো guchono *(WB)*

orientation *n* দিশা diśa

origin *n* উৎপত্তি utpôtti

original *adj (first)* আদিম adim; *(genuine)* আসল asôl

ornament *n* অলঙ্কার ɔlɔṅkar, ভূষণ bhūṣɔṇ

orphan *n* এতিম etim *(Bd)*, অনাথ ɔnath *(WB)*

orphanage *n* এতিমখানা etimkhana *(Bd)*, অনাথাশ্রম ɔnathaśrôm *(WB)*

oscillate *vb* দোলা dola, দুলা dula

ostentation *n* ভড়ক bhɔrôk

ostracism *n* নির্বাসন nirbasôn

other *adj* অন্য ɔnyô

otherwise *conj* না হলে na hôle; *adv* অন্যভাবে ɔnyôbhabe

ought *vb* উচিত ucit *adj*

out *adv* বাইরে baire

outcast *adj* জাতিচ্যুত jaticyutô

outcome *n* ফল phɔl

outdoors *adv* বাইরে baire

outer *adj* বাইরের bairer

outline *n (circumference)* সীমারেখা sīmarekha; *(sketch)* খসড়া khɔsṛa

outlook *n* দৃশ্য dr̥śyô

outside *adv, pp* বাইরে baire

outskirts *n* নগরপ্রান্ত nɔgôrprantô

outstanding *adj (remaining)* বাকি baki; *(excellent)* তোফা topha, সেরা sera, দারুণ daruṇ

oval *adj* উপবৃত্তাকার upôbr̥ttakar

oven *n* চুলা cula *(Bd)*, চুলো culo *(WB)*

over *adv (above, in excess of)* উপরে upôre, অতি– ôti; *(finished)* শেষ śeṣ

overall *adv* সব মিলে sɔb mile

overcast *adj* মেঘলা meghla

overdue *adv* মেয়াদ–উত্তির্ণ meŷad-uttirṇô

overflow *vb* চলকানো cɔlkano, চলকে পড়া côlke pɔṛa

overlook *vb* উপেক্ষা করা upekṣa kɔra

overseas *adv* বিদেশে bideśe

overtake *vb* আগে যাওয়া age yaoŷa

overwhelmed *adj* গরগর gɔrgɔr

overwhelmingly *adv* গরগরে gɔrgɔre

owe *vb* ঋণী থাকা r̥ṇī thaka

owl *n* পেচক pecôk, প্যাঁচা pyæ̃ca

own *vb* আছ– ach-, অধিকারে রাখা ôdhikare rakha; *adj* নিজের nijer, আপন apôn

owner *n* অধিকারী ôdhikarī, মালিক malik

ox *n* ষাঁড় ṣãṛ

oxygen *n* অম্লজান ɔmlôjan

oyster *n* ঝিনুক jhinuk

P

pace *n* পদক্ষেপ pɔdôkṣep

pack *vb* মোড়া mora

package *n* মোড়ক morôk

pad *n* কাগজের খণ্ড kagôjer khɔṇḍô

paddy *n* ধান dhan

padlock *n* তালা tala

pagan *adj* পৌত্তলিক pouttôlik

page *n* পাতা pata

pail *n* বালতি balti

pain *n* বেদনা bedôna, ব্যথা byæthạ

painful *adj* কষ্টকর kɔṣṭôkɔr

painless *adj* যন্ত্রণাহীন yɔntrônahīn

paint *vb (do artwork)* আঁকা āka;
(add color) রঙ করা rɔṅ kɔra

painter *n* চিত্রকর citrôkɔr

painting *n* ছবি chôbi

pair *n* জোড়া jora

pajamas *n* পায়জামা paŷjama

pal *n* বন্ধু bôndhu

palace *n* প্রাসাদ prasad

palate *n* তালু talu

pale *adj* ফেকাশে phækaśe, বিবর্ণ
bibɔrnô

pallet *n* খড়ভর্তি গদি khɔrbhôrti gôdi

palm *n (part of the hand)* তেলো
telo, তালু talu

palm tree *n* তালগাছ talgach

palpitation *n* ধড়ফড়ানি dhɔrphɔrani

pamphlet *n* পুস্তিকা pustika

pan *n* কড়াই kɔrai

pandemonium *n* গোলমাল golmal,
গণ্ডগোল gɔṇḍôgol

pander *vb* প্রশ্রয় দেওয়া prôśrɔŷ
deoŷa

panel *n* তক্ত tɔktô

panic *n* উদ্বেগ udbeg

pant *vb* হাঁপানো hāpano

panties *n* ছোট প্যান্ট chôṭô pyænṭ

pantry *n* ভাণ্ডার ঘর bhaṇḍar ghɔr

pants *n* প্যান্ট pyanṭ

papaya *n* পেঁপে pēpe

paper *n* কাগজ kagôj

paperback *n* পেপারব্যাক peparbyæk

parachute *n* প্যারাশুট pyæraśuṭ

parade *n (wide road)* ময়দান mɔŷdan; *(procession)* মিছিল michil

paradigm *n* নমুনা nômuna

paradise *n* স্বর্গ svɔrgô *(Hindu)*,
বেহেস্ত behestô *(Muslim)*

paragraph *n* অনুচ্ছেদ ônucched

parallel *adj* সমান্তরাল sɔmantɔral

paralysis *n* পক্ষাঘাত pɔkṣaghat

paralyzed *adj* অসাড় ɔsar

parameter *n* পরিসীমা pôrisīma

parasite *n* পরজীবী pɔrôjībī

parasitic *adj* পরজীবীয় pɔrôjībīŷô

parcel *n* মোড়ক morôk

pardon *n* ক্ষমা kṣɔma

parents *n* মা-বাবা ma-baba,
আম্মা-আব্বা amma-abba

parish *n* যাজক-পল্লি yajôk-pôlli

park *n* পার্ক park; *vb* গাড়ি রাখা gaṛi
rakha

parking space *n* গাড়ি রাখার জায়গা
gari rakhar jayga

parliament *n* সংসদ sɔṁsɔd

parliamentary *adj* সংসদীয়
sɔṁsɔdīŷô

parrot *n* টিয়া-পাখি ṭiya-pakhi

part *n (portion)* অংশ ɔṁśô, ভাগ
bhag; *(role)* ভূমিকা bhumika; *vb
(be separated)* বিছিন্ন হওয়া
bichinnô hɔoŷa

partial *adj (in part)* আংশিক aṁśik;
(biased) পক্ষপাতী pɔkṣôpatī

partiality n পক্ষপাত pɔkṣôpat

participate vb অংশগ্রহণ করা ɔṁśôgrôhôṇ kɔra

particle n কণিকা kôṇika

particular adj (special) বিশেষ biśeṣ; (specific) বিশিষ্ট biśiṣṭô

partition n বিভাজন bibhajôn

partner n অংশীদার ôṁśīdar

party n (group of people) দল dɔl, পার্টি parṭi; (feast) ভোজ bhoj

pass vb (occur) ঘটা ghɔṭa; (walk past) পার হওয়া par hɔôỹa; (time) কাটা kaṭa; (get through a test) পাস করা pas kɔra

passage n (act of passing) গমন gɔmôn, গতি gôti; (alley) গলি gôli; (piece of writing) অনুচ্ছেদ ônucched

passenger n যাত্রী yatrī

passion n (strong feeling) ভাবাবেগ bhababeg; (ardent love) আসক্তি asôkti

passionate adj আবেগপূর্ণ abegpūrṇô

passive adj অচেষ্টা ɔceṣṭa; n কর্মবাচ্য kɔrmôbacyô

passport n ছাড়-পত্র char-pɔtrô, পাসপোর্ট pasporṭ

past n অতীত ôtīt; adj গত gɔtô, বিগত bigɔtô; pp পরে pɔre

paste n লেই lei; vb লাগানো lagano, মাখা makha

pastime n আমোদ-প্রমোদ amod-prômod

pastry n কেক বানানোর মিশ্রণ kek bananor miśrôṇ

patch n তালি tali

patch up vb (repair) মেরামত করা meramôt kɔra, তালি মারা tali mara: (reconcile) মীমাংসা করা mīmaṁsa kɔra

patchwork n জোড়াতালি joṛatali

patent adj প্রকাশ্য prôkaśyô

path n পথ pɔth, রাস্তা rasta

pathetic adj করুণ kôruṇ

pathology n রোগবিদ্যা rogbidya

patience n ধৈর্য dhoiryô

patient n রোগী rogī; adj ধৈর্যশীল dhoiryôśīl

patriot n দেশপ্রেমিক deśpremik

patriotic adj দেশভক্ত deśbhɔktô

patrol n পাহারা pahara, পর্যবেক্ষণ pôryôbekṣôn

patron n সমর্থক sɔmôrthɔk

patter n টাপুর-টুপুর ṭapur-ṭupur

pattern n (model) আদর্শ adɔrśô; (sample) নমুনা nômuna; (design) নকশা nɔkśa

paunch n ভুঁড়ি bhũṛi, বড় পেট bɔṛô peṭ

pause n বিরাম biram, বিশ্রাম biśram; vb (stop) থামা thama, বিরত করা birôtô kɔra; (have a rest) বিশ্রাম করা biśram kɔra

pave vb রাস্তা বানানো rasta banano

pave the way vb পথ প্রস্তুত করা pɔth prôstut kɔra

pavement n ফুটপাথ phuṭpath

pavilion n মণ্ডপ mɔṇḍôp

paw n থাবা thaba

pawn n বন্ধক bɔndhôk; vb বন্ধক দেওয়া bɔndhôk deôỹa

pay n বেতন betôn, মাইনে maine; vb (give money) টাকা দেওয়া ṭaka deôỹa; (make amends) শোধ করা śodh kɔra

payment n প্রদান prôdan

pea n মটর mɔṭôr (Bd), মটরশুটি mɔṭôrśuṭi (WB)

peace n শান্তি śanti

peaceful adj শান্ত śantô

peacock n ময়ূর mɔŷūr

peak n চূড়া cūṛa (Bd), চূড়ো cūṛo (WB)

peanut n বাদাম badam

pear n নাশপাতি naśpati

pearl n মুক্তা mukta

peasant n চাষী caṣī

pebble n শিলাগুটি śilaguṭi, নুড়ি nuṛi

pedal n প্যাডেল pyæḍel

peddler n ফেরিওয়ালা pherioŷala

pedestrian n পদযাত্রী pɔdyatrī

pediatrician n শিশুদের ডাক্তার śiśuder ḍaktar

peek vb উঁকি মারা ūki mara

peel vb খসানো khɔsano; n ছাল chal, খোসা khosa

peg n গোঁজ gõj

pelvis n শ্রোণি śroṇi

pen n কলম kɔlôm

penalty n শাস্তি śasti

pencil n পেনসিল pensil

penetrate vb ঢোকা ḍhoka, ঢোকানো ḍhokano

penetration n অনুপ্রবেশ ônuprôbeś

penicillin n পেনিসিলিন penisilin

penis n লিঙ্গ liṅgô

penknife n পকেট ছুরি pɔkeṭ churi

penny n পয়সা pɔŷsa

pension n উত্তর-বেতন uttôr-betôn, পেনশন penśɔn

people n লোকজন lokjɔn

pepper n (black pepper) গোল মরিচ gol môric; (capsicum) লঙ্কা lɔṅka

peppermint n পুদিনা pudina

perceive vb (notice) টের পাওয়া ṭer paoŷa; (understand) বোঝা bojha; (feel) অনুভব করা ônubhɔb kɔra

perception n (feeling) অনুভব ônubhɔb; (sense) গোচর gocôr

perceptive adj সচেতন sɔcetɔn

perennial adj চিরন্তন cirôntɔn

perfect adj নিখুঁত nikhũt

perfidious adj বেইমান beiman

perform vb অভিনয় করা ôbhinɔŷ kɔra

performance n অভিনয় ôbhinɔŷ

perfume n সুগন্ধি sugôndhi

perhaps adv হয়তো hɔŷto, বোধ হয় bodh hɔŷ

peril n বিপদ bipɔd

period n (stretch of time) কাল kal; (stage, phase) পর্যায় pôryay; (menstruation) মাসিক masik

periodic adj পর্যাবৃত্ত pôryabṛttô

periodical n পত্রিকা pôtrika; adj সাময়িক samôŷik

periphery n পরিধি pôridhi, প্রান্ত prantô

perish vb (lose one's life) প্রাণ হারানো praṇ harano; (decay) পচে যাওয়া pôce yaoŷa

perishable adj পচনশীল pɔcônīl

permanence n স্থায়িত্ব sthaŷitvô

permanent adj চিরন্তন cirôntɔn, স্থায়ী sthaŷī

permission n অনুমতি ônumôti

permit vb অনুমতি দেওয়া ônumôti deoŷa

perpendicular adj খাড়া khaṛa

perpetual adj চিরস্থায়ী cirôsthaŷī

persist vb অধ্যবসায় করা ôdhyôbɔsaŷ kɔra

person n ব্যক্তি bykti (pron bekti), লোক lok, অমুক ômuk

personal adj ব্যক্তিগত byktigɔtô

personality n চরিত্র côritrô

perspective n পরিপ্রেক্ষিত pôriprekṣit

perspiration n ঘাম gham

perspire *vb* ঘামা ghama

persuade *vb* গছানো gɔchano, প্ররোচিত করা prôrocitô kɔra

persuasion *n* প্ররোচনা prôrocôna

perturb *vb* অস্থির করিয়ে দেওয়া ɔsthir kôriye deoýa

pervasive *adj* ব্যাপ্ত byæptô

perversion *n* বিকৃতি bikṛti

pessimist *n* দুঃখবাদী duhkhôbadī

pester *vb* জ্বালানো jvalano, নাজেহাল করা najehal kɔra, নাকাল করা nakal kɔra

pestle *n* নোড়া noṛa

pet *n* পোষা জন্তু poṣa jôntu

petal *n* পাপড়ি papṛi

petition *n* আবেদন abedôn

petroleum *n* পেট্রল peṭrôl

petty *adj (insignificant)* তুচ্ছ tucchô; *(small-minded)* ছোট মনের chôṭô môner

phantom *n (illusion)* মায়ামূর্তি maýamūrti, ছায়ামূর্তি chaýamūrti

pharmaceutical *adj* ওষুধপ্রস্তুতসংক্রান্ত ôsudhprôstutsɔṁkrantô

pharmacy *n* ওষুধের দোকান ôsudher dokan

phase *n* পর্যায় pôrýay

pheasant *n* জংলী মুর্গি jôṁlī murgi

phenomenon *n (incident)* ঘটনা ghɔṭôna; *(occurrence)* ব্যাপার byæpar; *(illusion)* প্রপঞ্চ prôpôñcô

philander *vb* ছিনালি করা chinali kɔra *(Bd)*, ছেনালি করা chenali kɔra *(WB)*

philanderer *n* ছিনাল chinal

philanthropy *n* পরহিত pɔrôhitô

philology *n* শব্দতত্ত্ব śɔbdôtɔttvô

philosopher *n* তত্ত্ববিৎ tɔttvôbit, দার্শনিক darśônik

philosophical *adj (of philosophy)* দার্শনিক darśônik; *(stoical)* নির্বিকার nirbikar

philosophy *n* দর্শনশাস্ত্র dɔrśônśastrô

phlegm *n* শ্লেষ্মা śleṣma

phlegmatic *adj* উদাসীন udasīn

phone *n* টেলিফোন ṭeliphon

phonetic *adj* ধ্বনি-অনুযায়ী dhvôni-ônuýaŷī

phonetics *n* ধ্বনি-তত্ত্ব dhvôni-tɔttvô

phosphorescent *adj* অনুপ্রভ ônuprôbhô

photo *n* তোলা ছবি tola chôbi, ফোটো photo

photocopy *n* ফোটোকপি photokɔpi

photograph *vb* ছবি তোলা chôbi tola

photographer *n* আলোকচিত্রকর alokcitrôkɔr

photography *n* আলোকচিত্র alokcitrô

phrase *n (expression)* উক্তি ukti; *(group of words)* শব্দসমষ্টি śɔbdôsɔmôṣṭi

physical *adj (real)* বাস্তব bastôb; *(natural)* প্রাকৃতিক prakṛtik; *(of the body)* শারীরিক śarīrik

physician *n* চিকিৎসক cikiṯsɔk

physicist *n* পদার্থবিজ্ঞানী pɔdarthôbijñænī

physics *n* পদার্থবিজ্ঞান pɔdarthôbijñæn

piano *n* পিয়ানো piýano

pickaxe *n* গাঁতি gãti, গাঁইতি gãiti

pick *vb (pluck)* তোলা tola; *(choose)* বেছে নেওয়া beche neoýa; *(take a small amount)* (~ **at**) খুঁটা khũṭa, খোঁটা khõṭa pickle *n (preservative)* আচার acar; *(plight)* দুরবস্থা durɔbôstha

pickpocket *n* গাঁটকাটা gãṭkaṭa, পকেটমার pɔkeṭmar

picnic *n* বনভোজন bônbhojôn, চড়াইভাতি cɔraibhati *(Bd)*, চড়ুইভাতি cɔruibhati *(WB)*

picture *n* ছবি chôbi, চিত্র citrô

picturesque *adj* চিত্রবৎ citrôbɔt, ছবির মত chôbir mɔtô

pie *n* পিঠা piṭha *(Bd)*, পিঠে piṭhe *(WB)*

piece *n (fragment)* টুকরা ṭukra *(Bd)*, টুকরো ṭukro *(WB)*; *(unit)* কিতা kita

pierce *vb* ছিদ্র করা chidrô kɔra

piety *n* ঈশ্বরভক্তি īśvôrbhôkti

pig *n* শূকর śūkôr *(Bd)*, শুয়োর śuŷor *(WB)*

pigeon *n* কবুতর kôbutôr *(Bd)*, পায়রা paŷra *(WB)*

pilau *(rice dish) n* পোলাও polao

pile *n* গাদা gada, রাশি raśi

pilgrim *n* পথিক pôthik, তীর্থযাত্রী tīrthôyatrī

pilgrimage *n* তীর্থযাত্রা tīrthôyatra *(Hindu)*, হজ hɔj *(Muslim)*

pill *n* বড়ি bôṛi

pillar *n* স্তম্ভ stɔmbhô

pillow *n* বালিশ baliś

pillowcase *n* বালিশের খোল baliśer khol

pilot *n* বিমানচালক bimancalôk

pimple *n* ফুসকুড়ি phuskuṛi, ব্রণ brônô

pin *n* আলপিন alpin, কাঁটা kãṭa

pincers *n* সাঁড়াশি sãṛaśi

pinch *vb* চিমটি কাটা cimṭi kaṭa

pine *n* পাইন–গাছ pain–gach; *vb*

আকাঙ্ক্ষা করা akaṅkṣa kɔra, কামনা করা kamôna kɔra

pineapple *n* আনারস anarɔs

pink *adj* গোলাপী golapī

pinnacle *n* চূড়া cūra *(Bd)*, চূড়ো cūro *(WB)*

pins and needles *n* ঝিঁঝিঁ jhĩjhĩ

pioneer *n* প্রবর্তক prôbɔrtɔk

pious *adj* ধার্মিক dharmik

pip *n* বীচি bīci

pipe *n (tube)* নল nɔl; *(whistle)* শিস śis

pirate *n* জলদস্যু jɔlôdôsyu

pistachio *n* পেস্তা pesta

pistol *n* পিস্তল pistɔl

pit *n (hole)* গর্ত gɔrtô; *(trap)* ফাঁদ phãd; *(mineshaft)* খনি khôni

pitch *n (fixed point)* তাক tak; *(sportsground)* খেলার মাঠ khælar maṭh

pitcher *n* কলসি kôlsi

pitiful *adj* বেচারা becara

pity *n* মায়া maya, দয়া dɔŷa

place *n* জায়গা jaŷga, স্থান sthan

plagiarism *n* উক্ত চৌর্যাপরাধ uktô couryapôradh

plagiarize *vb* উক্ত চুরি করা uktô curi kɔra

plague *n* প্লেগ–রোগ pleg-rog

plain *n (level land)* সমতল ভূমি sɔmôtɔl bhūmi; *adj (level)* সমতল sɔmôtɔl; *(unadorned)* সাদাসিধে sadasidhe; *(outspoken)* মনখোলা mônkhola

plan *n (draft)* নকশা nɔkśa; *(project)* প্রকল্প prôkɔlpô;

plane *n (level)* স্তর stɔr; *(airplane)* উড়ো জাহাজ uṛo jahaj, বিমান biman

planet *n* গ্রহ grôhô

plank *n* তক্তা tɔkta

plant *n* চারাগাছ caragach; *vb* লাগানো lagano

plasma *n* রক্তরস rɔktɔrɔs

plastic *n* প্ল্যাসটিক plyæstik

plate *n* থালা thala

platform *n* মঞ্চ mɔñcô

platinum *n* প্ল্যাটিনাম plyætinam

platitude *n* মামুলি কথা mamuli kɔtha

platonic *adj* নিষ্কাম niṣkam

play *vb* খেলা khæla; *n (game)* খেলা khæla; *(staged drama)* নাটক naṭôk

playing cards *n* তাস tas

playing field *n* খেলার মাঠ khælar maṭh

plea *n (lawsuit)* মামলা mamla; *(request)* আরজি arji; *(pretext)* অজুহাত ôjuhat

plead *vb* অনুরোধ করা ônurodh kɔra

pleasant *adj* চারু caru, মনোরম mônorɔm

please *int* দয়া করে dɔŷa kôre

pleasure *n* আনন্দ anôndô

plenty *adj* বহু bôhu

pliable *adj* নমনীয় nɔmônīŷô

plight *n* দুরবস্থা durɔbôstha,

plod *vb* থপথপ করে হাঁটা thɔpthɔp kôre hãṭa

plot *n (piece of land)* খণ্ড khɔṇḍô; *(scheme)* ফন্দি phôndi; *(storyline)* গল্পের ঘটনা gɔlper ghɔṭôna

plow *n* লাঙ্গল laṅgôl; *vb* চষা cɔṣa, চাষ করা caṣ kɔra

pluck *vb* তোলা tola

plucky *adj* তেজী tejī, সাহসী sahôsī

plug *n* ছিপি chipi

plum *n* প্লাম plam

plumber *n* কলের মিস্ত্রি kɔler mistri

plume *n* পালকগুচ্ছ palôkgucchô

plump *adj* মোটাসোটা moṭasoṭa, সুগোল sugol

plunder *vb* লোটা loṭa, লুটা luṭa, লুঠ করা luṭh kɔra

plunge *n* ডুবানো ḍubano *(Bd)*, ডুবানো ḍubono *(WB)*

plural *n* বহুবচন bôhubɔcôn

plus *adv* যোগসূচক yogsūcôk

pneumonia *n* ফুসফুস-প্রদাহ phus-phus-prôdahô, নিউমোনিয়া niumoniŷa

pocket *n* পকেট pɔkeṭ

pod *n* শুঁটি śũṭi

poem *n* কবিতা kôbita

poet *n* কবি kôbi

poetry *n* কাব্য kabyô

point *n* ফোঁটা phõṭa, বিন্দু bindu

poison *n* বিষ biṣ

poisonous *adj* বিষাক্ত biṣaktô

polarization *n* সমবর্তন sɔmôbɔrtôn

pole *n (staff)* দণ্ড dɔṇḍô; *(point of the earth's axis)* মেরু meru

polemic *adj* তার্কিক tarkik

police *n* পুলিশ puliś

police station *n* থানা thana

policy *n* কর্মসূচি kɔrmôsūci

polish *vb* মাজা maja, ঘষা ghɔṣa

polite *adj* শিষ্ট śiṣṭô, ভদ্র bhɔdrô

political *adj* রাজনৈতিক rajnoitik

politician *n* রাজনীতিক rajnītik

politics *n* রাজনীতি rajnīti

poll *n* ভোট-দান bhoṭ-dan

pollen *n* পরাগ pɔrag

pollute *vb* দূষিত করা dūṣitô kɔra

pollution *n* দূষণ dūṣɔṇ

pomegranate *n* ডালিম ḍalim

pomp *n* জাঁকজমক jãkjɔmôk

pond *n* পুকুর pukur

pony *n* টাট্টু ṭaṭṭu

pool *n* ডোবা ḍoba

poor *adj* গরিব gôrib

popcorn *n* খই khôi

pope *n* পোপ pop

poppyseed *n* পোস্ত postô

popular *adj* জনপ্রিয় jɔnôpriŷô

population *n* জনসংখ্যা jɔnôsɔṁkhya

porcelain *n* চীনামাটি cīnamaṭi

porch *n* বারান্দা baranda

pore *n* লোমকূপ lomkūp

pork *n* শূকরের মাংস śūkôrer maṁsô, শুঁয়োরের মাংস śũŷorer maṁsô

port *n* বন্দর bɔndôr

portable *adj* সুবহ subɔhô

porter *n* কুলি kuli

portion *n* ভাগ bhag

portrait *n* প্রতিকৃতি prôtikr̥ti

pose *n* ভঙ্গি bhôṅgi; *vb* ঢং করা ḍhɔṁ kɔra

position *n* অবস্থান ɔbôsthan

positive *adj* ভাল bhalô

possess *vb* আছ– ach–, অধিকারে রাখা ôdhikare rakha

possession *n* সম্পত্তি sɔmpôtti

possessive *adj* দখলি dɔkhôli

possibility *n* সম্ভাবনা sɔmbhabôna

possible *adj* সম্ভব sɔmbhɔb

post *n* থাম tham

post office *n* ডাক ঘর dak ghɔr

postage *n* ডাকমাসুল dakmasul

postcard *n* পোস্টকার্ড poṣṭkarḍ

posterity *n* উত্তরপুরুষ uttôrpuruṣ

postmark *n* ডাকঘরের ছাপ ḍakghɔrer chap

postpone *vb* মুলতবি রাখা multôbi rakha

pot *n* ডেকচি ḍekci, হাঁড়ি hãṛi

potato *n* আলু alu

pottery *n* পাত্রাদি patradi

pouch *n* বটুয়া bôṭuŷa

poultry *n* হাঁস–মুর্গি hãs–murgi

pound *vb* মাড়া maṛa; *n* আধ কেজি adh keji

pour *vb* ঢালা ḍhala

poverty *n* দারিদ্র্য daridryô

powder *n* চূর্ণ cūrṇô, গুঁড়ো gũṛo

power *n (ability)* ক্ষমতা kṣɔmôta; *(strength)* শক্তি śôkti

powerful *adj* ক্ষমতাবান kṣɔmôta-ban, প্রবল prôbɔl

powerless *adj* অক্ষম ɔkṣɔm

practical *adj* ব্যবহারিক bybôharik *(pron* bæboharik*)*

practically *adv (almost)* প্রায় praŷ, *(really)* আসলে asole

practice *n (custom)* রীতি rīti; *(exercise)* চর্চা côrca, অনুশীলন ônuśīlôn; *(application)* প্রয়োগ prôŷog

pragmatic *adj* প্রয়োগিক prôŷogik, বাস্তববাদী bastôbbadī

praise *n* প্রশংসা prôśɔṁsa

praiseworthy *adj* প্রশংসনীয় prôśɔṁsônīŷô

prattle *n* বকবক bɔkbɔk

prawn *n* চিংড়ি মাছ ciṁṛi mach

pray *vb* প্রার্থনা করা prarthôna kɔra

prayer *n (religious)* প্রার্থনা prarthôna; *(request)* আর্জি arji, অনুরোধ ônurodh; *(Muslim devotion)* নামাজ namaj

preach *vb* প্রচার করা prôcar kɔra

precarious *adj* পলকা pɔlka

precede *vb* আগে যাওয়া age yaoŷa

precedence *n* পূর্বাধিকার pūrbadhikar

precious *adj* (*dear*) প্রিয় priŷô; (*of high value*) মূল্যবান mūlyôban

precise *adj* ঠিক ṭhik, যথাযথ yɔthayɔth

predicate *n* বিধেয় bidheŷô

predict *vb* ভবিষ্যদ্বাণী করা bhôbiṣyɔdvaṇī kɔra

preface *n* ভূমিকা bhūmika

prefer *vb* পছন্দ করা pɔchôndô kɔra

preference *n* (*liking*) পছন্দ pɔchôndô; (*priority*) অগ্রাধিকার ɔgradhikar

prefix *n* অনুসর্গ ônusɔrgô

pregnant *adj* পোয়াতি poŷati, গর্ভবতী gɔrbhôbôtī

prejudice *n* (*superstition*) কুসংস্কার kusɔṁskar; (*bias*) পক্ষপাত pôkṣôpat

preparation *n* প্রস্তুতি prôstuti, আয়োজন aŷôjɔn

prepare *vb* প্রস্তুত করা prôstut kɔra, তৈরি করা toiri kɔra

prescribe *vb* নির্দিষ্ট করা nirdiṣṭô kɔra

prescription *n* (*directive*) নির্দেশ nirdeś; (*doctor's orders*) ডাক্তারের উপদেশপত্র ḍaktarer upôdeśpɔtrô

presence *n* উপস্থিতি upôsthiti

present *n* (*time now*) বর্তমান bɔrtô-man; (*gift*) উপহার upôhar; *adj* উপস্থিত upôsthit, হাজির hajir; *vb* উপহার দেওয়া upôhar deoŷa

presently *adv* তৎক্ষণাৎ tɔtkṣɔnaṭ

preserve *vb* (*keep*) রাখা rakha; (*protect*) রক্ষা করা rɔkṣa kɔra; *n* আচার acar

president *n* (*chairman*) সভাপতি sɔbhapôti; (*head of state*) রাষ্ট্রপতি raṣṭrôpôti

press *vb* (*push*) ঠেলা ṭhæla; (*exert pressure*) চাপ দেওয়া cap deoŷa, চাপা capa; *n* সংবাদিকতা sɔṁbadikɔta

pressure *n* চাপ cap

prestige *n* সম্মান sɔmman

presume *vb* মনে করা mône kɔra, ভাবা bhaba

pretend *vb* ভান করা bhan kɔra

pretension *n* ছল-ছুতা chɔl–chuta (*Bd*), ছল-ছতো chɔl–chuto (*WB*)

pretty *adj* (*beautiful*) সুন্দর sundôr, শোভন śobhôn; *adv* (*quite*) বেশ beś

prevailing *adj* প্রধান prôdhan

prevent *vb* প্রতিরোধ করা prôtirodh kɔra

prevention *n* প্রতিরোধ prôtirodh

preventive *adj* প্রতিরোধক prôtirodhôk

previous *adj* আগেকার agekar, আগের ager, প্রাক্তন prakton

price *n* দাম dam

priceless *adj* অমূল্য ɔmūlyô

prick *n* কাঁটা kāṭa

prickly *adj* খোঁচা-খোঁচা khõca-khõca

prickly heat *n* ঘামাচি ghamaci

pride *n* (*satisfaction*) গর্ব gɔrbô; (*vanity*) অহংকার ɔhômkar

priest *n* (*Hindu*) যাজক yajôk, পুরোহিত purôhit; (*Muslim*) মোল্লা molla; (*Christian*) পাদরি padri

primary *adj* (*first*) প্রথম prôthôm; (*original*) মৌলিক moulik

prime *adj* উত্তম uttôm

prime minister *n* প্রধান মন্ত্রী prôdhan môntrī

primitive *adj* আদিম adim

prince *n* রাজপুত্র rajputrô, রাজকুমার rajkumar

princess *n* রাজকুমারী rajkumarī

principal *adj* পরম pɔrôm

principle *n* তত্ত্ব tɔttvô, নিয়ম niŷôm

print *vb* ছাপা chapa, ছাপানো chapano

printing *n* ছাপাই chapai

priority *n* পূর্বিতা pūrbita, অগ্রাধিকার ɔgradhikar

prison *n* জেল jel, কারাগার karagar

prisoner *n* কয়েদি kɔŷedi

privacy *n* একান্তে ekante

private *adj* (*personal*) ব্যক্তিগত byktigɔtô (*pron* bektigɔto); (*secret*) গোপন gopôn

privilege *n* অধিকার ôdhikar

prize *n* পুরস্কার purôskar

probability *n* সম্ভাবনা sɔmbhabôna

probable *adj* সম্ভব sɔmbhɔb

probably *adv* সম্ভবত sɔmbhɔbɔtô

problem *n* সমস্যা sɔmôsya

procedure *n* পদ্ধতি pɔddhôti, কায়দা kaŷda

proceed *vb* অগ্রসর হওয়া ɔgrôsôr hɔoŷa

process *n* অগ্রগতি ɔgrôgôti

produce *vb* (*make*) করা kɔra; (*create*) সৃষ্টি করা sṛṣṭi kɔra; (*yield*) উৎপাদন করা utpadôn kɔra

product *n* (*thing*) বস্তু bôstu, জিনিস jinis; (*result, effect*) ফসল phɔsôl

profession *n* পেশা peśa

professional *adj* পেশাদার peśadar

professor *n* অধ্যাপক ôdhyapôk

profile *n* রেখাচিত্র rekhacitrô

profit *n* লাভ labh

profound *adj* গভীর gôbhīr

profuse *adj* অনর্গল ɔnɔrgɔl

program *n* পরিকল্পনা pôrikɔlpôna

programmer *n* পরিকল্পক pôrikɔlpôk

progress *n* (*development*) অগ্রগতি ɔgrôgôti; (*improvement*) উন্নতি unnôti

progressive *adj* (*ongoing*) ঘটমান ghɔṭôman; (*modern*) আধুনিকমনা adhunikmôna

prohibit *vb* নিষেধ করা niṣedh kɔra, বারণ করা barôn kɔra

prohibition *n* নিষেধ niṣedh, বারণ barôn

project *n* প্রকল্প prôkɔlpô

promenade *vb* বেড়ানো beṛano

promise *vb* কথা দেওয়া kɔtha deoŷa; *n* অঙ্গীকার ôṅgīkar, প্রতিজ্ঞা prôtijña

prompt *adj* তৎপর tɔtpɔr, চটপটে cɔtpɔṭe

pronoun *n* সর্বনাম sɔrbônam

pronounce *vb* উচ্চারণ করা uccarôn kɔra

pronunciation *n* উচ্চারণ uccarôn

proof *n* প্রমাণ prômaṇ

propaganda *n* প্রচার prôcar

propel *vb* চালানো calano

propeller *n* চালকযন্ত্র calôkyɔntrô

proper *adj* (*appropriate*) ঠিক ṭhik, যথাযথ yɔthaŷɔth; (*suitable*) উপযুক্ত upôyuktô

property *n* সম্পত্তি sɔmpôtti

prophet *n* নবী nôbī

proportion *n* মাপ map, অনুপাত ônupat

proposal *n* প্রস্তাব prôstab

propose *vb* প্রস্তাব করা prôstab kɔra

proprietor *n* মালিক malik

prose *n* গদ্য gôdyô

prospective *adj* প্রত্যাশিত prôtyaśitô

prosper *vb* সফল হওয়া sɔphôl hɔoŷa

prosperity *n* সাফল্য saphôlyô

prosperous *adj* শুভ śubhô

prostitute *n* বেশ্যা beśya

prostitution *n* বেশ্যাবৃত্তি beśyabr̊tti

protect *vb* রক্ষা করা rôkṣa kɔra

protection *n* রক্ষা rôkṣa

protein *n* দেহসার dehôsar, প্রোটিন proṭin

protest *vb* প্রতিবাদ করা prôtibad kɔra; *n* প্রতিবাদ prôtibad, আপত্তি apôtti

Protestant *adj* প্রটেস্ট্যান্ট prôṭesṭyænṭ

proud *adj* গর্বিত gôrbitô

prove *vb* প্রমাণ করা prôman kɔra

proverb *n* প্রবাদ prôbad

provide *vb* যোগানো yogano

province *n* প্রদেশ prôdeś

prudent *adj* বিচক্ষণ bicɔkṣôn

prune *vb* ছাঁটা chãṭa; *n* পিণ্ডী খেজুর piṇḍī khejur

pry *vb* উঁকি মারা ũki mara

psychiatrist *n* মনোরোগবিশেষজ্ঞ mônorogbiśeṣɔjñô *(pron* monorogbisheshɔggo)

psychological *adj* মনোবিদ্যাগত mônobidyagɔtô

psychologist *n* মনোবিজ্ঞানী mônobijñanī

psychology *n* মনোবিদ্যা mônobidya

pub *n* পানশালা panśala

public *n* জনসাধারণ jɔnôsadharôn; *adj* জনসাধারণের jɔnôsadharôner

publication *n* প্রকাশনা prôkaśôna

publicity *n* প্রচার prôcar

publish *vb* প্রকাশ করা prôkaś kɔra

publisher *n* প্রকাশক prôkaśɔk

pudding *n* পায়েস paŷes

puff *(of air) n* ফুঁ phũ; *vb* ফুঁ দেওয়া phũ deoŷa

pull *vb* টানা ṭana

pullover *n* গরম গেঞ্জি gɔrôm geñji, সোয়েটার soŷeṭar

pulp *n* মজ্জা mɔjja

pulse *n* *(heartbeat)* নাড়ী narī; *(lentils)* ডাল ḍal

pump *n* পাম্প pamp, নলকূপ nɔlkūp

pumpkin *n* কুমড়া kumra *(Bd)*, কুমড়ো kumro *(WB)*

punch *vb* ঘুষি মারা ghuṣi mara

punctual *adj* সময়মত sômôŷmɔtô

punctuation *n* যতি yôti

puncture *vb* খোঁচা khõca, ছিদ্র করা chidrô kɔra

pundit *n* পণ্ডিত pôṇḍit

punish *vb* শাস্তি দেওয়া śasti deoŷa

punishment *n* শাস্তি śasti

pupil *n* *(of the eye)* চোখের তারা cokher tara; *(student)* ছাত্র chatrô *(m)*, ছাত্রী chatrī *(f)*

puppet *n* পুতুল putul

puppy *n* কুকুর ছানা kukur chana

purchase *vb* কেনা kena; *n* সওদা sɔoda

pure *adj* খাঁটি khãṭi, শুচি śuci

purification *n* শোধন śodhôn

purify *vb* পরিষ্কার করা pôriṣkar kɔra, শুদ্ধ করা śuddhô kɔra

purity *n* শুদ্ধতা śuddhôta

purple *adj* বেগুনি beguni

purpose *n* উদ্দেশ্য uddeśyô

purse *n* মানিব্যাগ manibŷæg

pursue *vb* *(follow)* অনুসরণ করা ônusɔrôn kɔra; *(hunt)* শিকার করা śikar kɔra

pursuit *n* অনুধাবন ônudhabôn

pus *n* পুঁজ pūj

push *vb (knock)* ধাক্কা দেওয়া dhakka deoŷa; *(move forward)* ঠেলা ṭhæla

put *vb* রাখা rakha *(Bd, WB)*, থওয়া thɔoŷa *(Bd)*

put down *vb* বসানো bɔsano

put off *vb* মুলতবি রাখা multôbi rakha

put on *vb* পরা pɔra

put out *vb* নিবানো nibano

put up *vb* আশ্রয় দেওয়া aśrɔŷ deoŷa

put up with *vb* সহ্য করা sôhyô kɔra *(pron* shojjho kɔra)

putrid *adj* পচা pɔca

puzzle *n* ধাঁধা dhãdha

pyramid *n* পিরামিড piramiḍ

Q

quack *n* হাতুড়িয়া haturiŷa *(Bd)*, হাতুড়ে hature *(WB)*

quaint *adj (whimsical)* খেয়ালি kheŷali; *(old-fashioned)* সেকেলে sekele

qualification *n (condition)* শর্ত śɔrtô; *(expertise)* প্রশিক্ষণ prôśikṣôṇ

qualified *adj* যোগ্য yogyô

qualify *vb (gain expertise)* যোগ্য হওয়া yogyô hɔôŷa; *(restrict)* সীমিত করা sīmitô kɔra

quality *n (nature)* স্বভাব sʋɔbhab; *(merit)* গুণ guṇ

qualm *n* অস্বস্তিবোধ ɔsʋôstibodh

quantity *n* পরিমাণ pôrimaṇ

quarantine *n* সঙ্গরোধ sɔṅgôrodh

quarrel *n* ঝগড়া jhɔgṛa

quarry *n* খনি khôni

quarter *n* সিকি siki, পোয়া poŷa

quarter of an hour *n* পোয়া ঘণ্টা poŷa ghɔṇṭa, পনের মিনিট pɔnerô minit

quarter past *adv* সওয়া sɔôŷa

quarter to *adv* পৌনে poune

quarterly *adv* ত্রৈমাসিক troimasik

quartz *n* স্ফটিক sphôṭik

queasy *adj* বমিবমি bômibômi

queen *n* রানী ranī

queer *adj* অদ্ভুত ɔdbhut

quench *vb (put out)* নিবানো nibano, নেবানো nebano; *(~ thirst)* মেটানো meṭano

query *n* অনুসন্ধান ônusɔndhan

question *n* প্রশ্ন prôśnô, জিজ্ঞাসা jijñasa *(Bd)* জিজ্ঞেস jijñes *(WB)*; *vb* প্রশ্ন করা prôśnô kɔra, জিজ্ঞাসা করা jijñasa kɔra

questionable *adj* সন্দেহজনক sɔndehôjɔnôk

queue *n* সিরিয়াল siriŷal

quick *adj* দ্রুত drutô

quickly *adv* চটপটে cɔṭpɔṭe, শিগগির siggir, জলদি jôldi

quicksand *n* চোরাবালি corabali

quicksilver *n* পারদ parôd

quick-tempered *adj* রাগী ragī, বদমেজাজি bɔdmejaji

quiet *adj (silent)* চুপচাপ cupcap, নীরব nīrɔb; *(peaceful)* শান্ত śantô; *(still)* স্থির sthir

quill *n* পালক palôk

quilt *n* লেপ lep

quintessence *n* মর্ম mɔrmô

quit *vb* ছেড়ে যাওয়া chere yaoŷa, ছেড়ে দেওয়া chere deoŷa

quite *adv* বেশ beś

quiver *vb* কাঁপা kāpa

quiz *n* ক্রীড়াচ্ছলে পরীক্ষা krīṛacchôle pôrīkṣa, কুইজ kuij

quota *n* নির্দিষ্ট পরিমাণ nirdiṣṭô pôrimaṇ

quotation *n* উদ্ধৃতি uddhṙti

quotation mark *n* উদ্ধৃতি -চিহ্ন uddhṙti-cihnô

R

rabbit *n* খরগোশ khɔrgoś

rabies *n* ক্ষিপ্ততা kṣiptôta

race *n (group of people)* জাতি jati; *(competition)* প্রতিযোগিতা prôtiyogita; *vb* দৌড় দেওয়া douṛ deoŷa, ছুটা chuṭa

racial *adj* জাতিগত jatigɔtô

racism *n* জাতি–বিদ্বেষ jati-bidbeṣ

rack *n* আলনা alna

racket *n (uproar)* হৈচৈ hoicoi; *(sports equipment)* ব্যাট byæṭ

radiance *vb* দীপ্তি dīpti

radiant *adj* উজ্জ্বল ujjvôl, দীপ্তিমান dīptiman

radiation *n* বিকিরণ bikirɔṇ

radiator *n* হিটার hiṭar

radical *adj (fundamental)* মৌলিক moulik; *(thorough)* আমূল amūl

radio *n* বেতার betar, রেডিও reḍio

radioactive *adj* তেজস্ক্রিয় tejôskriŷô

radish *n* মূলা mūla *(Bd)*, মুলো mulo *(WB)*

radius *n* ব্যাসার্ধ byæsardhô

raffle *n* লটারি lɔṭari

raft *n* ভেলা bhæla

rafter *n* বরগা bɔrga

rag *n* নেকড়া nækṛa

rage *n (fit of passion)* ক্ষিপ্ততা kṣiptôta; *(anger)* রাগ rag, ক্রোধ krodh

ragged *adj* ছেঁড়াখোঁড়া chēṛakhoṛa, ছিন্নবিছিন্ন chinnôbichinnô

raid *n* হানা hana

rail *n (support)* ঠেকনো ṭhekno; *(transport)* রেল rel

railing *n* বেড়া beṛa

railroad, railway *n* রেলপথ relpɔth

rain *n* বৃষ্টি bṛṣṭi *(pron brishṭi)*

rainbow *n* রামধনু ramdhônu

rainy *adj* বৃষ্টিবহুল bṛṣṭibôhul

raise *vb (lift)* তোলা tola; *(bring up)* পালন করা palôn kɔra

raisin *n* কিশমিশ kiśmiś

rake *vb* আঁচড়ানো ācṛano; *n (harrow)* আঁচড় ācôṛ; *(rogue)* লম্পট lɔmpɔṭ

rally *n* জড় করা jɔrô kɔra

ram *n* মেষ meṣ; *vb (push)* ধাক্কা দেওয়া dhakka deoŷa

Ramadan *n* রমজান rɔmjan,

ramble *vb (talk randomly)* এলোমেলো কথা বলা elomelo kɔtha bɔla; *(walk about)* টোটো করা ṭoṭo kɔra

ramification *n* ফল phɔl

ramp *n* চালু স্তর calu stɔr

rampant *adj (forceful)* তেজস্বী tejôsvī

rancid *adj* পচা pɔca

random *adj* অকারণ ɔkarôṇ

range *n (extent)* প্রসার prôsar; *(reach)* নাগাল nagal

rank *n* শ্রেণি śreṇi

ransack *vb* লুট করা luṭ kɔra

ransom *n* মুক্তিপণ muktipɔṇ

rape *n* ধর্ষণ dhɔrṣôṇ; *vb* ধর্ষণ করা dhɔrṣôn kɔra

rapid *adj* দ্রুত drutô

rapidly *adv* দরদর dɔrdɔr

rapport *n* মনের মিল môner mil

rare *adj* বিরল birɔl, কম kɔm

rash *n* ঘামাচি ghamaci; *adj* হঠকারি hɔṭhôkari

rat *n* ইঁদুর īdur

rate *n* অনুপাত ônupat

rather *adv* বরং bɔrôm̐

ratification *n* চুক্তি cukti

ratify *vb* অনুমোদন করা ônumodôn kɔra

ratio *n* অনুপাত ônupat

ration *n* নির্দিষ্ট অংশ nirdiṣṭô ɔm̐śô

rational *n* যুক্তিসহ yuktisɔhô, যুক্তিবাদী yuktibadī

rattan *n* বেত bet

ravine *n* গিরিখাত girikhat

raw *adj* কাঁচা kāca

ray *n* কিরণ kirôṇ, রশ্মি rôśmi

razor *n* ক্ষুর kṣur

reach *vb* নাগাল পাওয়া nagal paoŷa; *n* নাগাল nagal

react *vb* সাড়া দেওয়া saṛa deoŷa

reaction *n* সাড়া saṛa, প্রতিক্রিয়া prôtikriŷa

read *vb* পড়া pɔra

reader *n* পাঠক paṭhôk

reading *n* (*study*) পাঠ paṭh, পড়া pɔra; (*recital*) আবৃত্তি abṙtti

ready *adj* (*prepared*) প্রস্তুত prôstut, তৈরি toiri; (*willing*) রাজি raji; (*prompt*) চটপট cɔṭpɔṭ

real *adj* আসল asôl, বাস্তব bastɔb

realism *n* বাস্তব–বাদ bastɔb–bad

reality *n* বাস্তবতা bastɔbôta

realize *vb* (*understand*) বুঝতে পারা bujhte para; (*profit*) লাভ করা labh kɔra

reap *vb* অর্জন করা ɔrjon kɔra

reappear *vb* ফিরে আসা phire asa

rear *n* পিছনদিক pichôndik (*Bd*), পেছনদিক pechôndik *WB*), পশ্চাৎ pɔścat; *vb* পালন করা palôn kɔra

reason *n* (*cause*) কারণ karôṇ; (*logic*) যুক্তি yukti; (*faculty of judgment*) বিচারবুদ্ধি bicarbuddhi

reasonable *adj* যুক্তিবাদী yuktibadī

reassurance *n* আশ্বাস aśvas

reassure *vb* আশ্বস্ত করা aśvɔstô kɔra, অভয় দেওয়া ɔbhɔŷ deoŷa

rebate *n* কমতি kômti

rebel *n* বিদ্রোহী bidrohī; *vb* বিদ্রোহ করা bidrohô kɔra

rebellion *n* বিদ্রোহ bidrohô

rebound *n* প্রতিক্ষেপ prôtikṣep

rebuff *n* ধমক dhɔmôk

rebuke *vb* তিরস্কার করা tirôskar kɔra

recall *vb* মনে পড়া mône pɔra

receipt *n* রসিদ rôsid

receive *vb* পাওয়া paoŷa

receiver *n* গ্রাহযন্ত্র grahôŷɔntrô

recent *adj* সাম্প্রতিক samprôtik

recently *adv* সম্প্রতি sɔmprôti, ইদানীং idanīm̐

reception *n* অভ্যর্থনা ôbhyôrthôna

recipe *n* রান্নার কায়দা rannar kaŷda

reciprocal *adj* পরস্পর pɔrôspɔr, পারস্পরিক parôspôrik

recital *n* আবৃত্তি abṙtti

recite *vb* আবৃত্তি করা abṙtti kɔra

reckless *adj* ডানপিটে ḍanpiṭe, বেপরোয়া bepɔrôŷa

reckon *vb* (*calculate*) হিসাব করা hisab kɔra; (*suppose*) মনে করা mône kɔra, অনুমান করা ônuman kɔra

reclaim *vb* (*recover*) পুনরুদ্ধার করা punôruddhar kɔra; (*want back*) ফেরত চাওয়া pherôt caoŷa

recognition *n* স্বীকৃতি svīkṙti

recognize *vb* চেনা cena

recommend *vb* সুপারিশ করা supariś kɔra

recommendation n সুপারিশ supariś

recompense vb শোধ করা śodh kɔra

reconcile vb মেটানো meṭano

reconciliation n মীমাংসা mīmamsa

record n দলিল dôlil; vb লিখে রাখা likhe rakha

recover vb সুস্থ হওয়া susthô hɔoŷa

recreation n আমোদপ্রমোদ amodprômod

recrimination n দোষারোপ doṣarop

recruit vb সংগ্রহ করা sɔmgrôhô kɔra

rectangle n আয়তক্ষেত্র aŷôtôkṣetrô

rectangular adj সমায়ত sɔmaŷôtô

rectify vb সংশোধন করা sɔmśodhôn kɔra

recuperate vb সুস্থ হওয়া susthô hɔoŷa

recur vb আবার হওয়া abar hɔoŷa

recurrence n পুনরুদ্ভব punôrudbhɔb

red adj লাল lal

reddish adj লালচে lalce

redeem vb (rescue) ত্রাণ করা traṇ kɔra; (get back) ফিরে পাওয়া phire paoŷa

reduce vb কমানো kɔmano

reduction n হ্রাস hras, লঘুকরণ lôghukɔrôṇ

reed n খাগড়া khagṛa

reef n সমুদ্রের শৈলশিরা sômudrer śoilśira

reel n লাটাই laṭai; vb টলটল করা ṭɔlṭɔl kɔra

refer vb পাঠানো paṭhano

refer to vb উল্লেখ করা ullekh kɔra

reference n উল্লেখ ullekh

referral n অরোপণ aropôṇ

refine vb শোধন করা śodhôn kɔra

refinement n শুদ্ধি śuddhi

reflect vb (throw back light) প্রতিফলিত হওয়া prôtiphôlitô hɔoŷa; (consider) বিবেচনা করা bibecôna kɔra

reflection n প্রতিফলন prôtiphɔlôn

reform vb উন্নত করা unnɔtô kɔra

refresh vb তরতাজা করা tɔrtaja kɔra

refreshment n (rejuvenation) সজীবতা sɔjībôta; (light meal) হালকা খাবার halka khabar, টিফিন ṭiphin

refrigerate vb ঠাণ্ডা করে রাখা ṭhaṇḍa kôre rakha

refrigerator n ফ্রিজ phrij, হিমায়নযন্ত্র himaŷônyɔntrô

refuge n আশ্রয় aśrɔŷ

refugee n আশ্রয়প্রার্থী aśrɔŷprarthī

refund n টাকা ফেরত ṭaka pherôt

refusal n প্রত্যাখ্যান prôtyakhyan

refuse n জঞ্জাল jɔñjal; vb না করা na kɔra, অসম্মত হওয়া ɔsɔmmɔtô hɔoŷa

regard vb (see) দেখা dækha; (consider) বিবেচনা করা bibecôna kɔra; (hold in esteem) সম্মান করা sɔmman kɔra; n (respect) শ্রদ্ধা śrôddha

regarding pp সম্পর্কে sɔmpɔrke, বিষয়ে biṣɔŷe

regime n শাসনব্যবস্থা śasôn-byæbôstha

region n এলাকা elaka

regional adj আঞ্চলিক añcôlik

register n তালিকা talika

registration n নিবন্ধন nibɔndhôn

regret n দুঃখ duḥkhô; আফশোস aphśos; vb দুঃখ করা duḥkhô kɔra

regular *adj* নিয়মিত niŷômitô

regulation *n* আইন ain, নিয়ম niŷôm

rehabilitation *n* পুনর্বাসন punôrbasôn

rehearsal *n* মহলা mɔhôla, চর্চা cɔrca, মহড়া mɔhôṛa

reign *n* আমল amɔl, শাসন śasôn; *vb* শাসন করা śasôn kɔra

reimburse *vb* টাকা ফেরত দেওয়া ṭaka pherôt deôŷa

rein *n* লাগাম lagam

reinforce *vb* শক্তি বাড়ানো śôkti baṛano

reject *vb* ফেলে দেওয়া phele deôŷa, অস্বীকার করা ɔsvīkar kɔra

rejection *n* অস্বীকার ɔsvīkar

rejoice *vb* আনন্দিত হওয়া anônditô hɔôŷa

relate *vb (tell)* বর্ণনা করা bɔrṇôna kɔra; *(connect)* যুক্ত করা yuktô kɔra

relationship *n* সম্পর্ক sɔmpɔrkô

relative *n* আত্মীয় atmŷô; *adj* তুলনামূলক tulônamūlɔk

relatives *n* আত্মীয়-স্বজন atmīŷô-svɔjôn

relax *vb (loosen)* আলগা দেওয়া alga deôŷa; *(rest)* জিরানো jirano *(Bd)*, জিরোনো jirono *(WB)*

relaxation *n* আরাম aram

release *vb* ছেড়ে দেওয়া cheṛe deôŷa, মুক্তি দেওয়া mukti deôŷa

relevant *adj* প্রাসঙ্গিক prasôṅgik

reliable *adj* নির্ভরযোগ্য nirbhɔryogyô

relief *n* উপশম upôśɔm

relieve *vb* উপশম করা upôśɔm kɔra

relieved *adj* উপশমিত upôśômitô

religion *n* ধর্ম dhɔrmô

religious *adj* ধার্মিক dharmik

reluctant *adj* নারাজ naraj, অনিচ্ছুক ɔnicchuk

rely on *vb* নির্ভর করা nirbhɔr kɔra

remain *vb* থাকা thaka, রওয়া rɔôŷa

remainder *n* বাকি baki

remaining *adj* বাকি baki

remark *n* মন্তব্য mɔntôbyô; *vb* মন্তব্য করা mɔntôbyô kɔra

remarkable *adj (noteworthy)* লক্ষণীয় lɔkṣôṇīŷô; *(special)* বিশেষ biśeṣ

remedy *n* চিকিৎসা cikitsa

remember *vb* মনে রাখা mône rakha

remembrance *n* স্মৃতি smṛti

remind *vb* মনে করিয়ে দেওয়া mône kôriŷe deôŷa

reminder *n (souvenir)* স্মারক smarôk; *(demand)* তাগাদা tagada

reminiscence *n* স্মৃতিচারণ smṛticarôṇ

remission *n* ক্ষমা kṣɔma, রেহাই rehai, হ্রাস hras

remnant *n* অবশিষ্ট ɔbôśiṣṭô

remorse *n* অনুতাপ ônutap

remote *adj* দূরবর্তী dūrôbôrtī

removal *n* অপসারণ ɔpôsarôṇ

remove *vb* সরানো sɔrano

renew *vb* আবার নতুন করা abar nôtun kɔra

renewal *n* নবীকরণ nôbīkɔrôṇ

renounce *vb* পরিত্যাগ করা pôrityæg kɔra

renovate *vb* ঘর নতুন করা ghɔr nôtun kɔra

rent *n* খাজনা khajna, ভাড়া bhaṛa; *vb* ভাড়া করা bhaṛa kɔra

repair *vb* মেরামত করা meramôt kɔra

repeat *vb* আবার বলা abar bɔla

repel *vb* প্রতিহত করা prôtihôtô kɔra

repent *vb* অনুতপ্ত হওয়া ônutɔptô hɔoŷa

repercussion *n* প্রতিক্রিয়া prôtikriŷa

repetition *n* পুনরাবৃত্তি punôrabṙtti

replace *vb* বদলানো bɔdlano, পাল্টানো palṭano

replete *adj* পূর্ণ pūrṇô

reply *vb* জবাব দেওয়া jɔbab deoŷa

report *n (narration)* বিবরণ bibɔrôṇ; *(statement)* প্রতিবেদন prôtibedôn

reporter *n* সাংবাদিক sambadik

represent *vb* প্রতিনিধি হওয়া prôtinidhi hɔoŷa

representative *n* প্রতিনিধি prôtinidhi

repression *n* দমন dɔmôn

reprimand *n* ধমক dhɔmôk; *vb* ধমকানো dhɔmkano

reprisal *n* প্রতিশোধ prôtiśodh

reproach *vb* তিরস্কার করা tirôskar kɔra

reproduce *vb (copy)* কপি করা kôpi kɔra; *(bring forth)* জন্ম দেওয়া jɔnmô deoŷa

reproduction *n* পুনর্গঠন punôrgɔṭhôn

reptile *n* সরিসৃপ sôrisṙp

republic *n* প্রজাতন্ত্র prôjatɔntrô

republican *adj* প্রজাতান্ত্রিক prôjatantrik

repulsive *adj* বীভৎস bībhɔ̂tsô

reputation *n* নাম nam

request *n* অনুরোধ ônurodh; *vb* অনুরোধ করা ônurodh kɔra

require *vb* লাগা laga, চাওয়া caoŷa

requirement *n* চাহিদা cahida

rescue *vb* বাঁচানো bācano, উদ্ধার করা uddhar kɔra

research *n* গবেষণা gɔbeṣɔṇa, অনুসন্ধান ônusɔndhan

resemblance *n* সাদৃশ্য sadṙśyô

resemble *vb* সদৃশ হওয়া sɔdṙśô hɔoŷa

resent *vb (dislike)* খারাপ লাগা kharap laga; *(be offended)* অপমান বোধ করা ɔpômaṇ bodh kɔra

reservation *n (doubt)* সন্দেহ sɔndehô; *(pre-booking)* আগের ব্যবস্থা ager bybôstha

reserve *n* সঞ্চয় sɔñcɔŷ; *vb* আগে বুক করা age buk kɔra

reserved *adj* সংরক্ষিত sɔmrôkṣitô

reservoir *n* ভাণ্ডার bhaṇḍar

reside *vb* বাস করা bas kɔra

residence *n* বাসভবন basbhɔbôn

resident *n* অধিবাসী ôdhibasī

residue *n* তলানি tɔlani

resign *vb* ছেড়ে দেওয়া cheṛe deoŷa

resignation *n* সমর্পণ sɔmɔrpôṇ

resin *n* রজন rɔjôn

resist *vb* রোধ করা rodh kɔra, বাধা দেওয়া badha deoŷa

resistance *n* রোধ rodh, বাধা badha

resistant *adj* বাধাদায়ক badhadaŷôk

resolution *n* সঙ্কল্প sɔṅkɔlpô

resolve *vb* সমাধান করা sɔmadhan kɔra

respect *n* শ্রদ্ধা śrɔddha

respectable *adj (honorable)* মাননীয় manônŷīô; *(considerable)* বেশ কিছু beś kichu

respond *vb* জবাব দেওয়া jɔbab deoŷa

response *n* জবাব jɔbab

responsibility *n* দায়িত্ব daŷitvô

responsible *adj* দায়ী daŷī

rest *n (relaxation)* বিশ্রাম biśram; *(remainder)* বাকি baki; *vb* জিরানো jirano

restaurant *n* রেস্তোরাঁ restorā

restless *adj* অস্থির ɔsthir

restlessness *n* ছটফটানি chɔṭphɔṭani

restore *vb* (*bring back*) ফিরিয়ে আনা phiriẏe ana; (*repair*) মেরামত করা meramɔt kɔra, ঠিক করা ṭhik kɔra

restrain *vb* আটকানো aṭkano

restrict *vb* সীমিত করা sīmitô kɔra

restriction *n* সীমানা sīmana, বাধা badha

result *n* ফল phɔl

resume *vb* পুনরারম্ভ করা punôrarômbhô kɔra

résumé *n* সংক্ষেপ sɔṁkṣep

retail *adj* খুচরা বিক্রি khucra bikri

retailer *n* খুচরা বিক্রেতা khucra bikreta

retain *vb* রাখা rakha, ধরে রাখা dhôre rakha

retina *n* অক্ষিপট ôkṣipɔṭ

retire *vb* (*retreat*) সরে যাওয়া sôre yaôẏa; (*give up one's career*) অবসর নেওয়া ɔbôsɔr neôẏa

retired *adj* অবসর প্রাপ্ত ɔbôsɔr praptô

retreat *vb* হটা hɔṭa, হটানো hɔṭano

retribution *n* প্রতিশোধ prôtiśodh

return *vb* ফেরা phera, ফিরে আসা phire asa, ফিরে যাওয়া phire yaôẏa

reunite *vb* পুনর্মিলিত করা punôr-militô kɔra

reveal *vb* প্রকাশ করা prôkaś kɔra

revelation *n* প্রকাশ prôkaś

revenge *n* প্রতিশোধ prôtiśodh

revenue *n* খাজনা khajna, তহসিল tɔhôsil

reverse *vb* উলটানো ulṭano, পালটানো palṭano; *adj* উলটা ulṭa, বিপরীত bipôrīt

revert *vb* প্রত্যাবর্তন করা prôtyæbɔrtôn kɔra

review *n* (*investigation*) সমীক্ষা sômīkṣa; (*reconsideration*) পুনর্বিচার punôrbicar; *vb* সমালোচনা করা sɔmalocôna kɔra

revise *vb* সংশোধন করা sɔṁśodhôn kɔra

revive *vb* বাঁচানো bācano

revocation *n* সংহরণ sɔṁhɔrôṇ

revoke *vb* বাতিল করা batil kɔra

revolt *vb* বিদ্রোহ করা bidrohô kɔra; *n* বিদ্রোহ bidrohô

revolution *n* (*rotation*) আবর্তন abɔrtôn; (*upheaval*) বিপ্লব biplɔb

revolve *vb* ঘোরা ghora, আবর্তিত হওয়া abôrtitô hɔôẏa

reward *n* পুরস্কার purɔskar

rheumatism *n* বাত bat

rhyme *n* ছড়া chɔra, মিত্রাক্ষর mitrakṣɔr

rhythm *n* ছন্দ chɔndô, তাল tal

rib *n* পাঁজর pājôr

ribbon *n* ফিতা phita (*Bd*), ফিতে phite (*WB*)

rice *n* (*paddy*) ধান dhan; (*uncooked grain*) চাল cal, চাউল caul; (*cooked grain*) ভাত bhat

rich *adj* ধনী dhônī

riches *n* ধনসম্পত্তি dhônsɔmpôtti

rickshaw *n* রিকশা rikśa

rid, **get ~ of** *vb* দূরে রাখা dūre rakha, ফেলে দেওয়া phele deôẏa

riddance *n* পরিত্যাগ pôrityæg

riddle *n* ধাঁধা dhādha

ride *vb* চড়া cɔra

ridge *n* শৈলশিরা śoilôśira

ridiculous *adj* হাস্যকর hasyôkɔr

rifle *n* বন্দুক bônduk

right *n* অধিকার ôdhikar; *adj (correct)* ঠিক ṭhik, সঠিক sɔṭhik; *(just)* ন্যায্য nyæyyô *(pron* næjjo); *(opposite of left)* ডান ḍan, ডাইন ḍain; *adv* **(to the ~)** ডানে ḍane, ডান–দিকে ḍan–dike

right-handed *adj* ডান হাতের ḍan hater

right-wing *adj* ডানপন্থী ḍanpônthī

rigid *adj* দৃঢ় dṛṛhô *(pron* drirho), শক্ত sɔktô

rim *n* কিনারা kinara, কানা kana

rind *n* খোসা khosa, ছাল chal

ring *n (circle)* বৃত্ত bṛttô; *(piece of jewelry)* আঙটি aṅṭi; *vb* বাজা baja, বাজানো bajano

rinse *vb* ধোয়া dhoŷa

riot *n* গোলমাল golmal, দাঙ্গা daṅga

rip *vb* ছেঁড়া chēṛa

ripe *adj* পাকা paka

rise *vb* ওঠা oṭha

risk *n* ঝুঁকি jhūki

risky *adj* ঝুঁকিপূর্ণ jhūkipūrṇô

ritual *n* নিয়ম niŷôm, রীতি rīti

rival *n* প্রতিদ্বন্দ্বী prôtidvôndvī

rivalry *n* প্রতিদ্বন্দ্বিতা prôtidvôndvita

river *n* নদী nôdī

riverbank *n* নদীর তীর nôdir tīr

road *n* রাস্তা rasta

roar *n* গর্জন gɔrjôn; *vb* গর্জানো gɔrjano

roast *vb* ঝলসানো jhôlsano

rob *vb* চুরি করে নেওয়া curi kôre neoŷa

robber *n* ডাকাত ḍakat

robbery *n* ডাকাতি ḍakati

robe *n* গাউন gaun

robot *n* রোবট robôṭ

robust *adj (of people)* স্বাস্থ্যপূর্ণ svasthyôpūrṇô, *(of things)* মজবুত mɔjbut

rock *n* পাথর pathôr; *vb (swing)* দোলা dola, দোলানো dolano

rocket *n* হাউই haui

rocky *adj* শিলাময় śilamɔŷ, পাথুরে pathure

rod *n* লাঠি laṭhi, দণ্ড dɔṇḍô

rogue *n* বদমায়েশ লোক bɔdmaŷeś lok

role *n* ভূমিকা bhūmika

roll *vb* গড়ানো gɔrano

roll about *vb* গড়াগড়ি করা gɔragôri kɔra

roll up *vb* গুটানো guṭano *(Bd)*, গুটোনো guṭono

romantic *adj (imaginary)* কাল্পনিক kalpônik; *(sentimental)* ভাবালু bhabalu, ভাবপ্রবণ bhabprôbôṇ

roof *n* ছাদ chad

room *n* ঘর ghɔr

roomy *adj* প্রশস্ত prôśɔstô

rooster *n* মোরগ morôg

root *n* শিকড় śikɔr, মূল mūl

rope *n* দড়ি dôri

rosary *n* জপমালা jɔpmala

rose *n* গোলাপ golap

rosy *adj* গোলাপী golapī

rot *vb* পচা pɔca

rotate *vb* আবর্তন করা abɔrtôn kɔra, ঘোরা ghora

rotation *n* আবর্তন abɔrtôn

rotten *adj* পচা pɔca

rough *adj (unpolished)* অমার্জিত ɔmarjitô; *(harsh)* রুক্ষ rukṣô, কড়া kɔra; *(unfinished)* একমেটে ekmeṭe

round *adj* গোল gol; *n* গোলক golôk

routine *n* পরম্পরা pɔrômpɔra

row *n (line)* সারি sari; *(argument)*

ঝগড়া jhɔgra; *(disturbance)* হৈচে
hôicôi; *vb* দাঁড় টানা dãṛ ṭana; *adv*
(in a ~) পরপর pɔrpɔr
rowboat *n* দাঁড়ের নৌকা dãṛer nouka
rowdy *adj* হৈচৈপূর্ণ hoicoipūrṇô
royal *adj* রাজকীয় rajôkīŷô
rub *vb* ঘষা ghɔṣa
rubber *n* রবার rɔbar
rubbish *n* বাজে কথা baje kɔtha,
আজেবাজে ajebaje
ruby *n* চুনি cuni
rucksack *n* হ্যাভারস্যাক
hyæbharsyæk
rudder *n* দাঁড় dãṛ
rude *adj* অসভ্য ɔsôbhyô, অভদ্র
ɔbhɔdrô
rude language *n* গালি gali,
গালাগালি galagali
ruffled *adj* এলো elo
rug *n* কম্বল kɔmbôl
ruin *n* সর্বনাশ śɔrbônaś, ধ্বংস
dhvɔṁsô; *vb* নষ্ট করা nɔṣṭô kɔra,
ধ্বংস করা dhvɔṁsô kɔra
rule *n (principle)* নিয়ম niŷôm;
(control) শাসন śason; *vb* শাসন
করা śason kɔra

ruler *n (tool for measuring)* রুলার
rular; *(leader)* শাসক śasôk
rumble *vb* গুড়গুড় শব্দ করা guṛguṛ
śɔbdô kɔra
rumor *n* রটনা rɔṭôna
run *vb* দৌড়ানো dourano *(Bd)*,
দৌড়োনো dourono, ছোটা choṭa
(also ছুটা chuṭa*)*
run away *vb* পালানো palano
running *n* দৌড় douṛ, ছুটাছুটি
chuṭachuṭi
rupture *n* ভঙ্গ bhôṅgô, ফাটল
phaṭôl
rush *n* তাড়া taṛa, তাড়াহুড়া
taṛahuṛa; *vb* তাড়াতাড়ি করা
taṛataṛi kɔra
Russia *n* রুশ দেশ ruś deś
Russian *adj* রুশ ruś
rust *n* মরচে môrce, জং jɔṁ
rustic *adj* গ্রাম্য gramyô, গেঁয়ো gẽŷo
rusty *adj* জং-ধরা jɔṁ-dhɔra,
মরচে-পড়া môrce-pɔṛa
ruthless *adj* নির্মম nirmɔm, কড়া
kɔṛa

S

sabotage *n* অন্তর্ঘাত ɔntôrghat

sack *n* বস্তা bɔsta

sacred *adj* পবিত্র pôbitrô

sacrifice *n* (*offering*) বলি bôli; (*relinquishment*) ত্যাগ tyæg; *vb* (*give up*) ত্যাগ করা tyæg kɔra; (*offer*) বলি দেওয়া bôli deôŷa

sad *adj* মন খারাপ môn kharap, বিষণ্ণ biṣɔṇṇô

sadden *vb* দুঃখ দেওয়া duḥkhô deôŷa

saddle *n* জিন jin

sadness *n* দুঃখ duḥkhô, বিষণ্ণতা biṣɔṇṇôta

safe *adj* (*secure*) নিরাপদ nirapɔd; (*unharmed*) অক্ষত ɔkṣɔtô; *n* সিন্দুক sinduk

safeguard *vb* রক্ষা করা rôkṣa kɔra

safety *n* নিরাপত্তা nirapɔtta

safety pin *n* সেফটিপিন sephṭipin

saffron *n* জাফরান japhran

sage *n* (*wise man*) ঋষি ṛṣi (*pron* rishi)

sago *n* সাগু sagu

sail *n* পাল pal; *vb* পাল তোলা pal tola

sailboat *n* পালতোলা নৌকা paltola nouka, নৌকো nouko

sailor *n* নাবিক nabik

saint *n* সাধু sadhu

salable *adj* বিক্রেয় bikreŷô

salad *n* সালাড salaḍ

salary *n* বেতন betɔn (*Bd*), মাইনে maine (*WB*)

sale *n* বিক্রি bikri

salesman *n* বিক্রেতা bikreta

saliva *n* থুথু thuthu, লালা lala

salt *n* লবণ lɔbôṇ (*Bd*), নুন nun (*WB*)

salty *adj* লবণাক্ত lɔbôṇaktô

salute *n* অভিবাদন ôbhibadôn

salvation *n* (*release*) উদ্ধার, uddhar, মুক্তি mukti; (*nirvana*) মোক্ষ mokṣô

salve *n* মলম mɔlôm

same *adj* একি eki

sample *n* নমুনা nômuna

sanction *n* (*permission*) অনুমতি ônumôti; (*penalty*) শাস্তি śasti

sanctioned *adj* মঞ্জুর môñjur

sanctuary *n* আশ্রয় aśrɔ̂ŷ

sand *n* বালু balu (*Bd*), বালি bali (*WB*)

sandal *n* চটি côṭi, স্যান্ডেল syænḍel

sandal tree *n* গন্ধসার gɔndhôsar, চন্দন গাছ cɔndôn gach

sandalwood *n* চন্দন cɔndôn

sandbank *n* চড়া cɔṛa

sandpaper *n* শিরিস–কাগজ śiris–kagôj

sandwich *n* স্যান্ডউইচ syænḍuic

sane *adj* সুস্থ মনের susthô môner

sanitary *adj* পরিষ্কার pôriṣkar

sanitation *n* স্বাস্থ্যব্যবস্থা svasthôby-bôstha

sanity *n* মতিস্থিরতা môtisthirôta

sap *vb* দুর্বল করা durbɔl kɔra; *n* রস rɔs

sapphire *n* নীলা nīla

sarcasm *n* শ্লেষ śleṣ

saree *n* শাড়ি śari

Satan *n* শয়তান śɔŷtan

satellite *n* উপগ্রহ upôgrôhô

satire *n* ব্যঙ্গ byæṅgô

satisfaction *n* তৃপ্তি tṛpti

satisfactory *adj* যথেষ্ট yɔtheṣṭô

satisfied *adj* সন্তুষ্ট sɔntuṣṭô, তৃপ্ত tṛptô

satisfy *vb* মেটানো meṭano, সন্তুষ্ট করা sɔntuṣṭô kɔra

Saturday *n* শনিবার śônibar

sauce *n* ঝোল jhol

saucepan *n* হাঁড়ি hāṛi

saucer *n* পিরিচ piric

sausage *n* কিমা মাংস kima maṁsô

savage *adj* বন্য bônyô, জঙ্গলী jôṅglī

save *vb (protect)* রক্ষা করা rôkṣa kɔra; *(rescue)* বাঁচানো bācano; *(accumulate)* জমানো jɔmano

savings *n* জমা jɔma

savior *n* পরিত্রাতা pôritrata

savor *vb* স্বাদ নেওয়া svad neoẏa

savory *adj* সুস্বাদু susvadu

saw *n* করাত kɔrat

sawdust *n* কাঠের গুঁড়ো kaṭher gūṛo

say *vb* বলা bɔla, কথা বলা kɔtha bɔla

saying *n (pronouncement)* উক্তি ukti; *(proverb)* প্রবাদ prôbad

scab *n* মামড়ি mamṛi

scabies *n* পাঁচড়া pācṛa

scaffold *n* ভারা bhara

scale *n* মাপনী mapônī

scan *vb* খুঁটিয়ে দেখা khūṭiẏe dekha

scandal *n* কলঙ্ক kɔlôṅkô

scandalous *adj* কলঙ্কময় kɔlôṅkômɔẏ

scar *n (mark)* দাগ dag, *(wound)* ক্ষতিচিহ্ন kṣôticihnô *(pron* khoticinho)

scarce *adj* কম kɔm, অপ্রচুর ɔprôcur

scare *vb* ভয় দেখানো bhɔẏ dekhano

scarf *n* ওড়না ɔrna

scarlet *adj* টকটকে লাল ṭɔkṭɔke lal, কস্তা kɔsta

scatter *vb* ছড়ানো chɔrano

scene *n (venue)* ঘটনাস্থল ghɔṭô-nasthɔl; *(part of a play)* দৃশ্য dṛśyô

scenery *n* দৃশ্য dṛśyô

scent *n* গন্ধ gɔndhô, ঘ্রাণ ghran

schedule *n (arrangement)* ব্যবস্থা bybôstha; *(timetable)* অনুসূচি ônusūci

scheme *n (system)* পদ্ধতি pɔddhôti; *(plot)* ফন্দি phôndi

scholar *n* পণ্ডিত pôṇḍit

scholarship *n (learning)* পাণ্ডিত্য paṇḍityô; *(grant)* ছাত্রবৃত্তি chatrôbṛtti

school *n* স্কুল skul, ইস্কুল iskul, বিদ্যালয় bidyalɔẏ

schoolchild *n* ইস্কুলের বাচ্চা iskuler bacca

schoolmate *n* সতীর্থ sɔtīrthô

schoolteacher *n* শিক্ষক śikṣɔk *(m)*, শিক্ষিকা śikṣika *(f)*

science *n* বিজ্ঞান bijñan

scientific *adj* বৈজ্ঞানিক boijñanik

scientist *n* বিজ্ঞানী bijñanī

scissors *n* কেচি keci *(Bd)*, কাঁচি kāci *(WB)*

scold *vb* বকা bɔka, বকুনি দেওয়া bôkuni deoẏa

scope *n (range)* পাল্লা palla; *(reach)* নাগাল nagal; *(extent)* প্রসার prôsar

score *n (mark)* দাগ dag; *(musical notation)* স্বরগ্রাম svɔrôgram; *(result)* ফল phɔl; *(record)* হিসাব hisab

scorn *n* অবজ্ঞা ɔbôjña

scorpion *n* কাঁকড়াবিছা kākṛabicha *(Bd)*, কাঁকড়াবিছে kākṛabiche

scour *vb* মাজা maja

scout *vb* তল্লাশ করা tɔllaś kɔra

scrap *n (small piece)* টুকরা ṭukra *(Bd)*, টুকরো ṭukro *(WB)*; *(fight)* ধস্তাধস্তি dhɔstadhôsti

scrape *vb (scour)* ঘষটানো ghɔṣṭano; *(scratch, comb)* আঁচড়ানো ācṛano

scratch *vb (itch)* চুলকানো culkano; *(erase)* তুলে দেওয়া tule deoẏa

scream *vb* চিৎকার করা citkar kɔra

screen *n (partition)* পর্দা pɔrda, আড়াল aṛal; *(window)* স্ক্রিন skrin

screw *n (tool)* ইস্ক্রুপ iskrup; *(twist)* মোচড় mocôṛ

script *n* লিপি lipi

scripture *n* শাস্ত্র śastrô

scrub *vb* মাজা maja, ঘষা ghɔṣa

scruple *n (conscience)* চেতনা cetôna; *(doubt)* সন্দেহ sɔndehô

scrupulous *adj (very thorough)* পুঙ্খানুপুঙ্খ puṅkhanupuṅkhô; *(conscientious)* বিবেকি bibeki

scrutiny *n* পরীক্ষা pôrīkṣa

scuffle *n* মারামারি maramari

sculptor *n* ভাস্কর bhaskɔr

sculpture *n* খুদাই khudai, খোদাই khodai, ভাস্কর্য bhaskɔryô

scum *n* ফেনা phæna

scythe *n* কাস্তে kaste

sea *n* সাগর sagôr, সমুদ্র sômudrô

seagull *n* গাঙচিল gaṅgôcil

seal *n (animal)* সিল sil; *(stamp)* চিহ্ন cinhô; *vb* এঁটে বন্ধ করা ēṭe bɔndhô kɔra

sealant *n* জতু jôtu

seam *n* সেলাইয়ের জোড় selaiẏer jɔṛ

seaport *n* সাগরের বন্দর sagôrer bɔndôr

search *vb* খোঁজা khõja; *n* অনুসন্ধান ônusɔndhan

seashore *n* সৈকত soikôt

seasickness *n* সমুদ্রপীড়া sômudrôpīṛa

season *n* ঋতু r̥tu, কাল kal

seasonal *adj* কালিক kalik

seat *n* চেয়ার ceẏar, বসার জায়গা bɔsar jaẏga

seatbelt *n* সিট-বেল্ট siṭ-belṭ

seaweed *n* শৈবাল śoibal

seclusion *n* নির্জনতা nirjɔnôta

second *n* সেকেন্ড sekenḍ; *adj* দ্বিতীয় dvitīẏô

second-born *adj* মেজো mejo

secret *n* গুপ্ত guptô, গোপন gopôn

secretary *n* কেরানি kerani

secretly *adv* লুকিয়ে lukiẏe, গোপনে gopône

section *n* অংশ ɔmśô, ভাগ bhag

secular *adj* ঐহিক oihik, লোকায়ত lokaẏɔtô

secure *adj* নিরাপদ nirapɔd

security *n* নিরাপত্তা nirapɔtta

sedate *adj* স্থির sthir

sedative *n* ঘুম পাড়ানি ওষুধ ghum paṛani oṣudh

seduce *vb (instigate)* ফুসলানো phuslano; *(entice)* প্রলোভন দেখানো prôlobhôn dækhano

seduction *n* প্রলোভন prôlobhôn

see *vb* দেখা dækha

seed *n* বিচি bici, বীজ bīj

seek *vb* খোঁজা khõja

seem *vb* মনে হওয়া mône hɔoẏa

seesaw *n* ওঠানামা oṭhanama

segment *n* ভাগ bhag

seize *vb* গ্রাস করা gras kɔra, জাপটানো japṭano

seizure *n (appropriation)* গ্রেপ্তার greptar, গ্রেফতার grephtar; *(convulsion)* খেঁচুনি khẽcuni

seldom *adv* কম kɔm

select *vb* বেছে নেওয়া beche neoŷa, পছন্দ করা pɔchôndô kɔra

selection *n* নির্বাচন nirbacôn

self *n* নিজ nij, নিজে nije

self-confidence *n* আত্মবিশ্বাস atmôbiśvas

self-control *n* আত্মশাসন atmôśasôn

self-defense *n* আত্মরক্ষা atmôrôkṣa

selfish *adj* স্বার্থপর svarthôpɔr

selfishness *n* স্বার্থ svarthô, স্বার্থপরতা svarthôpɔrôta

selfless *adj* ত্যাগী tyægī

self-respect *n* আত্মসম্মান atmôsɔmman

sell *vb* বেচা bæca, বিক্রি করা bikri kɔra

seller *n* ফেরিওয়ালা pherioŷala, বিক্রেতা bikreta

semen *n* শুক্র śukrô, বীর্য bīryô

semolina *n* সুজি suji

senate *n* সেনেট seneṭ

senator *n* সভ্য sôbhyô

send *vb* পাঠানো paṭhano

senior *n* বড় bɔrô

sensation *n* সংবেদন sɔmbedôn

sense *n* (*consciousness*) চেতনা cetôna; (*meaning*) অর্থ ɔrthô, মানে mane; (*reason*) যুক্তি yukti

senseless *adj* অচেতন ɔcetôn, অজ্ঞান ɔjñan (*pron* ɔggæn)

sensible *adj* যুক্তিবাদী yuktibadī

sensitive *adj* সুবেদী subedī

sentence *n* (*part of speech*) বাক্য bakyô; (*punishment*) শাস্তি śasti

sentiment *n* অনুভূতি ônubhūti

sentimental *adj* ভাবপ্রবণ bhabprôbôṇ

separate *adj* আলাদা alada, বিছিন্ন bichinnô; *vb* আলাদা করা alada kɔra, বিছিন্ন হওয়া bichinnô hɔɔŷa

separation *n* বিরহ birɔhô, বিয়োগ biŷog, বিচ্ছেদ bicched

September *n* সেপ্টেম্বর মাস septembɔr mas

septic *adj* বিষাক্ত biṣaktô

sequel *n* অনুগামী ônugamī

sequence *n* অনুক্রম ônukrôm

sequin *n* চুমকি cumki

sergeant *n* পুলিস-সার্জেন্ট pulis-sarjenṭ

serial *adj* পরম্পর pɔrômpɔr

serial order *n* পর্যায় pôryaŷ

series *n* সারি sari, মালা mala

serious *adj* (*solemn*) গম্ভীর gômbhīr; (*important*) গুরুত্বপূর্ণ gurutvôpūrṇô

sermon *n* ধর্মের বক্তৃতা dhɔrmer bôktr̥ta

serum *n* সিরাম siram

servant *n* চাকর cakôr

serve *vb* সেবা করা seba kɔra

service *n* সেবা seba

session *n* সত্র sɔtrô

set *vb* (*put*) রাখা rakha, বসানো bɔsano; (*fix*) ঠিক করা ṭhik kɔra; (*congeal*) জমাট হওয়া jɔmaṭ hɔɔŷa; (*go down*) নামা nama, অস্ত যাওয়া ɔstô yaoŷa

set off *vb* রওনা হওয়া rɔona hɔɔŷa

settle *vb* (*conclude*) মেটানো meṭano, সমাধান করা sɔmadhan kɔra; (*become fixed*) বসা bɔsa, স্থির হওয়া sthir hɔɔŷa

settlement *n* (*habitation*) লোকালয় lokalɔŷ; (*compromise*) রফা rɔpha, মীমাংসা mīmamsa

seven *num* সাত sat

seventeen *num* সতেরো sɔterô

seventh *num* সপ্তম sɔptôm

seventy *num* সত্তর sôttôr

several *adj* কয়েক kɔŷek

severe *adj (harsh)* কড়া kɔṛa, কঠোর kɔthor; *(intense)* তীব্র tībrô; *(powerful)* দুরন্ত durɔntô

sew *vb* সেলাই করা selai kɔra

sewer *n* নর্দমা nɔrdôma

sewing *n* সেলাই selai

sewing machine *n* সেলাইয়ের কল selaiŷer kɔl

sex *n (gender)* লিঙ্গ liṅgô; *(sexual activity)* যৌন মিলন younô milôn

sexual *adj* যৌন younô

shabby *adj* জীর্ণ jīrṇô

shade *n* ছায়া chaŷa

shadow *n* ছায়া chaŷa

shady *adj* ছায়াময় chaŷamɔŷ

shaft *n (rod, pole)* দণ্ড dɔṇḍô; *(quarry)* খনি khɔni; *(handle)* হাতল hatôl

shaggy *adj (uneven)* বন্ধুর bôndhur; *(hairy)* লোমশ lomôś

shake *vb* ঝাঁকা jhāka, ঝাঁকানো jhākano

shallow *adj* অগভীর ɔgôbhīr

sham *n* ফাঁকি phāki, ভান bhan

shame *n* লজ্জা lɔjja, শরম śɔrôm

shameless *adj* বেহায়া behaŷa

shampoo *n* স্যাম্পু syæmpu

shape *n* রূপ rūp, আকার akar, ঢক ḍhɔk; *vb* আকার দেওয়া akar deoŷa

share *vb* ভাগ করা bhag kɔra; *n* অংশ ɔṁśô, ভাগ bhag

shareholder *n* অংশীদার ôṁśīdar

shark *n* হাঙ্গর haṅgôr

sharp *adj* ধারালো dharalo

sharpen *vb* ধার দেওয়া dhar deoŷa

shave *vb* কামানো kamano

shaven *adj* নেড়া neṛa

shawl *n* শাল śal

she *pr* সে se, তিনি tini

sheaf *n* আঁটি āṭi, তাড়া taṛa

shear *vb* কাটা kaṭa

shed *vb* খসানো khɔsano; *n* গুদাম gudam

sheep *n* ভেড়া bheṛa

sheer *adj (translucent)* স্বচ্ছ svɔcchô; *(pure)* খাঁটি khāṭi

sheet *n* চাদর cadôr

sheikh *n* শেখ śekh

shelf *n* তাক tak

shell *n* খোলা khola

shellfish *n* খোলাওয়ালা মাছ kho-laoŷala mach

shelter *n* আশ্রয় aśrɔŷ

shepherd *n* মেষপালক meṣpalôk

shield *n* ঢাল ḍhal

shift *vb (move aside)* সরা sɔra; *(change)* বদলানো bɔdlano; *n* কাজের সময় kajer sômôŷ

shifty *adj* ছলপূর্ণ chɔlpūrṇô

shine *vb* আলো দেওয়া alo deoŷa; *n* আভা abha

shiny *adj* উজ্জ্বল ujjvɔl

ship *n* জাহাজ jahaj

shipwreck *n* জাহাজডুবি jahajḍubi

shirt *n* জামা jama, সার্ট sarṭ

shiver *vb* কাঁপা kāpa

shock *n* আঘাত aghat, দাগা daga

shoe *n* জুতা juta *(Bd)*, জুতো juto *(WB)*

shoelace *n* ফিতা phita *(Bd)*, ফিতে phite *(WB)*

shoot *vb* গুলি করা guli kɔra

shop *n* দোকান dokan; *vb* কেনাকাটা করা kenakaṭa kɔra

shopkeeper *n* দোকানদার dokandar

shopping *n* কেনা-কাটা kenakaṭa

shore *n* তীর tīr

short *adj* খাটো khaṭo, *(for people)* ছোট chotô, বেঁটে bēṭe

shortage *n* অভাব ɔbhab

shortcoming *n* ত্রুটি truṭi

shorten *vb* সংক্ষিপ্ত করা sɔṁkṣiptô kɔra

shortly *adv* শিগগির siggir, কিছুক্ষণের মধ্যে kichukṣɔṇer môdhye

shorts *n* হাফ প্যান্ট haph pyænṭ

should *vb* উচিত ucit

shoulder *n* কাঁধ kādh

shout *vb* চেঁচানো cēcano, চিৎকার করা ciṭkar kɔra

shove *vb* ঠেলা ṭhæla

shovel *n* বেলচা belca

show *vb* দেখানো dækhano; *n* প্রদর্শন prôdɔrśôn

show off *vb* ফুটানি করা phuṭani kɔra

shower *n* ফোয়ারা phoŷara

shrewd *adj* চতুর côtur

shrimp *n* চিংড়ি মাছ cimṛi mach

shrine *n* তীর্থস্থান tīrthôsthan

shrink *vb* সঙ্কুচিত হওয়া sɔṅkucit hɔŷa

shuffle *vb* *(mix cards)* তাস মিশিয়ে দেওয়া tas miśiŷe deoŷa

shut *vb* বন্ধ করা bɔndhô kɔra; *adj* বন্ধ bɔndhô

shutter *n* খড়খড়ি khɔrkhôṛi

shuttle *n* মাকু maku

shy *adj* লাজুক lajuk, ভীরু bhīru

sick *adj* অসুস্থ ɔsusthô

sickness *n* অসুখ ɔsukh

side *n* পাশ paś

side effect *n* প্রতিক্রিয়া prôtikriŷa

sidewalk *n* ফুটপাথ phuṭpath

sideways *adv* পাশদিকে paśdike

sieve *n* ছাঁকনি chākni

sift *vb* ছাঁকা chāka

sigh *n* দীর্ঘশ্বাস dīrghôśvas; *vb* দীর্ঘশ্বাস ফেলা dīrghôśvas phæla

sight *n* *(vision)* দৃষ্টি dṛṣṭi; *(attention)* নজর nɔjôr

sign *vb* সই করা sôi kɔra; *n* চিহ্ন cihnô *(pron* cinho)

sign language *n* আকারিঙ্গিত akariṅgit

signal *n* ইঙ্গিত iṅgit

signature *n* সই sôi

significance *n* *(importance)* গুরুত্ব gurutvô; *(meaning)* অর্থ ɔrthô, পদার্থ pɔdarthô

signify *vb* *(mean)* মানে হওয়া mane hɔŷa; *(indicate)* নিদর্শন হওয়া nidɔrśôn hɔŷa

silence *n* নীরবতা nīrɔbôta

silent *adj* নীরব nīrɔb, চুপচাপ cupcap

silk *n* রেশম reśɔm

silly *adj* *(stupid)* বোকা boka; *(naughty)* দুষ্টু duṣṭu, পাজি paji

silver *n* রূপা rupa *(Bd)*, রূপো rūpo *(WB)*

similar *adj* প্রায় একই praŷ eki, একই রকম eki rɔkôm

similarity *n* *(comparability)* তুল্যতা tulyôta; *(likeness)* আদল adôl

simmer *vb* টগবগ করা ṭɔgbɔg kɔra

simple *adj* সরল sɔrôl, সহজ sɔhôj

simplicity *n* সরলতা sɔrôlɔta

simply *adv* সহজে sɔhôje

simulate *vb* ভান করা bhan kɔra

simulation *n* ভান bhan

simultaneous *adj* একই সঙ্গে eki

sɔ̃ge, একই সময়ে eki sômôye

sin *n* পাপ pap

since *adv* অবধি ɔbôdhi; *pp* থেকে theke

sincere *adj* আন্তরিক antôrik, সত্যিকার sôtyikar

sincerity *n* সততা sɔtôta

sinew *n* পেশি peśi

sing *vb* গাওয়া gaoẏa

singer *n* গায়ক gaẏôk *(m)* গায়িকা gaẏika *(f)*

single *adj (one)* এক æk; *(unmarried)* অবিবাহিত ɔbibahitô

sinister *adj* অশুভ ɔśubhô

sink *vb* ডোবা ḍoba, ডোবানো ḍobano

sip *vb* চুমুক দেওয়া cumuk deoẏa

Sir *n* সার sar

sister *n (older)* দিদি didi *(Hindu)*, আপা apa *(Muslim)*; *(younger)* বোন bon

sister-in-law *n* ননদ nɔnôd, শালি śali

sit *vb* বসা bɔsa

site *n* স্থান sthan

situation *n* অবস্থা ɔbôstha, দশা dɔśa

six *num* ছয় chɔẏ

sixteen *num* ষোলো ṣolo

sixth *num* ষষ্ঠ ṣɔṣṭhô

sixty *num* ষাট ṣaṭ

size *n* মাপ map, সাইজ saij

skate *n* স্কেইট skeiṭ

skeleton *n* কঙ্কাল kɔṅkal

sketch *n* নকশা nɔkśa, খসড়া khɔsṛa

skid *vb* হড়কানো hɔṛkano

skill *n* দক্ষতা dôkṣôta

skillful *adj* দক্ষ dôkṣô

skim *vb* চোখ বুলানো cokh bulano

skin *n* চামড়া camṛa

skin rash *n* ছুলি chuli

skinny *adj* রোগা roga

skip *vb* লাফালাফি করা laphalaphi kɔra

skirt *n* স্কার্ট skarṭ

skull *n* খুলি khuli

sky *n* আকাশ akaś

slack *adj* মন্থর mɔnthôr

slander *vb* পরচর্চা pɔrôcɔrca

slang *n* অপভাষা ɔpôbhaṣa

slant *n* টাল ṭal; *vb* হেলানো helano

slanting *adj* তির্যক tiryɔk

slap *n* থাপ্পড় thappôr, চড় cɔṛ

slash *vb* কাটা kaṭa

slate *n* স্লেট পাথর sleṭ pathôr

slave *n* গোলাম golam

slavery *n* গোলামি golami

slay *vb* হত্যা করা hɔtya kɔra

sleep *vb* ঘুমানো ghumano; *n* ঘুম ghum, নিদ্রা nidra

sleepy *adj* নিদ্রালু nidralu, ক্লান্ত klantô

sleeve *n* জামার হাতা jamar hata

slender *adj* চিকন cikɔn, লিকলিকে liklike

slice *n* চাকলা cakla, ফালি phali

slide *vb* পিছলানো pichlano *(Bd)*, পেছলোনো pechlono *(WB)*

slight *adj* তুচ্ছ tucchô, সামান্য samanyô

slim *adj* পাতলা patla, রোগা roga

slimy *adj* চটচটে cɔṭcɔṭe

sling *n (catapult)* গুলতি gulti; *vb (throw)* ফেলা phæla, নিক্ষেপ করা nikṣep kɔra

slip *n (mistake)* ভুল bhul; *vb (lose one's footing)* হড়কানো hɔṛkano

slippery *adj* পিছলা pichla

slogan *n* স্লোগান slogan

slope *n* ঢল ḍhɔl

sloppy *adj (disorderly)* যেমন তেমন করে yæmôn tæmôn kôre

slot *n* নির্দিষ্ট জায়গা nirdiṣṭô jaŷga

slow *adj* ধীরে dhīre, মন্থর mɔnthôr

slowly *adv* আস্তে আস্তে aste aste

slug *n* শামুক śamuk

sluggish *adj* মন্থর mɔnthôr, অলস ɔlôs

sluice *n* জলকপাট jɔlkɔpaṭ

slum *n* বস্তি bôsti

small *adj (little)* ছোট chɔṭô; *(inferior)* পাতি pati; *(trivial)* তুচ্ছ tucchô, ক্ষুদ্র kṣudrô

smart *adj (clever)* চালাক calak; *(neat, trim)* ফিটফাট phiṭphaṭ

smash *vb* ধ্বংস করা dhvɔṁsô kɔra

smell *n* গন্ধ gɔndhô, ঘ্রাণ ghraṇ; *vb* গন্ধ পাওয়া gɔndhô paôŷa

smile *vb* হাসা hasa; *n* হাসি hasi

smith *n* সেকরা sekra

smog *n* ধোঁয়াশা dhõŷaśa

smoke *n* ধুম dhum, ধোঁয়া dhõŷa

smoky *adj* ধোঁয়াটে dhõŷaṭe

smooth *adj* সুস্থু susthu

smuggle *vb* চোরাই-চালান করা corai-calan kɔra

smuggling *n* চোরা আমদানি রপ্তানি cora amdani rɔptani

snack *n* জলখাবার jɔlkhabar, টিফিন ṭiphin

snag *n* বাধা badha

snail *n* শামুক śamuk

snake *n* সাপ sap

snake bean *n* পটোল pɔṭol

snake gourd *n* চিচিঙ্গা ciciṅga *(pron cicingga)*

snapshot *n* ফোটো phoṭo

snarl *n* রুক্ষ শব্দ rukṣô śɔbdô

snatch *vb* কাড়া kaṛa

sneak *vb* গুপ্তভাবে চলা guptôbhabe cɔla

sneaky *adj* প্রচ্ছন্ন prôchɔnnô

sneeze *vb* হাঁচি দেওয়া hãci deôŷa

snob *n* চালবাজ calbaj

snobbery *n* চালবাজি calbaji

snobbish *adj* চালবাজ calbaj

snore *vb* নাক ডাকা nak ḍaka

snort *vb* চিহিঁহি করা cīhĩhi kɔra

snout *n* তুণ্ড tuṇḍô

snow *n* তুষার tuṣar, বরফ bɔrôph; *vb* বরফ পড়া bɔrôph pɔṛa

snowflake *n* বরফের গুঁড়ি bɔrôpher gũṛi

snowstorm *n* তুষারঝড় tuṣarjhɔṛ

snub *vb* ধমক দেওয়া dhɔmôk deôŷa

so *adv (like this)* তাই tai; *(such)* এমন æmôn; *conj (therefore)* কাজেই kajei, সুতরাং sutôraṁ

so much *adv* এত ætô

soak *vb* ভেজানো bhejano

soap *n* সাবান saban

soar *vb (rise high)* উচ্চে ওড়া ucce oṛa, উঁচুতে ওড়া

sob *vb* ফুপানো phūpanô *(Bd)*, ফোঁপোনো phõpono *(WB)*

sociable *adj* মিশুক miśuk

social *adj (of society)* সামাজিক samajik; *(of the people)* লৌকিক loukik

socialism *n* সমাজতন্ত্র sɔmajtɔntrô

society *n* সমাজ sɔmaj

sock *n* মোজা moja

socket *n* কোটর kɔṭôr

soda *n* সোডা soḍa

sofa *n* কেদারা kedara

soft *adj (pliant)* নরম nɔrôm; *(gentle)* কোমল komôl

soil *n* মাটি maṭi

solace *n* সান্ত্বনা santvôna

solar *adj* সৌর sourô

soldier *n* সৈনিক soinik, সেনা sena

sole *n* (of the foot) পদতল pɔdôtɔl; *adj* (only) একমাত্র ækmatrô

solemn *adj* গম্ভীর gômbhīr

solid *adj* (compact) ঘন ghɔn

solidified *adj* গাঢ় gaṛhô

solitary *adj* একা æka, নিঃসঙ্গ niḥsɔṅgô

solitude *n* নির্জনতা nirjɔnôta

solution *n* (conclusion) সমাধান sɔmadhan; (reconciliation) মীমাংসা mīmamsa

solve *vb* সমাধান করা sɔmadhan kɔra

solvent *n* দ্রাবক drabôk

somber *adj* গম্ভীর gômbhīr

some *adj* কিছু kichu

somebody *n* কেউ keu

somehow *adv* যে কোনও ভাবে ye kono bhabe

someone *n* কেউ keu

something *n* কিছু kichu

sometime *adv* একদা ækôda, এক সময়ে æk sɔmɔŷe

sometimes *adv* সময় সময় sômôŷ sômôŷ, মাঝে মাঝে majhe majhe

somewhat *adv* কিছুটা kichuṭa

somewhere *adv* কোথাও kothao

son *n* পুত্র putrô, ছেলে chele, সন্তান sɔntan

song *n* গান gan

son-in-law *n* জামাই jamai

soon *adv* একটু পরে ekṭu pɔre

soot *n* ঝুল jhul

sore *adj* যন্ত্রণাপূর্ণ yɔntrônapūrṇô; *n* ঘা gha

sorrow *n* দুঃখ duḥkhô

sorry *adj* দুঃখিত duḥkhitô

sort *vb* গুছানো guchano (Bd), গুছোনো guchono (WB); *n* রকম rɔkôm, প্রকার prôkar

soul *n* আত্মা atma (pron atta)

sound *n* (noise) আওয়াজ aoŷaj, শব্দ śɔbdô; (air-vibration) ধ্বনি dhvôni; *adj* সুস্থ susthô

soup *n* সুপ sup

sour *adj* টক ṭɔk

source *n* (origin) উৎপত্তি utpôtti, উদ্ভব udbhɔb; (spring) নির্ঝর nirjhɔr

south *n* দক্ষিণ dôkṣiṇ

souvenir *n* স্মৃতিচিহ্ন smṛticihnô (pron sriticinho)

sovereign *adj* পরম pɔrôm

sow *vb* বীজ বোনা bīj bona

sowing *n* বপন bɔpôn

soybean *n* সয়াবীন sɔŷabīn

space *n* জায়গা jaŷga, স্থান sthan

spacious *adj* দরাজ dɔraj

spade *n* কোদাল kodal

spare *adj* বাড়তি barti

spark *n* স্ফুলিঙ্গ sphuliṅgô

sparkle *vb* জ্বলজ্বল করা jvɔljvɔl kɔra

sparkling *adj* জ্বলজ্বল jvɔljvɔl, ঝকঝক jhɔkjhɔk

sparrow *n* চড়াই cɔrai (Bd), চড়ুই cɔrui

sparse *adj* বিরল birôl

spasm *n* খেঁচুনি khẽcuni, খিঁচুনি khĩcuni

speak *vb* (utter) বলা bɔla; (converse) কথা বলা kɔtha bɔla

speaker *n* বক্তা bɔkta

special *adj* বিশেষ biśeṣ

specialist *n* বিশেষজ্ঞ biśeṣjɔnô

specific *adj* বিশিষ্ট biśiṣṭô

specify *vb* নির্ধারণ করা nirdharôṇ kɔra

specimen *n* নমুনা nômuna

spectator *n* দর্শক dɔrśôk

speech *n* (utterance) বচন bɔcon, উক্তি ukti; (lecture) বক্তৃতা bôktr̥ta

speed *n* (quickness) দ্রুততা drutôta; (velocity) বেগ beg

speedometer *n* দ্রুতিমাপক drutimapôk

spell *n* জাদুমন্ত্র jadumɔntrô; *vb* বানান করা banan kɔra

spelling *n* বানান banan

spend *vb* (money) খরচ করা khɔrôc kɔra; (time) সময় কাটানো sômɔ̂ŷ kaṭano

sphere *n* (globe) গোলক golôk; (domain) ক্ষেত্র kṣetrô, এলাকা elaka

spic and span *adj* ফিটফাট phiṭphaṭ

spice *n* মসলা mɔsla

spicy *adj* ঝাল jhal

spider *n* মাকড়সা makôrsa

spill *vb* চলকিয়ে ফেলা côlkiŷe phæla

spin *vb* (twist into thread) সুতি কাটা suta kaṭa; (turn) পাক দেওয়া pak deoŷa

spinach *n* শাক śak

spine *n* মেরুদণ্ড merudɔṇḍô

spiral *n* পেঁচ pêc

spire *n* চূড়া cūṛa (Bd), চূড়ো cūṛo (WB)

spirit *n* (energy) তেজ tej, সাহস sahôs; (ghost) ভূত bhūt

spiritual *adj* আধ্যাত্মিক adhyatmik

spit *vb* থুতু ফেলা thutu phæla

spite *n* আক্রোশ akroś, হিংসা hiṃsa; *conj* (in ~ of) সত্ত্বেও sɔttveo

splash *vb* ছিটকানো chiṭkano

splint *n* চটা cɔṭa

splinter *n* চোকলা cokla

split *vb* (separate) বিছিন্ন করা bichinnô kɔra; (cut) ফালি করা phali kɔra; (sever) চেরা cera, চিরা cira

spoil *vb* (destroy, corrupt) নষ্ট করা nɔṣṭô kɔra; (over-indulge) প্রশ্রয় দেওয়া prôśrɔŷ deoŷa

spoke *n* চাকার পাকি cakar paki; *v* see speak

sponge *n* স্পঞ্জ spɔñj

sponsor *n* (donor) দাতা data; (guarantor) জামিন jamin

spontaneous *adj* স্বতঃস্ফূর্ত svɔtɔ̂sphūrtô

spontaneously *adv* এমনি emni

spool *n* কাটিম kaṭim

spoon *n* চামচ camôc

sport *n* খেলাধুলা khæladhula (Bd), খেলাধুলো khæladhulo (WB)

sportsman *n* খেলোয়াড় khæloŷaṛ

spot *n* দাগ dag

spotless *adj* নির্মল nirmɔl

spout *n* নল nɔl

sprain *vb* মচকানো mɔckano, মচকে যাওয়া môcke yaoŷa

spray *n* জল সেচন jɔl secɔn

spread *vb* পাতা pata

spring *vb* লাফিয়ে ওঠা laphiŷe oṭha; *n* (fountain) ঝরনা jhɔrna; (season) বসন্তকাল bɔsôntôkal; (elasticity) স্থিতিস্থাপকতা sthitisthapôkôta

sprinkle *vb* ছিটিয়ে দেওয়া chiṭiŷe deoŷa

sprint *vb* দৌড়ানো douṛano

sprout *vb* গজানো gɔjano; *n* অঙ্কুর ônkur

spur *n* প্রেরণা prerôṇa

spy *n* গুপ্তচর guptôcɔr

square *n* বর্গক্ষেত্র bɔrgôkṣetrô

squash *vb* পিষা piṣa, পেষা peṣa

squeeze *vb* চাপ দেওয়া cap deôẏa, টিপা ṭipa

squirrel *n* কাঠবিড়ালি kaṭhbiṛali

stab *vb* ছোরা মারা chora mara

stable *n* আস্তাবল astabɔl; *adj* দৃঢ় dṛṛho (*pron* driṛho), স্থায়ী sthaẏī

stadium *n* স্টেডিয়াম sṭeḍiẏam

staff *n* লাঠি laṭhi

stage *n* মঞ্চ mɔñcô

stagger *vb* টলা ṭɔla, টলটলানো ṭɔlṭɔlano

stain *n* দাগ dag, ছোপ chop

stair *n* সিঁড়ি siṛi

staircase *n* সোপান sopan

stake *n* (*wager*) পণ pɔṇ; (*pole*) গুঁজি gūji

stale *adj* বাসি basi

stalk *n* বোঁটা bôṭa, বৃন্ত bṛntô (*pron* brinto)

stall *vb* থামানো thamano

stammer *vb* তোতলানো totlano; *n* তোতলামি totlami

stamp *vb* (*kick underfoot*) পদাঘাত করা pɔdaghat kɔra; (*mark, impress*) চাপ দেওয়া cap deôẏa; *n* টিকিট ṭikiṭ

stand *vb* (*be on one's feet*) দাঁড়ানো dāṛano; (*remain firm*) বলবৎ থাকা bɔlbɔt thaka; (*tolerate*) সহ্য করা sôhyô kɔra (*pron* shojjho kɔra)

stand by *vb* সমর্থন করা sɔmɔrthɔn kɔra

stand down *vb* পরিত্যাগ করা pôrityæg kɔra

stand out *vb* বিশিষ্ট হওয়া biśiṣṭô hɔôẏa

stand up to *vb* প্রতিরক্ষা করা prôtirɔkṣa kɔra

standard *n* আদর্শ adɔrśô; *adj* সাধারণ sadharôṇ

standing *n* গুরুত্ব gurutvô

stanza *n* স্তবক stɔbôk

staple *adj* প্রধান prôdhan

star *n* তারা tara

starboard *n* জাহাজের ডানদিকে jahajer ḍandike

starch *n* মাড় maṛ

stare *vb* তাকানো takano, চাওয়া caôẏa

starfish *n* তারামাছ taramach

starfruit *n* কামরাঙা kamraṅa

starry *adj* তারকাময় tarôkamɔẏ

start *n* (*beginning*) আরম্ভ arômbhô, শুরু śuru; (*introduction*) অনুবন্ধ ônubɔndhô; *vb* লাগা laga

startle *vb* চমকানো cɔmkano

starvation *n* অনাহার ɔnahar

starve *vb* অনাহারে থাকা ɔnahare thaka

state *n* (*condition*) অবস্থা ɔbôstha; (*circumstance*) হালচাল halcal; (*nation*) রাজ্য rajyô; *vb* ঘোষণা করা ghoṣôṇa kɔra

statement *n* উক্তি ukti

statesman *n* রাজশাসক rajyôśasôk

station *n* স্টেশন sṭeśôn, ইস্টেশন isṭeśôn

stationary *adj* নিশ্চল niścɔl, স্থির sthir

stationery *n* লেখার কাগজ lekhar kagôj

statistical *adj* পরিসাংখ্যিক pôrisamkhyik

statistics *n* পরিসংখ্যান pôrisɔmkhyan

statue *n* মূর্তি mūrti

status *n* প্রতিষ্ঠা prôtiṣṭha, অবস্থা ɔbôstha

status quo *n* বর্তমান অবস্থা bɔrtô-man ɔbôstha

statute *n* সংবিধি sɔmbidhi

statutory *adj* সংবিধিবদ্ধ sɔmbidhibɔddhô

stave *n* শ্লোক ślok, গানের স্তবক ganer stɔbôk

stay *vb* থাকা thaka, রওয়া rɔoýa

steadfast *adj* পলকহীন pɔlôkhīn

steady *adj* স্থায়ী sthaýī, অটল ɔtɔl

steak *n* মাংসের ফালি maṁser phali

steal *vb* চুরি করা curi kɔra

stealthily *adv* বেমালুম bemalum

steam *n* বাষ্প baṣpô

steamship *n* বাষ্পচালিত জাহাজ baṣpôcalitô jahaj

steel *n* ইস্পাত ispat

steep *adj* খাড়া khaṛa

steer *vb* চালানো calano, হাল ধরা hal dhɔra; *n* ষাঁড় ṣāṛ

steering-wheel *n* চালানোর চাকা calanor caka

stem *n* কাণ্ড kaṇdô

step *n* পদ pɔd

stepfather *n* সৎবাপ sɔtbap, সৎবাবা sɔtbaba

stepmother *n* সৎমা sɔtma

stereotype *n* ছাঁচ chāc

sterile *adj* (*aseptic*) জীবাণুমুক্ত jībaṇumuktô; (*infertile*) নিষ্ফল niṣphɔl

sterilize *vb* জীবাণুমুক্ত করা jībaṇumuktô kɔra

stern *adj* কড়া kɔra

stethoscope *n* স্টেথোস্কোপ sṭethoskop

stew *n* সিদ্ধ মাংস siddhô maṁsô

steward *n* (*manager*) দেওয়ান deoŷan; (*flight attendant*) বিমানের সেবক bimaner sebɔk (*m*) বিমানের সেবিকা bimaner sebika (*f*)

stick *n* লাঠি lathi; *vb* লাগা laga, আটকানো aṭkano

sticky *adj* চিটা ciṭa (*Bd*) চিটে ciṭe (*WB*), আঠাল aṭhalô

stiff *adj* (*hard*) শক্ত śɔktô; (*severe*) কড়া kɔra; (*formal*) কঠিন kôthin

stiffen *vb* শক্ত করা śɔktô kɔra

stigma *n* কলঙ্ক kɔlôṅkô

still *adj* নীরব nīrôb, শান্ত śantô; *adv* এখনো ækhôno

stillness *n* নিস্তব্ধতা nistɔbdhôta

stimulant *n* উদ্দীপক uddīpɔk

stimulate *vb* উদ্দীপিত করা uddīpitô kɔra

sting *n* হুল hul; *vb* হুল ফোটানো hul phoṭano

stink *n* দুর্গন্ধ durgɔndhô

stipulation *n* শর্ত śɔrtô

stir *vb* (*move*) নড়া nɔra, নড়াচড়া করা nɔracɔra kɔra; (*cause to move*) নাড়া nara

stitch *n* (*in sewing*) সুচের ফোঁড় sucer phõṛ; (*sudden pain*) খিল-ধরা ব্যথা khil-dhɔra bytha

stock *n* (*stored goods*) সম্ভার sɔmbhar; (*roots, family*) বংশ bɔṁśô; (*investment*) ফটকা phɔṭka; (*livestock*) পালিত জীবজন্তু palitô jībjôntu

stockbroker *n* দালাল dalal

stocking *n* মোজা moja

stomach *n* পেট peṭ

stomachache *n* পেটের ব্যথা peṭer bytha

stone n (rock) পাথর pathôr; (pip) আঁটি āṭi, বীচি bīci; (jewel) মণি môṇi

stool n টুল ṭul, পিঁড়ি pīṛi

stop vb (cease) থামা thama; (cause to cease) থামানো thamano

storage n সঞ্চয় sɔñcɔy̆

store vb জমানো jɔmano; n দোকান dokan

storeroom n গুদাম gudam

stork n সারস sarôs

storm n ঝড় jhɔr, তুফান tuphan

stormy adj ঝোড়ো jhoṛô

story n (tale) গল্প gɔlpô, কাহিনী kahinī; (floor) তলা tɔla

stout adj মোটা moṭa

stove n চুলা cula (Bd), চুলো culo (WB)

straight adj (ahead) সোজা soja; (direct) সরাসরি sɔrasôri; (honest) সরল sɔrôl, সৎ sɔṭ; (horizontal) সটান sɔṭan

strain vb (stretch) টান–টান করা ṭan-ṭan kɔra; (sieve) ছাঁকা chāka; n (injury) খাটনির ব্যথা khaṭnir bytha, (effort) প্রচেষ্টা prôcesṭa, খাটনি khaṭni; (flow) ধারা dhara, প্রবাহ prôbahô

strainer n ছাঁকনি chākni

strand n সূত্র sūtrô

strange adj (unknown) অচেনা ɔcena; (weird) অদ্ভুত ɔdbhut

stranger n অচেনা লোক ɔcena lok

strangle vb দমন করা dɔmôn kɔra

strap n বন্ধনী bɔndhônī

strategy n কৌশল kouśôl

straw n খড় khɔr

stray vb বিপথে যাওয়া bipɔthe yaoŷa

streak n রেখা rekha

stream n (flow) ধারা dhara, প্রবাহ prôbahô; (current) স্রোত srot

street n রাস্তা rasta, পথ pɔth

strength n শক্তি śôkti, বল bɔl

strengthen vb সবল করা sɔbɔl kɔra

strenuous adj কষ্টকর kɔṣṭôkɔr

stress n (emphasis) জোর jor; (pressure) চাপ cap

stretch vb (pull) টানা ṭana; n (reach) নাগাল nagal

stretcher n সচল শয্যা sɔcɔl śɔyya (pron shɔcɔl shɔjja)

strict adj (exact) যথাযথ yɔthayɔth; (stern) কড়া kɔra

strife n বিবাদ bibad

strike vb (hit) আঘাত করা aghat kɔra; (knock) ধাক্কা দেওয়া dhakka deoŷa;(realise) খেয়াল হওয়া kheŷal hɔoŷa; n হরতাল hɔrtal

striking adj আকর্ষণীয় akôrṣôṇīŷô

string n (thread) সুতা suta; (rope) দড়ি dôri

strip n ফালি phali; vb কাপড় খোলা kapôr khola

stripe n ডোরা ḍora

striped adj ডুরে ḍure

stroke n আঘাত aghat; vb হাত বুল–িনো hat bulano

stroll n পায়চারি paŷcari

strong n (powerful) শক্তিশালী śôk-tiśalī, প্রবল prôbɔl; (healthy) সুস্থ susthô; (intense) গভীর gôbhīr

structure n গঠন gɔṭhôn, কাঠামো kaṭhamo

struggle vb যুঝা yujha, সংগ্রাম করা sɔmgram kɔra; n সংগ্রাম sɔmgram

stubble n কুশ kuś

stubborn n জেদী jedī, গোঁয়ার gõŷar

student *n* ছাত্র chatrô *(m)*, ছাত্রী chatrī *(f)*

study *n (exercise)* অনুশীলন ônuśīlôn; *(pursuit of knowledge)* অধ্যয়ন ɔdhyɔŷôn; *(room for reading)* পড়ার ঘর pɔṛar ghɔr; *vb* পড়া pɔṛa

stuff *n* পদার্থ pɔdarthô

stuffy *adj* গুমট gumôt

stumble *vb* হোঁচট খাওয়া hõcôṭ khaoŷa

stun *vb* বিস্মিত করা bismitô kɔra

stunned *adj* স্তম্ভিত stɔmbhitô

stunning *adj* চমৎকার cɔmôṭkar

stupid *adj* বোকা boka

style *n* ধরন dhɔrôn, রীতি rīti

stylish *adj* জাঁকালো jākalo

subdue *vb* দমন করা dɔmôn kɔra

subdued *adj* শায়েস্তা śaŷesta

subject *n (topic)* বিষয় biṣɔŷ; *(citizen)* নাগরিক nagôrik; *adj* অধীন ôdhīn

subjective *adj* মনোমত mônomɔtô

sublime *adj* সেরা sera, শ্রেষ্ঠ śreṣṭhô

submarine *n* ডুবো-জাহাজ ḍubo-jahaj

submit *vb* নিবেদন করা nibedôn kɔra

subordinate *adj* অধস্তন ɔdhɔstɔnô

subscribe *vb* চাঁদা দেওয়া cāda deoŷa

subscription *n* চাঁদা cāda

subsequent *adj* পরবর্তী pɔrôbôrtī

subservient *adj* অনুবর্তী ônubôrtī

subsidy *n* অনুদান ônudan

subsistence *n* বিদ্যমানতা bidyô-manôta

substance *n* সত্ত্ব sɔttvô

substantial *adj* বাস্তবিক bastôbik

substitute *n* বিকল্প bikɔlpô

subterfuge *n* ফন্দি phôndi, ফাঁকি phāki

subtle *adj (delicate)* মিহি mihi; *(refined)* বিদগ্ধ bidɔgdhô

subtract *vb* বিয়োগ করা biŷog kɔra

suburb *n* সহরতলি sɔhôrtôli

succeed *vb (follow)* অনুসরণ করা ônusɔrôṇ kɔra; *(be successful)* সফল হওয়া sɔphɔl hɔoŷa

success *n* সফলতা sɔphɔlôta

such *adj* এমন æmôn

suck *vb* চোষা coṣa

sudden *adj* হঠাৎ hɔṭhaṭ

suffer *vb* কষ্ট পাওয়া kɔṣṭô paoŷa, ভোগ করা bhog kɔra

suffice *vb* কুলানো kulano *(Bd)*, কুলোনো kulono *(WB)*

sufficient *adj* যথেষ্ট yɔtheṣṭô

suffix *n* বিভক্তি bibhôkti

sugar *n* চিনি cini

sugarcane *n* আখ akh

suggest *vb* প্রস্তাব করা prôstab kɔra

suggestion *n* প্রস্তাব prôstab

suicide *n* আত্মহত্যা atmôhɔtya

suit *vb* মানানো manano; *n (legal action)* মামলা mamla; *(men's outfit)* স্যুট syuṭ

suitable *adj* উপযুক্ত upôyuktô, যোগ্য yogyô

suitcase *n* স্যুটকেস syuṭkes

suite *n* আসবাব সমষ্টি asbab sɔmôṣṭi

suitor *n* আবেদক abedôk

sullen *adj* গোমড়া gomṛa

sulphur *n* গন্ধক gɔndhôk

sultry *adj* গুমট gumôt

sum *n* সমষ্টি sɔmôṣṭi

summary *n* সারাংশ sarâṁśô, সংক্ষেপ sɔṁkṣep

summer *n* গরমকাল gɔrômkal,

গ্রীষ্মকাল grīṣmôkal (*pron* grisshokal)

summit *n* শিখর śikhôr

summon *vb* ডাকা ḍaka

sun *n* সূর্য sūryô, রোদ rod

sunbathe *vb* রোদে পোহানো rode pohano

sunbeam *n* সূর্যকিরণ sūryôkirôṇ

sunburnt *adj* রোদে পোড়া rode poṛa (*also* পুড়া puṛa)

Sunday *n* রবিবার rôbibar

sunflower *n* সূর্যমুখী ফুল sūryô-mukhī phul

sunglasses *n* রঙীন চশমা rôṅīn cɔśma

sunny *adj* রৌদ্রোজ্জ্বল roudrôjjvɔl

sunrise *n* সূর্যোদয় sūryodɔŷ, উদয় udɔŷ

sunset *n* সূর্যাস্ত sūryastô

sunshine *n* রোদ rod, আতপ atôp

sunstroke *n* সদিগরমি sôrdigɔrômi

superb *adj* সেরা sera, চমৎকার cɔmôtkar

superficial *adj* উপরিগত upôrigɔtô

superfluous *adj* অপর্যাপ্ত ɔpôryaptô, বেশি beśi

superior *adj* উচ্চতর uccôtɔr

supermarket *n* সুপারমার্কেট supar-markeṭ

supernatural *adj* আলৌকিক aloukik

superstition *n* কুসংস্কার kusɔṁskar

supervise *vb* দেখাশেনো করা dækhaśona kɔra, খেয়াল রাখা kheŷal rakha

supervision *n* তত্ত্বাবধান tɔttvabdhan

supper *n* রাতের খাবার rater khabar

supplement *n* সম্পূরক sɔmpūrôk

supply *vb* যোগানো yogano

support *n* সমর্থন sɔmɔrthɔn

supporter *n* সপক্ষ sɔpɔkṣô

suppose *vb* অনুমান করা ônuman kɔra, মনে হওয়া mône hɔoŷa

supposition *n* অনুমান ônuman

suppress *vb* দমন করা dɔmôn kɔra

supreme *adj* চরম cɔrôm

surcharge *n* অধিভার ôdhibhar

sure *adj* নিশ্চিত niścitô

surely *adv* অবশ্য ɔbôśyô, অবশ্যই ɔbôśyôi

surety *n* জামিন jamin

surface *n* উপরের স্তর upôrer stɔr

surfeit *n* আতিশয্য atiśôṣyyô

surge *n* তরঙ্গ tɔrôṅgô

surgeon *n* অস্ত্রচিকিৎসক ɔstrôcikitsɔk

surgery *n* অস্ত্রচিকিৎসা ɔstrôcikitsa

surly *adj* বদমেজাজী bɔdmejajī

surname *n* পদবি pɔdôbi

surpass *vb* অতিক্রম করা ôtikrôm kɔra

surplus *n* বাড়তি bɑṛti

surprise *n* বিস্ময় bismɔŷ, আশ্চর্য aścôryô

surrender *vb* (give up) ছেড়ে দেওয়া cheṛe deoŷa; (be defeated) পরাজিত হওয়া pɔrajitô hɔoŷa

surrogate *adj* বদলি bôdli

surround *vb* ঘেরা ghera

surrounding *adj* চারদিকের cardiker

surroundings *n* পরিবেশ pôribeś

surveillance *n* পাহারা pahara, নজর nɔjôr

survive *vb* বাঁচা bãca, বেঁচে থাকা bẽce thaka

suspect *vb* সন্দেহ করা sɔndehô kɔra

suspend *vb* (hang) ঝোলানো jholano; (dismiss) বরখাস্ত করা bɔrkhastô kɔra

suspense *n* উৎকণ্ঠা utkɔntha

suspicion *n* সন্দেহ sɔndehô

suspicious *adj* সন্দিগ্ধ sɔndigdhô

sustain *vb* তুলে রাখা tule rakha

swallow *vb* গেলা gela (*also* গিলা gila); *n* চাতক catôk

swamp *n* জলাজমি jɔlajômi, বিল, bil

swan *n* রাজহাঁস rajhās

swarm *n* ঝাঁক jhāk

swear *vb* (*take an oath*) শপথ করা śɔpɔth kɔra; (*use abusive language*) গালি দেওয়া gali deôya

sweat *vb* ঘামা ghama; *n* ঘাম gham

sweater *n* গরম গেঞ্জি gɔrôm geñji

sweep *vb* ঝাড়ু দেওয়া jharu deôya (*Bd*), ঝাঁট দেওয়া jhāt deôya

sweet *adj* মিষ্টি miṣṭi

sweeten *vb* মিষ্টি দেওয়া miṣṭi deôya

swell *vb* (*increase in size*) স্ফীত হওয়া sphītô hɔôya; (*distend in pain*) ফোলা phola, ফুলে ওঠা phule otha

swelling *n* ফুলা phula

swift *adj* চটপটে cɔtpɔte, শিগগির śiggir

swim *vb* সাঁতার কাটা sātar kata

swimmer *n* সাঁতারু sātaru

swimming *n* সাঁতার sātar

swimming pool *n* সাঁতার কাটার পুল sātar katar pul

swindle *vb* ঠকানো thɔkano, প্রতারণা করা prôtarôṇa kɔra

swindler *n* প্রতারক prôtarɔk

swing *vb* দোলা dola; *n* দোলনা dolna

switch *vb* বদলানো bɔdlano; *n* সুইচ suic

sword *n* তরোয়াল tɔrôyal

syllable *n* অক্ষর ɔkṣôr

symbol *n* প্রতীক prôtīk, চিহ্ন cihnô (*pron* cinho)

symbolic *adj* চিহ্নগত cihnôgɔtô (*pron* cinhogɔto)

symmetry *n* প্রতিসাম্য prôtisamyô

sympathetic *adj* সহানুভূতিপূর্ণ sɔhanubhūtipūrṇô

sympathize *vb* মায়া লাগা maya laga

sympathy *n* সহানুভূতি sɔhanubhūti

symptom *n* লক্ষণ lɔkṣôn

synagogue *n* ইহুদিদের ভক্তিরস্থান ihudider bhôktirsthan

synchronic *adj* সমকালীন sɔmkalīn

synonym *n* সমার্থ শব্দ sɔmarthô śɔbdô

syntax *n* বাক্যগঠন bakyôgɔthôn

synthesis *n* সমন্বয় sɔmônvɔŷ

synthetic *adj* সাংশ্লেষিক saṁślesik

syringe *n* সিরিঞ্জ siriñj

syrup *n* সিরাপ sirap

system *n* (*structure*) গঠনতন্ত্র gɔthôntɔntrô; (*method*) নিয়ম niŷôm, পদ্ধতি pɔddhôti

systematic *adj* নিয়মানুযায়ী niŷômanuyaŷī

table 251 taste

T

table n (piece of furniture) টেবিল ṭebil; (set of facts and figures) তথ্যাদি tôthyadi; (index) সূচি sūci

tablet n বড়ি bôṛi

taboo adj (forbidden utterance) অকথ্য ɔkɔthyô; n (religious ban) ধর্মীয় নিষেধ dhɔrmīŷô niṣedh

tacit adj অকথিত ɔkôthitô

tack n ছোট পেরেক chôṭô perek

tact n সুবিচার subicar

tactful adj সুবেদী subedī, শোভন śobhôn

tactic n কৌশল kouśôl

tag n ট্যাগ ṭyæg

tail n লেজ lej

tail-end n শেষাংশ śeṣaṁśô

tailor n দরজি dôrji

taint n দাগ dag, কলঙ্ক kɔlôṅkô; vb কলঙ্কিত করা kɔlôṅkitô kɔra

take vb নেওয়া neoŷa

take after vb অনুযায়ী হওয়া ônuyaŷī hɔoŷa

take away vb সরিয়ে নিয়ে যাওয়া sôriŷe niŷe yaoŷa

take off vb (shed) খোলা khola; (flourish) সমৃদ্ধ হওয়া sɔmr̥ddhô hɔoŷa; (leave) অপসরণ করা ɔpôsɔrôṇ kɔra

take on vb গ্রহণ করা grôhôṇ kɔra

take over vb নিয়ন্ত্রণ করা niŷôntrôṇ kɔra

take to vb আসক্ত হওয়া asɔktô hɔoŷa

take up vb ব্যাপ্ত করা byaptô kɔra

tale n কাহিনী kahinī, গল্প gɔlpô

talent n দক্ষতা dôkṣôta

talented adj দক্ষ dôkṣô

talk n আলাপ alap; vb কথা বলা kɔtha bɔla

talkative adj বাচাল bacal, আলাপী alapī

tall adj লম্বা lɔmba

tamarind n তেঁতুল tētul

tame adj (domesticated) পোষা poṣa; (subdued) দমিত dômitô

tamper vb হস্তক্ষেপ করা hɔstôkṣep kɔra

tampon n ট্যাম্পন ṭyampôn

tan adj (tawny-brown) তামাটে tamaṭe; vb (color in the sun) রোদে পুড়ে যাওয়া rode puṛe yaoŷa

tangerine n কমলালেবু kɔmlalebu

tangle n জট jɔṭ, পেঁচ pēc

tank n জলাধার jɔladhar

tanker n তেলবাহ জাহাজ telbahô jahaj

tantalize vb উত্ত্যক্ত করা uttyôktô kɔra

tap vb (touch lightly) টোকা দেওয়া ṭoka deoŷa; (draw out) টেনে বের করা ṭene ber kɔra

tape n ফিতা phita (Bd), ফিতে phite (WB)

tape measure n মাপার ফিতা mapar phita

tape recorder n টেপরেকর্ডার ṭeprekɔrḍar

tapeworm n ফিতা-কৃমি phita-krimi

tar n আলকাতরা alkatra

target n লক্ষ্য lôkṣyô

tariff n শুল্ক śulkô

tart adj টক ṭɔk

task n করণীয় kɔrôṇīŷô

taste n (discernment) রুচি ruci;

(flavor) স্বাদ svad; *vb* স্বাদ নেওয়া svad neoŷa

tasteful *adj* রুচিকর rucikɔr

tasteless *adj* বিস্বাদ bisvad

tasty *adj* সুস্বাদু susvadu

tattle *n (chatter)* বকবকানি bɔkbɔkani

tattoo *n* উলকি ulki

taunt *n* উপহাস upôhas

taut *adj* আঁটো ãṭo

tax *n* কর kɔr, খাজনা khajna

taxi *n* ট্যাক্সি ṭyæksi

tea *n* চা ca

tea leaves *n* চা-পাতা ca–pata

teach *vb* শেখানো śekhano, পড়ানো pɔrano

teacher *n (in a school)* শিক্ষক śikṣôk *(m)*, শিক্ষিকা sikṣika *(f)*; *(spiritual guide)* গুরু guru

teaching *n* শিক্ষাদান śikṣadan

team *n* টিম ṭim, দল dɔl

teapot *n* চায়ের পাত্র caŷer patrô

tear *n* চোখের জল cokher jɔl, কান্না kanna; *vb* ছেঁড়া chẽra, ছিন্ন করা chinnô kɔra

tear up *vb* ছিঁড়ে ফেলা chĩre phæla

tease *vb (comb)* আঁচড়ানো ãcrano; *(irritate)* জ্বালানো jvalano; *(make fun of)* ঠাট্টা করা ṭhaṭṭa kɔra, তামাশা করা tamaśa kɔra

teaspoon *n* ছোট চামচ choṭo camôc, চা–চামচ ca–camôc

technical *adj* প্রযুক্তিগত prôyuktigɔtô

technology *n* প্রযুক্তিবিদ্যা prôyuktibidya

teenager *n* যুবক yubôk *(m)* যুবতি yubôti *(f)*

telegram *n* টেলিগ্রাম ṭeligram

telepathy *n* পরস্পরের মনের জানাজানি pɔrôspɔrer môner janajani

telephone *n* টেলিফোন ṭeliphon

telescope *n* দূরবীন dūrbīn

television *n* টেলিভিশন ṭelibhiśôn, টি ভি ṭi bhi

tell *vb* বলা bɔla, জানানো janano

temper *n* মেজাজ mejaj

temperance *n* মিতাচার mitacar

temperate *adj (of mild climate)* নাতিশীতোষ্ণ natiśītoṣṇô; *(moderate)* মিতাচারী mitacarī

temperature *n* তাপ tap

temple *n (house of worship)* মন্দির môndir, *(side of face)* ললাট lɔlaṭ

tempo *n* বেগমাত্রা begmatra

temporary *adj* অস্থায়ী ɔsthaŷī

tempt *vb (put to the test)* পরীক্ষা করা pôrīkṣa kɔra; *(entice)* প্রলুব্ধ করা prôlubdhô kɔra

temptation *n* প্রলোভন prôlobhôn

ten *num* দশ dɔś

ten million *num* কোটি koṭi, ক্রোড় kror

tenacious *adj* নাছোড়বান্দা nachor-banda, গোঁয়ার gõŷar

tenacity *n* সংসক্তি sɔmsôkti, জিদ jid *(also* জেদ jed)

tenant *n* ভাড়াটে bharaṭe

tend *vb (look after)* দেখাশোনা করা dækhaśona kɔra; *(be inclined to)* প্রবণ হওয়া prôbɔṇ hɔoŷa

tendency *n* ঝোঁক jhõk, প্রবণতা prôbɔṇta

tender *adj* কোমল komôl; *n* প্রস্তাব prôstab

tendon *n* পেশি peśi

tennis *n* টেনিস ṭenis

tense *n* ক্রিয়ার কাল kriŷar kal; *adj* চাপের মধ্যে caper môdhye, পীড়িত pīṛitô

tension *n* টেনশন ṭenśôn

tent *n* তাঁবু tābu

tentacle *n* কর্ষিকা kôrṣika

tentative *adj* কাঁচা kāca, পরীক্ষামূলক pôrīkṣamūlɔk

tenth *num* দশম dɔśôm

tenuous *adj* হালকা halka

tepid *adj* অল্প গরম ɔlpô gɔrôm

term *n* *(word)* শব্দ śɔbdô; *(fixed period)* স্থিতিকাল sthitikal; *(condition)* শর্ত śɔrtô

terminal *adj* প্রান্তিক prantik; *n* টার্মিনাল ṭarminal

terminate *vb* *(finish)* সারা sara, শেষ করা śeṣ kɔra; *(complete)* সমাপ্ত করা sɔmaptô kɔra, ফুরানো phurano

termination *n* *(completion)* সমাপন sɔmapɔn; *(abortion)* গর্ভনাশ gɔrbhônaś

terminology *n* পরিভাষা pôribhaṣa

termite *n* উইপোকা uipoka

terrace *n* *(row of houses)* ভবন-শ্রেণি bhɔbôn-śreṇi, *(verandah)* বারান্দা baranda

terrestrial *adj* স্থলজ sthɔlôjô

terrible *adj* ভীষণ bhīṣôṇ, ভয়ঙ্কর bhɔŷôṅkɔr

terribly *adv* খুবই khubi

terrific *adj* দারুণ daruṇ

territory *n* এলাকা elaka

terror *n* ত্রাস tras, সন্ত্রাস sɔntras, আতঙ্ক atôṅkô

terrorism *n* সন্ত্রাসবাদ sɔntrasbad

terrorist *n* সন্ত্রাসী sɔntrasī

test *n* পরীক্ষা pôrīkṣa

testicle *n* মুষ্ক muṣkô

testify *vb* সাক্ষ্য দেওয়া sakṣyô deoŷa

testimony *n* সাক্ষ্য sakṣyô

text *n* পাঠ paṭh

textbook *n* পাঠ্যপুস্তক paṭhyôpustɔk

textile *n* কাপড় kapôṛ

than *conj* চেয়ে ceŷe

thank *vb* ধন্যবাদ দেওয়া dhɔnyôbad deoŷa

thankful *adj* কৃতজ্ঞ kr̥tôjñô

thankfulness *n* কৃতজ্ঞতা kr̥tôjñôta

thanks *int* ধন্যবাদ dhɔnyôbad

that *pr* তা ta; *conj* যে ye; *det* সে se

thaw *vb* গলা gɔla

the *det sg* –টা –ṭa, –টি –ṭi; *pl* –রা –ra, –গুলো –gulo, –গুলি –guli

theater *n* রঙ্গমঞ্চ rɔṅgômɔñcô

theft *n* চুরি curi

theme *n* *(topic)* বিষয় biṣɔŷ; *(main thread)* সূত্র sūtrô

then *adv, conj* তখন tɔkhôn, সে সময় se sômôŷ

theology *n* ধর্মশাস্ত্র dhɔrmôśastrô

theoretical *adj* তাত্ত্বিক tattvik

theory *n* তত্ত্ব, মতবান mɔtôban

therapeutic *adj* চিকিৎসাবিদ্যাগত cikiṯsabidyagɔtô

therapist *n* চিকিৎসক cikiṯsôk

therapy *n* চিকিৎসা cikiṯsa

there *adv* সেখানে sekhane

therefore *conj* তাই tai, অতএব ɔtôeb, সে জন্য se jônyô

thermometer *n* তাপমাপক-যন্ত্র tapômapôk-yɔntrô

thermos *n* থার্মোফ্লাস্ক tharmophlask

thermostat *n* তাপস্থাপক tapôsthapôk

these *pr* এগুলো egulo, এগুলি eguli

thesis *n* প্রবন্ধ prôbɔndhô

they *pr* তারা tara

thick *adj (bulky, heavy)* মোটা moṭa; *(dense)* ঘন ghɔnô

thicken *vb* ঘনানো ghɔnano

thickness *n* ঘনতা ghɔnôta

thief *n* চোর cor

thigh *n* ঊরু uru

thimble *n* আঙুলের টুপি aṅguler ṭupi

thin *adj* পাতলা patla, রোগা roga

thing *n* জিনিস jinis, বস্তু bôstu

think *vb* ভাবা bhaba, মনে করা mône kɔra

third *num* তৃতীয় tŕtīŷô

thirst *n* পিপাসা pipasa

thirsty *adj* পিপাসিত pipasitô

thirteen *num* তের terô, তেরো tero

thirty *num* ত্রিশ triś *(Bd)*, তিরিশ tiriś *(WB)*

this *det, pr* এই ei, এটা eṭa

thorn *n* কাঁটা kãṭa

thorough *adj (conscientious)* যত্নশীল yɔtnôśīl; *(meticulous)* তন্নতন্ন tɔnnôtɔnnô

thoroughfare *n* মধ্যবর্তী পথ môd-hyôbôrtī pɔth

thoroughly *adv* পুঙ্খানুপুঙ্খভাবে puṅkhanupuṅkhôbhabe

those *pr* ওগুলো ogulo, ওগুলি oguli

though *conj* যদিও yôdio

thought *n (reflection)* চিন্তা cinta, ভাবনা bhabna; *(consideration)* বিবেচনা bibecôna

thoughtful *adj (imaginative)* ভাবুক bhabuk; *(considerate)* বিবেচক bibecôk

thousand *num* হাজার hajar

thread *n (connecting element)* সূত্র sūtrô, *(cloth)* সুতা suta *(Bd)*, সুতো suto *(WB)*

threat *n* শাসানি śasani, হুমকি humki

threaten *vb* ভয় দেখানো bhɔŷ dækhano

three *num* তিন tin

threshold *n (doorstep)* গোবরাট gobôraṭ; *(outset)* সূত্রপাত sūtrôpat

thrift *n* মিতব্যায়িতা mitôbyæŷita

thrifty *adj* মিতব্যায়ী mitôbyæŷī *(pron* mitobæŷi)

thrill *n* শিহরণ śihôrôṇ

thrive *vb* সতেজ হয়ে ওঠা sɔtej hôŷe oṭha, ফোটা phoṭa

throat *n* গলা gɔla

throb *vb* দপদপ করা dɔpdɔp kɔra

throne *n (seat for a king)* সিংহাসন simhasôn; *(royalty)* রাজপদ rajpɔd

throttle *vb* শ্বাসরোধ করা svasrodh kɔra

through *pp* দিয়ে diŷe

throughout *adv* সারাক্ষণ sarakṣɔṇ

throw *vb* ছুড়ে ফেলা chuṛe phæla

throw away *vb* ফেলে দেওয়া phele deoŷa

thrust *vb* ঠেলে দেওয়া ṭhele deoŷa, ধাক্কা দেওয়া dhakka deoŷa

thumb *n* বুড়ো আঙুল buṛo aṅgul

thunder *n* মেঘের ডাক megher ḍak

thunderbolt *n* বজ্রপাত bɔjrôpat

Thursday *n* বৃহস্পতিবার bŕhôspôtibar

ticket *n* টিকিট ṭikiṭ

tickle *vb* কাতুকুতু দেওয়া katukutu kɔra

tidal *adj* স্রোত-সংক্রান্ত srot-sɔṁkrantô

tidal wave *n* বেলোর্মি belormi

tide *n (current, flow)* প্রবাহ prôbahô; *(ebb and flow)* জোয়ার-ভাটা joŷar-bhaṭa

tidy *adj* পরিপাটি pôripaṭi, ছিমছাম chimcham

tie *vb* বাঁধা bādha; *n* টাই ṭai

tiger *n* বাঘ bagh

tight *adj* কষা kɔṣa, চিপা cipa *(Bd)*, চেপা cepa *(WB)*

tighten *vb* কষা kɔṣa, আঁটা āṭa

tile *n* টালি ṭali

tilt *vb* হেলা hæla

tilted *adj* কাত kat

timber *n* কাঠ kaṭh

time *n* সময় sômôŷ

timetable *n* সময়সূচি sômôŷsūci

timid *adj* ভীরু bhīru

tin *n* টিন ṭin

tingle *n* শিহরণ śihɔrôṇ

tint *vb* আভা abha

tiny *adj* ক্ষুদ্র kṣudrô, ছোট ছোট chotô chotô

tip *n (extreme end)* ডগা ḍɔga; *(highest point)* চূড়া cūṛa *(Bd)*, চূড়ো cūṛo *(WB)*; *(hint)* ইঙ্গিত iṅgit; *vb* উলটিয়ে দেওয়া ulṭiŷe deoŷa

tirade *n* তিরস্কার tirôskar

tire *n* চাকা caka; *vb* ক্লান্ত হওয়া klantô hɔoŷa

tired *adj* ক্লান্ত klantô, কাহিল kahil

tiredness *n* ক্লান্তি klanti

tireless *adj* অক্লান্ত ɔklantô

tissue *n* কাপড় kapôṛ

title *n* শিরনাম śirônam

to *pp* দিকে dike, পর্যন্ত pôryôntô

toad *n* ব্যাঙ byæṅ

tobacco *n* তামাক tamak

today *adv* আজ aj, আজকে ajke

toe *n* পায়ের আঙুল paŷer aṅgul

together *adv* একসঙ্গে æksɔṅge

toil *n* পরিশ্রম pôriśrôm, কষ্ট kɔṣṭô

toilet *n* টয়লেট ṭɔŷleṭ, পায়খানা paŷkhana

token *n* চিহ্ন cihnô *(pron* cinho)

tolerance *n* সহ্যশক্তি sôhyôśôkti *(pron* shojjhoshokti)

tolerate *vb* সহ্য করা sôhyô kɔra *(pron* shojjho kɔra)

toll *n* তোলা tola

tomato *n* টমেটো ṭômeṭo

tomb *n* কবর kɔbôr, সমাধি sɔmadhi

tomorrow *adv* কালকে kalke, আগামীকাল agamīkal

tomtom *n* ঢোল ḍhol

ton *n* টন ṭɔn

tone *n* সুর sur

tongs *n* চিমটা cimṭa *(Bd)*, চিমটে cimṭe *(WB)*, সাঁড়াশি sāṛaśi

tongue *n* জিব jib, জিভ jibh

tonsils *n* টনসিল ṭônsil

too *adv (also)* ও o; *(excessively)* বেশি beśi

tool *n* যন্ত্র yɔntrô

tooth *n* দাঁত dāt

toothache *n* দাঁতের ব্যথা dāter byæetha

toothbrush *n* দাঁতের ব্রাশ dāter braś

toothpaste *n* দাঁতের মাজন dāter majôn

top *n* চূড়া cūṛa, উপরিভাগ upôribhag; *adj* উচ্চ uccô, উপর upôr

topic *n* বিষয় biṣôŷ, প্রসঙ্গ prôsôṅgô

topical *adj* প্রাসঙ্গিক prasôṅgik

topsy-turvy *adj* উলটা-পালটা ulṭa-palṭa *(Bd)*, উলটো-পালটা ulṭo-palṭa *(WB)*

torch *n* টর্চলাইট ṭɔrclaiṭ

torment *n* যন্ত্রণা yɔntrôṇa; *vb* পীড়ন করা pīṛôn kɔra, যন্ত্রণা দেওয়া yɔntrôṇa deoŷa tornado *n* ঘূর্ণিঝড় ghurṇijhɔr

torrent *n* প্রবল স্রোত prôbɔl srot

torso *n* ধড় dhɔr

tortoise *n* কচ্ছপ kɔcchôp *(Bd)*, কাছিম kachim *(WB)*

torture *n* যন্ত্রণা yɔntrôṇa

toss *vb* ছুড়ে ফেলা chure phæla

total *adj* মোট moṭ, সব মিলে sɔb mile, সম্পূর্ণ sɔmpūrṇô

totalitarian *adj* সর্বগ্রাসী sɔrbôgrasī

totally *adv* সম্পূর্ণভাবে sɔmpūrṇô-bhabe, একেবারে ækebare

touch *n* স্পর্শ spɔrśô; *vb* ছোঁয়া chỗẏa, স্পর্শ করা spɔrśô kɔra

touching *adj* মর্মস্পর্শী mɔrmôspɔrśī

touchy *adj* ভঙ্গুর bhôṅgur

tough *adj* বলিষ্ঠ bôlisṭhô

toughen *vb* শক্ত করা śɔktô kôra

toughness *n* শক্তি śôkti

tour *n* সফর sɔphôr

tourism *n* প্রমোদভ্রমণের ব্যবসা prômodbhrômôṇer bybsa

tourist *n* ভ্রমণকারী bhrômôṇkarī

tow *vb* টেনে নিয়ে যাওয়া ṭene niẏe yaoẏa

toward *pp* দিকে dike

towel *n* গামছা gamcha, তোয়ালে toẏale

tower *n* দুর্গ dūrgô, বুরুজ buruj

town *n* শহর śɔhôr, নগর nɔgôr

toy *n* খেলনা khelna

trace *n (quest)* সন্ধান sɔndhan; *(evidence)* সাক্ষ্য saksyô

trachea *n* শ্বাসনালী svasônalī

track *n* পথ pɔth

traction *n* আকর্ষণ akôrṣôṇ

tractor *n* ট্র্যাক্টর ṭryækṭɔr

trade *n* বিনিময় binimɔẏ, ক্রয়-বিক্রয় krɔẏ-bikrɔẏ

trader *n* বণিক bôṇik, ব্যবসায়ী bybsaẏī

tradition *n* ঐতিহ্য oitihyô *(pron oitijjho)*

traditional *adj* ঐতিহ্যিক oitihyik *(pron oitijjhik)*

traffic *n* চলাচল cɔlacɔl, যাতায়াত yatayat

tragedy *n (sad incident)* দুঃখদায়ক ঘটনা duḥkhôdayôk ghɔṭôna; *(drama)* বিয়োগান্ত নাটক biẏogantô naṭôk

tragic *adj* বিয়োগান্ত biẏogantô

trail *n* গমনপথ gɔmônpɔth

trailer *n (climbing plant)* লতা lɔta; *(back part of a truck)* টানাগাড়ি ṭanagari

train *n* রেলগাড়ি relgari; *vb* শিক্ষা দেওয়া śiksa deoẏa

training *n* শিক্ষা śiksa

trait *n* বৈশিষ্ট্য boiśisṭyô

traitor *n* বিশ্বাসঘাতক biśvasghaṭôk

tram *n* ট্রামগাড়ি ṭramgari

tramp *n* ভবঘুরে bhɔbôghure

trance *n* সমাধি sɔmadhi

transaction *n* লেনদেন lenden

transcript *n* প্রতিলিপি prôtilipi

transfer *n* পরিবৃত্তি pôribṛtti

transform *vb* রূপান্তর করা rūpantɔr kɔra

transformation *n* রূপান্তর rūpantɔr

transit *n* চলার পথ cɔlar pɔth

translate *vb* অনুবাদ করা ônubad kɔra

translation *n* অনুবাদ ônubad

translator *n* অনুবাদক ônubadôk

transmission *n* প্রেরণ prerɔṇ

transmit *n* পাঠিয়ে দেওয়া paṭhiẏe deoẏa

transparent *adj* স্বচ্ছ svɔcchô

transport *n* যান yan, পরিবহণ pôribɔhɔn

trap *n* ফাঁদ phãd; *vb* ফাঁদে ফেলা phãde phæla

trash *n* ময়লা mɔyla, আবর্জনা abôrjɔna

trashy *adj* বাজে baje

travel *n* ভ্রমণ bhrômôn; *vb* ভ্রমণ করা bhrômôn kɔra

travesty *n* ভান bhan

treacherous *adj* মায়াময় maɣamɔɣ, বেইমান beiman

treachery *n* বেইমানী beimanī

tread *vb* মাড়ানো marano

treason *n* রাষ্ট্রদ্রোহ raṣṭrôdrohô

treasure *n* ধন dhɔn, সম্পদ sɔmpôd

treasurer *n* খাজাঞ্চি khajañci

treasury *n* ধনাগার dhɔnagar

treat *vb (handle)* ব্যবহার করা byæbôhar kɔra, আচরণ করা acôrôn kɔra; *(heal)* চিকিৎসা করা cikitsa kɔra

treatise *n* বিজ্ঞাপন bijñapôn

treatment *n* চিকিৎসা cikitsa

treaty *n* মধ্যস্থতা môdhyôsthôta

tree *n* গাছ gach

trellis *n* মাচা maca

tremble *vb* কাঁপা kãpa

tremendous *adj* প্রকাণ্ড prôkaṇdô

tremor *n* কম্প kɔmpô

tremulous *adj* কম্পমান kɔmpôman

trend *n (inclination)* প্রবণতা prôbônɔta, ঝোঁক jhōk; *(fashion)* হালচাল halcal

trespass *vb* লঙ্ঘন করা lɔnghôn kɔra

trespassing *n* অনধিকার প্রবেশ ɔnôdhikar prôbeś

trial *n* আদালতের বিচার adalɔter bicar

triangle *n* ত্রিভুজ tribhuj

triangular *adj* ত্রিভুজীয় tribhujīɣô

tribe *n* গোষ্ঠী goṣṭhī, বংশ bɔṁśô

tribute *n* প্রদান prôdan

trick *n* ফন্দি phôndi, চালাকি calaki

trickle *vb* ফোঁটা ফোঁটা পড়া phōṭa phōṭa pɔra

trifle *n* তুচ্ছতা tucchôta

trigger *vb* ঘটানো ghɔṭano

trilogy *n* তিন খণ্ডের গ্রন্থ tin khɔṇder grônthô

trip *n* ভ্রমণ bhrômôn; *vb* হোঁচট খাওয়া hōcôṭ khaoɣa

trite *adj* মামুলি mamuli

triumph *n (victory celebration)* বিজয়োল্লাস bijɔɣollas; *(joy of success)* সাফল্যের আনন্দ saphɔlyer anôndô

trivia *n* তুচ্ছ জিনিস tucchô jinis

trivial *adj* মামুলি mamuli

troops *n* সেনাবাহিনী senabahinī

tropical *adj* গরমের দেশের gɔrômer deśer

tropics *n* গ্রীষ্মপ্রধান grīṣmôprôdhan

trouble *n* ঝামেলা jhamela, অসুবিধা ɔsubidha

troublesome *adj* বিরক্তিকর birôktikɔr

trousers *n* প্যান্ট pyæṇṭ

truant *adj* স্কুল-পালানে skul-palane

truce *n* যুদ্ধবিরতি yuddhôbirôti

truck *n* মালগাড়ি malgari, লরি lɔri

true *adj (real)* সত্যিকার sôtyikar; *(actual)* আসল asôl, বাস্তব bastɔb; *(accurate)* যথাযথ yɔthaɣɔthô; *(genuine)* শুদ্ধ śuddhô, খাঁটি khãṭi

truly *adv* সত্যি sôtyi

trump *n* তুরুপ turup

trunk *n* বাক্স baksô, সিন্দুক sinduk

trust *n* আস্থা astha

trustworthy *adj* বিশ্বাসী biśvasī

trusty *adj* বিশ্বস্ত bisvɔstô

truth *n (essence, validity)* তত্ত্ব tɔttvô; *(reality)* সত্য sôtyô, সত্যি sôtyi

truthful *adj* সত্যবাদী sôtyôbadī

try *vb* চেষ্টা করা ceṣṭa kɔra

tryst *n* অভিসার ôbhisar

tube *n* নল, পাইপ nɔl, paip

tuberculosis *n* টিবি ṭibi, যক্ষ্মারোগ yɔkṣmarog

tuberose *n* রজনীগন্ধা rɔjônīgɔndha

tubewell *n* নলকূপ nɔlkūp

Tuesday *n* মঙ্গলবার môṅgôlbar

tug *vb* সবলে টানা sɔbɔle ṭana

tugboat *n* টানার পোত ṭanar pot

tumble *vb* হোঁচট খাওয়া hõcôṭ khaoẏa

tumor *n* স্ফীতি sphīti, টিউমার ṭiumar

tune *n* সুর sur

tunnel *n* সুরঙ্গ surɔṅgô

turban *n* পাগড়ি pagṛi

Turkey *n* তুরস্ক turôskô

Turkish *adj* তুকী turkī

turmoil *n* অশান্তি ɔśanti

turn *vb (revolve)* ঘোরা ghora; *(go back)* ফিরে যাওয়া phire yaoẏa; *(change)* পরিবর্তন করা pôribôrtôn kɔra, বদলানো bɔdlano; *(bend)* বাঁকা bāka, বাঁকানো bākano; *(set upside-down)* উলটানো ulṭano

turn down *vb* অগ্রাহ্য করা ɔgrahyô kɔra *(pron* ɔgrajjho kɔra), না বলা na bɔla

turn off *vb* বন্ধ করা bɔndhô kɔra

turn on *vb* ছাড়া chara

turn up *vb* হাজির হওয়া hajir hɔoẏa

turnip *n* শালগম salgɔm

turpentine *n* তার্পিন tarpin

turtle *n* কচ্ছপ kɔcchôp, কাছিম kachim

twang *n* টং শব্দ ṭɔṁ śɔbdô

tweak *n* খিমচি khimci

tweezers *n* চিমটে cimṭe

twelve *num* বার barô, বারো baro

twenty *num* বিশ biś *(Bd)*, কুড়ি kuṛi *(WB)*

twice *adv* দুই বার dui bar

twig *n* ফেঁকড়ি phẽkṛi

twilight *n* গোধূলি godhūli

twin *n* জমজ jɔmôj, যমজ yɔmôj

twinge *n* তীব্র ব্যথা tībrô bytha

twinkle *vb* পলক ফেলা pɔlôk phæla

twist *vb* বাঁকানো bākano, পেঁচানো pæcano

two *num* দুই dui

type *n* ধরন dhɔrôn, রকম rɔkôm; *vb* টাইপ করা taip kɔra

typewriter *n* টাইপরাইটার ṭaipraiṭar

typhoid *n* আন্ত্রিক জ্বর antrik jvɔr, টাইফয়েড ṭaiphôẏeḍ

typhoon *n* তুফান tuphan

typical *adj* বৈশিষ্ট্যমূলক boiśiṣṭyômūlôk

tyranny *n* অত্যাচার ɔtyacar

U

ugly *adj* বিশ্রী biśrī, কুৎসিত kuṯsit

ulcer *n* ক্ষত kṣɔtô, ঘা gha

ulterior *adj* অন্য ɔnyô

ultimate *adj* চরম cɔrôm, শেষ śeṣ

ultimately *adv* শেষ পর্যন্ত śeṣ pôryôntô

ultra- *pref* অতি- ôti-

umbilical cord *n* গর্ভনাড়ি gɔrbhônaṛi

umbrella *n* ছাতা, ছাতি chata, chati

unable *adj* অক্ষম ɔkṣɔm

unacceptable *adj* অগ্রাহ্য ɔgrahyô (*pron* ɔgrajjho)

unaccountable *adj* অকারণে ɔkarôṇe

unadulterated *adj* অকৃত্রিম ɔkr̥trim

unaided *adj* নিঃসহায় niḥsɔhaŷ

unanimous *adj* একমত ekmɔt

unarmed *adj* নিরস্ত্র nirɔstrô

unassuming *adj* নিরহংকার nirɔhôṁkar

unauthorized *adj* অননুমত ɔnônumɔtô

unavoidable *adj* অপরিহার্য ɔpôriharyô

unaware *adj* অজ্ঞাত ɔjñætô

unbearable *adj* অসহ্য ɔsɔhyô (*pron* ɔsojjho)

unbounded *adj* অসীম ɔsīm

uncertain *adj* অনিশ্চিত ɔniścitô

uncle *n* (*father's older brother*) বড় চাচা bɔrô caca *Muslim*, জেঠা, জ্যাঠা jæṭha *Hindu*; (*father's younger brother*) চাচা caca *Muslim*, কাকা kaka *Hindu*; (*mother's brother*) মামা mama *Muslim*, মামা mama *Hindu*; (*mother's sister's husband*) খালু khalu *Muslim*, মেসো meso, মেসোমশায় mesomɔśaŷ *Hindu*; (*father's sister's husband*) ফুফা phupha *Muslim*, পিসা pisa, পিসামশায় pisamɔśaŷ *Hindu*

unclean *adj* অপরিষ্কার ɔpôriskar

uncomfortable *adj* অস্বস্তি ɔsvôsti

uncommon *adj* অসাধারণ ɔsadharôṇ

unconditional *adj* নিঃশর্ত niḥśɔrtô

unconquered *adj* অপরাজিত ɔpɔrajitô

unconscious *adj* অচেতন ɔcetôn, অজ্ঞান ɔjñæn

uncontrollable *adj* উদ্দাম uddam

uncover *vb* প্রকাশ করা prôkaś kɔra

undaunted *adj* অশঙ্কিত ɔśôṅkitô, সাহসী sahôsī

undecided *adj* অনিশ্চিত ɔniścitô

undefeated *adj* অপরাজিত ɔpɔrajitô

under *pp* নিচে nice

undercover *adv* গোপনে gopône

undergo *vb* ভোগ করা bhog kɔra

underground *adj* মাটির নিচে maṭir nice

undergrowth *n* ঝোপ jhop

underline *vb* জোর দেওয়া jor deôŷa

underneath *adv* নিচে nice, তলায় tɔlaŷ

undernourished *adj* অপুষ্ট ɔpuṣṭô

undershirt *n* গেঞ্জি geñji

undershorts *n* হাফ প্যান্ট haph pyænṭ

undersign *vb* সই করা sôi kɔra

understand *vb* বোঝা bojha

understanding *n* বোধশক্তি bodhśôkti, জ্ঞান jñæn

undertake *vb* হাতে নেওয়া hate neoŷa

undeveloped *adj* অনুন্নত ɔnunnɔtô

undivided *adj* অবিচ্ছিন্ন ɔbichinnô

undo *vb (open)* খুলে দেওয়া khule deoŷa; *(spoil)* নাশ করা naś kɔra

unease *n* অস্বস্তি ɔsvôsti

uneasy *adj* অস্থির ɔsthir

uneducated *adj* অশিক্ষিত ɔśikṣitô

unemployed *adj* বেকার bekar

unemployment *n* বেকারি bekari

unending *adj* অশেষ ɔśeṣ, অনন্ত ɔnôntô

unequal *adj* অসম ɔsɔmô, অসমকক্ষ ɔsɔmôkɔkṣô

unexpected *adj* অপ্রত্যাশিত ɔprôtyæśitô

unfair *adj* অন্যায্য ɔnyayyô (*pron* ɔnnajjô)

unfamiliar *adj* অপরিচিত ɔpôricitô, অচেনা ɔcena

unfasten *vb* খোলা khola

unfit *adj* অযোগ্য ɔyogyô

unfortunate *adj* হতভাগ্য hɔtôb- hagyô

unfortunately *adv* দুর্ভাগ্যবশতঃ durbhagyôbɔśôtôḥ

unfriendly *adj* অমিশুক ɔmiśuk, অমিশুকে ɔmiśuke

unhappy *adj* বিষণ্ণ biṣɔnnô, নিরানন্দ niranôndô

unhealthy *adj* অস্বাস্থ্যকর ɔsvasthyôkɔr

uniform *adj* একরকম ækrɔkôm

unimportant *adj* তুচ্ছ tucchô

unintentional *adj* অনিচ্ছাকৃত ɔnicchakr̥tô

union *n* *(joining)* সংযোগ sɔṁyog, মিলন milɔn; *(organization)* সমিতি sômiti

unique *adj* একমাত্র ækmatrô

unit *n* একক ekɔk

unite *vb* সংযুক্ত করা sɔṁyuktô kɔra

United Kingdom *n* যুক্তরাজ্য yuktôrajyô

United Nations *n* রাষ্ট্রসংঘ raṣṭrôsôṁghô

United States *n* যুক্তরাষ্ট্র yuktôraṣṭrô

unity *n* একত্ব ækôtvô

universal *adj* বিশ্বজনীন biśvôjônīn

universe *n* বিশ্ব bisvô, জগৎ jɔgôt

university *n* বিশ্ববিদ্যালয় biśvôbidyalɔŷ

university department *n* অনুষদ ônuṣɔd

unknown *adj* অচেনা ɔcena

unless *conj* যদি ... না, পাছে yôdi ... na, pache

unlike *adj* অসম ɔsɔmô

unload *vb* মাল নামানো mal namano

unlucky *adj* ভাগ্যহীন bhagyôhīn

unnecessary *adj* অপ্রয়োজনীয় ɔprôŷojônīŷô

unofficial *adj* বেসরকারি besɔrkari

unpack *vb* খোলা khola

unpleasant *adj* বিরস birɔs

unpopular *adj* অপ্রিয় ɔpriŷô

unrest *n* অস্থিরতা ɔsthirɔta

unsafe *adj* বিপজ্জনক bipôjjɔnôk

unsatisfied *adj* অসন্তুষ্ট ɔsɔntuṣṭô

unskilled *adj* অদক্ষ ɔdôkṣô

unstable *adj* ঠুনকো ṭhunko

unsuccessful *adj* ব্যর্থ byærthô

unsuitable *adj* অনুপযুক্ত ɔnupôŷuktô

untie *vb* খুলে দেওয়া khule deoŷa

until *pp* পর্যন্ত pôryôntô

untrue *adj* মিথ্যা mithya *(Bd)*, মিথ্যে mithye *(WB)*

unusual *adj* অসাধারণ ɔsadharôṇ

unwell *adj* অসুস্থ ɔsusthô

unwieldy *adj* বেকায়দা bekaŷda

unwilling *adj* নারাজ naraj, অনিচ্ছুক ɔnicchuk

up *adv* উপরের দিকে upôrer dike

upkeep *n* সমর্থন sɔmɔrthɔn

upon *pp* উপরে upôre

upper *adj* উপরের upôrer

uproar *n* গণ্ডগোল gɔṇḍôgol, হইচই hôicôi

upset *n* ঝামেলা jhamela; *vb* উলটানো ulṭano

upside down *adv* উলটা ulṭa (Bd), উলটো ulṭo (WB)

upstairs *adj* উপরতলায় upôrtɔlaŷ

upstream *adj* উজানে ujane

up-to-date *adj* বর্তমান bɔrtôman

urban *adj* নাগরিক nagôrik

urge *vb (insist on)* জিদ jid (জেদ jed) ধরা dhɔra; *(goad, impel)* তাড়না করা taṛna kɔra

urgency *n* ত্বরা tvɔra

urgent *adj* জরুরি jôruri

urinate *vb* মোতা mota *(also* মুতা muta), পেচ্ছাব করা pecchab kɔra

urine *n* পেচ্ছাব pecchab, প্রস্রাব prôsrab

urn *n* কলসি kôlsi

us *pr* আমাদের amader

usage *n* প্রয়োগ prôŷog

use *vb* ব্যবহার করা bybôhar kɔra; *n (treatment)* ব্যবহার bybôhar; *(custom, practice)* প্রথা prôtha

used *adj* পুরাতন puratôn

used to *adj* অভ্যস্ত ôbhyôstô

useful *adj* কেজো kejo, ব্যবহারিক bybôharik

useless *adj (futile)* ব্যর্থ byrthô; *(superfluous)* ফালতু phaltu

usual *adj* সাধারণ sadharôṇ

usually *adv* সাধারণত sadharôṇôtô

utensil *n* যন্ত্র yɔntrô

uterus *n* জরায়ু jɔraŷu

utilize *vb* কাজে লাগানো kaje lagano

utmost *adj* চরম cɔrôm

utter *vb* উচ্চারণ করা uccarôṇ kɔra; *adj* অত্যন্ত ôtyôntô

V

vacancy *n* (gap) ফাঁক phāk; (emptiness) শূন্যতা sūnyôta

vacant *adj* ফাঁকা phāka, খালি khali

vacation *n* ছুটি chuṭi

vaccinate *vb* টিকা দেওয়া ṭika deoýa

vaccination *n* টিকা ṭika

vacuum *n* শূন্যস্থান sūnyôsthan

vagina *n* যোনি yoni

vague *adj* অস্পষ্ট ɔspɔṣṭô

vain *adj* অহংকারি ɔhɔṁkari

valet *n* বেয়ারা beýara

valiant *adj* সাহসী sahôsī

valid *adj* (legal) বৈধ boidhô; (logical) যুক্তিপূর্ণ yuktipūrṇô

validity *n* যুক্তি yukti

valley *n* উপত্যকা upôtyoka

valuable *adj* মূল্যবান mūlyoban

value *n* (worth) মূল্য mūlyô; (price) দাম dam

valve *n* কপাটক kɔpaṭôk

van *n* মালগাড়ি malgaṛi

vanilla *n* ভ্যানিলা bhyænila

vanish *vb* হাওয়া হয়ে যাওয়া haoýa hôýe yaoýa

vanity *n* ফুটানি phuṭani, গুমর gumôr

vapor *n* বাষ্প baspô

variable *adj* বিচিত্র bicitrô

variation *n* বিভিন্নতা bibhinnôta

variety *n* বিচিত্রতা bicitrôta

various *adj* নানা nana

varnish *vb* বার্নিশ barniś

vary *vb* বদলানো bɔdlano

vault *n* সমাধিকক্ষ sɔmadhikôkṣô

veal *n* বাছুরের মাংস bachurer maṁsô

vegetable *n* সবজি sôbji

vegetarian *n*, *adj* নিরামিষ niramiṣ

vegetation *n* গাছপালা gachpala

vehement *adj* প্রবল prôbɔl, জোরে jore

vehicle *n* গাড়ি gaṛi

veil *n* ঘোমটা ghomṭa

vein *n* শিরা śira

velvet *n* মখমল mɔkhmɔl

venerate *vb* শ্রদ্ধা করা śrɔddha kɔra

venereal *adj* রতিবাহিত rôtibahitô

venereal disease *n* রতিবাহিত রোগ rôtibahitô rog

vengeance *n* প্রতিশোধ prôtiśodh

venom *n* বিষ biṣ

vent *n* ফাটল phaṭôl

ventilate *vb* বাতাস দেওয়া batas deoýa

ventilation *n* বাতাস চলাচল batas cɔlacɔl

ventilator *n* ঘুলঘুলি ghulghuli

ventricle *n* নিলয় nilɔý

venture *n* প্রচেষ্টা prôceṣṭa

verb *n* ক্রিয়াপদ kriýapɔd

verbal *adj* মৌখিক moukhik

verdict *n* রায় raý

verge *n* সীমানা sīmana, প্রান্ত prantô

verification *n* প্রমাণ prômaṇ

verify *vb* প্রমাণ করা prômaṇ kɔra

versatile *adj* বহুমুখী bôhumukhī

verse *n* পদ্য pɔdyô

version *n* রূপ rūp

versus *pp* বনাম bɔnam

vertebra *n* কশেরুকা kɔśeruka

vertical *adj* খাড়া khaṛa, লম্বালম্বি lɔmbalômbi

very *adv* খুব khub

vessel *n* পাত্র patrô

vest *n* গেঞ্জি geñji

veteran *n* অভিজ্ঞ ব্যক্তি ôbhijñô bykti *(pron* obhiggo bekti)

veterinarian *n* পশুর ডাক্তার pôśur ḍaktar

via *pp* হয়ে hôŷe

vibrate *vb* কাঁপা kāpa

vibration *n* কম্প kɔmpô

vice *n (fault)* দোষ doṣ; *(sin)* পাপ pap

vice president *n* উপ-সভাপতি upô-sɔbhapôti

vicinity *n* কাছ kach

vicious *adj* খারাপ kharap, উগ্র ugrô

victim *n* বলি bôli

victory *n* বিজয় bijɔŷ

view *n (outlook)* দৃশ্য dr̥śyô *(pron* drissho); *(opinion)* মত mɔt

vigor *n* তেজ tej

vigorous *adj* তেজী tejī

villa *n* বাসভবন basbhɔbôn

village *n* গ্রাম gram, গাঁ gã

villain *n* দুর্জন ব্যক্তি durjɔn bykti

vine *n* আঙুরলতা aṅgurlɔta

vinegar *n* সির্কা sirka

vintage *adj* অতীত কালের ôtīt kaler

violate *n (attack)* আক্রমণ করা akrômɔn kɔra; *(damage)* ক্ষতি করা kṣôti kɔra

violation *n* ক্ষতি kṣôti

violence *n* হিংস্রতা hiṁsrôta

violent *adj (cruel)* হিংস্র hiṁsrô; *(out of control)* উদ্দাম uddam

violet *adj* বেগুনি beguni

violin *n* বেহালা behala

virgin *n* কুমারী kumarī

virtual *adj* অপ্রকৃত ɔprôkr̥tô

virtue *n* গুণ gun

virus *n* রোগের বীজ roger bīj

visa *n* ভিসা bhisa

visibility *n* দৃশ্য dr̥śyô *(pron* drissho)

visible *adj* দৃশ্যমান dr̥śyôman

vision *n* দৃষ্টি dr̥ṣṭi *(pron* drishti)

visit *vb (go to see)* দেখতে যাওয়া dekhte yaoŷa; *(go on an excursion)* বেড়ানো beṛano

visitor *n* অতিথি ôtithi, মেহমান mehôman

visor *n* মুখোশ mukhoś

visual *adj* চাক্ষুষ cakṣuṣ

vital *adj* জীবিত jībitô

vitality *n* জীবনীশক্তি jībônīśôkti

vitamin *n* ভিটামিন bhiṭamin

vivid *adj* জীবন্ত jībôntô

vocabulary *n* শব্দকোষ śɔbdôkoṣ

vocal *adj* কণ্ঠাগত kɔṇṭhagɔtô

voice *n (power of speech)* স্বর svɔr; *(tone, pitch)* সুর sur; *vb* বলা bɔla

void *n* শূন্যতা śūnyôta; *adj* খালি khali, শূন্য śūnyô

volcano *n* আগ্নেয়গিরি agneŷôgiri

volt *n* বিদ্যুতের মাপ bidyuter map

volume *n (extent, bulk)* আয়তন aŷôtôn; *(sound level)* জোর jor; *(one of a set of books)* খণ্ড khɔṇḍô

voluntary *adj* ইচ্ছাজনিত icchajônit

volunteer *n* স্বেচ্ছাকর্মী svecchakɔrmī

vomit *vb* বমি করা bômi kɔra

vote *n* নির্বাচন nirbacôn, ভোট bhoṭ; *vb* ভোট দেওয়া bhoṭ deoŷa

voter *n* ভোটদাতা bhoṭdata

vow *n* শপথ śɔpɔth, প্রতিজ্ঞা prôtijña

vowel *n* স্বরবর্ণ svɔrôbɔrṇô

voyage *n* ভ্রমণ bhrômɔn

vulgar *adj (unspeakable)* অবদ্য ɔbɔdyô; *(base, common)* ইতর itôr; *(obscene)* অশ্লীল ɔślīl

vulnerable *adj* অরক্ষিত ɔrôkṣitô

vulture *n* শকুন śôkun, শকুনি śôkuni

W

wage *n* বেতন betôn

wagon *n* শকট śôkôt

waist *n* কোমর komôr

wait *vb* অপেক্ষা করা ɔpekṣa kɔra

waiter *n* পরিবেশক pôribeśôk

waiver *n* পরিত্যাগ pôrityæg

wake *vb* জাগা jaga; *n* পাহারা pahara

wake s.o. up *vb* জাগানো jagan

walk *vb* হাঁটা hāṭa; *n* পায়চারি paŷcari

wall *n* দেওয়াল deôŷal

wallet *n* মানিব্যাগ manibyag

walnut *n* কাঠবাদাম kaṭhbadam

wand *n* দণ্ড dɔṇḍô

wander *vb* বেড়ানো berano, হাঁটাহাঁটি করা hāṭahāṭi kɔra

want *vb* চাওয়া caoŷa; *n (require-ment)* চাহিদা cahida; *(lack)* অভাব ɔbhab

war *n* যুদ্ধ yuddhô

wardrobe *n* আলমারি almari

warehouse *n* গুদাম gudam

wares *n* পসরা pɔsôra

warm *adj* গরম gɔrôm

warmth *n* তাপ tap

warn *vb (make aware)* জ্ঞাপন করা jñæpôn kɔra; *(alert)* সতর্ক করা sɔtɔrkô kɔra

warp *vb* বাঁকা bāka, বাঁকানো bākano

warrant *n (receipt)* রসিদ rôsid; *(proof)* প্রমাণ prôman

warranty *n* জামিন jamin

wart *n* আঁচিল ācil

wary *adj* সতর্ক sɔtɔrkô, সাবধানে sabdhane

wash *vb* ধোয়া dhoŷa

washerman *n* ধোপা dhopa

washing machine *n* কাপড়-কাচার মেসিন kapôṛ-kacar mesin

wasp *n* বোলতা bolta

waste *n (failure)* নিষ্ফলতা niṣphɔlôta; *(ruin)* নষ্ট *adj* nɔṣṭô *adj; vb (decline, shrink)* অপচয় হওয়া ɔpôcɔŷ hɔoŷa; *(fail to use)* নষ্ট করা nɔṣṭô kɔra

wasteful *adj* অপব্যয়ী ɔpôbyæŷī

watch *n* ঘড়ি ghôṛi; *vb* নজর রাখা nɔjôr rakha

watchful *adj* সতর্ক sɔtɔrkô

watchman *n* চৌকিদার coukidar

water *n* পানি pani *(Bd)*, জল jɔl *(WB)*

water buffalo *n* মহিষ môhiṣ

water lily *n* শাপলা śapla

water supply *n* জল-সরবরাহ jɔl-sɔrbôrahô

waterfall *n* জলপ্রপাত jɔlprôpat

waterlogged *adj* জলময় jɔlômɔŷ

watermelon *n* তরমুজ tôrmuj

waterproof *adj* জলাভেদ্য jɔlabhedyô

watery *adj* জলীয় jôlīŷô

wave *n* ঢেউ ḍheu, তরঙ্গ tɔrôṅgô; *vb (swing)* দোলা dola; *(beckon)* হাত নাড়া hat naṛa

wavelength *n* তরঙ্গদৈর্ঘ্য tɔrôṅgô-doirgyô

waver *vb* টলা ṭɔla

wavy *adj* তরঙ্গিত tɔrôṅgitô

wax *n* মোম mom

way *n* পথ pɔth, উপায় upaŷ

wayward *adj* খেয়ালী kheŷalī

we *pr* আমরা amra

weak *adj (lacking strength)* দুর্বল durbɔl; *(listless)* নিস্তেজ nistej; *(lacking intensity)* হালকা halka

weaken *vb* দুর্বল করা durbɔl kɔra

weakness *n* দুর্বলতা durbɔlôta

wealth *n* ধন dhôn

wealthy *adj* ধনী dhônī

weapon *n* অস্ত্র ɔstrô

wear *vb* (be dressed in) পরা pɔra; (last, endure) টিকা ṭika

wear out *vb* (exhaust) পরিশ্রান্ত করা pôriśrantô kɔra

weariness *n* ক্লান্তি klanti

weary *adj* ক্লান্ত klantô

weather *n* আবহাওয়া abhaoŷa

weave *vb* বোনা bona, বুনা buna

weaver *n* তাঁতি tāti

weaverbird *n* বাবুইপাখি babuipakhi

web *n* জাল jal

wedding *n* বিয়ে biŷe, বিবাহ bibahô

wedge *n* গোঁজ gōj

Wednesday *n* বুধবার budhbar

weed *n* আগাছা agacha

week *n* সপ্তাহ sɔptahô

weekend *n* সাপ্তাহিক ছুটি saptahik chuṭi

weekly *adj* সাপ্তাহিক saptahik

weep *vb* কাঁদা kāda

weft *n* বুনানি bunani (Bd), বুনুনি bununi (WB)

weigh *vb* (balance) তৌল করা toul kɔra; (measure weight) ওজন করা ojôn kɔra

weight *n* (measure) ওজন ojôn; (burden, heaviness) ভার bhar

weird *adj* অদ্ভুত ɔdbhut

welcome *n* স্বাগতম svagɔtôm

weld *vb* ঢালাই করা ḍhalai kɔra

welding *n* ঢালাই ḍhalai

welfare *n* মঙ্গল môṅgôl, কল্যাণ kôlyaṇ

well *n* (spring) ঝরনা jhɔrna; (shaft for drawing water) কূপ kūp, কুয়া kuŷa; *adj* সুস্থ susthô; *adv* ভালভাবে bhalôbhabe

west *n* পশ্চিম pôścim

western *adj* পশ্চিমা pôścima

wet *adj* ভিজা bhija (Bd), ভিজে bhije (WB)

whale *n* তিমি timi

wharf *n* ঘাট ghaṭ

what *pr* কি ki, কী kī

whatever *adv, rel* যা কিছু ya kichu, যে কোনও ye kono

wheat *n* গম gɔm

wheel *n* চাকা caka

wheelbarrow *n* ঠেলাগাড়ি ṭhælagaṛi

wheeze *vb* হাঁপ ধরা hāp dɔra

when *adv* কখন kɔkhôn, কবে kɔbe; *rel* যখন yɔkhôn, যে সময় ye sômôŷ

where *adv* কোথা kotha, কই kôi; *rel* যেখানে yekhane

wherever *adv* কোথাও kothao

whether *conj* কিনা kina

whetstone *n* শানপাথর śanpathôr

which *pr* কোন kon

whichever *adv* যে কোনও ye kono

whiff *n* ফুঁ phũ

while *n* ক্ষণ kṣɔṇ; *conj, rel* যতক্ষণ yɔtôkṣɔṇ

whip *n* চাবুক cabuk

whirl *vb* বেগে চলা bege cɔla

whirlpool *n* জলঘূর্ণি jɔlghūrṇi

whisk *vb* ফেটানো pheṭano

whisker *n* জুলপি julpi

whisper *vb* ফিসফিস করা phisphis kɔra

whistle *vb* শিস দেওয়া śis deoŷa

white *adj* সাদা sada

whiten *vb* সাদা করা sada kɔra

who *pr* কে ke (sg), কারা kara (pl); *pr, rel* যে ye (sg), যারা yara (pl)

whoever *pr, rel* কেউ keu

whole *adj* সারা sara, সমস্ত sɔmôstô, পুরা pura *(Bd)*, পুরো puro *(WB)*

wholesale *n* পাইকারী paikarī

wholesome *adj (healthy)* স্বাস্থ্যকর svasthyôkɔr; *(honorable)* সত্যিকার sôtyikar

why *adv* কেন kænô

wick *n* পলিতা pôlita *(Bd)*, পলতে pɔlte *(WB)*

wicked *adj* পাজি paji, দুষ্টু duṣṭu, খারাপ kharap

wickedness *n* শয়তানি śɔŷtani

wicker *n* বেত bet

wicker stool *n* মোড়া moṛa

wide *adj* চওড়া cɔoṛa

widespread *adj* ব্যাপক byæpôk

widow *n* বিধবা bidhôba

width *n* প্রসার prôsar

wield *vb* হাতে ধরা hate dhɔra

wife *n* স্ত্রী strī, বউ bôu

wig *n* পরচুল pɔrcul

wild *adj (in a natural state)* বন্য bɔnyô; *(untamed)* জঙ্গলী jôṅglī; *(unruly)* অবাধ ɔbadh

wilderness *n* মরু môru

wildlife *n* বন্য পশু-পাখি bɔnyô pôśu-pakhi

will *n* ইচ্ছা iccha *(Bd)*, ইচ্ছে icche *(WB)*

willful *adj* স্বেচ্ছাচারী svecchacarī, ছন্দানুগামী chɔndanugamī

willfulness *n* ছন্দানুগমন chɔndanugɔmôn

willing *adj* ইচ্ছুক icchuk

willpower *n* ইচ্ছাশক্তি icchaśôkti

win *vb (beat opponent)* জেতা jeta, জিতা jita, বিজয়ী হওয়া bijɔŷī hɔôŷa; *(succeed)* সফল হওয়া sɔphɔl hɔôŷa

wind *n* বাতাস batas, হাওয়া haoŷa; *vb* পাকানো pakano, পেঁচানো pēcano

windmill *n* বাতচক্র batcɔkrô

window *n* জানালা janala

windpipe *n* শ্বাসনালী śvasɔnalī

windy *adj* ঝড়ো jhoṛô

wine *n* মদ mɔd

wing *n* ডানা ḍana

wink *n* পলক pɔlôk; *vb* পলক ফেলা pɔlôk phæla

winner *n* বিজয়ী bijɔŷī

winter *n* শীতকাল śītkal

wipe *vb* মোছা mocha, মুছা mucha

wire *n* তার tar

wisdom *n* বুদ্ধি buddhi

wise *adj* বুদ্ধিমান buddhiman

wish *n* ইচ্ছা iccha, কামনা kamôna, আকাঙ্ক্ষা akaṅkṣa; *vb* ইচ্ছা করা iccha kɔra

wit *n (understanding)* মনীষা mônīṣa; *(humor)* রসিকতা rôsikôta

witch *n* ডাইনী ḍainī

with *pp (in company of)* সঙ্গে sɔṅge, সাথে sathe; *(making use of)* দিয়ে diŷe, নিয়ে niŷe

withdraw *vb (retreat)* হটা hɔṭa; *(take back)* ফেরত নেওয়া pherôt neoŷa

withhold *vb (keep back)* ঠেকিয়ে রাখা ṭhekiŷe rakha

within *pp* ভিতরে bhitôre *(Bd)*, ভেতরে bhetôre *(WB)*

without *pp* ছাড়া chaṛa, বিনা bina

withstand *vb* বাধা দেওয়া badha deoŷa

witness *n* সাক্ষী sakṣī

witty *adj (intelligent)* বিদগ্ধ bidɔgdhô; *(humorous)* রসিক rôsik

wolf *n* নেকড়ে nekṛe

woman *n* মহিলা môhila, নারী narī

womb *n* জরায়ু jɔraŷu

wonder *vb* বিস্মিত হওয়া bismito
hɔŷa; *n (amazement)* বিস্ময়
bismɔŷ; *(miracle)* অলৌকিক
ব্যাপার ɔloukik byæpar

wonderful *adj* আশ্চর্য aścôryô,
চমৎকার cɔmôtkar

wood *n* কাঠ kaṭh

wood-apple *n* বেল bel

wool *n* পশম pɔśôm

woollen *adj* পশমী pɔśômī

word *n (uttered sound)* শব্দ śɔbdô;
(fact, statement) কথা kɔtha;
(promise) প্রতিজ্ঞা prôtijña

wordless *adj* অকথিত ɔkôthitô,
শব্দহীন śɔbdôhīn

wordy *adj* শব্দবহুল śɔbdôbôhul

work *n* কাজ kaj; *vb* কাজ করা kaj
kɔra

worker *n* কর্মচারী kɔrmôcarī

workshop *n* কর্মকক্ষ kɔrmôkôkṣô

world *n* বিশ্ব biśvô, পৃথিবী pṛthibī,
দুনিয়া duniŷa

World Bank *n* বিশ্বব্যাংক
biśvôbyæṁk

World Health Organization *n*
বিশ্ব স্বাস্থ্য সংস্থা biśvô svasthyô
sɔṁstha

worldwide *adj* বিশ্বজোড়া biśvôjoṛa

worm *n (creepy-crawly)* পোকা
poka; *(in the human body)* ক্রিমি
krimi

worn out *adj* কাহিল kahil

worried *adj* চিন্তিত cintitô, উদ্বিগ্ন
udbignô

worry *n* চিন্তা cinta, দুশ্চিন্তা
duścinta; *vb* চিন্তা করা cinta kɔra,
অস্থির হওয়া ɔsthir hɔŷa

worship *vb (adore)* ভক্তি করা
bhôkti kɔra; *(perform religious
ceremony, Hindu)* পূজা করা pūja
(Bd), পুজো করা pujo *(WB)*; *n (adoration)* ভক্তি bhôkti; *(religious ceremony)* পূজা pūja

worth *n* মূল্য mūlyô, দাম dam

worthless *adj* বাজে baje, মূল্যহীন
mūlyôhīn, ফালতু phaltu

worthwhile *adj* লাভজনক labhjɔnôk

worthy *adj* যোগ্য yogyô

would-be *adj* হবু hôbu

wound *n* ঘা gha

wrap *n* চাদর cadôr; *vb* মোড়া mɔṛa,
মুড়া muṛa

wrap around *vb* লেপটানো lepṭano

wrap up *vb* চোকানো cokano,
চুকিয়ে ফেলা cukiŷe phela

wrath *n* ক্রোধ krodh

wreath *n* শিরোমালা śiromala

wreck *n* ধ্বংসাবশেষ dhvɔṁsabôśeṣ

wrench *vb* মোচড়ানো mocṛano

wrestle *vb* মল্লযুদ্ধ করা mɔllôyuddhô
kɔra

wrestler *n* মল্ল mɔllô, মল্লবীর
mɔllôbīr

wrinkle *n* বলিরেখা bôlirekha

wrist *n* কবজি kôbji

wristwatch *n* হাতঘড়ি hatghôṛi

write *vb* লেখা lekha

writer *n* লেখক lekhɔk

writing *n* লেখা lekha, লিপি lipi

wrong *n (injustice)* অন্যায় ɔnyaŷ;
(fault) দোষ doṣ; *(mistake)* ভুল
bhul; *adj (mistaken)* ভুল bhul;
(unjust) অন্যায্য ɔnyayyô *(pron
ɔnnajjo)*

wrongful *adj* বেআইনী beainī

XYZ

xenophobia *n* বিদেশিদের ভয় bideśider bhɔŷ

xerox *n* ফোটোকপি phoṭokôpi

Xmas *n* বড়দিন bɔrôdin

X-ray *n* রঞ্জন-রশ্মি rɔñjôn-rôśmi

yacht *n* পালতোলা নৌকা paltola nouka

yank *vb* টানা ṭana

yard *n* *(measurement)* গজ gɔj; *(enclosed space)* উঠান uṭhan *(Bd)*, উঠোন uṭhon *(WB)*

yarn *n* সুতা suta *(Bd)*, সুতো suto *(WB)*

yawn *vb* হাই তোলা hai tola

year *n* বছর bɔchôr

yearly *adj* বার্ষিক barṣik, বাৎসরিক baṭsôrik

yearn *vb* কামনা করা kamôna kɔra

yeast *n* গাঁজলা gājla

yell *vb* চিৎকার করা ciṭkar kɔra

yellow *adj* হলুদ hôlud *(Bd)*, হলদে hɔlde *(WB)*

yes *adv* হাঁ hyæ̃

yesterday *adv* গতকাল gɔtôkal, কালকে kalke

yet *adv* এখনও ekhôno; *conj* তবে tɔbe, কিন্তু kintu

yield *vb* দেওয়া deoŷa, উৎপাদন করা utpadôn kɔra

yoga *n* যোগশাস্ত্র yogśastrô

yogurt *n* দই dôi

yoke *n* জোয়াল joŷal, যুগল yugôl

yolk *n* ডিমের কুসুম ḍimer kusum

you *pr* তুমি tumi *(fam)*, আপনি apni *(pol)*, তুই tui *(intim)*

young *adj* *(opposite of old)* অল্পবয়স্ক ɔlpôbɔŷôskô; *(new, fresh)* তরুণ tôruṇ; *(delicate)* কচি kôci, তাজা taja

youth *n* *(time of life)* যৌবন youbôn, যুবাকাল yubakal; *(young person)* যুবক yubôk *(m)*, যুবতি yubôti *(f)*

youthful *adj* যুবা yuba

zeal *n* *(interest)* আগ্রহ agrôhô; *(exuberance)* উদ্দীপনা uddīpôna

zealous *adj* উৎসাহী utshahī, উদ্দীপ্ত uddīptô, আগ্রহী agrôhī

zebra *n* জেবরা jebra

zenith *n* সুবিন্দু subindu

zero *n* শূন্য śūnyô

zest *n* তেজ tej

zigzag *adj* আঁকাবাঁকা ākabāka

zinc *n* দস্তা dɔsta

zip *vb* লাগানো lagano

zipper *n* চেইন cein, জিপ jip

zodiac *n* রাশিচক্র raśicɔkrô

zone *n* *(area)* এলাকা ælaka; *(sphere, region)* বলয় bɔlɔŷ

zoo *n* চিড়িয়াখানা ciriŷakhana

zoological *adj* প্রাণিবিদ্যাগত praṇibidyagɔtô

zoology *n* প্রাণিবিদ্যা praṇibidya

Common Bangla verbs in alphabetical order

Only the base forms are given here. Variants can be found in the main part of the dictionary.

Bangla	Roman	Meaning	Bangla	Roman	Meaning
আঁকা	āka	draw	গেলা	gela	swallow
আঁচড়ানো	ācṛano	comb	গোছানো	gochano	tidy up
আটা	aṭa	tighten	গোনা	gona	count
আছ–	ach	be, have	ঘটা	ghɔṭa	happen
আটকানো	aṭkano	arrest	ঘামা	ghama	sweat
আনা	ana	bring	ঘুমানো	ghumano	sleep
আসা	asa	come	ঘোরা	ghora	move, turn
এগনো	egôno	advance	চটা	cɔṭa	be angry
এড়ানো	æṛano	avoid	চড়া	cɔṛa	climb
এলানো	elano	loosen	চলা	cɔla	move
ওঠা	oṭha	rise	চাওয়া	caoŷa	want
ওড়া	oṛa	fly	চাটা	caṭa	lick
কওয়া	kɔoŷa	speak	চাপা	capa	press
কমা	kɔma	decrease	চেনা	cena	know
কমানো	kɔmano	reduce	চুলকানো	culkano	scratch
করা	kɔra	do	চুষা	cuṣa	suck
কাঁদা	kāda	cry, weep	চেঁচানো	cecano	shout
কাঁপা	kāpa	shiver	ছড়া	chɔṛa	spread
কাচা	kaca	wash	ছাঁকা	chāka	sieve
কাটা	kaṭa	cut	ছাড়া	chaṛa	leave
কামড়ানো	kamṛano	bite	ছুলা	chula	peel
কুলানো	kulano	be sufficient	ছেঁড়া	chēṛa	tear
কেনা	kena	buy	ছোঁয়া	chõŷa	touch
খাওয়া	khaoŷa	eat	ছোড়া	choṛa	throw
খাটা	khaṭa	work hard	জমা	jɔma	pile up
খেলা	khæla	play	জমানো	jɔmano	collect
খোঁজা	khõja	search	জাগা	jaga	wake
খোলা	khola	open	জানা	jana	know
গড়া	gɔṛa	make, shape	জুটা	juṭa	collect
গলা	gɔla	melt	জুড়ানো	juṛano	cool
গাওয়া	gaoŷa	sing	জ্বলা	jvɔla	burn

জ্বালানো	jvalano	ignite	পোড়া	pora	burn
ঝাড়া	jhara	thresh	পোষা	poṣa	bring up, tame
ঝোলা	jhola	hang			
টানা	ṭana	pull	পৌঁছানো	põuchano	arrive
টিকা	ṭika	last	ফাটা	phaṭa	burst
টেপা	ṭepa	press	ফুটানো	phuṭano	boil
টোকা	ṭoka	imitate	ফেরা	phera	return
ঠকানো	ṭhɔkano	cheat	ফেলা	phæla	throw
ঠেকা	ṭheka	touch	বকা	bɔka	scold
ডাকা	ḍaka	call	বলা	bɔla	speak
ডোবা	ḍoba	sink	বসা	bɔsa	sit
ঢাকা	ḍhaka	cover	বাঁচা	bãca	survive
ঢোকা	ḍhoka	enter	বাঁচানো	bãcano	save
তাকানো	takano	look at	বাঁধা	bãdha	tie up
তোলা	tola	lift	বাছা	bacha	select
থাকা	thaka	stay	বাজানো	bajano	play music
থামা	thama	stop	বাড়া	baṛa	grow
দাঁড়ানো	dãṛano	stand	বাড়ানো	baṛano	increase
দেওয়া	deoẏa	give	বাধা	badha	obstruct
দেখা	dekha	see	বেঁধানো	bẽdhano	pierce
দোলা	dola	swing	বেচা	beca	sell
দৌড়ানো	douṛano	run	বেরনো	berôno	go out
ধরা	dhora	hold	বোঝা	bojha	understand
ধোয়া	dhoẏa	wash	বোঝানো	bojhano	explain
নড়া	nɔṛa	move	বোনা	bona	knit
নাচা	naca	dance	ভরা	bhɔra	fill
নাড়া	naṛa	stir	ভাঙা	bhaṅa	break
নামা	nama	descend	ভাজা	bhaja	fry
নিবানো	nibano	extinguish	ভাবা	bhaba	think
নেওয়া	neoẏa	take	ভালবাসা	bhalôbasa	love
পড়া	pɔṛa	read, fall	ভাসা	bhasa	float
পাওয়া	paoẏa	get	ভেজা	bheja	get wet
পাকানো	pakano	ripen	ভোগা	bhoga	suffer
পাঠানো	paṭhano	send	ভোলা	bhola	forget
পালানো	palano	flee	মরা	mɔra	die
পেঁচানো	pẽcano	twist	মাজা	maja	brush

মানা	mana	mind	শেখা	śekha	learn
মাপা	mapa	measure	শেখানো	śekhano	teach
মারা	mara	beat	শুকানো	śukano	dry
মেলা	mæla	mix	শোনা	śona	listen, hear
মেশা	meśa	mix	শোয়া	śoŷa	lie down
মোছা	mocha	wipe	সওয়া	sɔoŷa	endure
যাওয়া	yaoŷa	go	সরা	sɔra	move
রওয়া	rɔoŷa	remain	সাজা	saja	dress up
রাঁধা	rādha	cook	সারা	sara	finish
রাগা	raga	get angry	হওয়া	hɔoŷa	be
লাগা	laga	attach	হাঁটা	hāṭa	walk
লাগানো	lagano	employ	হারা	hara	be lost
লাফা	lapha	jump	হারানো	harano	lose
লুকানো	lukano	hide	হাসা	hasa	laugh
লেখা	lekha	write			

Verb Charts – Conjugation Tables

Bangla has five distinctive verb endings for the following persons:

(1) 1st person আমি ami *I*. The plural আমরা amra *we* has the same verb endings.
(2) 2nd person familiar তুমি tumi *you*. The plural তোমরা tomra *you* has the same verb endings.
(3) 2nd person intimate তুই tui *you*. The plural তোরা tora *you* has the same verb endings.
(4) 3rd person ordinary সে se *he, she*. The plural তারা tara *they* has the same verb endings.
(5) 2nd person polite আপনি apni *you*. The plural আপনারা apnara has the same verb endings.
3rd person honorific তিনি tini *he, she*. The plural তাঁরা tāra has the same verb endings.

Note that the verb endings for 2nd person polite and 3rd person honorific are always the same.

A more detailed overview of Bangla pronouns is given below.

Bangla has eight tenses: simple present = pres.s., present continuous = pres.c., present perfect = pres.pf., future tense = fut, simple past = p.s., past continuous = p.c., past perfect = p. pf, and past habitual = p.hab.

CVC (consonant-vowel-consonant): করা kɔra *do, make*

tenses	1 আমি ami	2 তুমি tumi	3 তুই tui	4 সে se	5 আপনি, তিনি apni, tini
pres.s.	করি kôri	কর kɔrô	করিস kôris	করে kɔre	করেন kɔren
pres.c.	করছি kôrchi	করছ kôrchô	করছিস kôrchis	করছে kôrche	করছেন kôrchen
pres. pf.	করেছি kôrechi	করেছ kôrechô	করেছিস kôrechis	করেছে kôreche	করেছেন kôrechen
fut	করব kôrbô	করবে kôrbe	করবি kôrbi	করবে kôrbe	করবেন kôrben
p.s.	করলাম kôrlam	করলে kôrle	করলি kôrli	করল kôrlô	করলেন kôrlen
p.c.	করছিলাম kôrchilam	করছিলে kôrchile	করছিলি kôrchili	করছিল kôrchilô	করছিলেন kôrchilen
p.pf.	করেছিলাম kôrechilam	করেছিলে kôrechile	করেছিলি kôrechili	করেছিল kôrechilô	করেছিলেন kôrechilen
p.hab.	করতাম kôrtam	করতে kôrte	করতিস kôrtis	করত kôrtô	করতেন kôrten

VC (vowel-consonant): ওঠা oṭha *rise, get up*

Tenses	1 আমি ami	2 তুমি tumi	3 তুই tui	4 সে se	5 আপনি, তিনি apni, tini
pres.s.	উঠি uṭhi	ওঠ oṭhô	উঠিস uṭhis	ওঠে oṭhe	ওঠেন oṭhen
pres.c.	উঠছি uṭhchi	উঠছ uṭhchô	উঠছিস uṭhchis	উঠছে uṭhche	উঠছেন uṭhchen

pres.pf.	উঠেছি	উঠেছ	উঠেছিস	উঠেছে	উঠেছেন
	uṭhechi	uṭhechô	uṭhechis	uṭheche	uṭhechen
fut	উঠব	উঠবে	উঠবি	উঠবে	উঠবেন
	uṭhbô	uṭhbe	uṭhbi	uṭhbe	uṭhben
p.s.	উঠলাম	উঠলে	উঠলি	উঠল	উঠলেন
	uṭhlam	uṭhle	uṭhli	uṭhlô	uṭhlen
p.c.	উঠছিলাম	উঠছিলে	উঠছিলি	উঠছিল	উঠছিলেন
	uṭhchilam	uṭhchile	uṭhchili	uṭhchilô	uṭhchilen
p.pf.	উঠেছিলাম	উঠেছিলে	উঠেছিলি	উঠেছিল	উঠেছিলেন
	uṭhechilam	uṭhechile	uṭhechili	uṭhechilô	uṭhechilen
p.hab.	উঠতাম	উঠতে	উঠতিস	উঠত	উঠতেন
	uṭhtam	uṭhte	uṭhtis	uṭhtô	uṭhten

CaC (consonant-a-consonant): থাকা thaka *stay*

tenses	1	2	3	4	5
	আমি	তুমি	তুই	সে	আপনি, তিনি
	ami	tumi	tui	se	apni, tini
pres.s.	থাকি	থাক	থাকিস	থাকে	থাকেন
	thaki	thakô	thakis	thake	thaken
pres.c.	থাকছি	থাকছ	থাকছিস	থাকছে	থাকছেন
	thakchi	thakchô	thakchis	thakche	thakchen
pres.pf.	থেকেছি	থেকেছ	থেকেছিস	থেকেছে	থেকেছেন
	thekechi	thekechô	thekechis	thekeche	thekechen
fut	থাকব	থাকবে	থাকবি	থাকবে	থাকবেন
	thakbô	thakbe	thakbi	thakbe	thakben
p.s.	থাকলাম	থাকলে	থাকলি	থাকল	থাকলেন
	thaklam	thakle	thakli	thaklô	thaklen
p.c.	থাকছিলাম	থাকছিলে	থাকছিলি	থাকছিল	থাকছিলেন
	thakchilam	thakchile	thakchili	thakchilô	thakchilen
p.pf.	থেকেছিলাম	থেকেছিলে	থেকেছিলি	থেকেছিল	থেকেছিলেন
	thekechilam	thekechile	thekechili	thekechilô	thekechilen
p.hab.	থাকতাম	থাকতে	থাকতিস	থাকত	থাকতেন
	thaktam	thakte	thaktis	thaktô	thakten

aC (a-consonant): আনা ana *bring*

tenses	1	2	3	4	5
	আমি	তুমি	তুই	সে	আপনি, তিনি
	ami	tumi	tui	se	apni, tini
pres.s.	আনি	আন	আনিস	আনে	আনেন
	ani	anô	anis	ane	anen
pres.c.	আনছি	আনছ	আনছিস	আনছে	আনছেন
	anchi	anchô	anchis	anche	anchen
pres.pf.	এনেছি	এনেছ	এনেছিস	এনেছে	এনেছেন
	enechi	enechô	enechis	eneche	enechen
fut	আনব	আনবে	আনবি	আনবে	আনবেন
	anbô	anbe	anbi	anbe	anben
p.s.	আনলাম	আনলে	আনলি	আনল	আনলেন
	anlam	anle	anli	anlô	anlen
p.c.	আনছিলাম	আনছিলে	আনছিলি	আনছিল	আনছিলেন
	anchilam	anchile	anchili	anchilô	anchilen
p.pf.	এনেছিলাম	এনেছিলে	এনেছিলি	এনেছিল	এনেছিলেন
	enechilam	enechile	enechili	enechilô	enechilen
p.hab.	আনতাম	আনতে	আনতিস	আনত	আনতেন
	antam	ante	antis	antô	anten

CV (consonant-vowel): হওয়া hɔoŷa *be, become*

tenses	1	2	3	4	5
	আমি	তুমি	তুই	সে	আপনি, তিনি
	ami	tumi	tui	se	apni, tini
pres.s.	হই	হও	হস	হয়	হন
	hôi	hɔo	hôs	hɔŷ	hɔn
pres.c.	হচ্ছি	হচ্ছ	হচ্ছিস	হচ্ছে	হচ্ছেন
	hôcchi	hôcchô	hôcchis	hôcche	hôcchen
pres.pf.	হয়েছি	হয়েছ	হয়েছিস	হয়েছে	হয়েছেন
	hôŷechi	hôŷechô	hôŷechis	hôŷeche	hôŷechen
fut	হব	হবে	হবি	হবে	হবেন
	hɔbô	hɔbe	hôbi	hɔbe	hɔben

p.s.	হলাম	হলে	হলি	হল	হলেন
	hôlam	hôle	hôli	hôlô	hôlen
p.c.	হচ্ছিলাম	হচ্ছিলে	হচ্ছিলি	হচ্ছিল	হচ্ছিলেন
	hôcchilam	hôcchile	hôcchili	hôcchilô	hôcchilen
p.pf.	হয়েছিলাম	হয়েছিলে	হয়েছিলি	হয়েছিল	হয়েছিলেন
	hôŷechilam	hôŷechile	hôŷechili	hôŷechilô	hôŷechilen
p.hab.	হতাম	হতে	হতিস	হত	হতেন
	hôtam	hôte	hôtis	hôtô	hôten

CV (consonant-vowel): দেওয়া deoŷa *give*

(This has some irregularities. নেওয়া neoŷa *take* conjugates the same way.)

tenses	1	2	3	4	5
	আমি	তুমি	তুই	সে	আপনি, তিনি
	ami	tumi	tui	se	apni, tini
pres.s.	দেই, দিই	দাও	দিস	দেয়	দেন
	dei, dii	dao	dis	deŷ	den
pres.c.	দিচ্ছি	দিচ্ছ	দিচ্ছিস	দিচ্ছে	দিচ্ছেন
	dicchi	dicchô	dicchis	dicche	dicchen
pres.pf.	দিয়েছি	দিয়েছ	দিয়েছিস	দিয়েছে	দিয়েছেন
	diŷechi	diŷechô	diŷechis	diŷeche	diŷechen
fut	দেব, দিব	দেবে	দেবি	দেবে	দেবেন
	debô, dibô	debe	debi	debe	deben
p.s.	দিলাম	দিলে	দিলি	দিল	দিলেন
	dilam	dile	dili	dilô	dilen
p.c.	দিচ্ছিলাম	দিচ্ছিলে	দিচ্ছিলি	দিচ্ছিল	দিচ্ছিলেন
	dicchilam	dicchile	dicchili	dicchilô	dicchilen
p.pf.	দিয়েছিলাম	দিয়েছিলে	দিয়েছিলি	দিয়েছিল	দিয়েছিলেন
	diŷechilam	diŷechile	diŷechili	diŷechilô	diŷechilen
p.hab.	দিতাম	দিতে	দিতিস	দিত	দিতেন
	ditam	dite	ditis	ditô	diten

Ca (consonant-a): যাওয়া yaoŷa *go*

(This has some irregularities.)

tenses	1 আমি ami	2 তুমি tumi	3 তুই tui	4 সে se	5 আপনি, তিনি apni, tini
pres.s.	যাই yai	যাও yao	যাস yas	যায় yaŷ	যান yan
pres.c.	যাচ্ছি yacchi	যাচ্ছ yacchô	যাচ্ছিস yacchis	যাচ্ছে yacche	যাচ্ছেন yacchen
pres.pf.	গিয়েছি giŷechi	গিয়েছ giŷechô	গিয়েছিস giŷechis	গিয়েছে giŷeche	গিয়েছেন giŷechen
fut	যাব yabô	যাবে yabe	যাবি yabi	যাবে yabe	যাবেন yaben
p.s.	গেলাম gelam	গেলে gele	গেলি geli	গেল gelô	গেলেন gelen
p.c.	যাচ্ছিলাম yacchilam	যাচ্ছিলে yacchile	যাচ্ছিলি yacchili	যাচ্ছিল yacchilô	যাচ্ছিলেন yacchilen
p.pf.	গিয়েছিলাম giŷechilam	গিয়েছিলে giŷechile	গিয়েছিলি giŷechili	গিয়েছিল giŷechilô	গিয়েছিলেন giŷechilen
p.hab.	যেতাম yetam	যেতে yete	যেতিস yetis	যেত yetô	যেতেন yeten

Ca (consonant-a): খাওয়া khaoŷa *eat*

tenses	1 আমি ami	2 তুমি tumi	3 তুই tui	4 সে se	5 আপনি, তিনি apni, tini
pres.s.	খাই khai	খাও khao	খাস khas	খায় khaŷ	খান khan
pres.c.	খাচ্ছি khacchi	খাচ্ছ khacchô	খাচ্ছিস khacchis	খাচ্ছে khacche	খাচ্ছেন khacchen
pres.pf.	খেয়েছি kheŷechi	খেয়েছ kheŷechô	খেয়েছিস kheŷechis	খেয়েছে kheŷeche	খেয়েছেন kheŷechen
fut	খাব khabô	খাবে khabe	খাবি khabi	খাবে khabe	খাবেন khaben

	1	2	3	4	5
p.s.	খেলাম khelam	খেলে khele	খেলি kheli	খেল khelô	খেলেন khelen
p.c.	খাচ্ছিলাম khacchilam	খাচ্ছিলে khacchile	খাচ্ছিলি khacchili	খাচ্ছিল khacchilô	খাচ্ছিলেন khacchilen
p.pf.	খেয়েছিলাম kheŷechilam	খেয়েছিলে kheŷechile	খেয়েছিলি kheŷechili	খেয়েছিল kheŷechilô	খেয়েছিলেন kheŷechilen
p.hab.	খেতাম khetam	খেতে khete	খেতিস khetis	খেত khetô	খেতেন kheten

CVCA (consonant-vowel-consonant-a): ঘুমানো ghumano *sleep*

tenses	1 আমি ami	2 তুমি tumi	3 তুই tui	4 সে se	5 আপনি, তিনি apni, tini
pres.s.	ঘুমাই ghumai	ঘুমাও ghumao	ঘুমাস ghumas	ঘুমায় ghumaŷ	ঘুমান ghuman
pres.c.	ঘুমাচ্ছি ghumacchi	ঘুমাচ্ছ ghumacchô	ঘুমাচ্ছিস ghumacchis	ঘুমাচ্ছে ghumacche	ঘুমাচ্ছেন ghumacchen
pres.pf.	ঘুমিয়েছি ghumiŷechi	ঘুমিয়েছ ghumiŷechô	ঘুমিয়েছিস ghumiŷechis	ঘুমিয়েছে ghumiŷeche	ঘুমিয়েছেন ghumiŷechen
fut	ঘুমাব ghumabô	ঘুমাবে ghumabe	ঘুমাবি ghumabi	ঘুমাবে ghumabe	ঘুমাবেন ghumaben
p.s.	ঘুমালাম ghumalam	ঘুমালে ghumale	ঘুমালি ghumali	ঘুমাল ghumalô	ঘুমালেন ghumalen
p.c.	ঘুমাচ্ছিলাম ghumac–chilam	ঘুমাচ্ছিলে ghumac–chile	ঘুমাচ্ছিলি ghumac–chili	ঘুমাচ্ছিল ghumac–chilô	ঘুমাচ্ছিলেন ghumac–chilen
p.pf.	ঘুমিয়েছিলাম ghumiŷe–chilam	ঘুমিয়েছিলে ghumiŷe–chile	ঘুমিয়েছিলি ghumiŷe–chili	ঘুমিয়েছিল ghumiŷe–chilô	ঘুমিয়েছিলেন ghumiŷe–chilen
p.hab.	ঘুমাতাম ghumatam	ঘুমাতে ghumate	ঘুমাতিস ghumatis	ঘুমাত ghumatô	ঘুমাতেন ghumaten

incomplete verb: আছ্- ach *be, exist, be present*

tenses	1 আমি ami	2 তুমি tumi	3 তুই tui	4 সে se	5 আপনি, তিনি apni, tini
pres.s.	আছি achi	আছ achô	আছিস achis	আছে ache	আছেন achen
p.s.	ছিলাম chilam	ছিলে chile	ছিলি chili	ছিল chilô	ছিলেন chilen

Bangla Pronouns

Personal and Possessive Pronouns

fam = familiar, pol = polite, ord = ordinary, hon = honorific

Singular

Nominative

1st ps	আমি ami	*I*
2nd ps (fam)	তুমি tumi	*you*
2nd ps (pol)	আপনি apni	*you*
3rd ps (ord)	সে se / এ e / ও o	*he, she*
3rd ps (hon)	তিনি tini / ইনি ini / উনি uni	*he, she*

Genitive

1st ps	আমার amar	*my*
2nd ps (fam)	তোমার tomar	*your*
2nd ps (pol)	আপনার apnar	*your*
3rd ps (ord)	তার tar / এর er / ওর or	*his, her*
3rd ps (hon)	তাঁর tãr / এঁর ẽr / ওঁর õr / ওনার onar	*his, her*

Objective

1st ps	আমাকে amake	*me*
2nd ps (fam)	তোমাকে tomake	*(to) you*
2nd ps (pol)	আপনাকে apnake	*(to) you*
3rd ps (ord)	তাকে take / একে eke / ওকে oke	*him, her*
3rd ps (hon)	তাঁকে tãke / ওঁকে õke / ওনাকে onake	*him, her*

Note: 3rd person pronouns, whether animate or inanimate, distinguish three degrees of proximity to the speaker:

> এ e = close to the speaker (near)
>
> ও o = at a distance from the speaker (far)
>
> সে se = neutral

This explains why there are always more 3rd person pronouns than any others.

Plural

Nominative

1st ps	আমরা amra	*we*
2nd ps (fam)	তোমরা tomra	*you*
2nd ps (pol)	আপনারা apnara	*you*
3rd ps (ord)	তারা tara / ওরা ora	*they*
3rd ps (hon)	তাঁরা tāra / এঁরা ēra / ওঁরা õra	*they*

Genitive and Object Case

1st ps	আমাদের amader	*our, us*
2nd ps (fam)	তোমাদের tomader	*your, to you*
2nd ps (pol)	আপনাদের apnader	*your, to you*
3rd ps (ord)	তাদের tader / ওদের oder	*their, them*
3rd ps (hon)	তাঁদের tāder / এঁদের ēder / ওঁদের õder	*their, them*

Interrogative (Question) Pronouns

Nominative

singular	কে ke	*who*
plural	কারা kara	

Genitive

singular	কার kar	*whose*
plural	কাদের kader	

Objective

singular	কাকে kake	*(to) whom*
plural	কাদের kader	

Relative Pronouns

Nominative

singular	যে ye	*who*
plural	যারা yara	

Genitive

singular	যার yar	*whose*
plural	যাদের yader	

Objective

singular	যাকে yake	*(to) whom*
plural	যাদের yader	

Indefinite Personal Pronouns

Nominative	কেউ keu	*someone*	যে কেউ ye keu	*anyone*
Genitive	কারও karo	*someone's*	যে কারও ye karo	*anyone's*
Objective	কাউকে kauke	*to someone*	যে কাউকে ye kauke	*to anyone*

Inanimate Pronouns

Nominative, Objective

Demonstrative	তা ta	*it*
	এ e / এটা eṭa	*this*
	ও o / ওটা oṭa	*that*
Interrogative	কি ki	*what*
Relative	যা ya	*what*
Indefinite	কিছু kichu	*something*

Genitive

Demonstrative	তার tar	*of it*
	এটার eṭar	*of this*
	ওটার oṭar	*of that*
Interrogative	কিসের kiser	*of what*
Relative	যার yar	*of what*
Indefinite	কিছুর kichur	*of something*

Locative

Demonstrative	তাতে tate	*in it*
	এতে ete	*in this*
	ওতে ote	*in that*
Interrogative	কিসে kise	*in what*
Relative	যাতে yate	*in what*
Indefinite	কিছুতে kichute	*in something*

Numbers

1 ১ এক æk	34 ৩৪ চৌত্রিশ coutriś
2 ২ দুই dui	35 ৩৫ পঁয়ত্রিশ pɔ̃ytriś
3 ৩ তিন tin	36 ৩৬ ছত্রিশ chôtriś
4 ৪ চার car	37 ৩৭ সাঁইত্রিশ sãitriś
5 ৫ পাঁচ pãc	38 ৩৮ আটত্রিশ aṭtriś
6 ৬ ছয় chɔy	39 ৩৯ উনচল্লিশ unôcôlliś
7 ৭ সাত sat	40 ৪০ চল্লিশ côlliś
8 ৮ আট aṭ	41 ৪১ একচল্লিশ ækcôlliś
9 ৯ নয় nɔy	42 ৪২ বিয়াল্লিশ biyalliś
10 ১০ দশ dɔś	43 ৪৩ তেতাল্লিশ tetalliś
11 ১১ এগারো ægaro	44 ৪৪ চুয়াল্লিশ cuyalliś
12 ১২ বারো baro	45 ৪৫ পঁয়তাল্লিশ pɔ̃ytalliś
13 ১৩ তেরো tero	46 ৪৬ ছেচল্লিশ checôlliś
14 ১৪ চৌদ্দো couddo	47 ৪৭ সাতচল্লিশ satcôlliś
15 ১৫ পনেরো pɔnero	48 ৪৮ আটচল্লিশ aṭcôlliś
16 ১৬ ষোলো ṣolo	49 ৪৯ উনপঞ্চাশ unôpɔñcaś
17 ১৭ সতেরো sɔtero	50 ৫০ পঞ্চাশ pɔñcaś
18 ১৮ আঠারো aṭharo	51 ৫১ একান্ন ækannô
19 ১৯ উনিশ uniś	52 ৫২ বাহান্ন bahannô
20 ২০ বিশ biś / কুড়ি kuri	53 ৫৩ তিপ্পান্ন tippannô
21 ২১ একুশ ekuś	54 ৫৪ চুয়ান্ন cuyannô
22 ২২ বাইশ baiś	55 ৫৫ পঞ্চান্ন pɔñcannô
23 ২৩ তেইশ teiś	56 ৫৬ ছাপ্পান্ন chappannô
24 ২৪ চব্বিশ côbbiś	57 ৫৭ সাতান্ন satannô
25 ২৫ পঁচিশ pɔ̃ciś	58 ৫৮ আটান্ন aṭannô
26 ২৬ ছাব্বিশ chabbiś	59 ৫৯ উনষাট unôṣaṭ
27 ২৭ সাতাশ sataś / সাতাইশ sataiś	60 ৬০ ষাট ṣaṭ
28 ২৮ আটাশ aṭaś/ আটাইশ aṭaiś	61 ৬১ একষট্টি ækṣôṭṭi
29 ২৯ উনত্রিশ unôtriś	62 ৬২ বাষট্টি baṣôṭṭi
30 ৩০ ত্রিশ triś	63 ৬৩ তেষট্টি teṣôṭṭi
31 ৩১ একত্রিশ ektriś	64 ৬৪ চৌষট্টি couṣôṭṭi
32 ৩২ বত্রিশ bôtriś	65 ৬৫ পঁয়ষট্টি pɔ̃yṣôṭṭi
33 ৩৩ তেত্রিশ tetriś	66 ৬৬ ছেষট্টি cheṣôṭṭi
	67 ৬৭ সাতষট্টি satṣôṭṭi

68 ৬৮ আটষট্টি aṭṣôṭṭi

69 ৬৯ উনসত্তর unôsôttôr

70 ৭০ সত্তর sôttôr

71 ৭১ একাত্তর ækattôr

72 ৭২ বাহাত্তর bahattôr

73 ৭৩ তিয়াত্তর tiŷattôr

74 ৭৪ চুয়াত্তর cuŷattôr

75 ৭৫ পঁচাত্তর pɔ̃cattôr

76 ৭৬ ছিয়াত্তর chiŷattôr

77 ৭৭ সাতাত্তর satattôr

78 ৭৮ আটাত্তর aṭattôr

79 ৭৯ উনআশি unôaśi

80 ৮০ আশি aśi

81 ৮১ একাশি ækaśi

82 ৮২ বিরাশি biraśi

83 ৮৩ তিরাশি tiraśi

84 ৮৪ চুরাশি curaśi

85 ৮৫ পঁচাশি pɔ̃caśi

86 ৮৬ ছিয়াশি chiŷaśi

87 ৮৭ সাতাশি sataśi

88 ৮৮ আটাশি aṭaśi / অষ্টাশি ɔṣṭôaśi

89 ৮৯ উননব্বই unônɔbbôi

90 ৯০ নব্বই nɔbbôi

91 ৯১ একানব্বই ækanɔbbôi

92 ৯২ বিরানব্বই biranɔbbôi

93 ৯৩ তিরানব্বই tiranɔbbôi

94 ৯৪ চুরানব্বই curanɔbbôi

95 ৯৫ পঁচানব্বই pɔ̃canɔbbôi

96 ৯৬ ছিয়ানব্বই chiŷanɔbbôi

97 ৯৭ সাতানব্বই satanɔbbôi

98 ৯৮ আটানব্বই aṭanɔbbôi

99 ৯৯ নিরানব্বই niranɔbbôi

100 ১০০ এক শ ek śô

200 ২০০ দু শ du śô

1000 ১০০০ হাজার hajar

100.000 ১,০০,০০০ এক লাখ æk lakh

one million ১০, ০০, ০০০ দশ লাখ dɔś lakh

ten million ১,০০,০০,০০০ এক কোটি æk koṭi/ এক ক্রোড় æk kroṛ

zero ০ শূন্য śūnyô

one and a half দেড় deṛ

two and a half আড়াই aṛai

Weights, Fractions and Time

কিলো kilo is used for kilometers, the word মাইল mail is also in use.
কেজি keji *(kg)* is used for kilograms.

আধ adha/ আধা adh half

    আধ ঘণ্টা adh ghɔnṭa half an hour

    আধা কেজি adha keji 500 grams

পোয়া poŷa a quarter

    তিন পেওয়া tin poŷa three quarters

তেহাই tehai a third

সাড়ে saṛe plus one half

    সাড়ে ছয় মাইল saṛe chɔy mail six and a half miles

    সাড়ে তিন ঘণ্টা saṛe tin ghɔnṭa three and a half hours

    সাড়ে পাঁচটা saṛe pãcṭa half past five

পৌনে poune minus one quarter, three quarters

    পৌনে দুই কেজি poune dui keji 1,750 grams

    পৌনে সাটটা poune satṭa quarter to seven

সোয়া soŷa (*pron* showa) plus one quarter

    সোয়া ঘণ্টা soŷa ghɔnṭa an hour and a quarter

    সোয়া চার মাইল soŷa car mail four and a quarter miles

    সোয়া দশটা soŷa dosṭa quarter past ten

Ordinal Numbers

প্রথম prothom first

দ্বিতীয় dvitīŷô second

তৃতীয় trtīŷô third

চতুর্থ côturthô fourth

পঞ্চম pɔñcôm fifth

ষষ্ঠ ṣɔṣṭhô sixth

সপ্তম sɔptôm seventh

অষ্টম ɔṣṭôm eighth

নবম nɔbôm ninth

দশম dɔśôm tenth

Days of the Week

রবিবার rôbibar Sunday
সোমবার sombar Monday
মঙ্গলবার mɔṅgôlbar Tuesday
বুধবার budhbar Wednesday
বৃহস্পতিবার br̈hôspôtibar Thursday
শুক্রবার śukrôbar Friday
শনিবার śônibar Saturday

Bengali Months and Seasons

The Bengali calendar is still in use with monolingual publishers and news-
papers. The Bengali new century 1400 began on 15 April 1993. The second
half of the year 2010 was therefore 1417 in Bengali counting. Bengalis count
six seasons, lasting two months each.

Months	Seasons
বৈশাখ boiśakh (April – May)	গ্রীষ্ম grīṣmô summer
জ্যৈষ্ঠ jyoiṣṭhô (May – June)	
আষাঢ় aṣaṛh (June –July)	বর্ষা bɔrṣa rainy season
শ্রাবণ śrabôṇ (July – August)	
ভাদ্র bhadrô (August – September)	শরৎ śɔrôṯ early autumn
আশ্বিন aśvin (September – October	
কার্তিক kartik (October – November)	হেমন্ত hemôntô late autumn
অগ্রহায়ণ ɔgrôhaŷôṇ (November – December)	
পৌষ pouṣ (December – January)	শীত śīt winter
মাঘ magh (January – February)	
ফালগুন phalgun (February – March)	বসন্ত bɔsôntô spring
চৈত্র coitrô (March – April)	

More Dictionary & Phrasebooks…

Arabic-English/English-Arabic
Dictionary & Phrasebook
3,000 entries · ISBN 0-7818-0973-8 · $13.95pb

Dari-English/English-Dari Dictionary & Phrasebook
5,000 entries · ISBN 0-7818-0971-1 · $14.95pb

Gujarati-English/English-Gujarati
Dictionary & Phrasebook
6,800 entries · ISBN 0-7818-1051-5 · $13.95pb

Hindi-English/English-Hindi Dictionary & Phrasebook
3,400 entries · ISBN 0-7818-0983-5 · $12.95pb

Kurdish (Sorani)-English/English-Kurdish (Sorani)
Dictionary & Phrasebook
4,000 entries · ISBN 0-7818-1245-3 · $12.95pb

Marathi-English/English-Marathi
Dictionary & Phrasebook
ISBN 978-0-7818-1142-2 · $14.95pb

Nepali-English/English-Nepali Dictionary & Phrasebook
Romanized
1,500 entries · ISBN 0-7818-0957-6 · $13.95pb

Pashto-English/English-Pashto Dictionary & Phrasebook
Romanized
3,000 entries · ISBN 0-7818-0972-X · $13.95pb

Tajik-English/English-Tajik Dictionary & Phrasebook
1,400 entries · ISBN 0-7818-0662-3 · $11.95pb

Tamil-English/English-Tamil Dictionary & Phrasebook
Romanized
6,000 entries · ISBN 0-7818-1016-7 · $13.95pb

Urdu-English/English-Urdu Dictionary & Phrasebook
Romanized
3,000 entries · ISBN 0-7818-0970-3 · $13.95pb

Also from Hippocrene Books…

India: An Illustrated History
Prem Kishore & Anuradha Kishore Ganpati

This volume succinctly recounts 4,500 years of Indian history, from the earliest Indus valley settlements to the twentieth-century struggle against British imperial rule, including the challenges facing the country today. Sections on cultural traditions, regional cuisine, and dress being the various facets of this nation to life.

234 pages · 50 photos/illus./maps · ISBN 0-7818-0944-4 · $14.95pb

Voices of American Muslims: Twenty-Three Profiles
Linda Brandi Cateura

What is new about this volume? It is that it brings together the voices of many different American Muslims, female and male, Sunni and Shia, immigrant, African-American and white, scholar and imam, taxi-driver and activist, high school student and writer, in one volume. It allows American Muslims to speak for themselves."

—from the introductory essay by Omid Safi.

In this long-overdue book, Muslims from all walks of life introduce themselves and speak out on pressing questions. They speak loudly and clearly, declaring their individuality and deep devotion to the United States. Linda Brandi Cateura's interviews and first person narratives are frank and full of remarkable insights, and they make for an exceptionally warm and vitally informative book.

284 pages · ISBN 0-7818-1054-X · $24.95

Women in Islam:
An Anthology from the Qur'ān and Hadīths
Translated and edited by Nicholas Awde

What does Islam really say about women? Much of the answer may be found in this collection of major references to women in the Qur'ān and Hadīths—the two holy writings on which Islamic legislation and social practice are based. The role of women in islam is a growing area of study and this collection fulfills the need for e definitive resource which gathers together all significant material on the subject and presents it in an accessible way. Extensive notes and short biographies of the women of the Prophet's household draws a vivid picture of their lives and culture.

256 pages · ISBN 0-7818-1090-6 · $18.95pb

CUISINE

Flavorful India
Priti Chitnis Gress

Flavorful India showcases the cuisine of Gujarat—from street foods like crunchy snack mix and vegetable fritters, to traditional home-cooked dishes that feature an abundance of locally available vegetables like okra, eggplant, bottle gourd, and many varieties of beans. Spicy dals, delicate flatbreads, and traditional sweets and beverages bring the Gujarati dining experience full circle. This collection of authentic family recipes will introduce simple, delectable recipes written for the home cook and adapted to the North American kitchen. An introduction to Gujarati culture, sections on spices, ingredients, and utensils, and charming line drawings by the author's father bring the flavors of India to life.

Two-color · ISBN 978-0-7818-1207-8 · $14.95pb

Healthy South Indian Cooking *Expanded Edition*
Alamelu Vairavan & Dr. Patricia Marquardt

With an emphasis on the famed Chettinad cooking tradition of southern India, these 197 mostly vegetarian recipes will allow home cooks to create exotic fare like Masala Dosa, Pearl Onion and Tomato Sambhar, and Eggplant Masala Curry. Each of these low-fat, low-calorie recipes includes complete nutritional analysis. Also included are sample menus of complementary dishes and innovative suggestions for integrating

South Indian dishes into traditional Western meals. A multi-lingual glossary of spices and ingredients, a section on the preparation of *dals* (a staple lentil dish), and 16 pages of color photographs make this book a clear and concise introduction to the healthy, delicious cooking of south India.

16-page color photo insert · ISBN 978-0-7818-1189-7 · $35.00hc

The Kerala Kitchen: Recipes and Recollections from the Syrian Christians of South India
Lathika George

Long before the time of Christ, the lure of spices drew sea-farers to Kerala, a lush, tropical state on the Malabar Coast of South India. Saint Thomas also traveled this spice route, converting several Brahmin families who later intermarried with Syrians who had settled here; giving birth to the vibrant Syrian Christian community of Kerala. Featured here are 150 delectable recipes such as *Meen Vevichathu* (Fish Curry Cooked in a Clay Pot), *Parippu* (Lentils with Coconut Milk) and *Thiyal* (Shallots with Tamarind and Roasted Coconut). Equally mouthwatering are a variety of rice preparations, *Puttu* (Steamed Rice Cake) and *Paalappam* (Lace-Rimmed Pancakes), and tempting desserts like *Karikku* Pudding (Tender Coconut Pudding). These dishes are adapted for the North American kitchen, and accompanied by a guide to spices, herbs, and equipment, as well as a glossary of food terms. Full of beautiful photographs, charming illustrations and lyrical memories of food and family.

16-page color photo insert · ISBN 0-7818-1184-2 · $35.00hc

Menus and Memories of Punjab
Veronica "Rani" Sidhu

Arguably India's most popular cuisine, Punjabi food boasts mouthwatering tandoori kebabs, satisfying curries, and an array of delectable breads. These twenty-two menus feature a wide range of dishes, from rustic, roadside *dhaba* offerings like Buttermilk Stew with Vegetable *Pakoras* and the famous *Saag* and *Mukke Di Roti* (Stewed Mixed Greens with Corn Flatbread), to elegant Roast Leg of Lamb and Royal Bread Pudding that have graced the tables of Maharajahs. Remarkably healthful, over 125 of these recipes are designated vegetarian or vegan. Whether you wish to re-create an Indian restaurant dish that you love, or one from your grandmother's kitchen, this will be your trusted guide, providing step-by-step, easy-to-follow recipes and advice on shopping, prepping, and creating menus with harmonious elements. Glossaries of food and religious terms, color photos, a resource section for finding Indian ingredients, and bibliography round out this collection.

16-page color photo insert · ISBN 0-7818-1220-7 · $29.95hc

Taste of Nepal
Jyoti Pandey Pathak

One of the very few Nepali cookbooks on the market, *Taste of Nepal* is a thorough and comprehensive guide to this cuisine, featuring more than 350 authentic recipes, a section on well-known Nepali herbs and spices, menu planning, Nepalese kitchen equipment, and delightful illustrations. Instructions are clearly detailed with illustrations, and most ingredients are readily available stateside. There is something for everyone in this book—for the most timid cook Fried Rice (*Baasi-Bhaat Bhutuwa*) or Stir-Fried Chicken (*Kukhura Taareko*) are easily achievable, but the adventurous will be tempted to try Goat Curry (*Khasi-Boka ko Maasu*) and Sun-Dried Fish with Tomato Chutney (*Golbheda ra Sidra Maacha*).

ISBN 0-7818-1121-X · $27.50hc

Prices subject to change without prior notice. **To purchase Hippocrene Books** contact your local bookstore, visit www.hippocrenebooks.com, call (212) 685-4373, or write to: HIPPOCRENE BOOKS, 171 Madison Avenue, New York, NY 10016.